Alice in the Country of Joker

~Circus and Liar's Game~

- STORY -

This is a love adventure game based on Lewis Carroll's *Alice in Wonderland* that develops into a completely different storyline. This Wonderland is a fairy tale gone very wrong—or very *right*, if you like a land of gunfights where the "Hatters" are a mafia syndicate.

The main character is far from a romantic. In fact, she's especially sick of love relationships.

In *Alice in the Country of Joker*, Alice can experience the changing seasons that were absent in the other storylines. The Circus comes along with April Season, the season of lies. The Circus's dazzle and glitter hides its terrible purpose, and as Alice tries to wrap her head around the shifting world, she falls deeper and deeper into a nefarious trap.

When this story begins, Alice is already close to the inhabitants of Wonderland but hasn't fallen in love. Each role-holder treasures Alice differently with their own bizarre love—those who want to *protect* Alice from the Joker are competing with those who would rather be jailers. In the Country of Joker, there's more at stake than Alice's romantic affections...

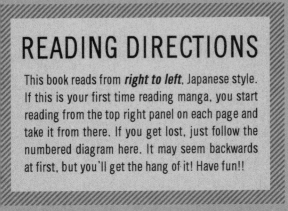

Alice

IN THE COUNTRY OF

Joker

VOLUME 2

story by **QuinRose**
art by **Mamenosuke Fujimaru**

STAFF CREDITS

translation	**Angela Liu**
adaptation	**Lianne Sentar**
lettering	**Laura Scoville**
cover design	**Nicky Lim**
proofreader	**Shanti Whitesides**
assistant editor	**Bambi Eloriaga-Amago**
editor	**Adam Arnold**
publisher	**Jason DeAngelis** **Seven Seas Entertainment**

ALICE IN THE COUNTRY OF JOKER: CIRCUS AND LIAR'S GAME VOL. 2
Copyright © Mamenosuke Fujimaru / QuinRose 2012
First published in Japan in 2012 by ICHIJINSHA Inc., Tokyo.
English translation rights arranged with ICHIJINSHA Inc., Tokyo, Japan.

ISBN: 978-1-937867-25-6

Printed in Canada

First Printing: May 2013

10 9 8 7 6 5 4 3 2 1

Seven Seas

FOLLOW US ONLINE: www.gomanga.com

READING DIRECTIONS

This book reads from *right to left*, Japanese style.
If this is your first time reading manga, you start
reading from the top right panel on each page and
take it from there. If you get lost, just follow the
numbered diagram here. It may seem backwards
at first, but you'll get the hang of it! Have fun!!

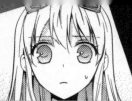

Alice Liddell

An average teenage girl...with a heavy complex. After being dragged to Wonderland by the White Rabbit, she's managed to adapt and even enjoy her bizarre surroundings.

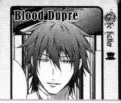

Blood Dupre
The Hatter

The dangerous, shadowy leader of the mafia group known as the Hatter Family. He's incredibly smart, but due to his temperamental moods and his desire to keep things "interesting," he often digs his own grave—and the graves of many others.

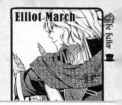

Elliot March
The Hatter

The No. 2 of the Hatter Family and Blood's right-hand man, Elliot is an ex-criminal and an escaped convict. After partnering with Blood, he improved his violent nature and thinks for several seconds before shooting. In his mind, this is a vast improvement.

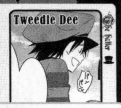

Tweedle Dee
The Hatter

Gatekeeper of the Hatter territory, Dee loves days off. He and his brother can be innocent at times, but their (frequent) malice and unsavory activities earned them the nickname "Bloody Twins." He can shifts his body between a child and an adult version of itself.

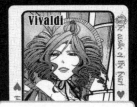

Vivaldi
The Castle of the Heart

Ruthless and cruel, Vivaldi is an arrogant beauty with a wild temper. She takes her fury out on everyone around her, including her poor subordinates. Although a picture-perfect Mad Queen, she cares for Alice as if Alice were her little sister... or a very interesting plaything.

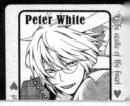

Peter White
The Castle of the Heart

Prime Minister of Heart Castle who has rabbit ears growing out of his head. He loves Alice and hates everything else. His cruel, irrational actions are disturbing, but he acts like a completely different person—er, rabbit?—when in the throes of his love for Alice.

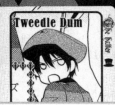

Tweedle Dum
The Hatter

The other Bloody Twin, Dum loves money. He can also become an adult when he feels like it.

Alice IN THE COUNTRY OF Joker

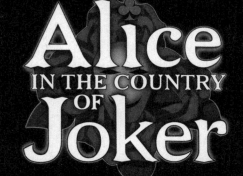

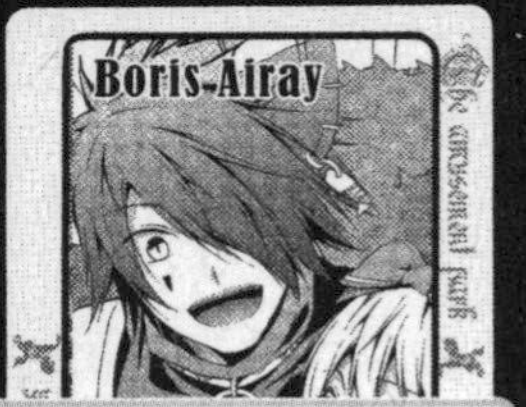
Boris Airay
The amusement park

A riddle-loving cat with a signature smirk, he has a tendency to pose questions and never answer them. Since seeing the Sleepy Mouse whets his appetite, he carries a fork and knife at all times.

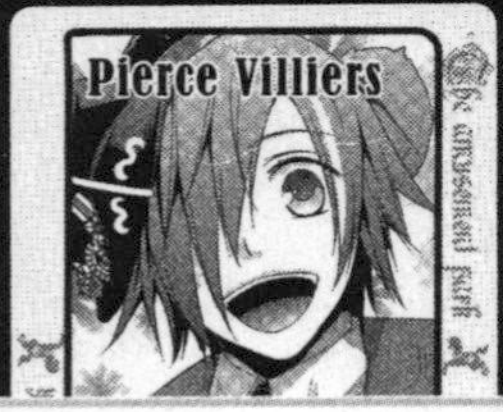
Pierce Villiers
The amusement park

An insomniac mouse who drinks too much coffee. He's terrified of Boris but loves Nightmare, who brings precious sleep. He used to be a part of the Hatter family, but after relentless bullying from the cat and twins, he's become a runaway.

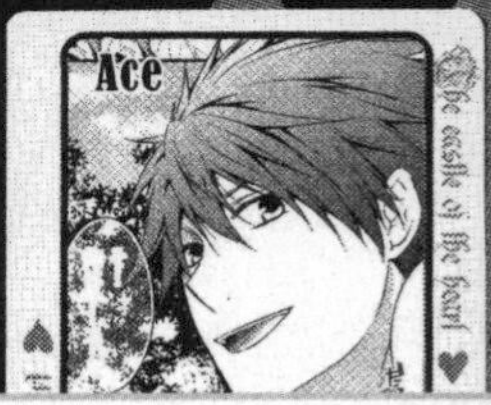
Ace
The castle of the heart

The Knight of Hearts and subordinate of Vivaldi. He's a very unlucky (yet strangely positive) man...who tends to plow forward and only worsen his situation. Ace is one of the Clockmaker's few friends and visits Julius frequently—usually getting lost on the way.

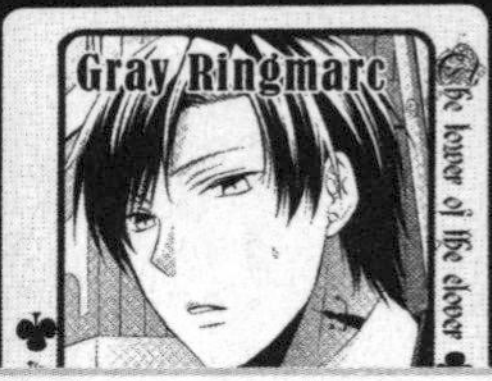
Gray Ringmarc
The tower of the clover

Nightmare's subordinate. This sound thinker with a strong work ethic is surprisingly good with a blade. Elliot considers Gray a comrade, since they share a strong dedication to their bosses...which annoys Gray.

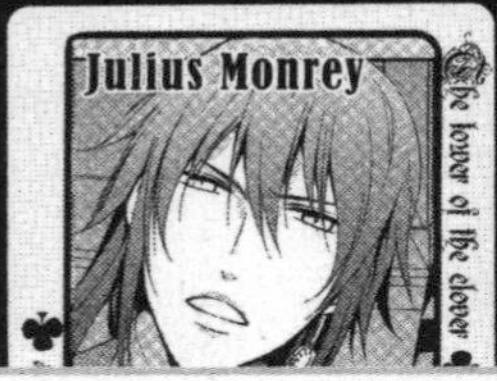
Julius Monrey
The tower of the clover

This gloomy Clockmaker is also known as the Undertaker. Despite being a sarcastic workaholic, he gets along with Ace. He had some part in the imprisonment of Elliot, the March Hare, and is thus the target for hatred.

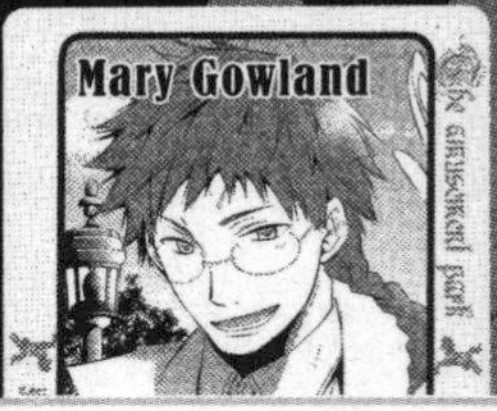
Mary Gowland
The amusement park

The owner of the Amusement Park. He hides his hated first name, Mary, but pretty much everyone already knows it. His full name is a play on words that sounds like "Merry Go Round" when said quickly. He's a terrible, terrible musician.

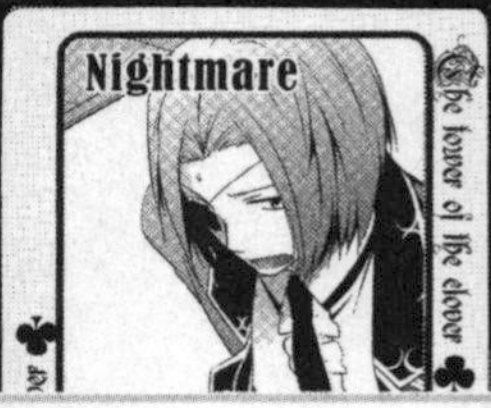
Nightmare
The tower of the clover

A sickly nightmare who often coughs up blood. He has the power to read people's thoughts and enter dreams. He technically holds a high position and has many subordinates, but since he can't even take care of his own health, he leaves most things to Gray.

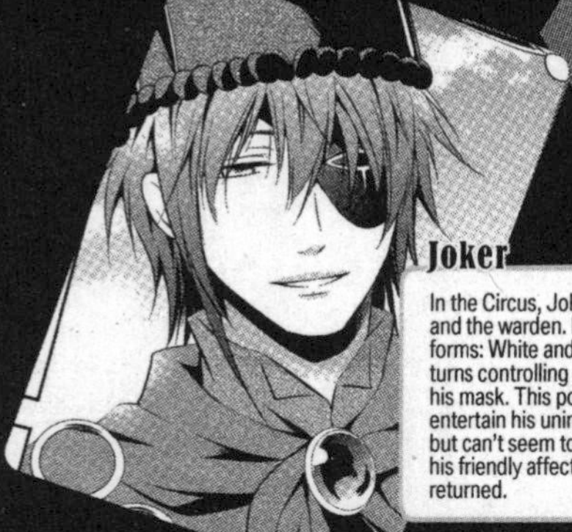
Joker

In the Circus, Joker is the leader... and the warden. He exists in two forms: White and Black, which take turns controlling either his body or his mask. This poor card loves to entertain his uninterested peers, but can't seem tounderstand why his friendly affections are rarely returned.

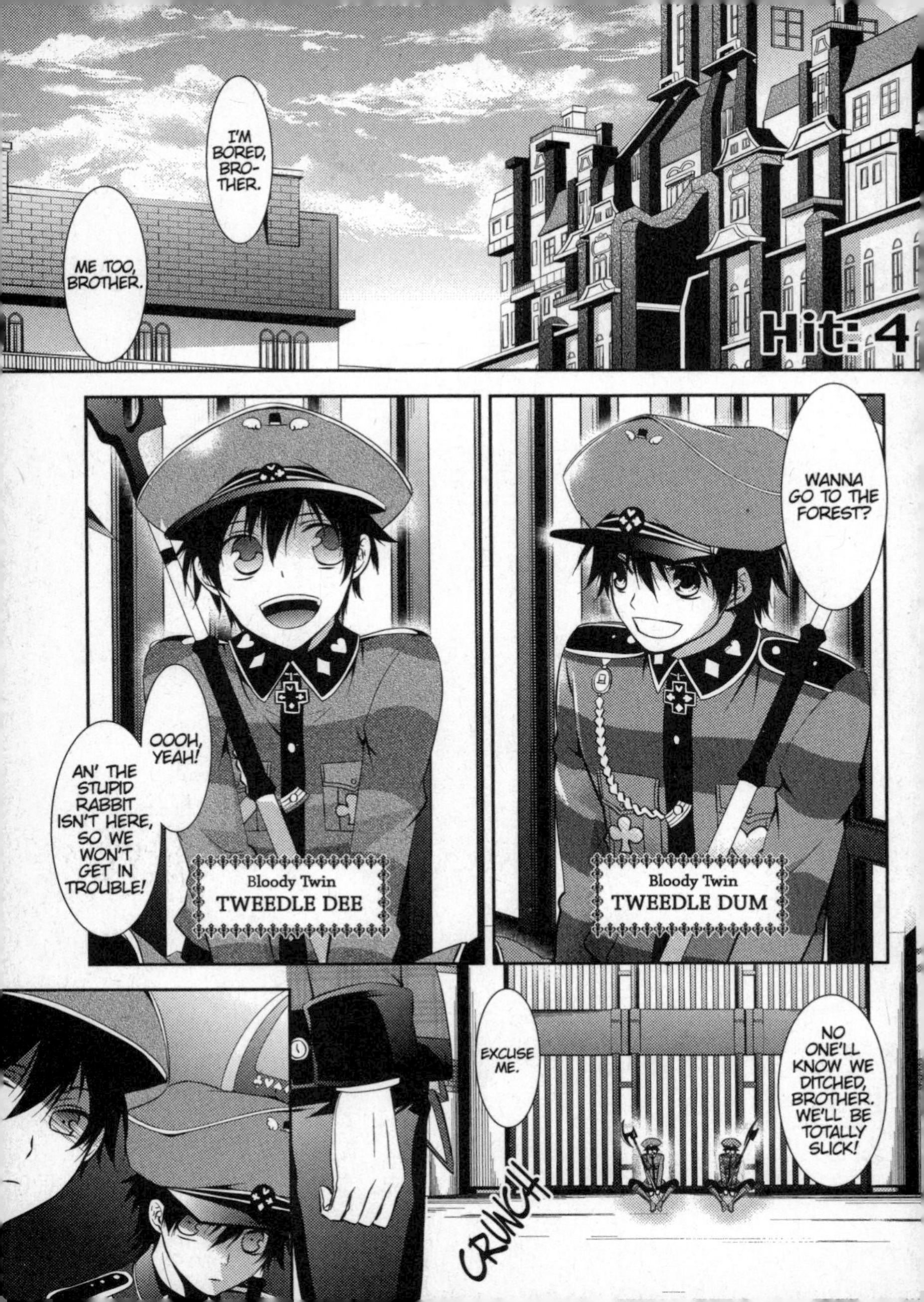
Hit: 4
I'M BORED, BROTHER.
ME TOO, BROTHER.
WANNA GO TO THE FOREST?
Bloody Twin TWEEDLE DUM
OOOH, YEAH!
AN' THE STUPID RABBIT ISN'T HERE, SO WE WON'T GET IN TROUBLE!
Bloody Twin TWEEDLE DEE
NO ONE'LL KNOW WE DITCHED, BROTHER. WE'LL BE TOTALLY SLICK!
EXCUSE ME.
CRUNCH

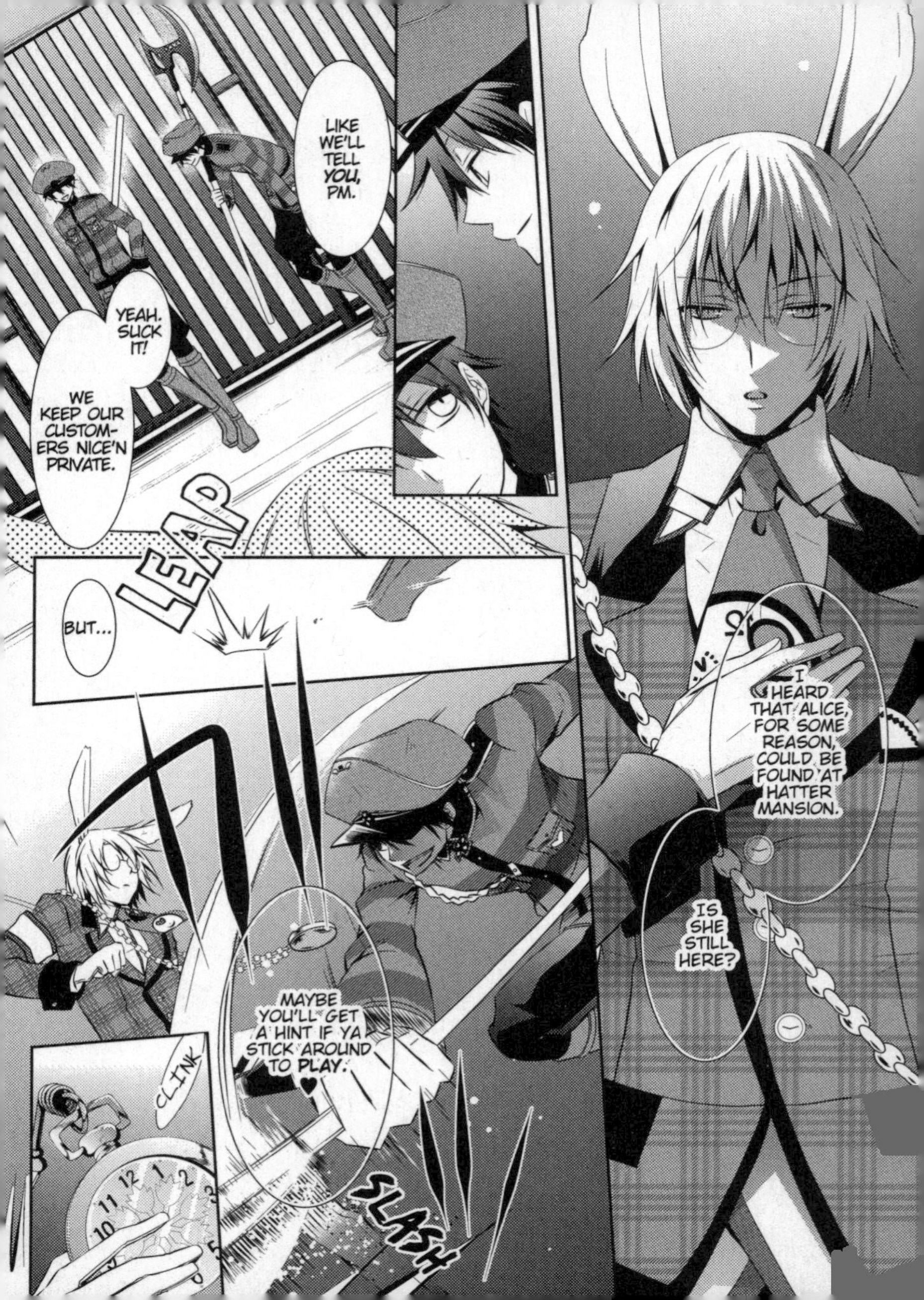
I HEARD THAT ALICE, FOR SOME REASON, COULD BE FOUND AT HATTER MANSION.
IS SHE STILL HERE?
LIKE WE'LL TELL YOU, PM.
YEAH. SUCK IT!
WE KEEP OUR CUSTOMERS NICE'N PRIVATE.
BUT...
LEAP
MAYBE YOU'LL GET A HINT IF YA STICK AROUND TO PLAY. ♥
SLASH
CLINK

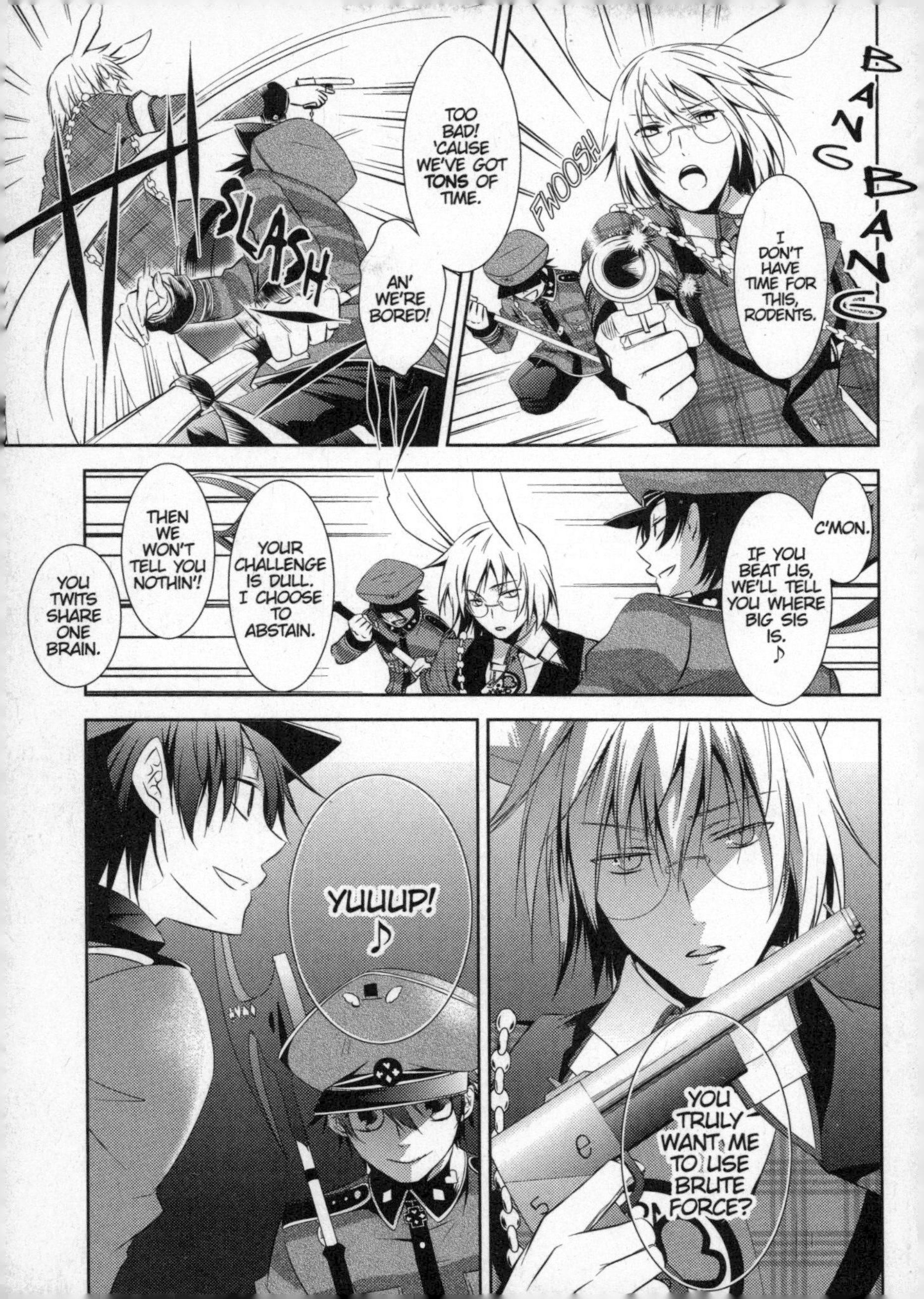
BANG BANG
I DON'T HAVE TIME FOR THIS, RODENTS.
FWOOSH!
TOO BAD! 'CAUSE WE'VE GOT TONS OF TIME.
AN' WE'RE BORED!
SLASH
C'MON.
IF YOU BEAT US, WE'LL TELL YOU WHERE BIG SIS IS. ♪
YOUR CHALLENGE IS DULL. I CHOOSE TO ABSTAIN.
THEN WE WON'T TELL YOU NOTHIN'!
YOU TWITS SHARE ONE BRAIN.
YOU TRULY WANT ME TO USE BRUTE FORCE?
YUUUP! ♪

Hit: 4

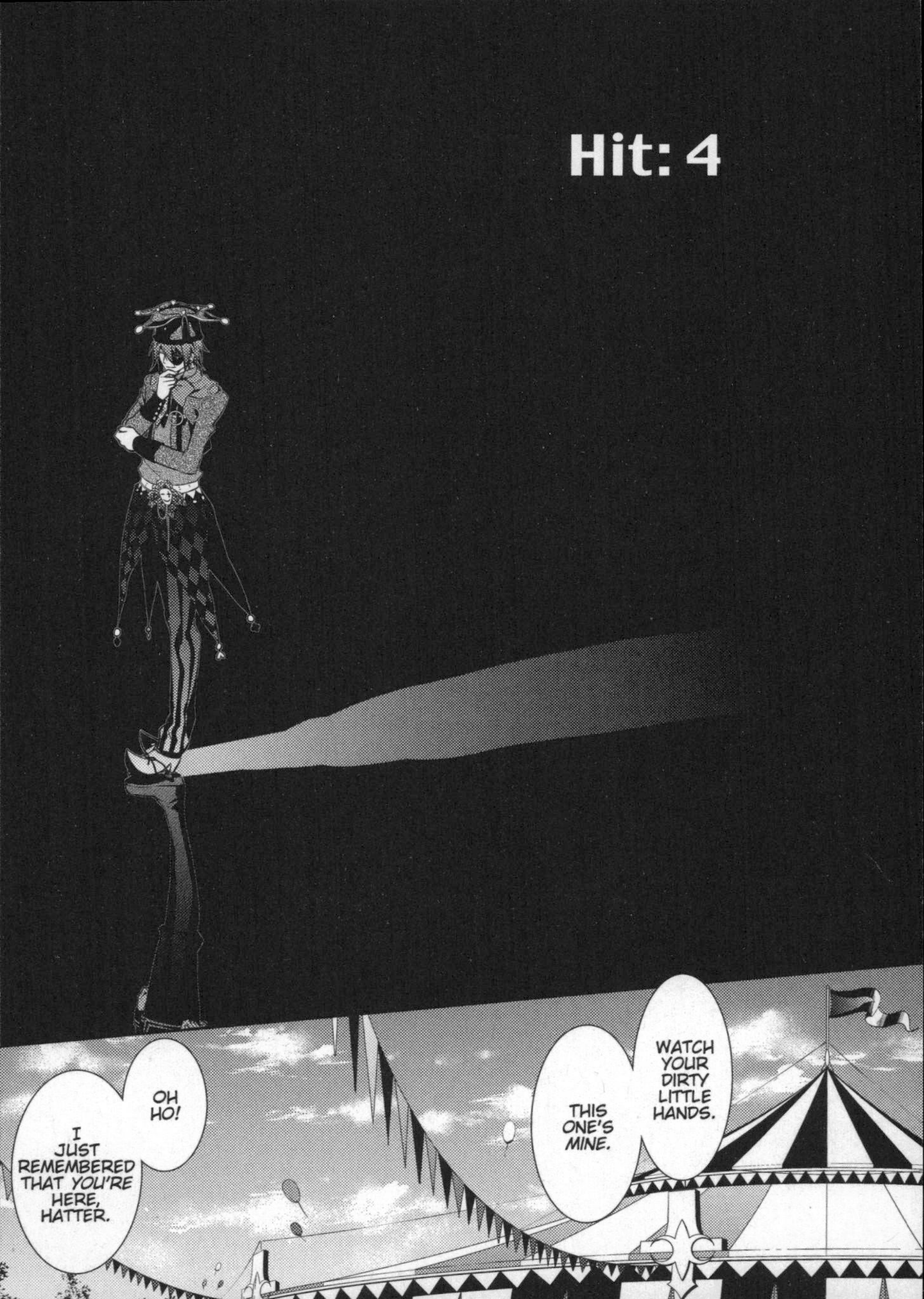
WATCH YOUR DIRTY LITTLE HANDS.
THIS ONE'S MINE.
OH HO!
I JUST REMEMBERED THAT *YOU'RE* HERE, HATTER.

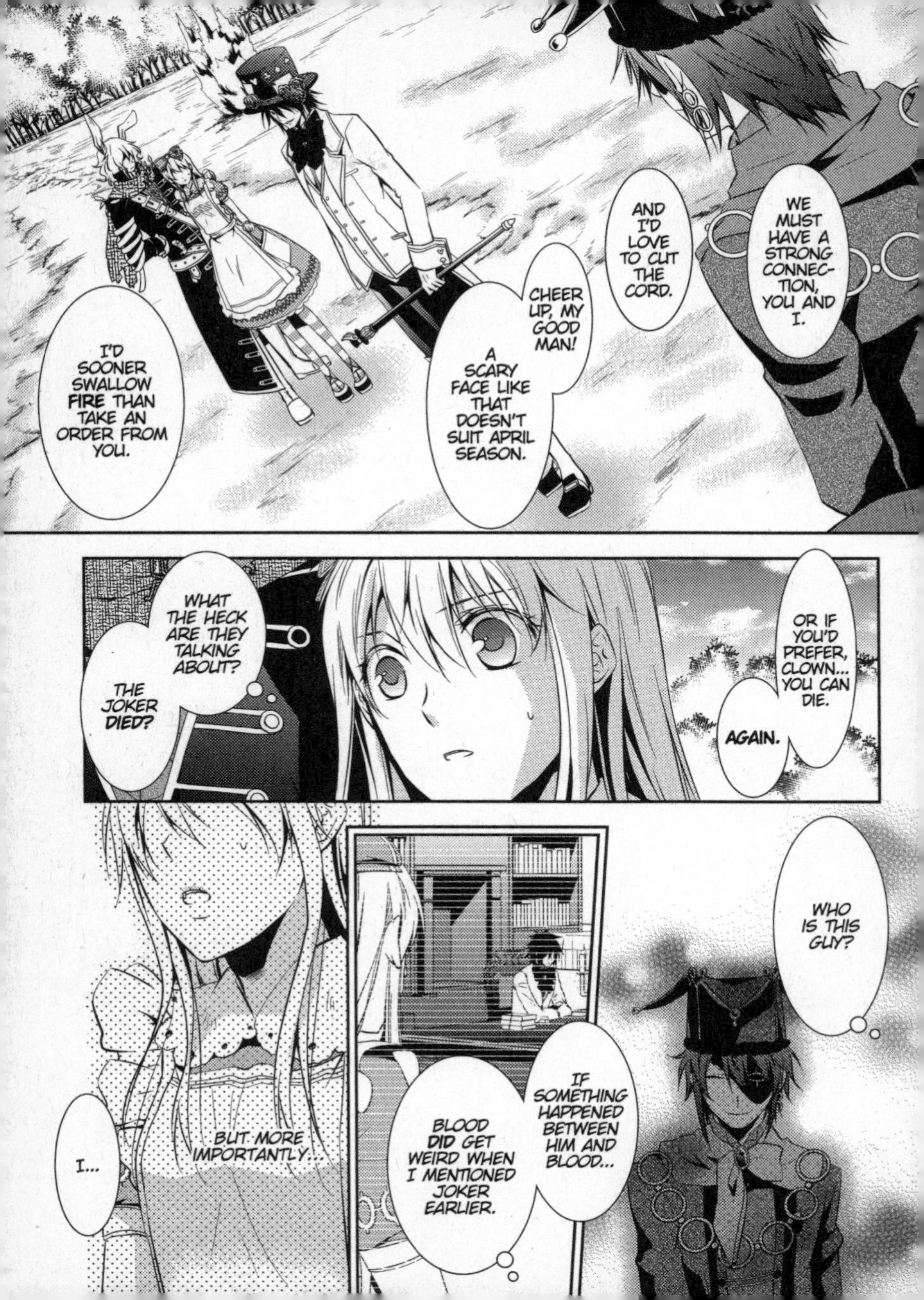
WE MUST HAVE A STRONG CONNECTION, YOU AND I.
AND I'D LOVE TO CUT THE CORD.
CHEER UP, MY GOOD MAN!
A SCARY FACE LIKE THAT DOESN'T SUIT APRIL SEASON.
I'D SOONER SWALLOW **FIRE** THAN TAKE AN ORDER FROM YOU.
OR IF YOU'D PREFER, CLOWN... YOU CAN DIE.
AGAIN.
WHAT THE HECK ARE THEY TALKING ABOUT?
THE JOKER **DIED**?
WHO IS THIS GUY?
IF SOMETHING HAPPENED BETWEEN HIM AND BLOOD...
BLOOD **DID** GET WEIRD WHEN I MENTIONED JOKER EARLIER.
BUT MORE IMPORTANTLY...
I...

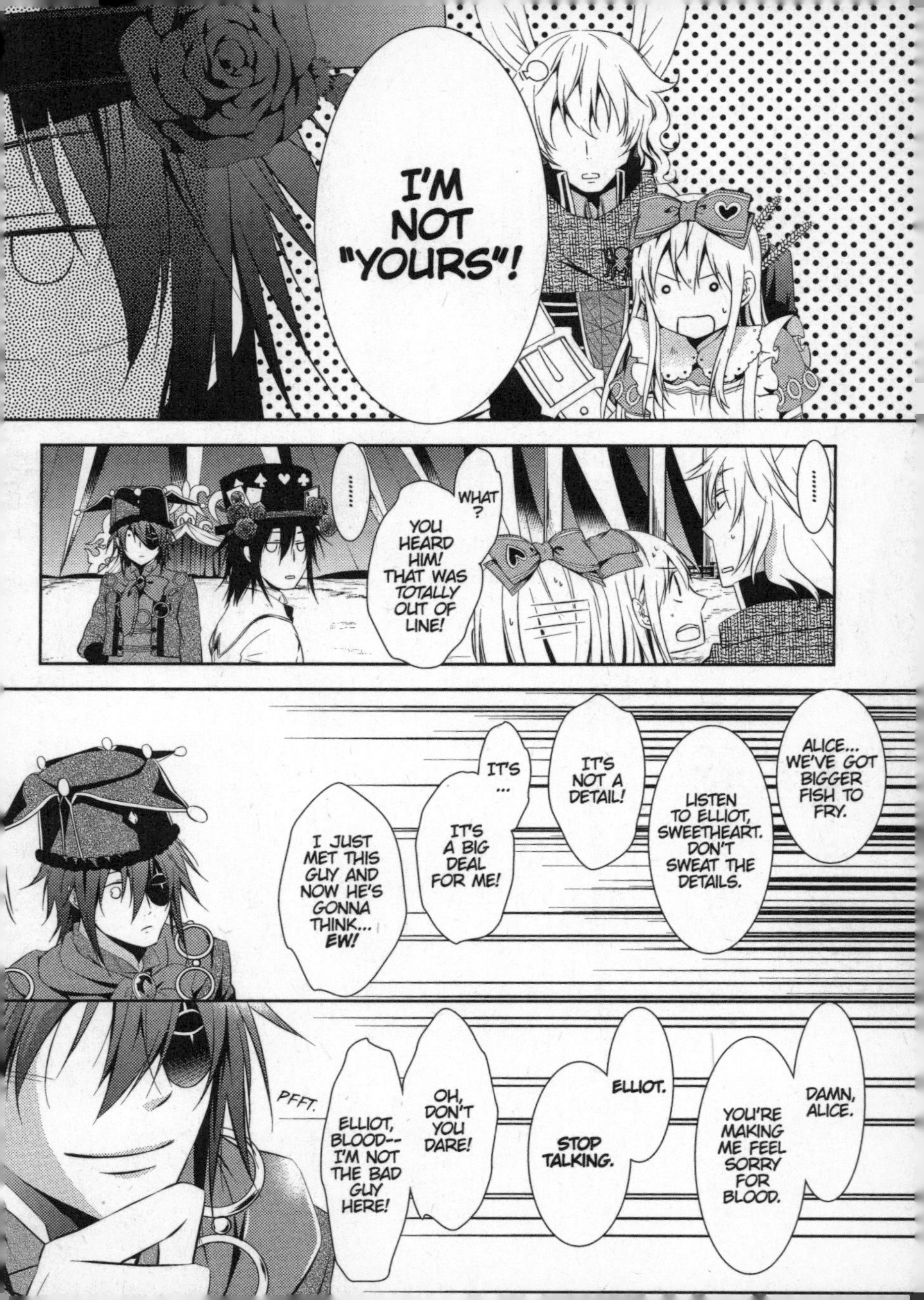

I'M NOT "YOURS"!
......
WHAT? YOU HEARD HIM! THAT WAS TOTALLY OUT OF LINE!
......
ALICE... WE'VE GOT BIGGER FISH TO FRY.
LISTEN TO ELLIOT, SWEETHEART. DON'T SWEAT THE DETAILS.
IT'S NOT A DETAIL!
IT'S ...
IT'S A BIG DEAL FOR ME!
I JUST MET THIS GUY AND NOW HE'S GONNA THINK... EW!
DAMN, ALICE.
YOU'RE MAKING ME FEEL SORRY FOR BLOOD.
ELLIOT.
STOP TALKING.
OH, DON'T YOU DARE!
ELLIOT, BLOOD-- I'M NOT THE BAD GUY HERE!
PFFT.

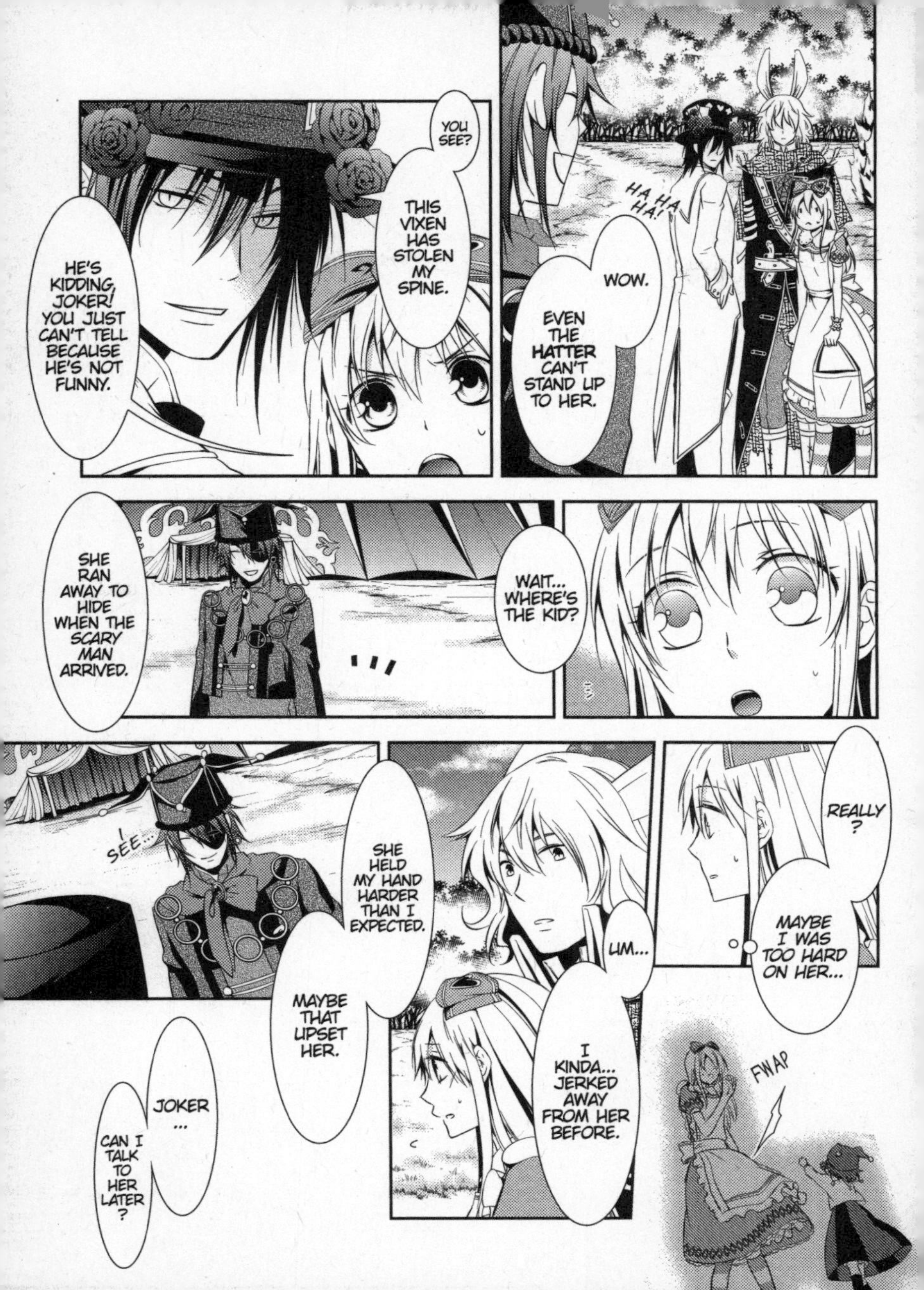
HA HA HA!
WOW.
EVEN THE HATTER CAN'T STAND UP TO HER.
YOU SEE?
THIS VIXEN HAS STOLEN MY SPINE.
HE'S KIDDING, JOKER! YOU JUST CAN'T TELL BECAUSE HE'S NOT FUNNY.
WAIT... WHERE'S THE KID?
SHE RAN AWAY TO HIDE WHEN THE SCARY MAN ARRIVED.
REALLY?
MAYBE I WAS TOO HARD ON HER...
SHE HELD MY HAND HARDER THAN I EXPECTED.
UM...
I SEE...
I KINDA... JERKED AWAY FROM HER BEFORE.
FWAP
MAYBE THAT UPSET HER.
JOKER...
CAN I TALK TO HER LATER?

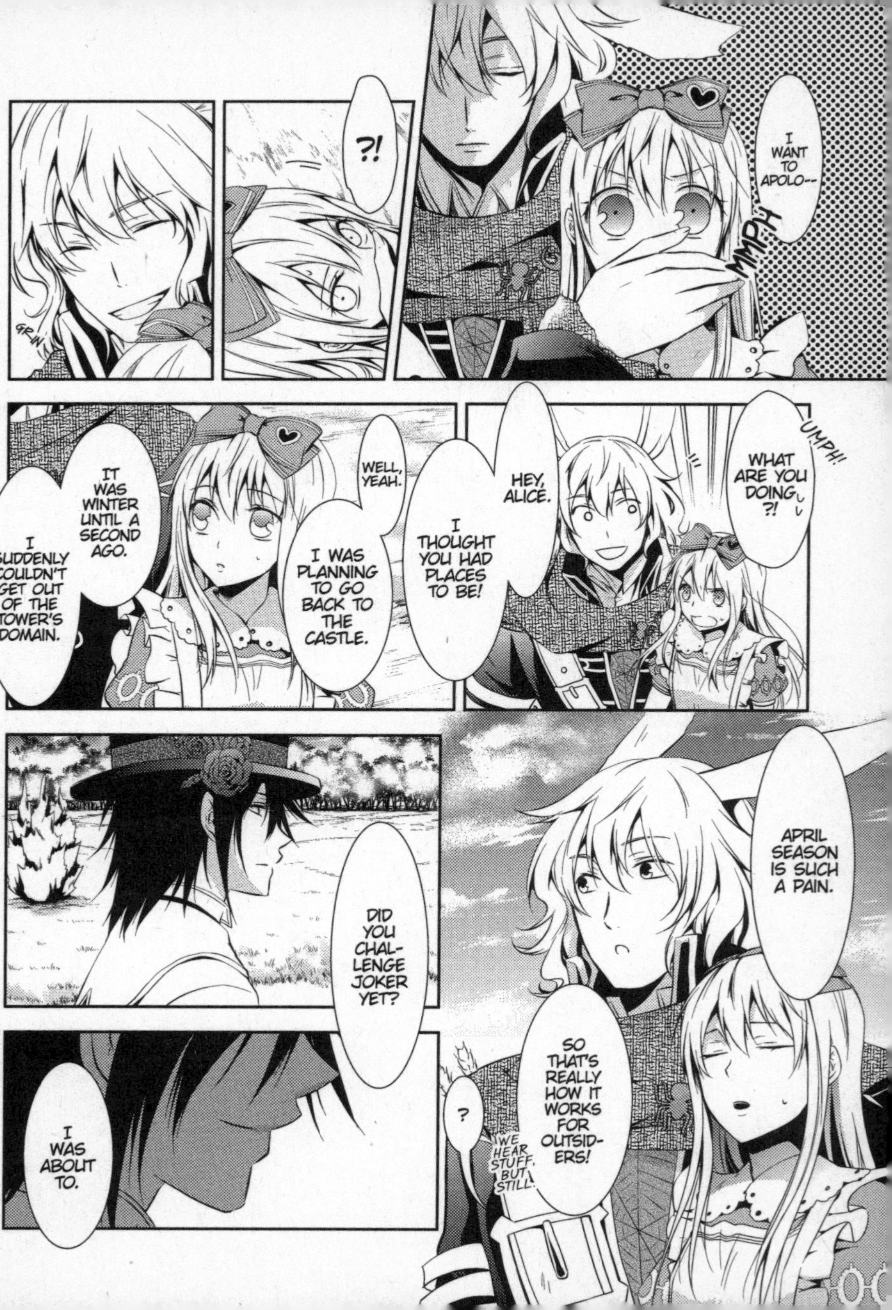
I WANT TO APOLO--
MMPH
?!
GRIN
UMPH!!
WHAT ARE YOU DOING?!
HEY, ALICE.
I THOUGHT YOU HAD PLACES TO BE!
WELL, YEAH.
I WAS PLANNING TO GO BACK TO THE CASTLE.
IT WAS WINTER UNTIL A SECOND AGO.
I SUDDENLY COULDN'T GET OUT OF THE TOWER'S DOMAIN.
APRIL SEASON IS SUCH A PAIN.
SO THAT'S REALLY HOW IT WORKS FOR OUTSIDERS!
WE HEAR STUFF, BUT STILL.
?
DID YOU CHALLENGE JOKER YET?
I WAS ABOUT TO.

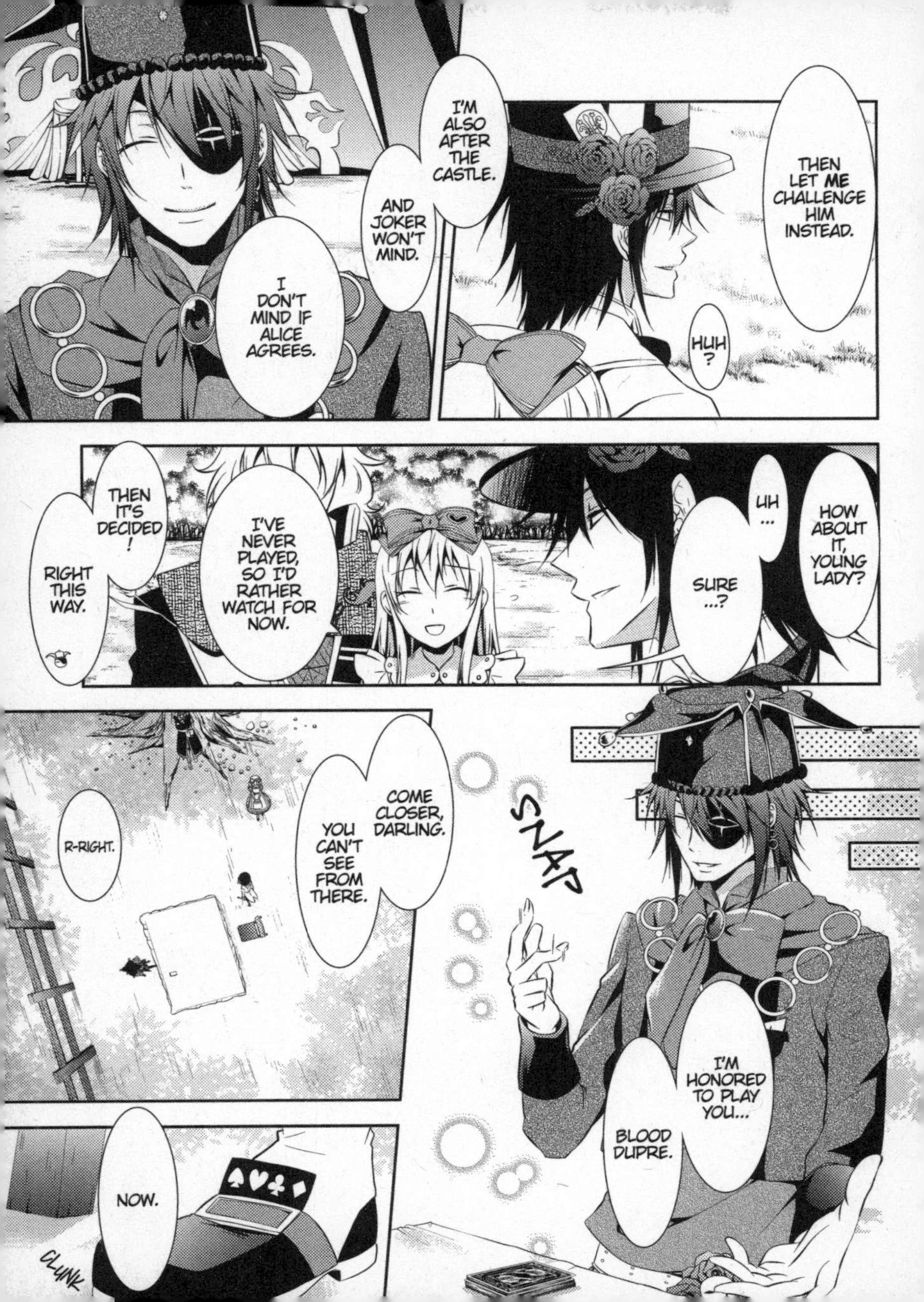
THEN LET ME CHALLENGE HIM INSTEAD.
HUH?
I'M ALSO AFTER THE CASTLE.
AND JOKER WON'T MIND.
I DON'T MIND IF ALICE AGREES.
HOW ABOUT IT, YOUNG LADY?
UH... SURE...?
I'VE NEVER PLAYED, SO I'D RATHER WATCH FOR NOW.
THEN IT'S DECIDED! RIGHT THIS WAY.
SNAP
I'M HONORED TO PLAY YOU...
BLOOD DUPRE.
COME CLOSER, DARLING.
YOU CAN'T SEE FROM THERE.
R-RIGHT.
NOW.
CLUNK

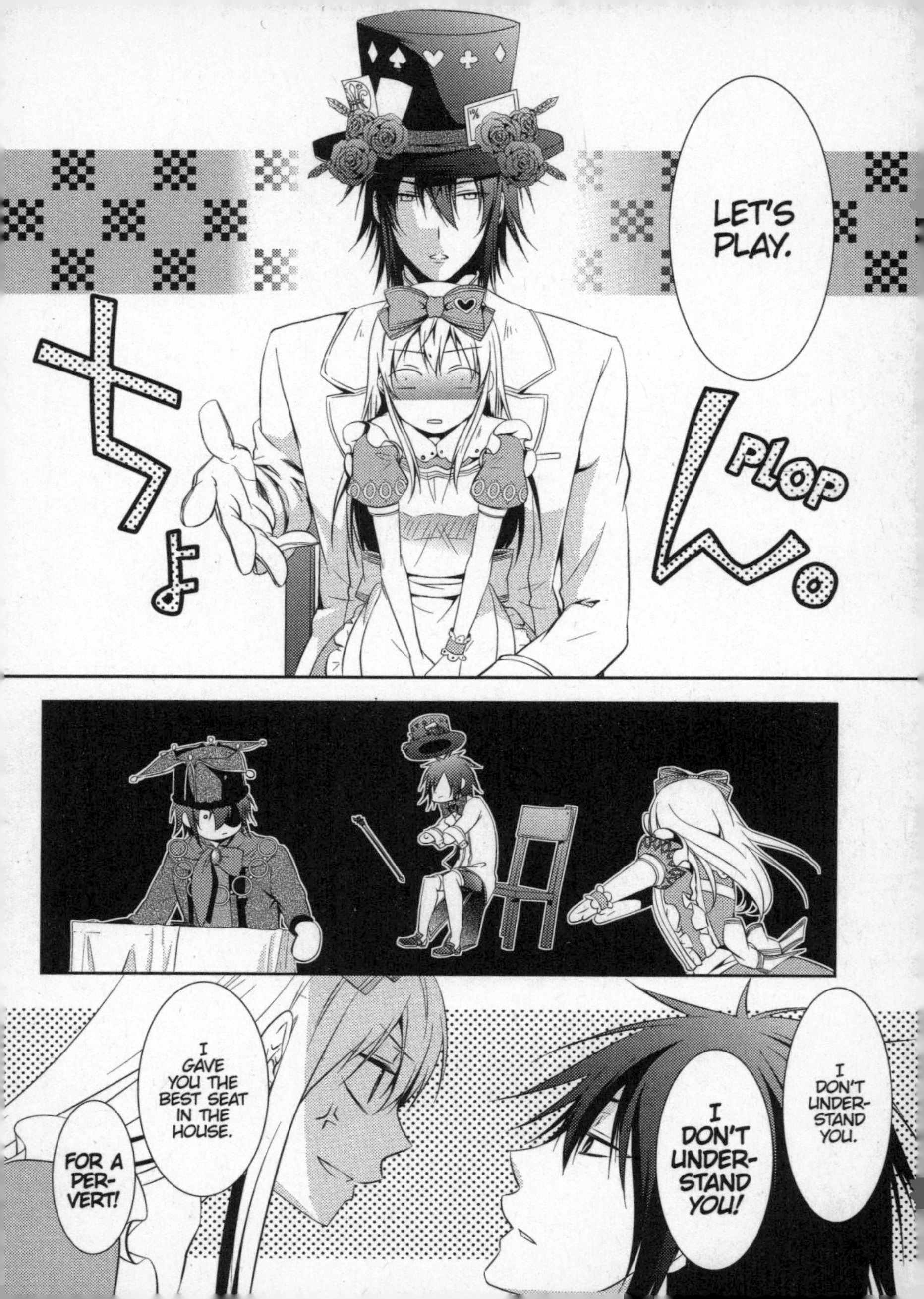
LET'S PLAY.
ん。
PLOP
ちょ
I DON'T UNDER-STAND YOU.
I DON'T UNDER-STAND YOU!
I GAVE YOU THE BEST SEAT IN THE HOUSE.
FOR A PER-VERT!

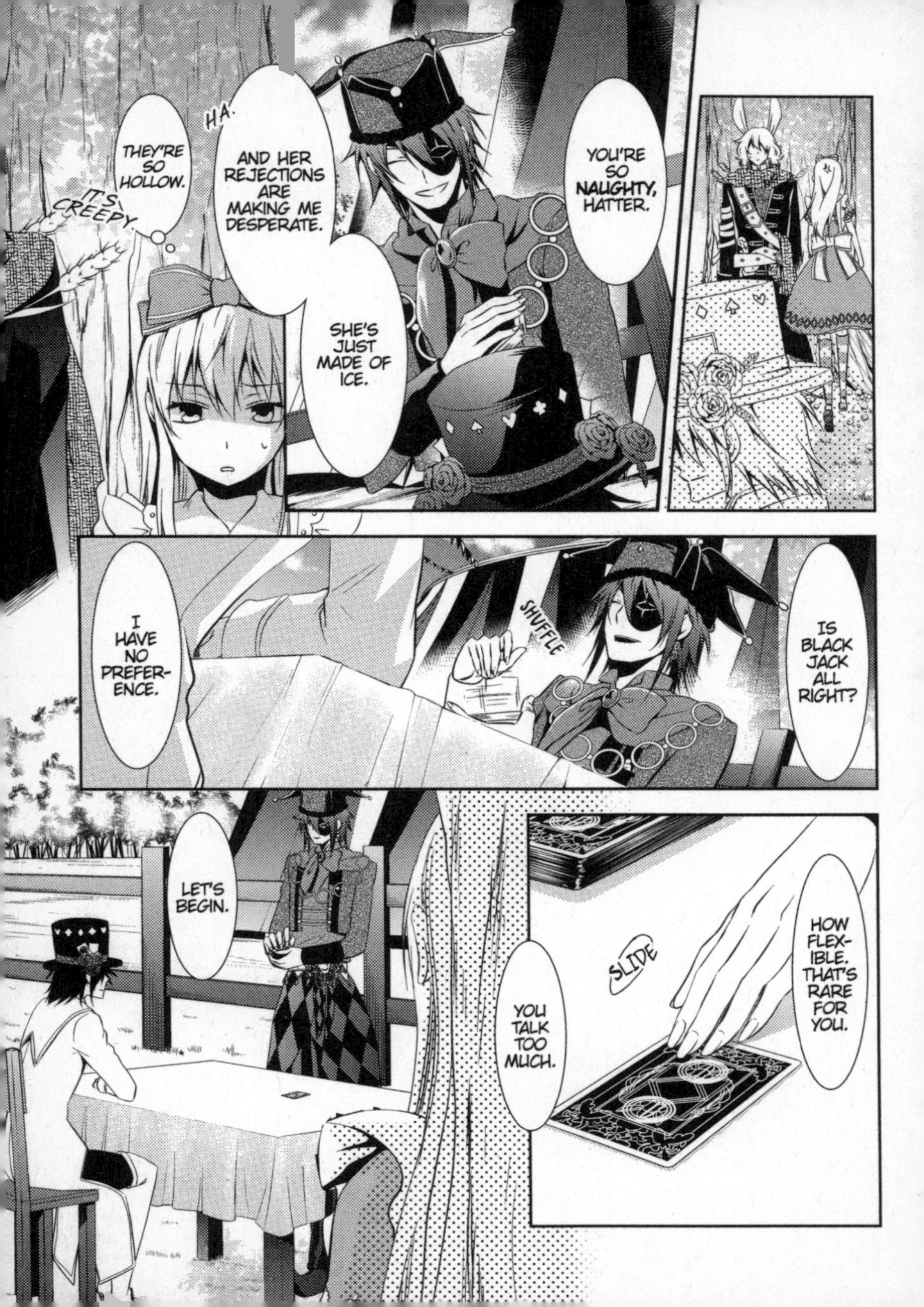
YOU'RE SO NAUGHTY, HATTER.
AND HER REJECTIONS ARE MAKING ME DESPERATE.
HA.
SHE'S JUST MADE OF ICE.
THEY'RE SO HOLLOW.
IT'S CREEPY.
IS BLACK JACK ALL RIGHT?
SHUFFLE
I HAVE NO PREFERENCE.
HOW FLEXIBLE. THAT'S RARE FOR YOU.
SLIDE
YOU TALK TOO MUCH.
LET'S BEGIN.

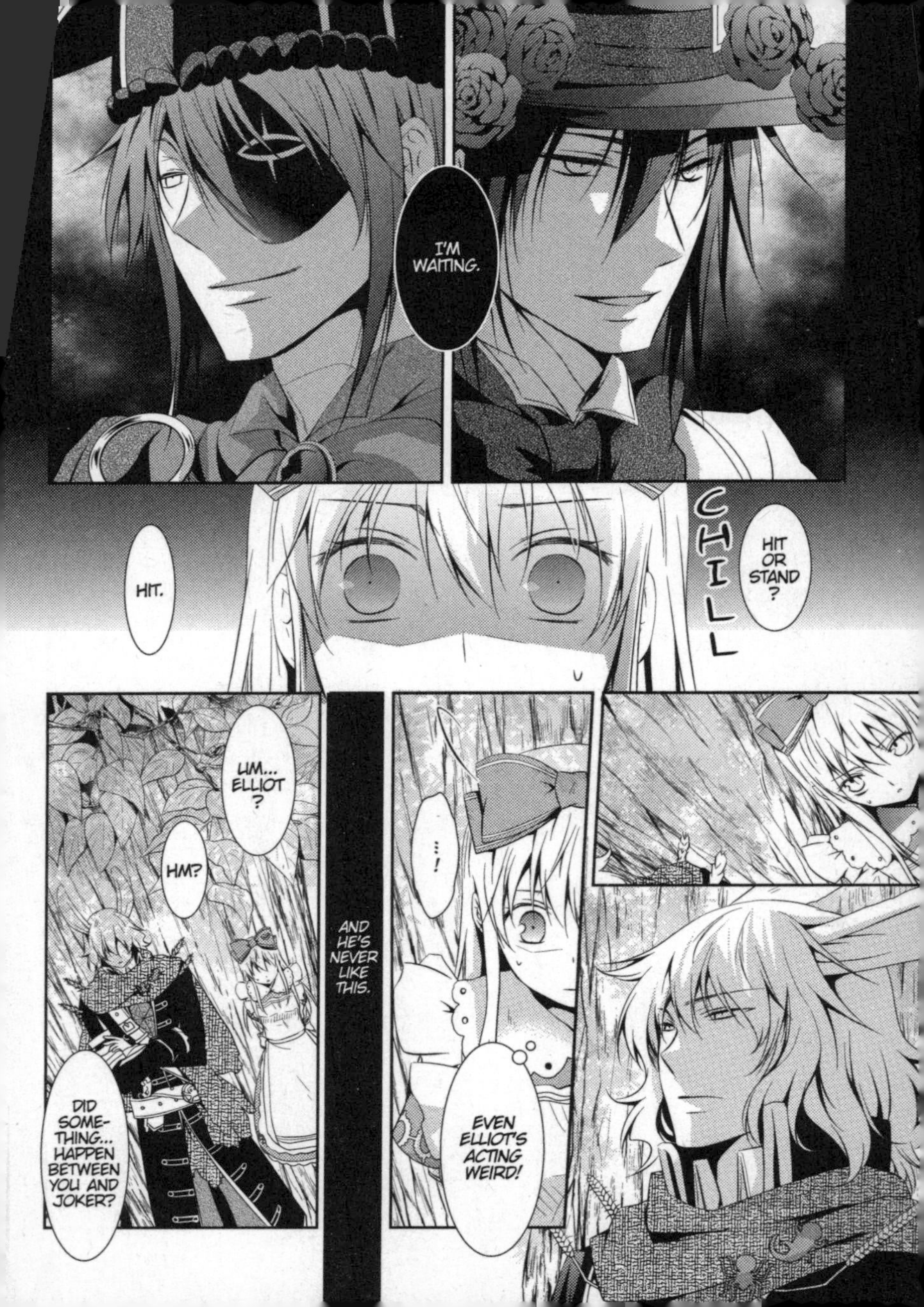
I'M WAITING.
HIT OR STAND?
CHILL
HIT.
...!
EVEN ELLIOT'S ACTING WEIRD!
AND HE'S NEVER LIKE THIS.
UM... ELLIOT?
HM?
DID SOME-THING... HAPPEN BETWEEN YOU AND JOKER?

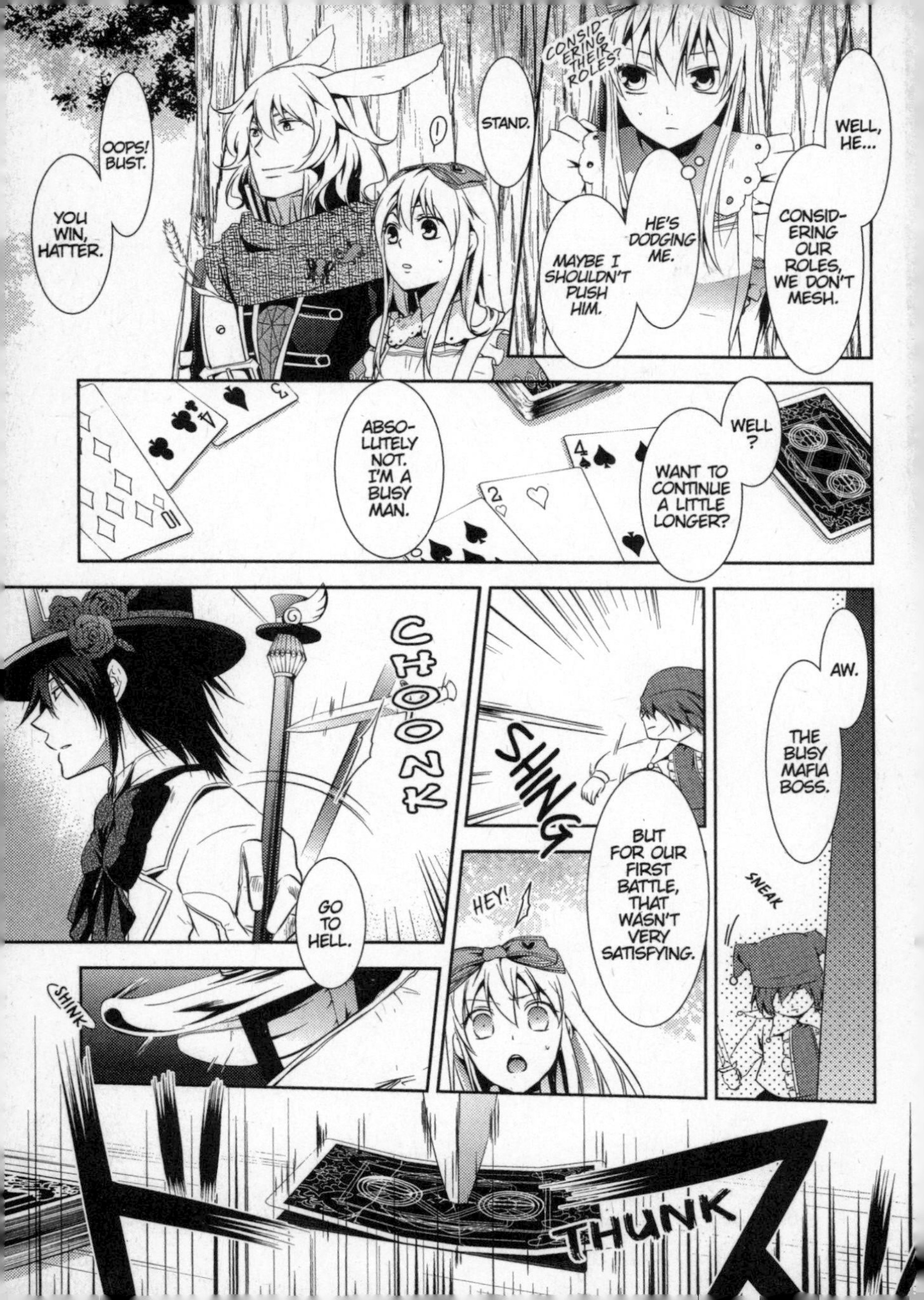

WELL, HE...
CONSID-ERING OUR ROLES, WE DON'T MESH.
CONSID-ERING THEIR ROLES?
HE'S DODGING ME.
MAYBE I SHOULDN'T PUSH HIM.
STAND.
!
OOPS! BUST.
YOU WIN, HATTER.
WELL? WANT TO CONTINUE A LITTLE LONGER?
ABSO-LUTELY NOT. I'M A BUSY MAN.
AW. THE BUSY MAFIA BOSS.
BUT FOR OUR FIRST BATTLE, THAT WASN'T VERY SATISFYING.
SHING
CHOONK
GO TO HELL.
SNEAK
HEY!
SHINK
THUNK

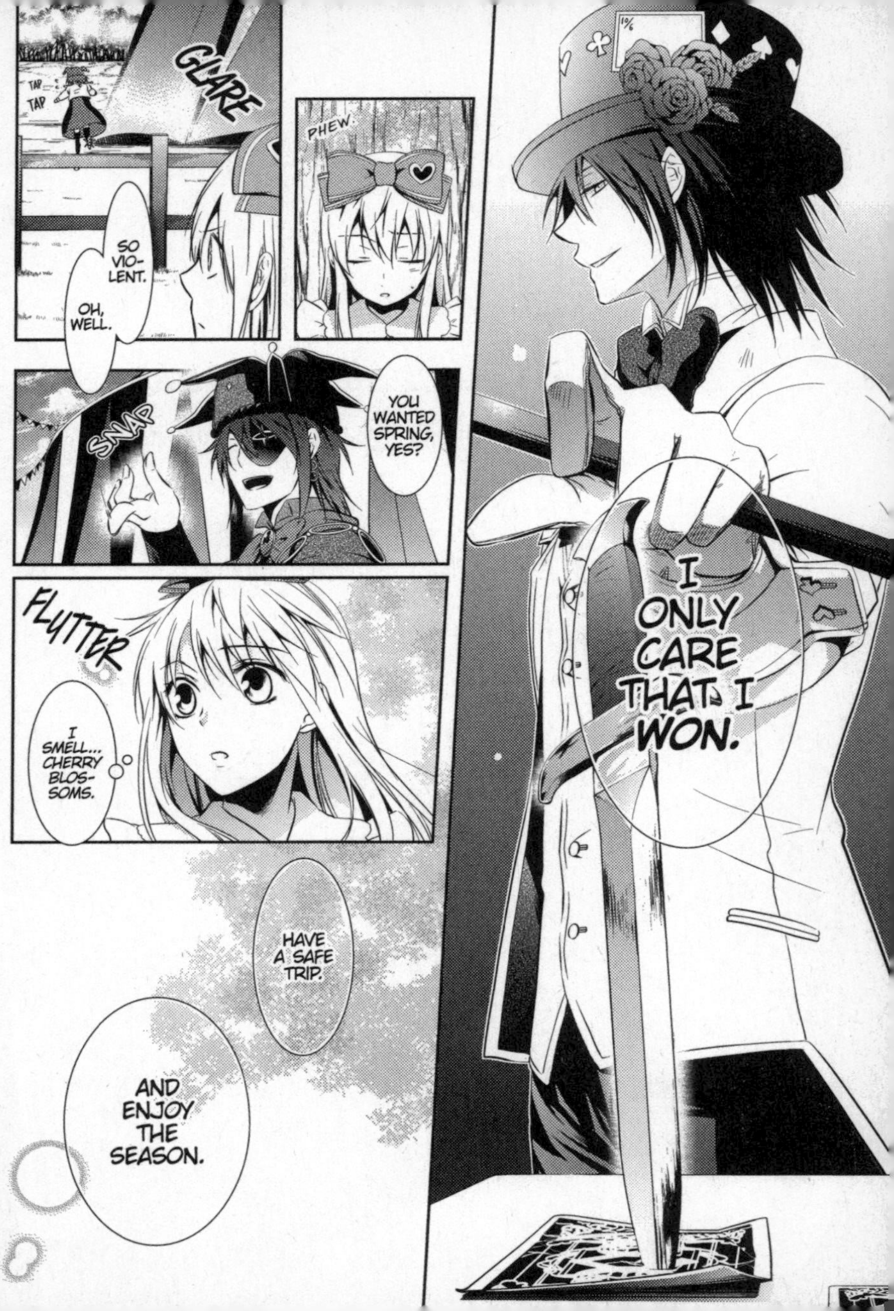
I ONLY CARE THAT I WON.
PHEW.
GLARE
TAP
TAP
SO VIO-LENT.
OH, WELL.
YOU WANTED SPRING, YES?
SNAP
FLUTTER
I SMELL... CHERRY BLOS-SOMS.
HAVE A SAFE TRIP.
AND ENJOY THE SEASON.

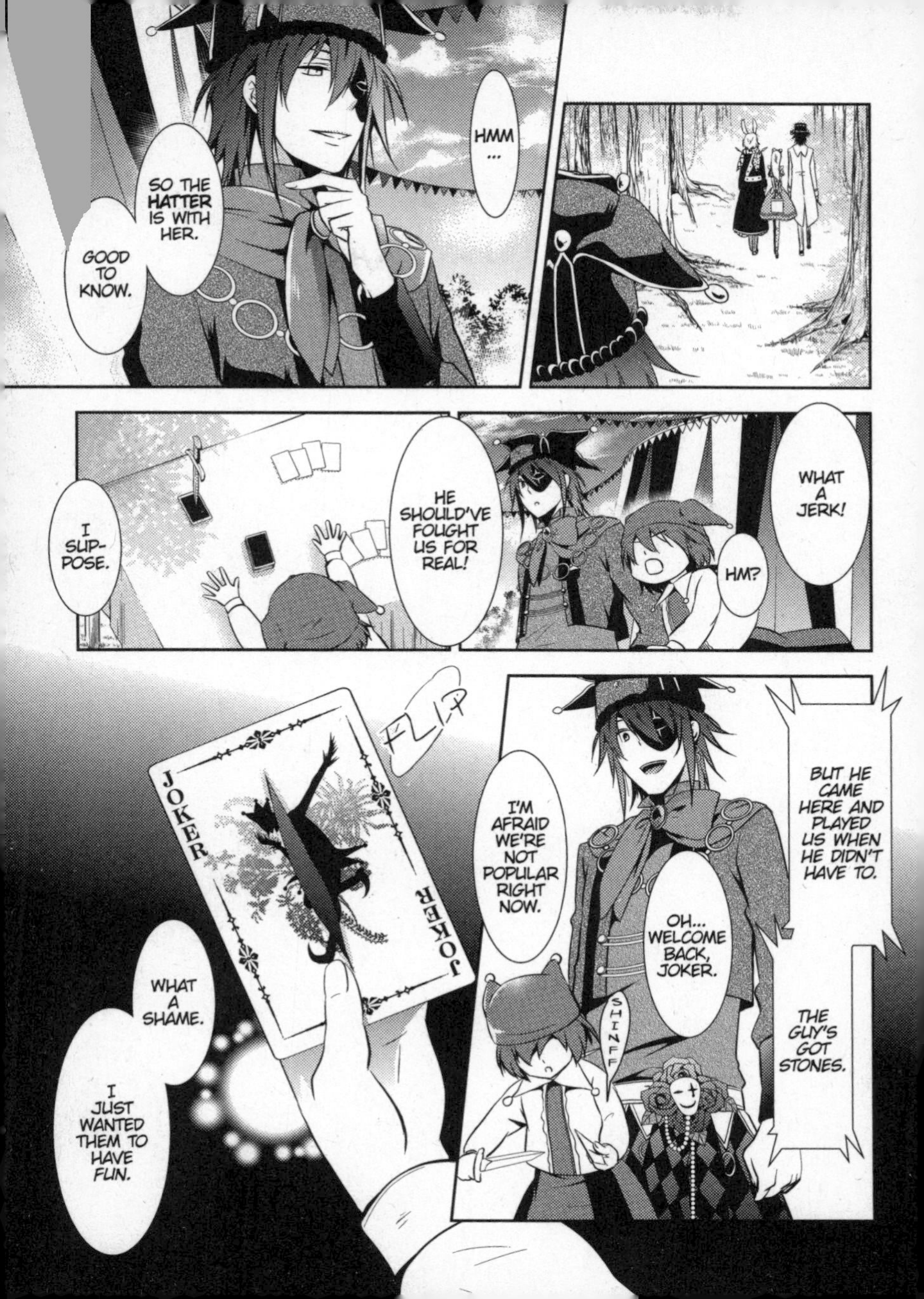
HMM...
SO THE HATTER IS WITH HER.
GOOD TO KNOW.
WHAT A JERK!
HM?
HE SHOULD'VE FOUGHT US FOR REAL!
I SUP-POSE.
BUT HE CAME HERE AND PLAYED US WHEN HE DIDN'T HAVE TO.
I'M AFRAID WE'RE NOT POPULAR RIGHT NOW.
OH... WELCOME BACK, JOKER.
THE GUY'S GOT STONES.
SHINFF
FLIP
JOKER
JOKER
WHAT A SHAME.
I JUST WANTED THEM TO HAVE FUN.

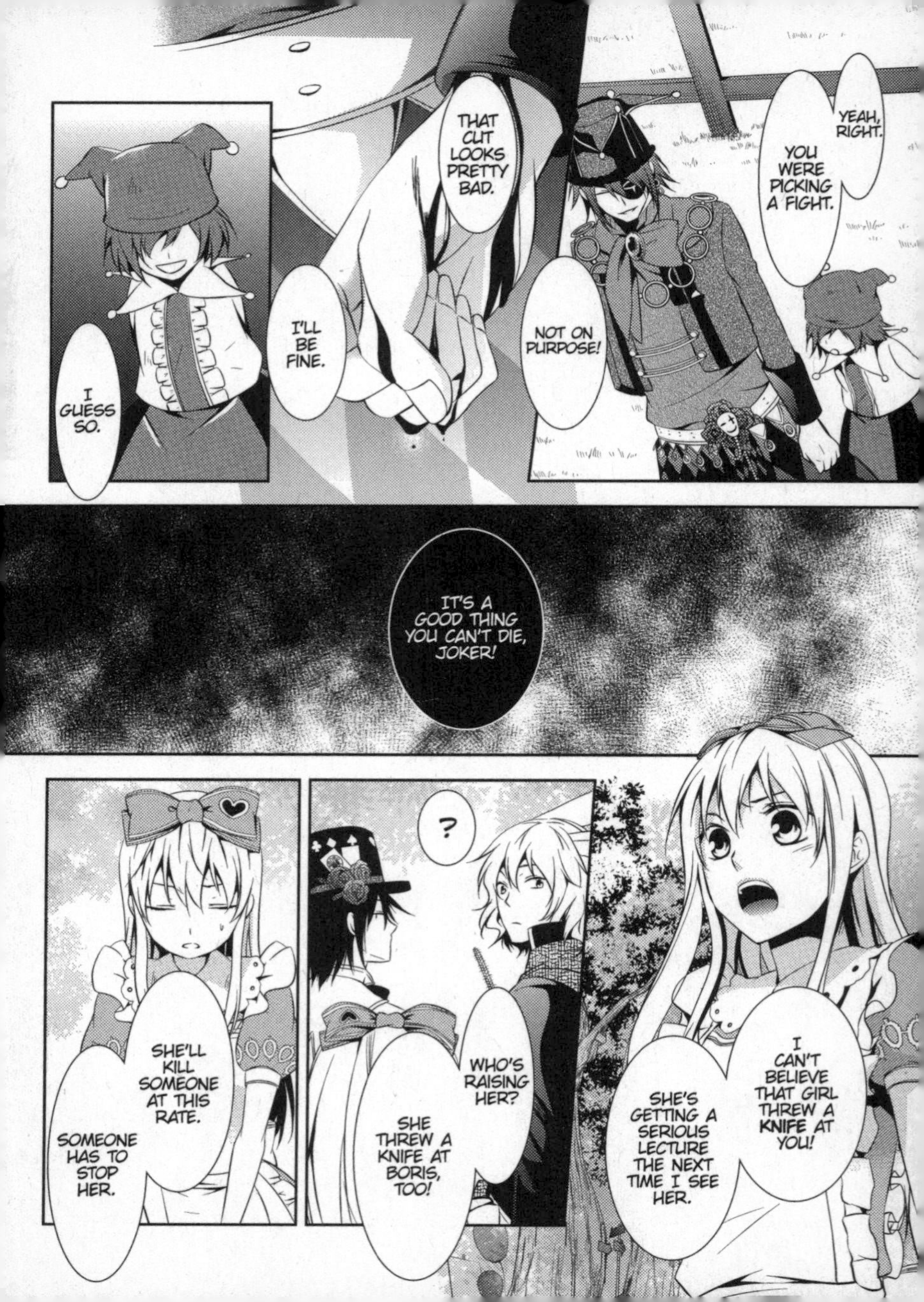

YEAH, RIGHT.
YOU WERE PICKING A FIGHT.
THAT CUT LOOKS PRETTY BAD.
NOT ON PURPOSE!
I'LL BE FINE.
I GUESS SO.
IT'S A GOOD THING YOU CAN'T DIE, JOKER!
I CAN'T BELIEVE THAT GIRL THREW A KNIFE AT YOU!
SHE'S GETTING A SERIOUS LECTURE THE NEXT TIME I SEE HER.
?
WHO'S RAISING HER?
SHE THREW A KNIFE AT BORIS, TOO!
SHE'LL KILL SOMEONE AT THIS RATE.
SOMEONE HAS TO STOP HER.

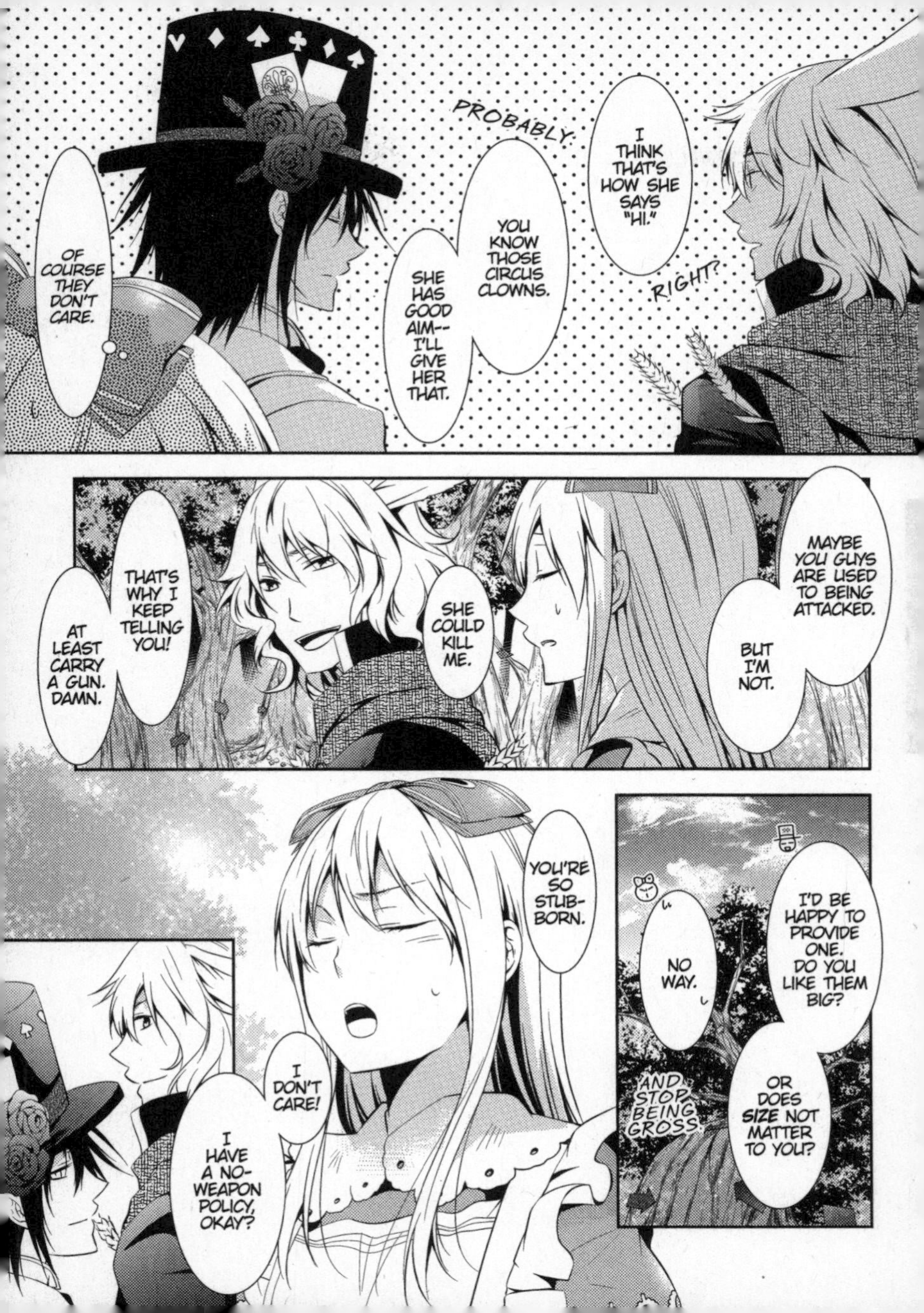
I THINK THAT'S HOW SHE SAYS "HI."
RIGHT?
PROBABLY.
YOU KNOW THOSE CIRCUS CLOWNS.
SHE HAS GOOD AIM-- I'LL GIVE HER THAT.
OF COURSE THEY DON'T CARE.
MAYBE YOU GUYS ARE USED TO BEING ATTACKED.
BUT I'M NOT.
SHE COULD KILL ME.
THAT'S WHY I KEEP TELLING YOU!
AT LEAST CARRY A GUN. DAMN.
I'D BE HAPPY TO PROVIDE ONE. DO YOU LIKE THEM BIG?
OR DOES SIZE NOT MATTER TO YOU?
NO WAY.
AND STOP BEING GROSS.
YOU'RE SO STUB-BORN.
I DON'T CARE!
I HAVE A NO-WEAPON POLICY, OKAY?

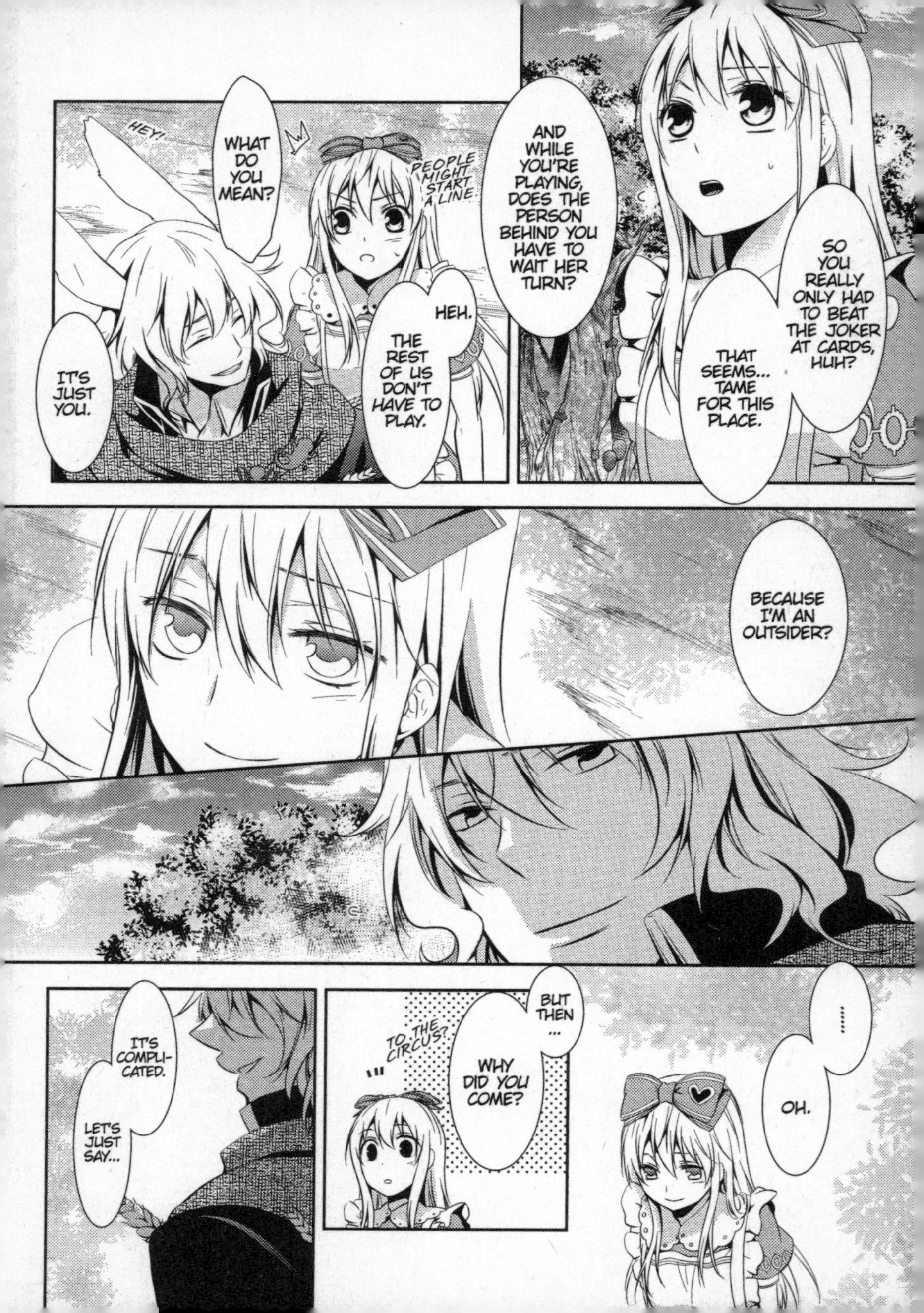

SO YOU REALLY ONLY HAD TO BEAT THE JOKER AT CARDS, HUH?
THAT SEEMS... TAME FOR THIS PLACE.
AND WHILE YOU'RE PLAYING, DOES THE PERSON BEHIND YOU HAVE TO WAIT HER TURN?
PEOPLE MIGHT START A LINE.
HEH.
THE REST OF US DON'T HAVE TO PLAY.
IT'S JUST YOU.
WHAT DO YOU MEAN?
HEY!
BECAUSE I'M AN OUTSIDER?
......
OH.
BUT THEN...
WHY DID YOU COME?
TO THE CIRCUS?
IT'S COMPLICATED.
LET'S JUST SAY...

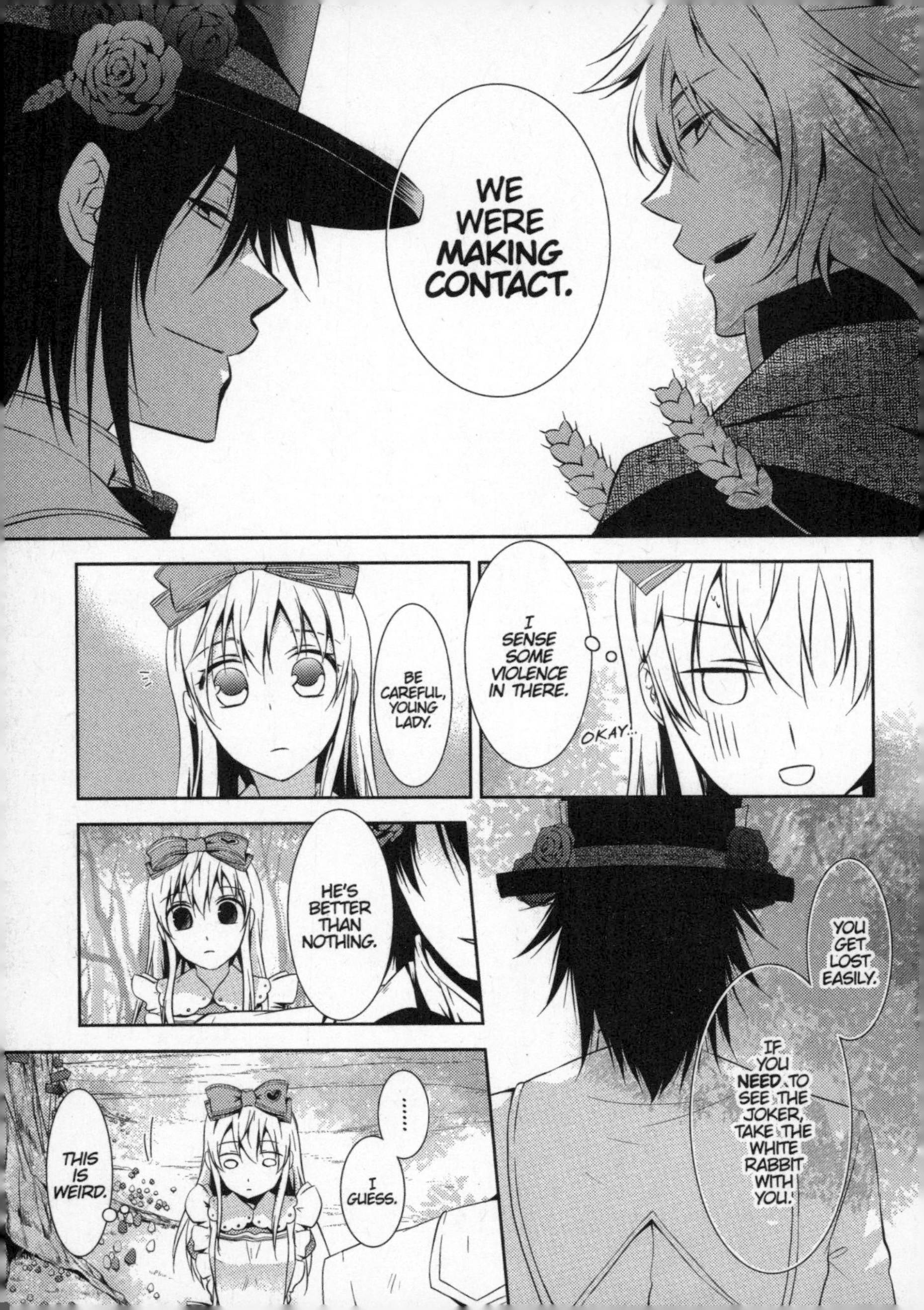
WE WERE MAKING CONTACT.
I SENSE SOME VIOLENCE IN THERE.
OKAY...
BE CAREFUL, YOUNG LADY.
YOU GET LOST EASILY.
IF YOU NEED TO SEE THE JOKER, TAKE THE WHITE RABBIT WITH YOU.
HE'S BETTER THAN NOTHING.
......
I GUESS.
THIS IS WEIRD.

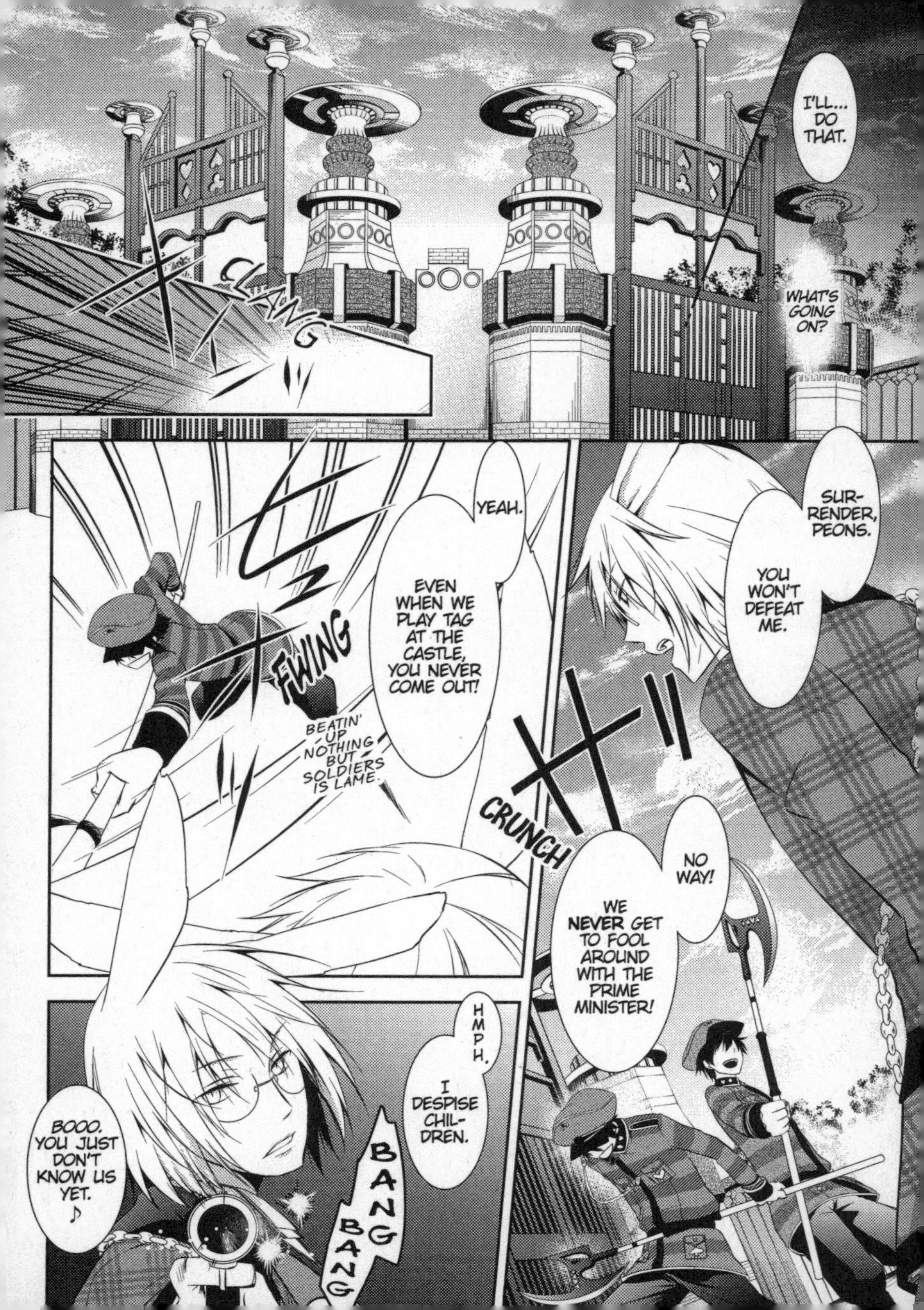
I'LL... DO THAT.
WHAT'S GOING ON?
CLANG
SUR-RENDER, PEONS.
YOU WON'T DEFEAT ME.
CRUNCH
NO WAY!
WE NEVER GET TO FOOL AROUND WITH THE PRIME MINISTER!
YEAH.
EVEN WHEN WE PLAY TAG AT THE CASTLE, YOU NEVER COME OUT!
FWING
BEATIN' UP NOTHING BUT SOLDIERS IS LAME.
HMPH.
I DESPISE CHIL-DREN.
BOOO. YOU JUST DON'T KNOW US YET. ♪
BANG
BANG

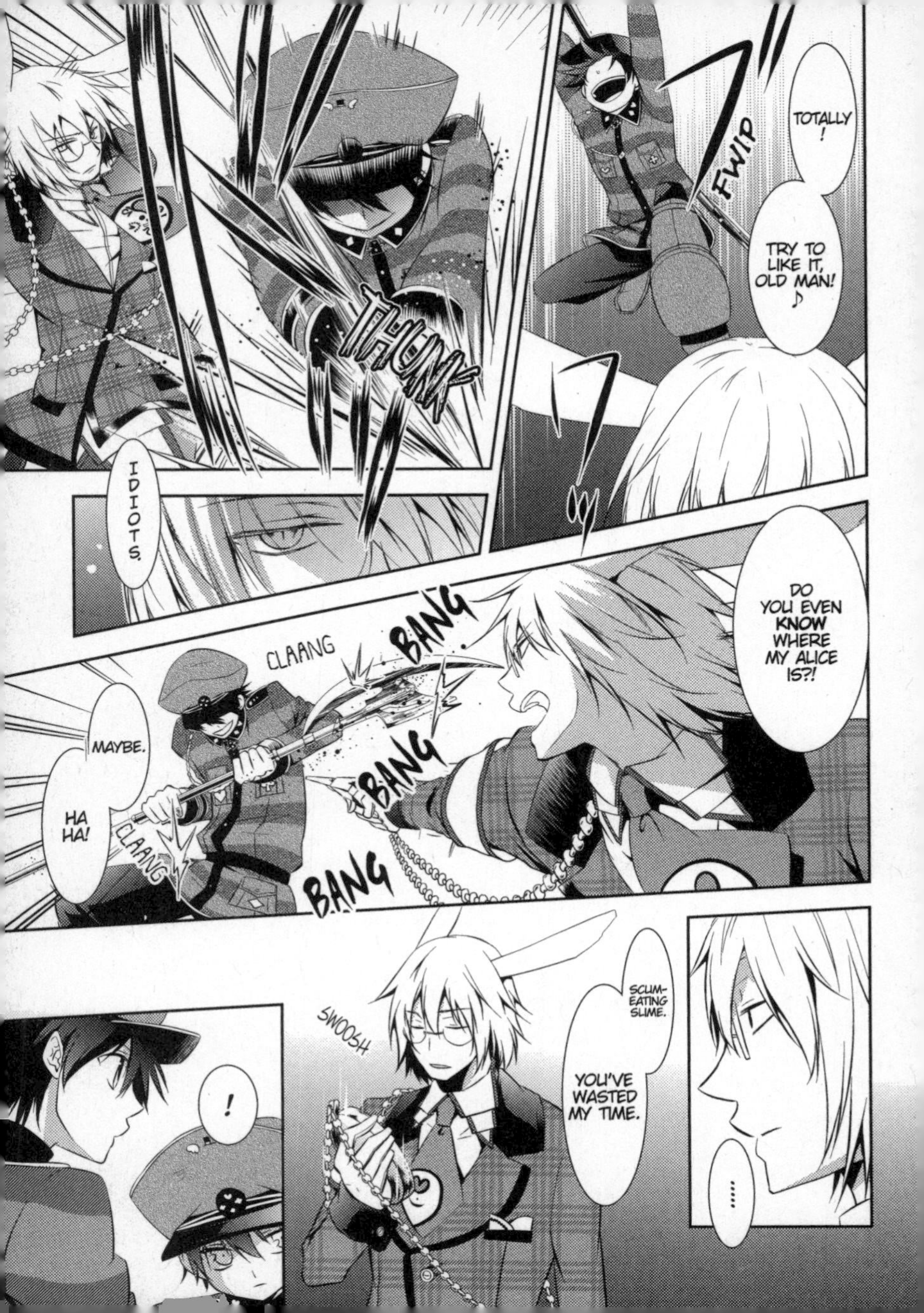

TOTALLY!
FWIP
TRY TO LIKE IT, OLD MAN! ♪
THUNK
IDIOTS.
DO YOU EVEN KNOW WHERE MY ALICE IS?!
BANG
CLAANG
BANG
MAYBE.
HA HA!
CLAANG
BANG
.....
SCUM-EATING SLIME.
YOU'VE WASTED MY TIME.
SWOOSH
!

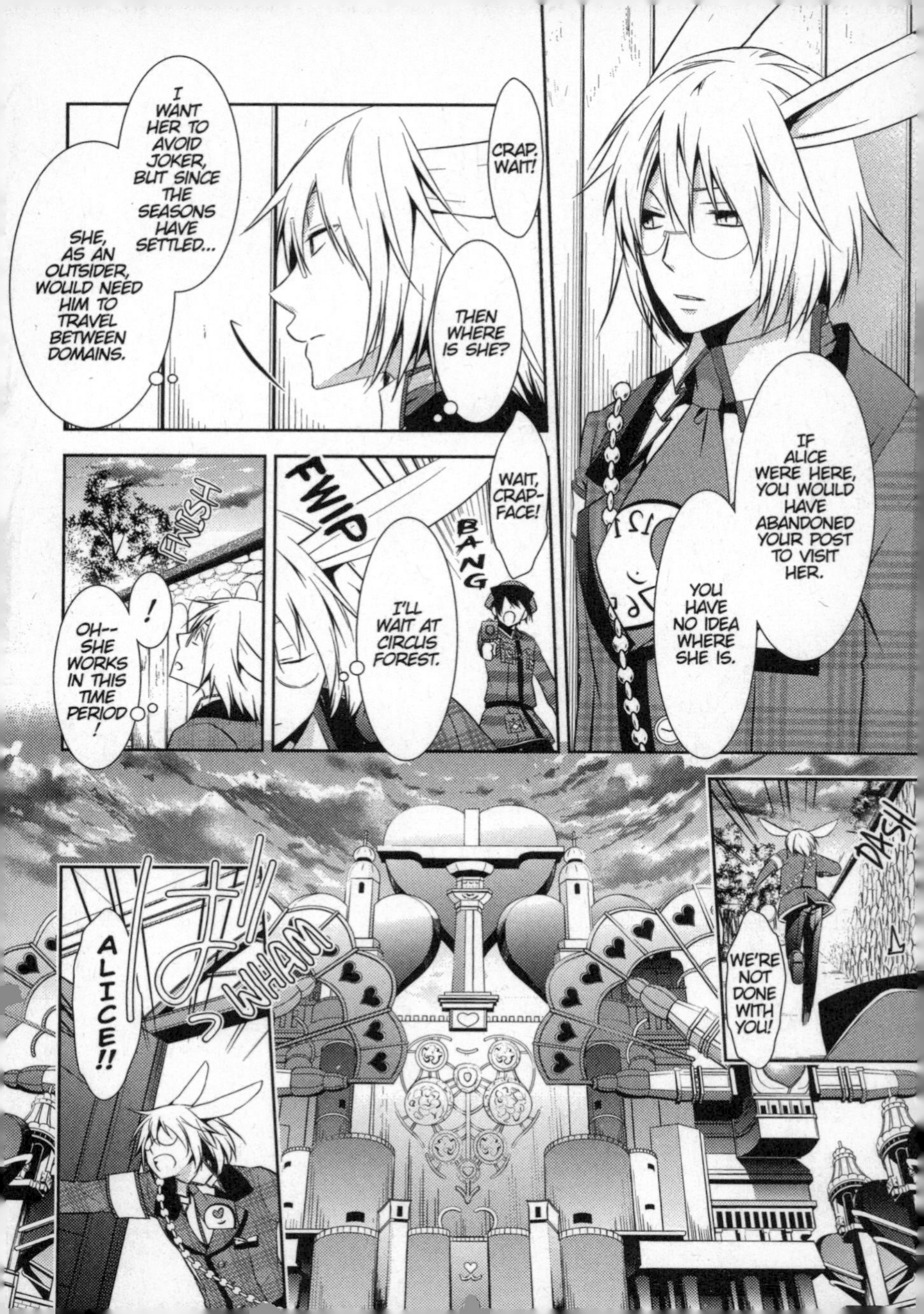
IF ALICE WERE HERE, YOU WOULD HAVE ABANDONED YOUR POST TO VISIT HER.
YOU HAVE NO IDEA WHERE SHE IS.
CRAP. WAIT!
THEN WHERE IS SHE?
I WANT HER TO AVOID JOKER, BUT SINCE THE SEASONS HAVE SETTLED...
SHE, AS AN OUTSIDER, WOULD NEED HIM TO TRAVEL BETWEEN DOMAINS.
WAIT, CRAP-FACE!
BANG
FWIP
I'LL WAIT AT CIRCUS FOREST.
FWISH
!
OH-- SHE WORKS IN THIS TIME PERIOD!
DASH
WE'RE NOT DONE WITH YOU!
WHAM
ALICE!!

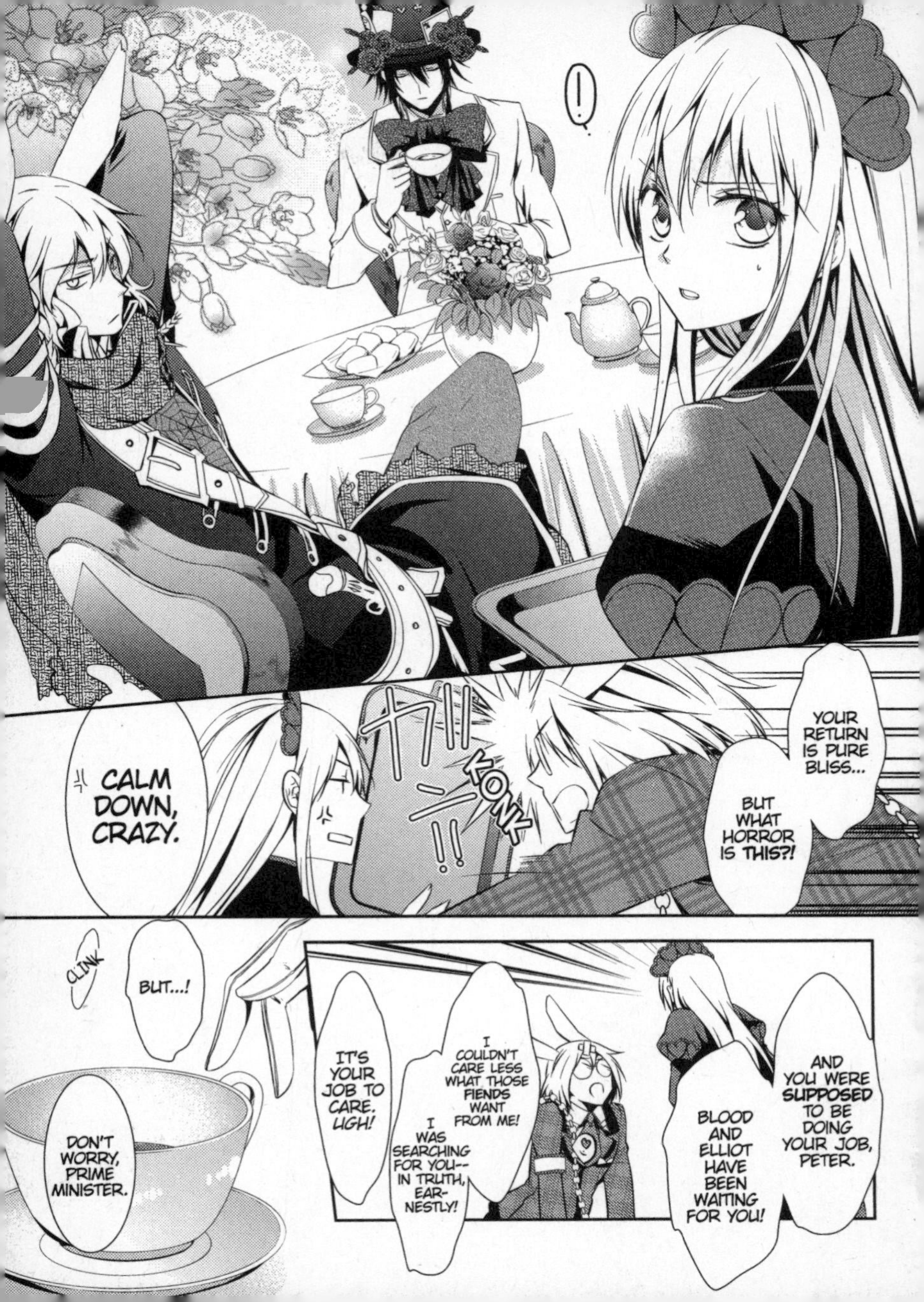
!
YOUR RETURN IS PURE BLISS...
BUT WHAT HORROR IS THIS?!
KONK
CALM DOWN, CRAZY.
AND YOU WERE SUPPOSED TO BE DOING YOUR JOB, PETER.
BLOOD AND ELLIOT HAVE BEEN WAITING FOR YOU!
I COULDN'T CARE LESS WHAT THOSE FIENDS WANT FROM ME!
I WAS SEARCHING FOR YOU-- IN TRUTH, EAR-NESTLY!
IT'S YOUR JOB TO CARE. UGH!
BUT...!
CLINK
DON'T WORRY, PRIME MINISTER.

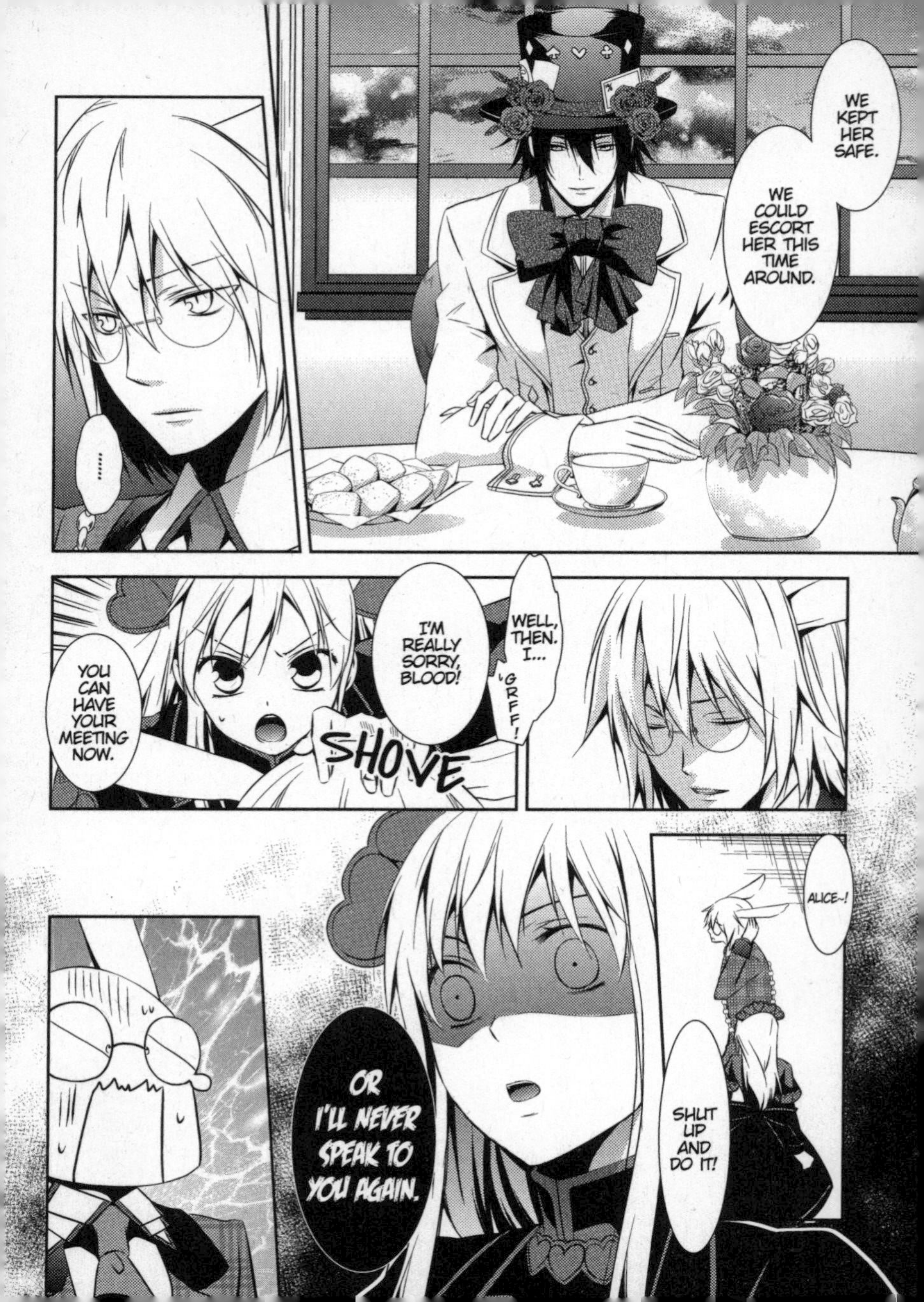
WE KEPT HER SAFE.
WE COULD ESCORT HER THIS TIME AROUND.
......
WELL, THEN. I...
GRFF!
I'M REALLY SORRY, BLOOD!
YOU CAN HAVE YOUR MEETING NOW.
SHOVE
ALICE~!
SHUT UP AND DO IT!
OR I'LL NEVER SPEAK TO YOU AGAIN.

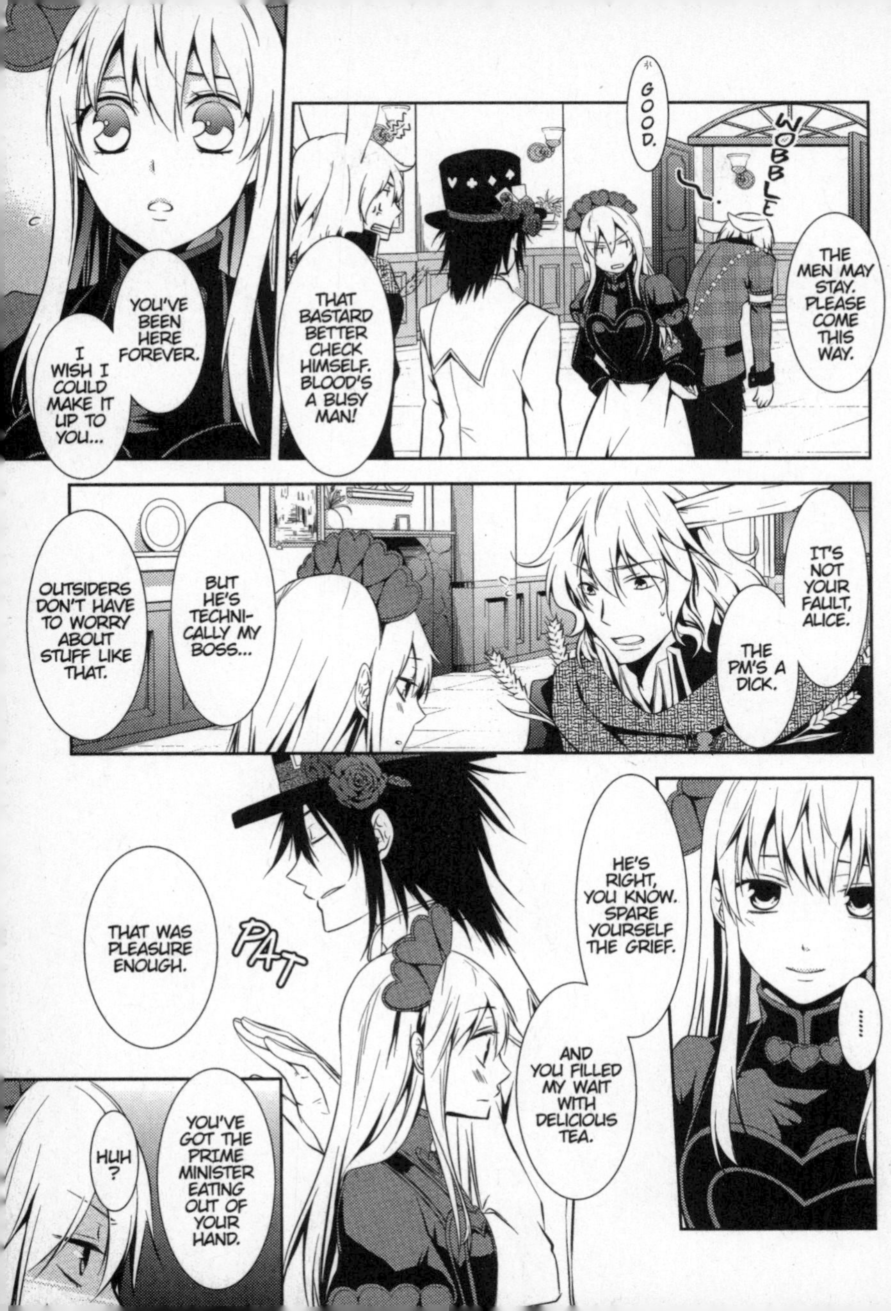
WOBBLE
GOOD.
THE MEN MAY STAY. PLEASE COME THIS WAY.
THAT BASTARD BETTER CHECK HIMSELF. BLOOD'S A BUSY MAN!
YOU'VE BEEN HERE FOREVER.
I WISH I COULD MAKE IT UP TO YOU...
IT'S NOT YOUR FAULT, ALICE.
THE PM'S A DICK.
BUT HE'S TECHNICALLY MY BOSS...
OUTSIDERS DON'T HAVE TO WORRY ABOUT STUFF LIKE THAT.
......
HE'S RIGHT, YOU KNOW. SPARE YOURSELF THE GRIEF.
PAT
THAT WAS PLEASURE ENOUGH.
AND YOU FILLED MY WAIT WITH DELICIOUS TEA.
YOU'VE GOT THE PRIME MINISTER EATING OUT OF YOUR HAND.
HUH?

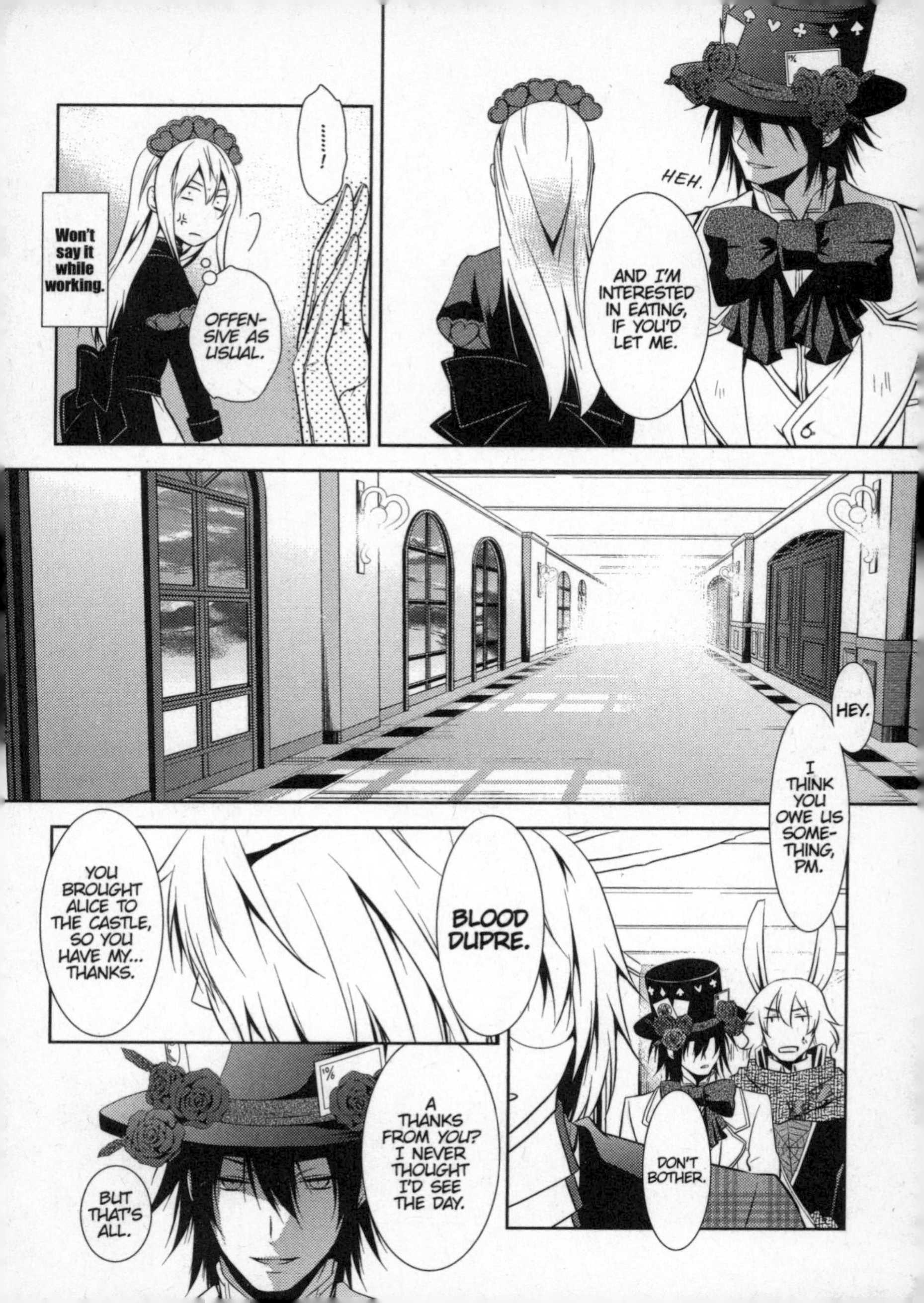
HEH.
AND I'M INTERESTED IN EATING, IF YOU'D LET ME.
......!
OFFEN-SIVE AS USUAL.
Won't say it while working.
HEY.
I THINK YOU OWE US SOME-THING, PM.
BLOOD DUPRE.
YOU BROUGHT ALICE TO THE CASTLE, SO YOU HAVE MY... THANKS.
DON'T BOTHER.
A THANKS FROM YOU? I NEVER THOUGHT I'D SEE THE DAY.
BUT THAT'S ALL.

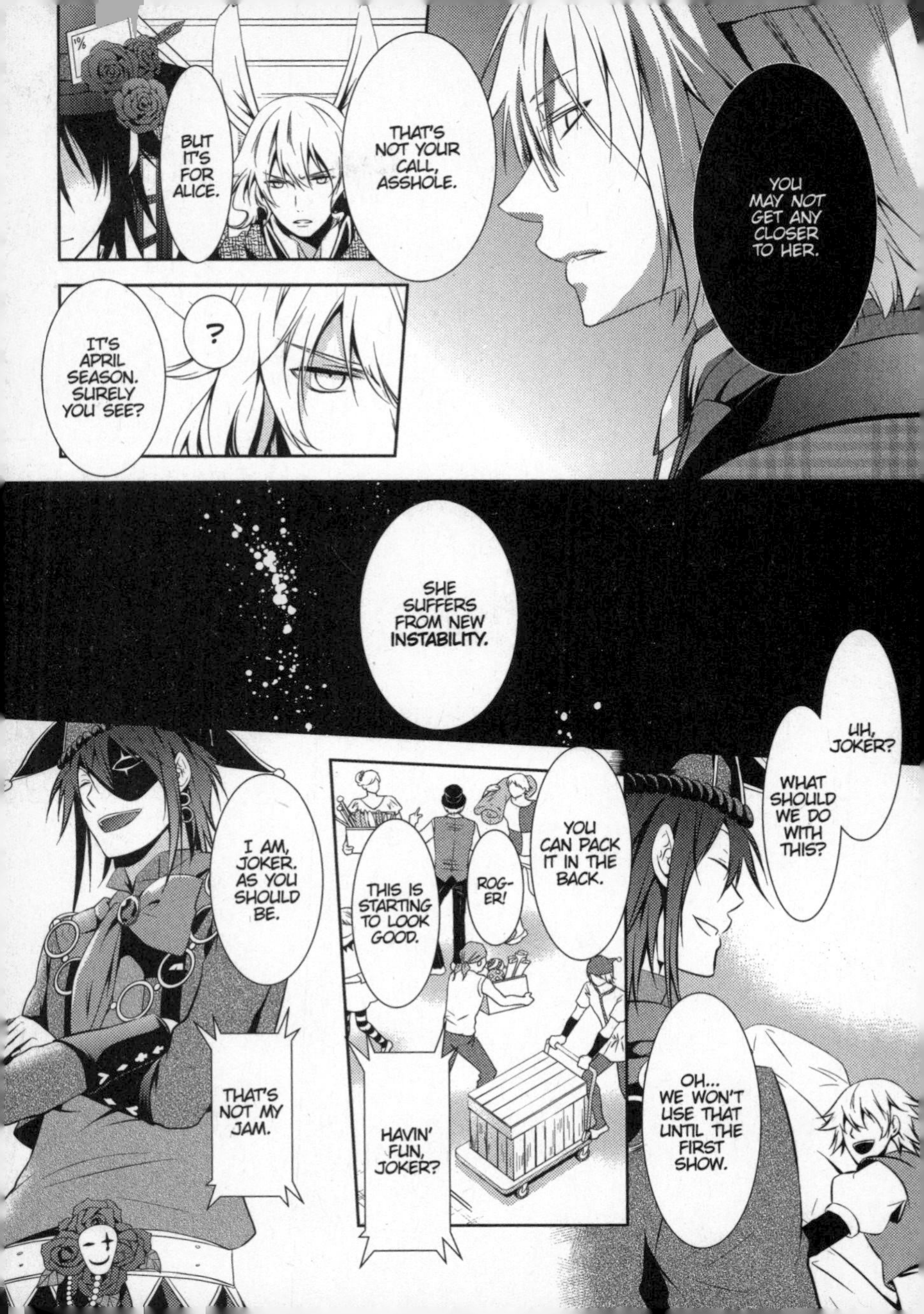
YOU MAY NOT GET ANY CLOSER TO HER.
THAT'S NOT YOUR CALL, ASSHOLE.
BUT IT'S FOR ALICE.
?
IT'S APRIL SEASON. SURELY YOU SEE?
SHE SUFFERS FROM NEW INSTABILITY.
UH, JOKER? WHAT SHOULD WE DO WITH THIS?
YOU CAN PACK IT IN THE BACK.
OH... WE WON'T USE THAT UNTIL THE FIRST SHOW.
ROG-ER!
THIS IS STARTING TO LOOK GOOD.
HAVIN' FUN, JOKER?
I AM, JOKER. AS YOU SHOULD BE.
THAT'S NOT MY JAM.

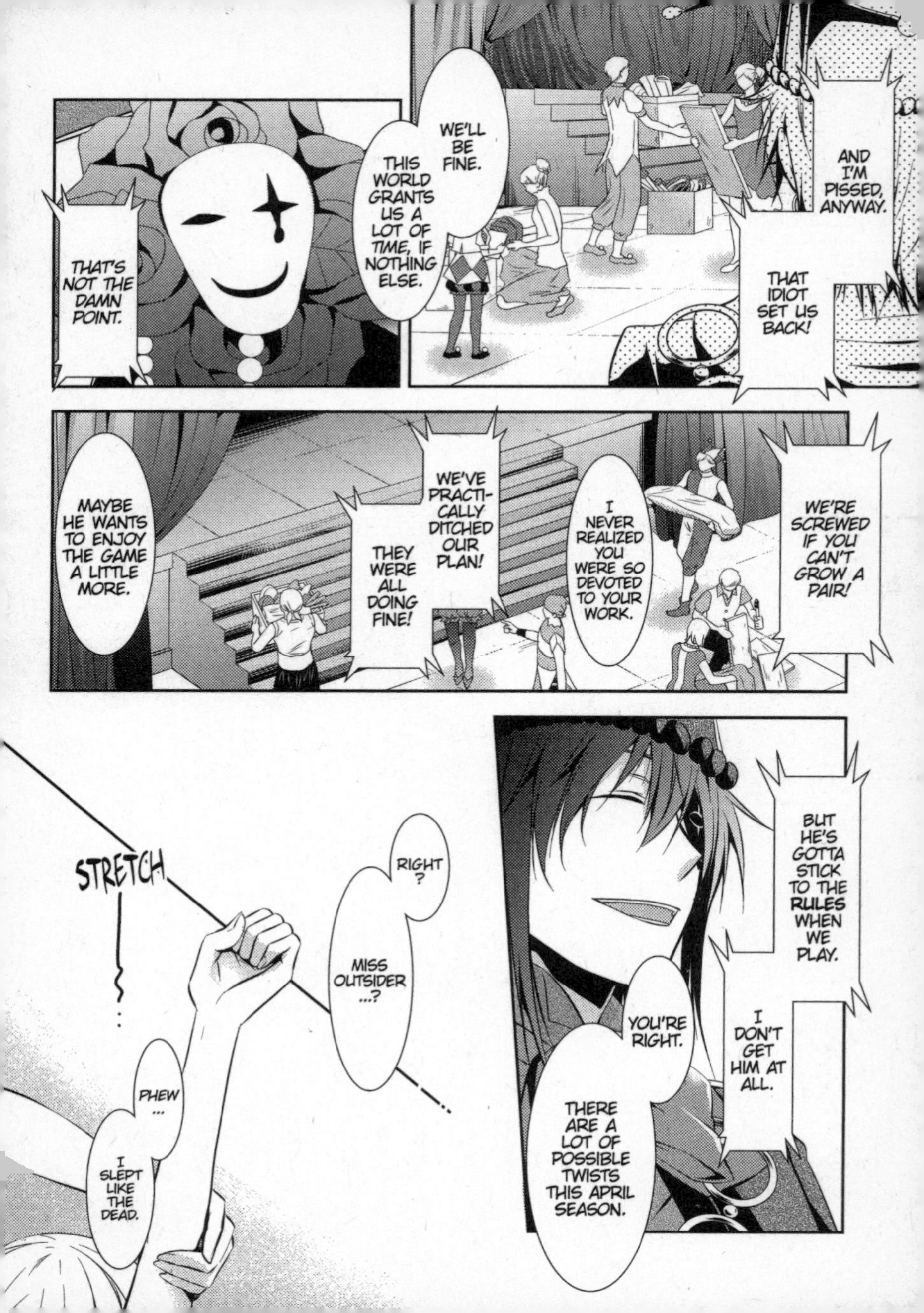
AND I'M PISSED, ANYWAY.
THAT IDIOT SET US BACK!
WE'LL BE FINE.
THIS WORLD GRANTS US A LOT OF TIME, IF NOTHING ELSE.
THAT'S NOT THE DAMN POINT.
WE'RE SCREWED IF YOU CAN'T GROW A PAIR!
I NEVER REALIZED YOU WERE SO DEVOTED TO YOUR WORK.
WE'VE PRACTICALLY DITCHED OUR PLAN!
THEY WERE ALL DOING FINE!
MAYBE HE WANTS TO ENJOY THE GAME A LITTLE MORE.
BUT HE'S GOTTA STICK TO THE RULES WHEN WE PLAY.
I DON'T GET HIM AT ALL.
YOU'RE RIGHT.
THERE ARE A LOT OF POSSIBLE TWISTS THIS APRIL SEASON.
RIGHT?
MISS OUTSIDER...?
STRETCH
PHEW...
I SLEPT LIKE THE DEAD.

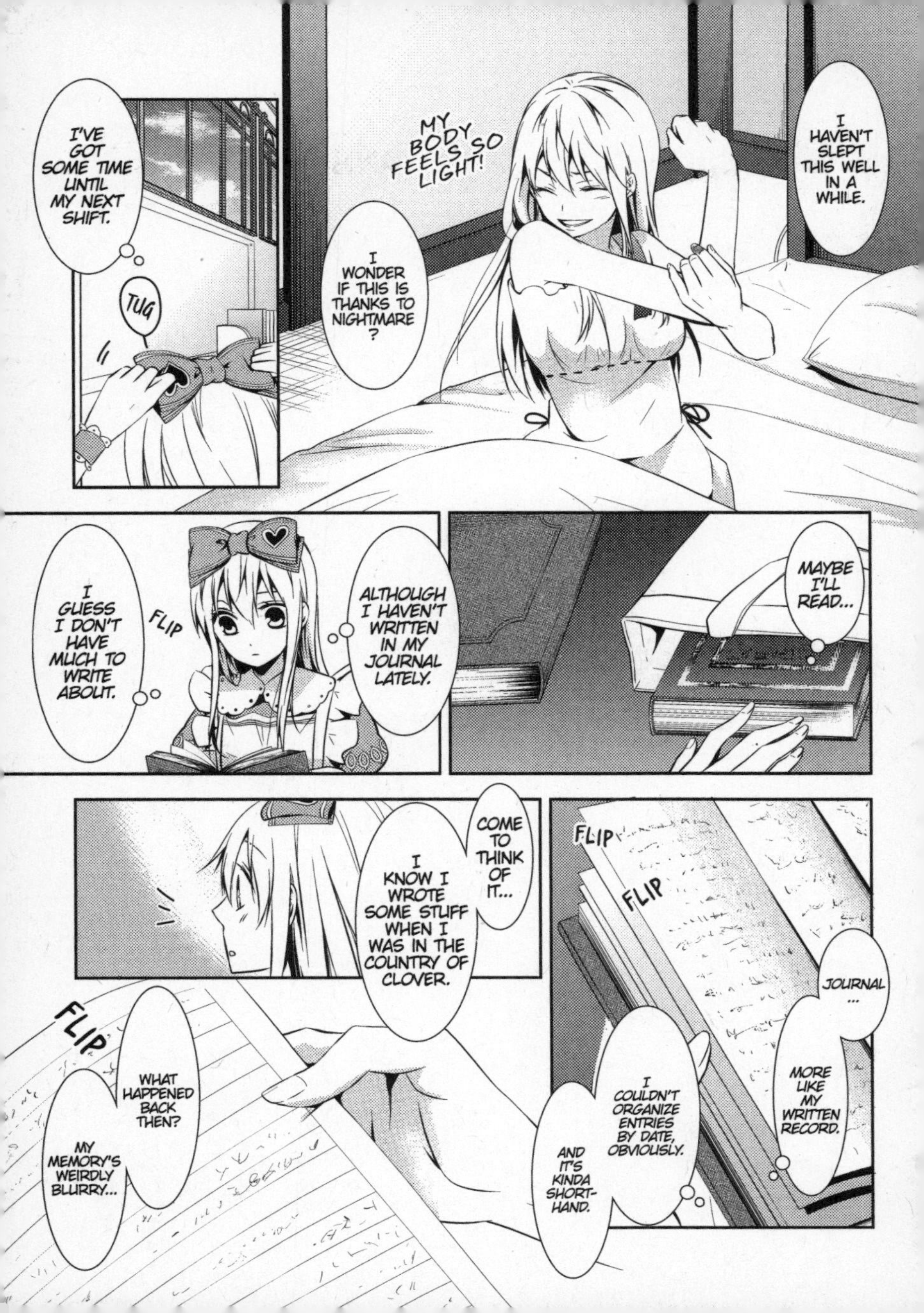
I HAVEN'T SLEPT THIS WELL IN A WHILE.
MY BODY FEELS SO LIGHT!
I WONDER IF THIS IS THANKS TO NIGHTMARE?
I'VE GOT SOME TIME UNTIL MY NEXT SHIFT.
TUG
MAYBE I'LL READ...
ALTHOUGH I HAVEN'T WRITTEN IN MY JOURNAL LATELY.
FLIP
I GUESS I DON'T HAVE MUCH TO WRITE ABOUT.
FLIP
FLIP
JOURNAL...
MORE LIKE MY WRITTEN RECORD.
I COULDN'T ORGANIZE ENTRIES BY DATE, OBVIOUSLY.
AND IT'S KINDA SHORT-HAND.
COME TO THINK OF IT...
I KNOW I WROTE SOME STUFF WHEN I WAS IN THE COUNTRY OF CLOVER.
FLIP
WHAT HAPPENED BACK THEN?
MY MEMORY'S WEIRDLY BLURRY...

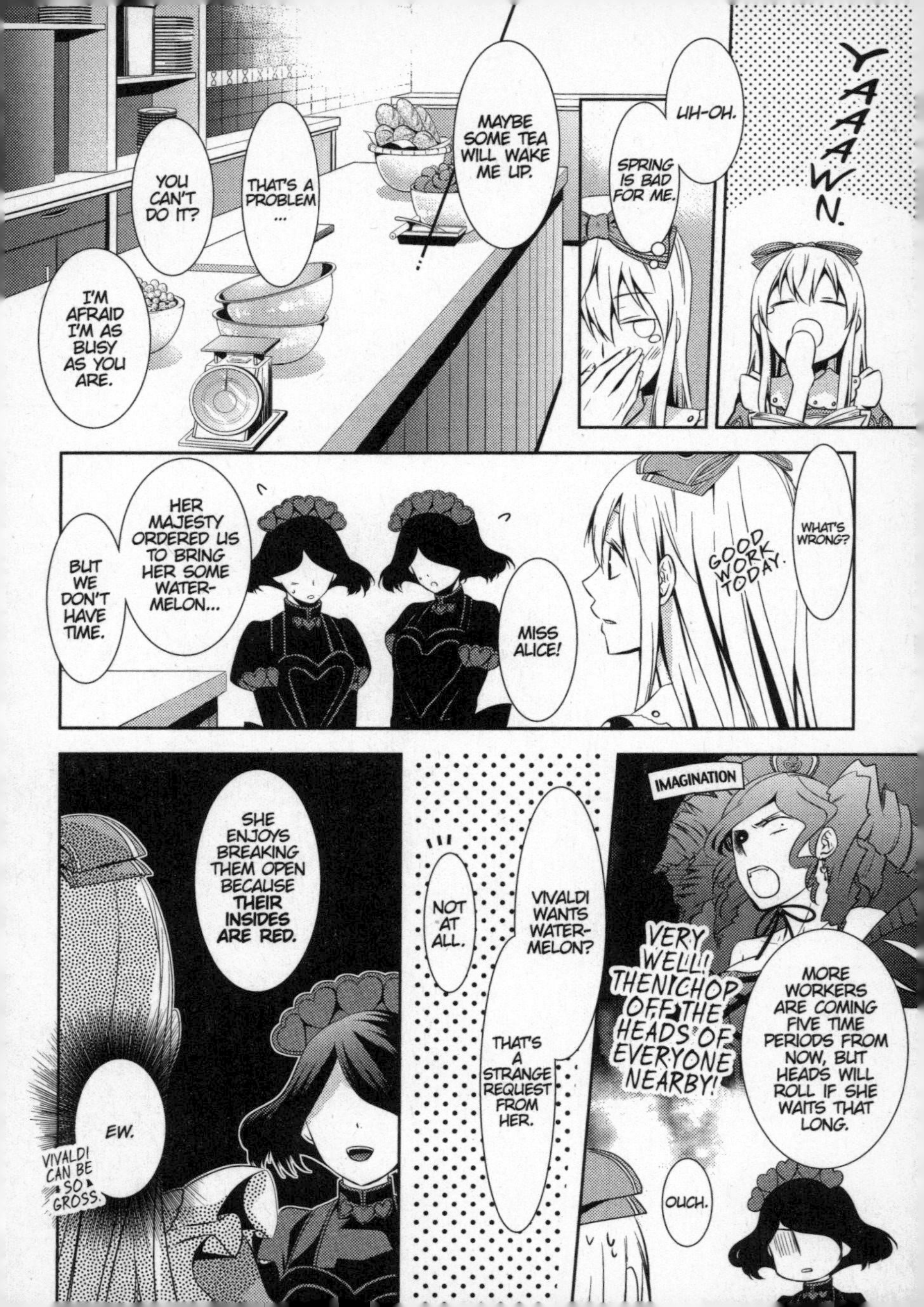
YAAAWN.
UH-OH.
SPRING IS BAD FOR ME.
MAYBE SOME TEA WILL WAKE ME UP.
THAT'S A PROBLEM...
YOU CAN'T DO IT?
I'M AFRAID I'M AS BUSY AS YOU ARE.
WHAT'S WRONG?
GOOD WORK TODAY.
MISS ALICE!
HER MAJESTY ORDERED US TO BRING HER SOME WATER-MELON...
BUT WE DON'T HAVE TIME.
IMAGINATION
VERY WELL! THEN I CHOP OFF THE HEADS OF EVERYONE NEARBY!
MORE WORKERS ARE COMING FIVE TIME PERIODS FROM NOW, BUT HEADS WILL ROLL IF SHE WAITS THAT LONG.
OUCH.
VIVALDI WANTS WATER-MELON?
NOT AT ALL.
THAT'S A STRANGE REQUEST FROM HER.
SHE ENJOYS BREAKING THEM OPEN BECAUSE THEIR INSIDES ARE RED.
EW.
VIVALDI CAN BE SO GROSS.

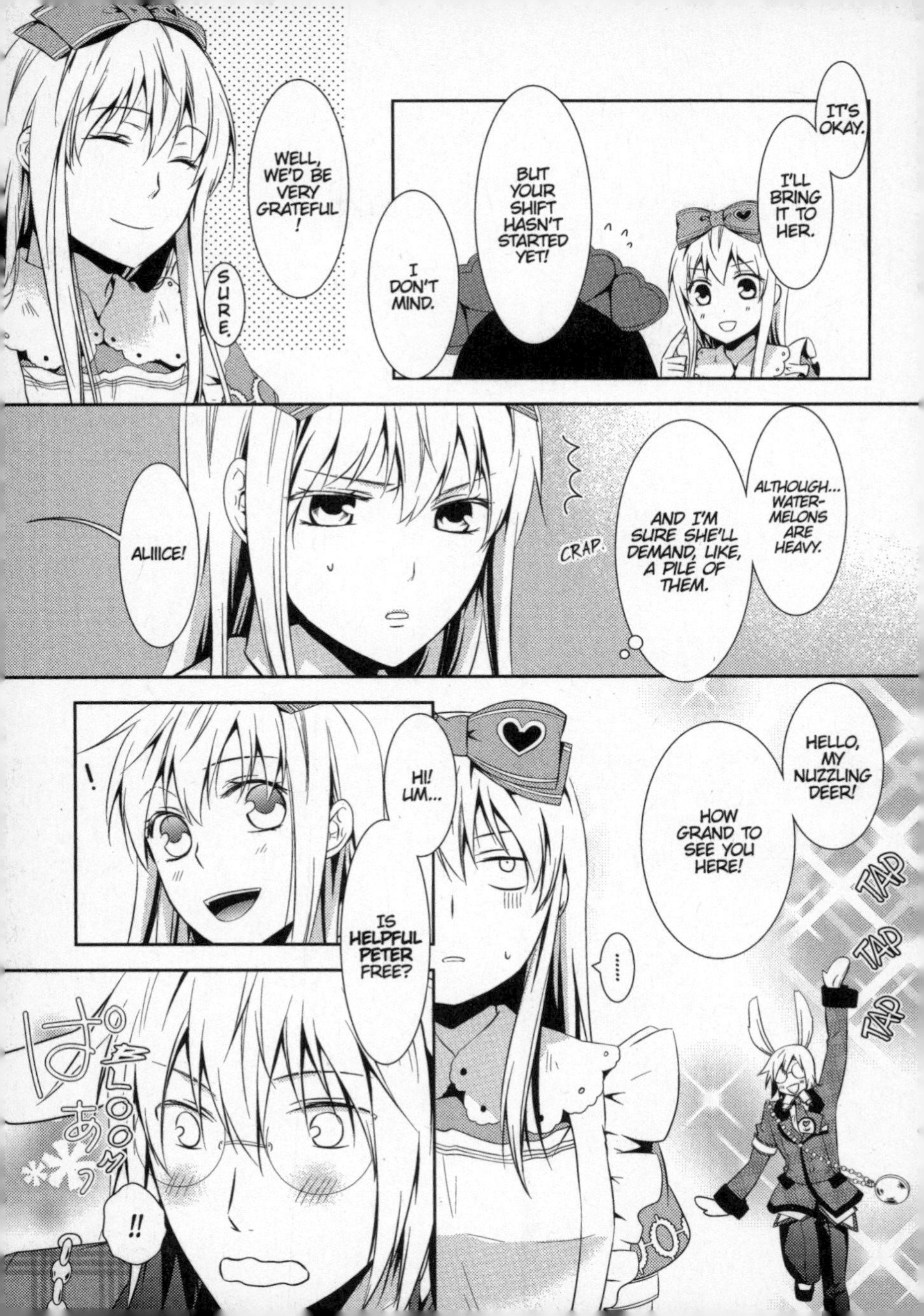
IT'S OKAY.
I'LL BRING IT TO HER.
BUT YOUR SHIFT HASN'T STARTED YET!
I DON'T MIND.
WELL, WE'D BE VERY GRATEFUL!
SURE.
ALTHOUGH... WATER-MELONS ARE HEAVY.
AND I'M SURE SHE'LL DEMAND, LIKE, A PILE OF THEM.
CRAP.
ALIIICE!
HELLO, MY NUZZLING DEER!
HOW GRAND TO SEE YOU HERE!
TAP TAP TAP
......
!
HI! UM...
IS HELPFUL PETER FREE?
ぱあっ
BLOOOM
!!

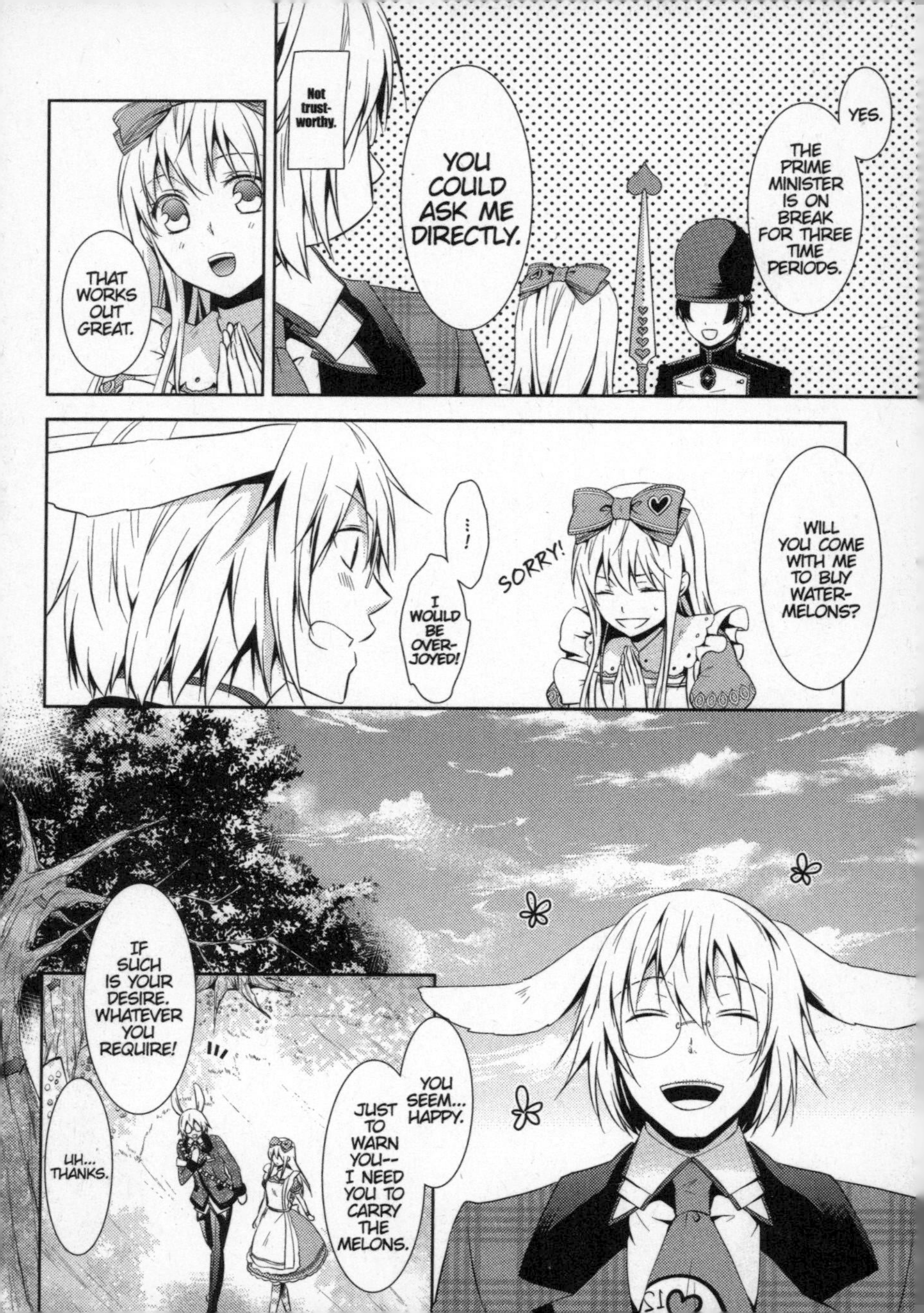
YES.
THE PRIME MINISTER IS ON BREAK FOR THREE TIME PERIODS.
YOU COULD ASK ME DIRECTLY.
Not trust-worthy.
THAT WORKS OUT GREAT.
WILL YOU COME WITH ME TO BUY WATER-MELONS?
SORRY!
...!
I WOULD BE OVER-JOYED!
IF SUCH IS YOUR DESIRE. WHATEVER YOU REQUIRE!
YOU SEEM... HAPPY.
JUST TO WARN YOU-- I NEED YOU TO CARRY THE MELONS.
UH... THANKS.

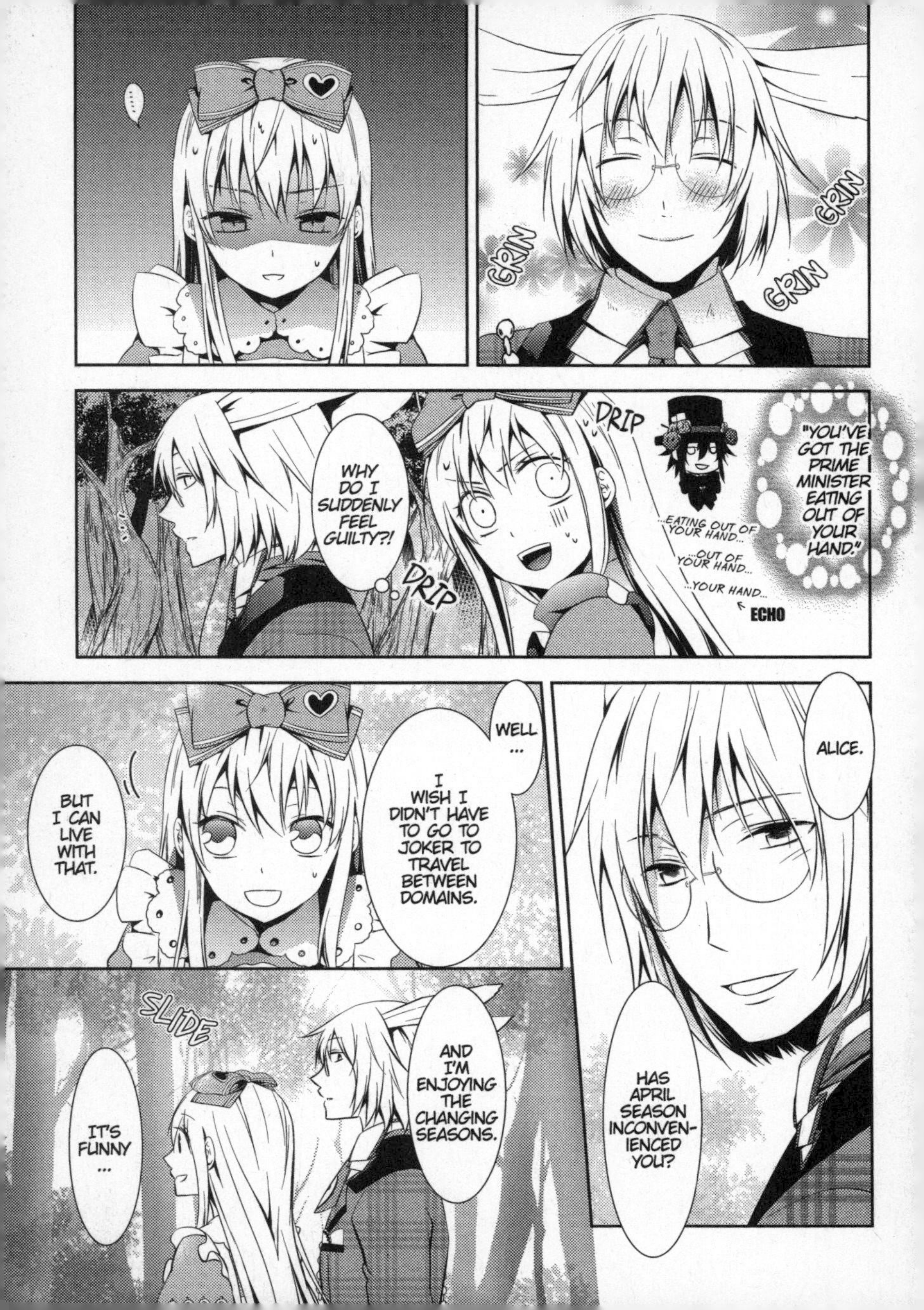
GRIN
GRIN
GRIN
...
"YOU'VE GOT THE PRIME MINISTER EATING OUT OF YOUR HAND."
...EATING OUT OF YOUR HAND...
...OUT OF YOUR HAND...
...YOUR HAND...
ECHO
DRIP
WHY DO I SUDDENLY FEEL GUILTY?!
DRIP
ALICE.
HAS APRIL SEASON INCONVEN-IENCED YOU?
WELL ...
I WISH I DIDN'T HAVE TO GO TO JOKER TO TRAVEL BETWEEN DOMAINS.
BUT I CAN LIVE WITH THAT.
AND I'M ENJOYING THE CHANGING SEASONS.
SLIDE
IT'S FUNNY ...

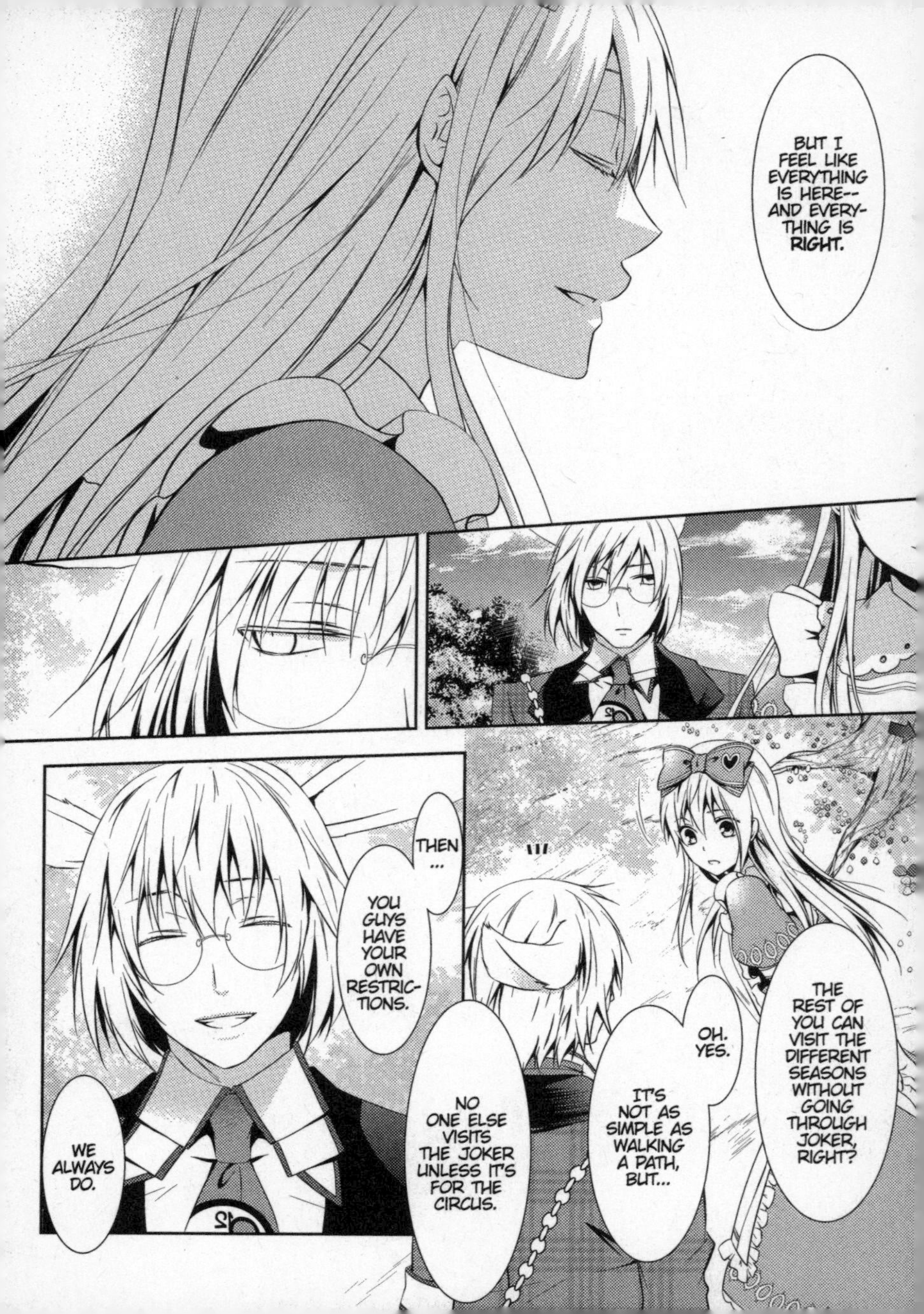
BUT I FEEL LIKE EVERYTHING IS HERE--AND EVERYTHING IS RIGHT.
THE REST OF YOU CAN VISIT THE DIFFERENT SEASONS WITHOUT GOING THROUGH JOKER, RIGHT?
OH. YES.
IT'S NOT AS SIMPLE AS WALKING A PATH, BUT...
NO ONE ELSE VISITS THE JOKER UNLESS IT'S FOR THE CIRCUS.
THEN ...
YOU GUYS HAVE YOUR OWN RESTRICTIONS.
WE ALWAYS DO.

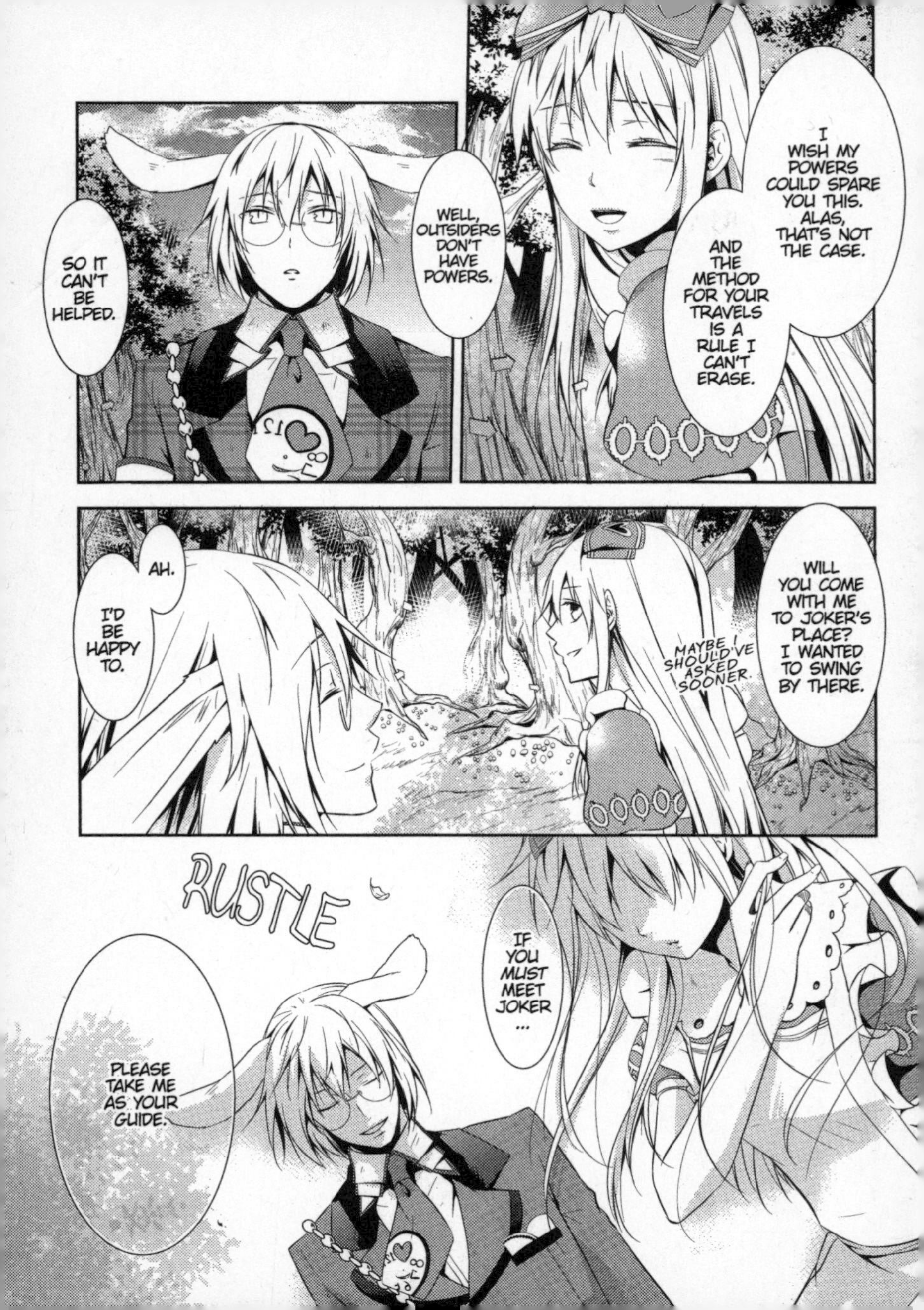
I WISH MY POWERS COULD SPARE YOU THIS. ALAS, THAT'S NOT THE CASE.
AND THE METHOD FOR YOUR TRAVELS IS A RULE I CAN'T ERASE.
WELL, OUTSIDERS DON'T HAVE POWERS.
SO IT CAN'T BE HELPED.
WILL YOU COME WITH ME TO JOKER'S PLACE? I WANTED TO SWING BY THERE.
MAYBE I SHOULD'VE ASKED SOONER.
AH.
I'D BE HAPPY TO.
RUSTLE
IF YOU MUST MEET JOKER...
PLEASE TAKE ME AS YOUR GUIDE.

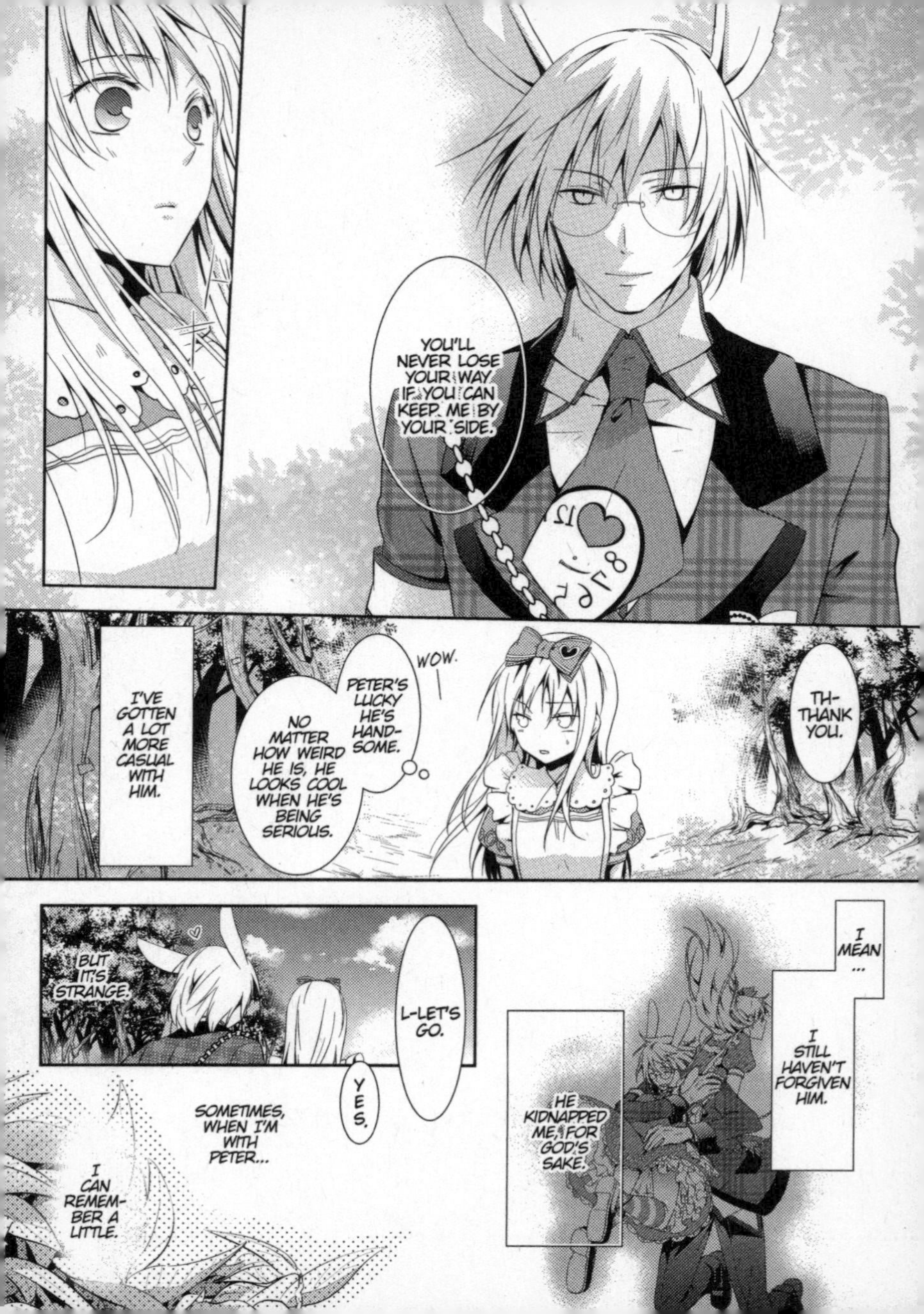
YOU'LL NEVER LOSE YOUR WAY IF YOU CAN KEEP ME BY YOUR SIDE.
TH-THANK YOU.
WOW.
PETER'S LUCKY HE'S HANDSOME.
NO MATTER HOW WEIRD HE IS, HE LOOKS COOL WHEN HE'S BEING SERIOUS.
I'VE GOTTEN A LOT MORE CASUAL WITH HIM.
I MEAN...
I STILL HAVEN'T FORGIVEN HIM.
HE KIDNAPPED ME, FOR GOD'S SAKE.
L-LET'S GO.
YES.
BUT IT'S STRANGE.
SOMETIMES, WHEN I'M WITH PETER...
I CAN REMEMBER A LITTLE.

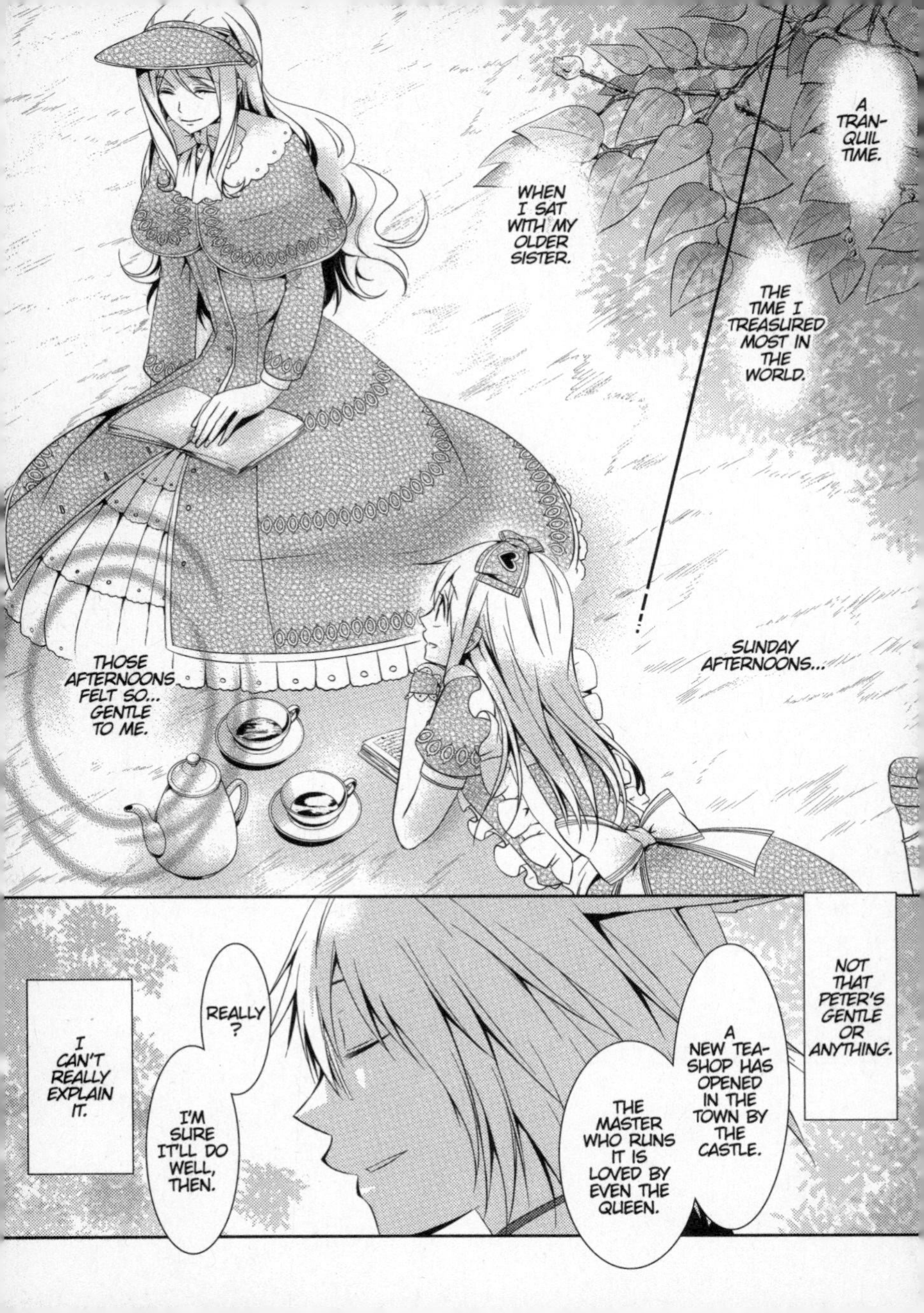
A TRAN-QUIL TIME.
WHEN I SAT WITH MY OLDER SISTER.
THE TIME I TREASURED MOST IN THE WORLD.
SUNDAY AFTERNOONS...
THOSE AFTERNOONS FELT SO... GENTLE TO ME.
NOT THAT PETER'S GENTLE OR ANYTHING.
A NEW TEA-SHOP HAS OPENED IN THE TOWN BY THE CASTLE.
THE MASTER WHO RUNS IT IS LOVED BY EVEN THE QUEEN.
REALLY?
I'M SURE IT'LL DO WELL, THEN.
I CAN'T REALLY EXPLAIN IT.

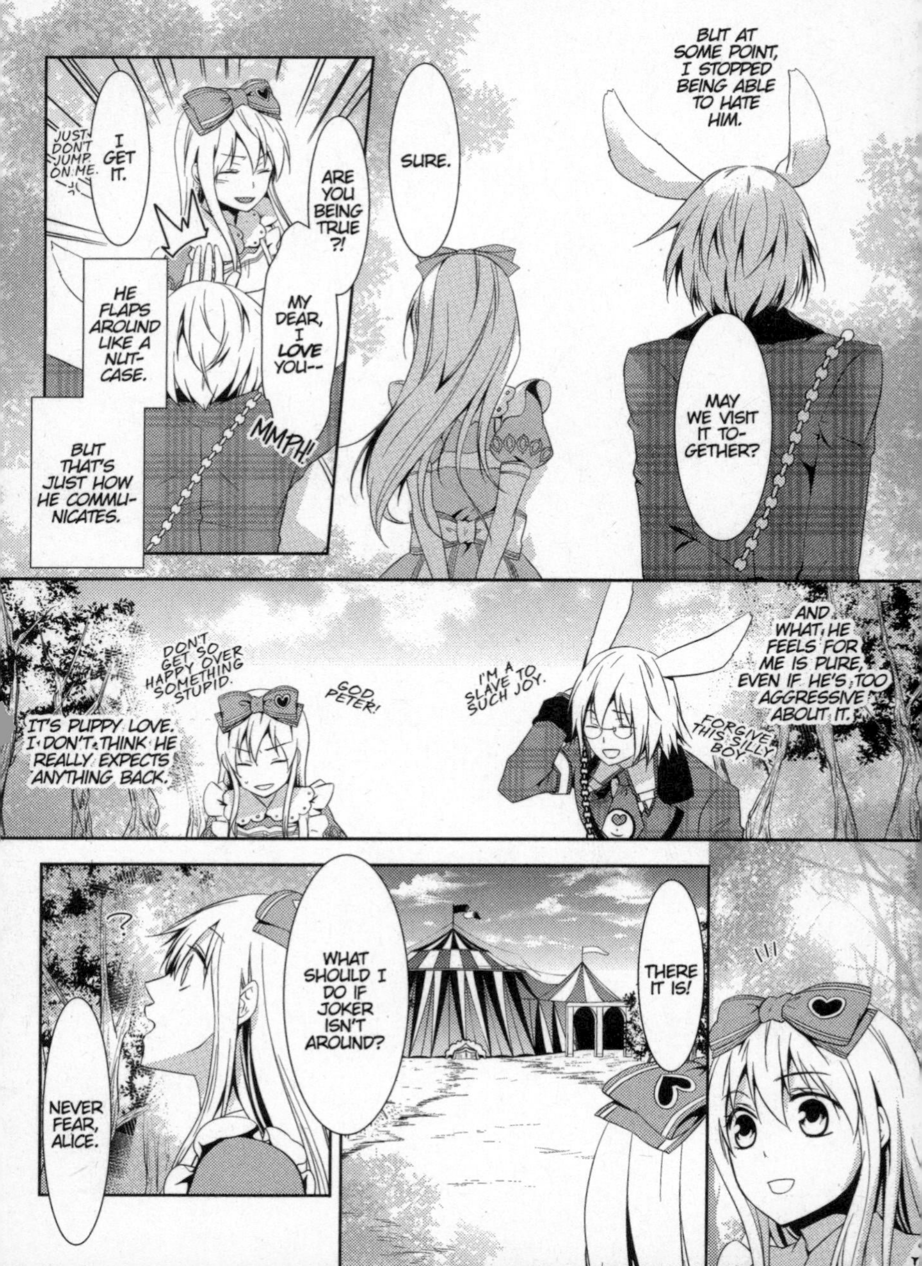
BUT AT SOME POINT, I STOPPED BEING ABLE TO HATE HIM.
MAY WE VISIT IT TO-GETHER?
SURE.
ARE YOU BEING TRUE?!
MY DEAR, I LOVE YOU--
MMPH!
I GET IT.
JUST DON'T JUMP ON ME.
HE FLAPS AROUND LIKE A NUT-CASE.
BUT THAT'S JUST HOW HE COMMUNICATES.
AND WHAT HE FEELS FOR ME IS PURE, EVEN IF HE'S TOO AGGRESSIVE ABOUT IT.
FORGIVE THIS SILLY BOY.
I'M A SLAVE TO SUCH JOY.
GOD, PETER!
DON'T GET SO HAPPY OVER SOMETHING STUPID.
IT'S PUPPY LOVE. I DON'T THINK HE REALLY EXPECTS ANYTHING BACK.
THERE IT IS!
WHAT SHOULD I DO IF JOKER ISN'T AROUND?
NEVER FEAR, ALICE.

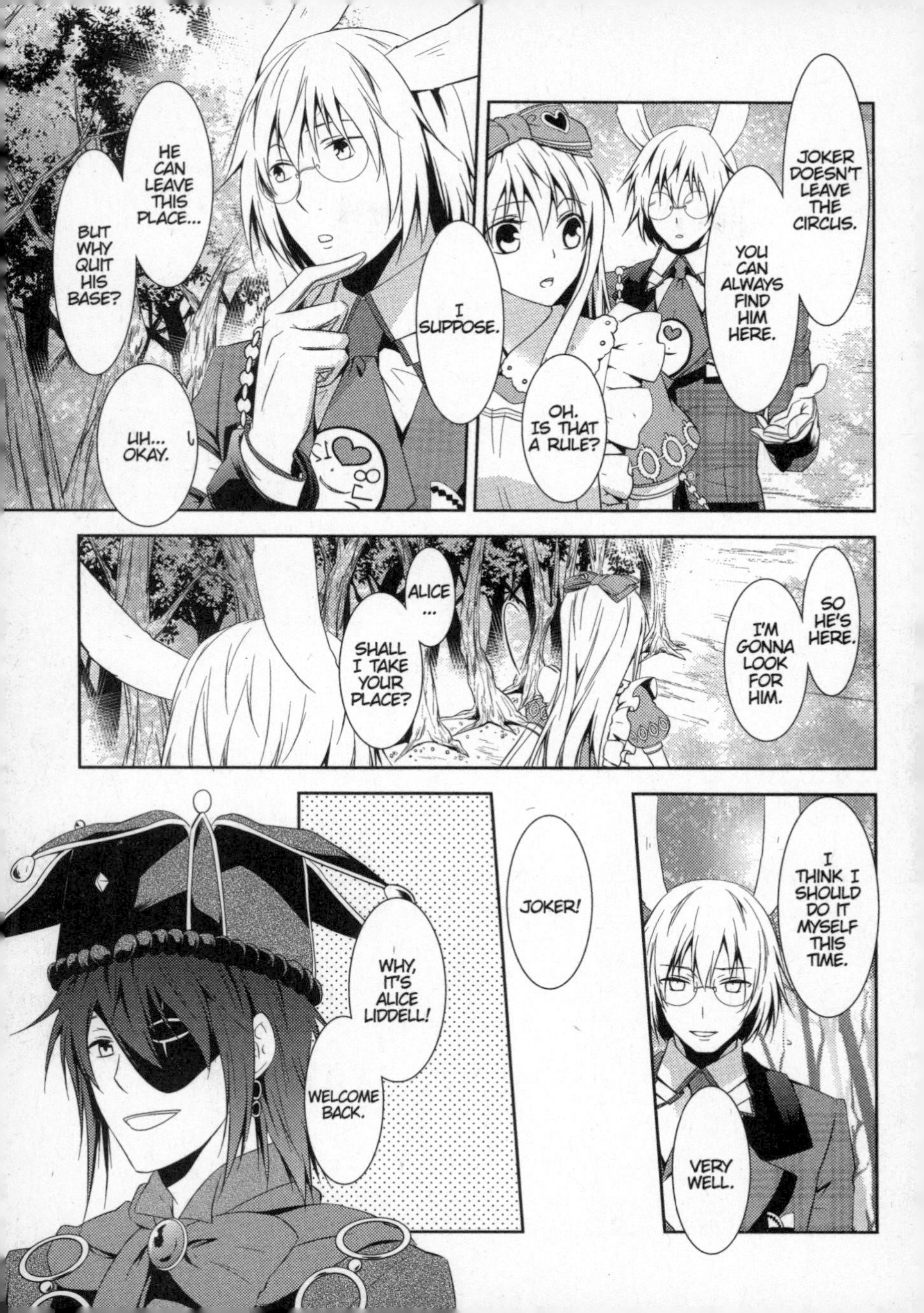
JOKER DOESN'T LEAVE THE CIRCUS.
YOU CAN ALWAYS FIND HIM HERE.
OH. IS THAT A RULE?
I SUPPOSE.
HE CAN LEAVE THIS PLACE...
BUT WHY QUIT HIS BASE?
UH... OKAY.
SO HE'S HERE.
I'M GONNA LOOK FOR HIM.
ALICE ...
SHALL I TAKE YOUR PLACE?
I THINK I SHOULD DO IT MYSELF THIS TIME.
VERY WELL.
JOKER!
WHY, IT'S ALICE LIDDELL!
WELCOME BACK.

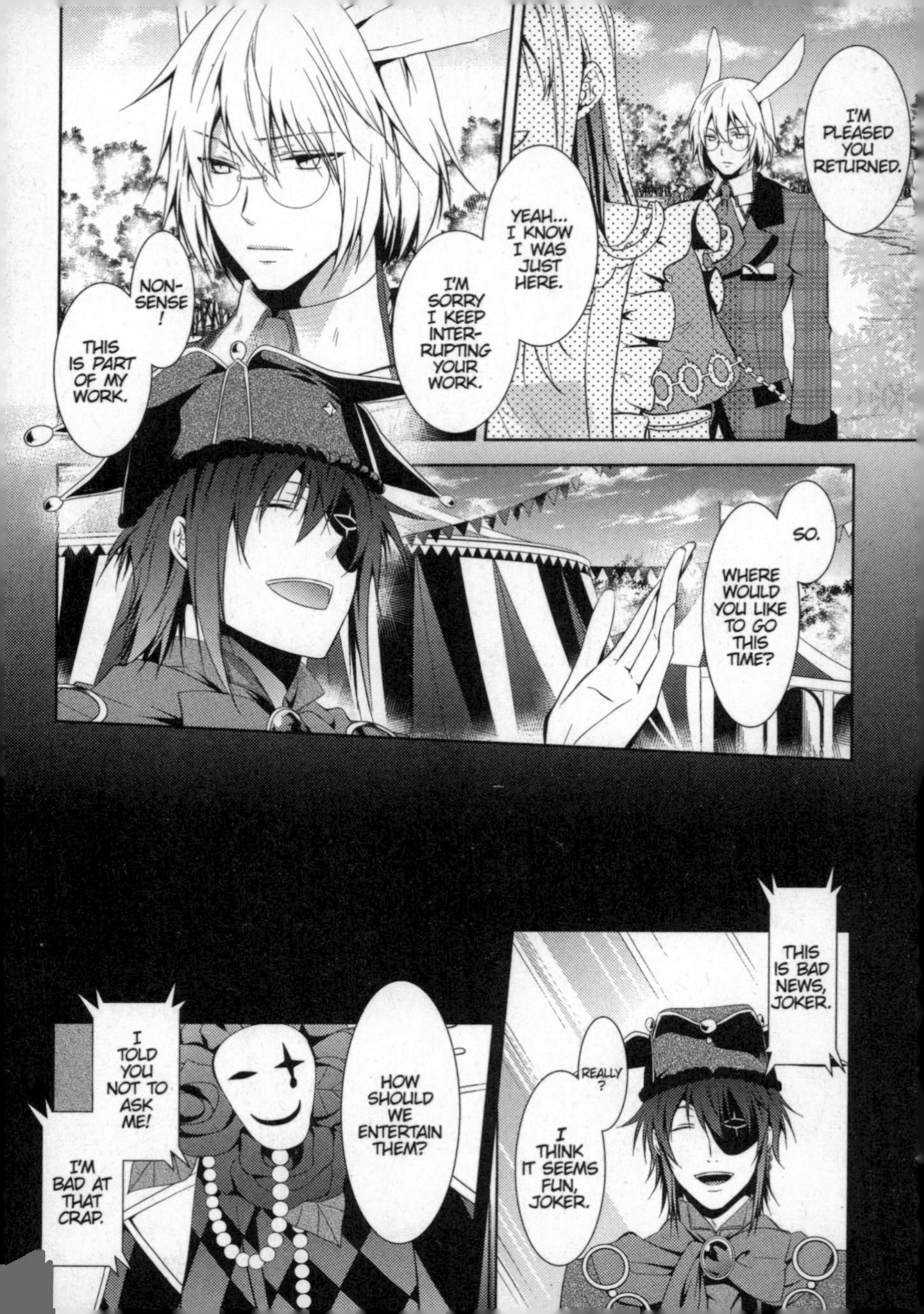
I'M PLEASED YOU RETURNED.
YEAH... I KNOW I WAS JUST HERE.
I'M SORRY I KEEP INTER-RUPTING YOUR WORK.
NON-SENSE!
THIS IS PART OF MY WORK.
SO.
WHERE WOULD YOU LIKE TO GO THIS TIME?
THIS IS BAD NEWS, JOKER.
REALLY?
I THINK IT SEEMS FUN, JOKER.
HOW SHOULD WE ENTERTAIN THEM?
I TOLD YOU NOT TO ASK ME!
I'M BAD AT THAT CRAP.

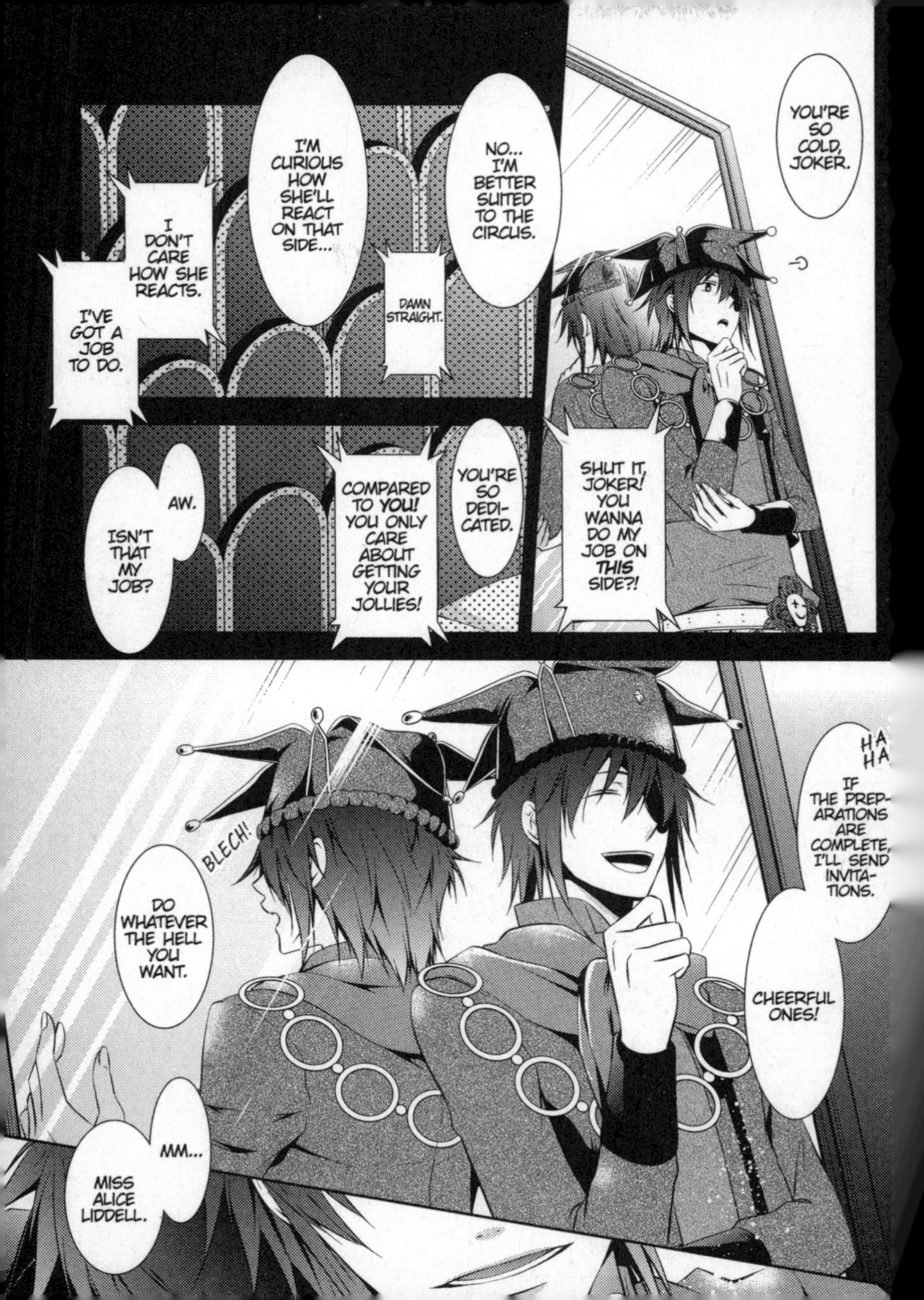
YOU'RE SO COLD, JOKER.
SHUT IT, JOKER! YOU WANNA DO MY JOB ON THIS SIDE?!
NO... I'M BETTER SUITED TO THE CIRCUS.
DAMN STRAIGHT.
I'M CURIOUS HOW SHE'LL REACT ON THAT SIDE...
I DON'T CARE HOW SHE REACTS.
I'VE GOT A JOB TO DO.
YOU'RE SO DEDICATED.
COMPARED TO YOU! YOU ONLY CARE ABOUT GETTING YOUR JOLLIES!
AW.
ISN'T THAT MY JOB?
HA HA
IF THE PREPARATIONS ARE COMPLETE, I'LL SEND INVITATIONS.
CHEERFUL ONES!
BLECH!
DO WHATEVER THE HELL YOU WANT.
MM...
MISS ALICE LIDDELL.

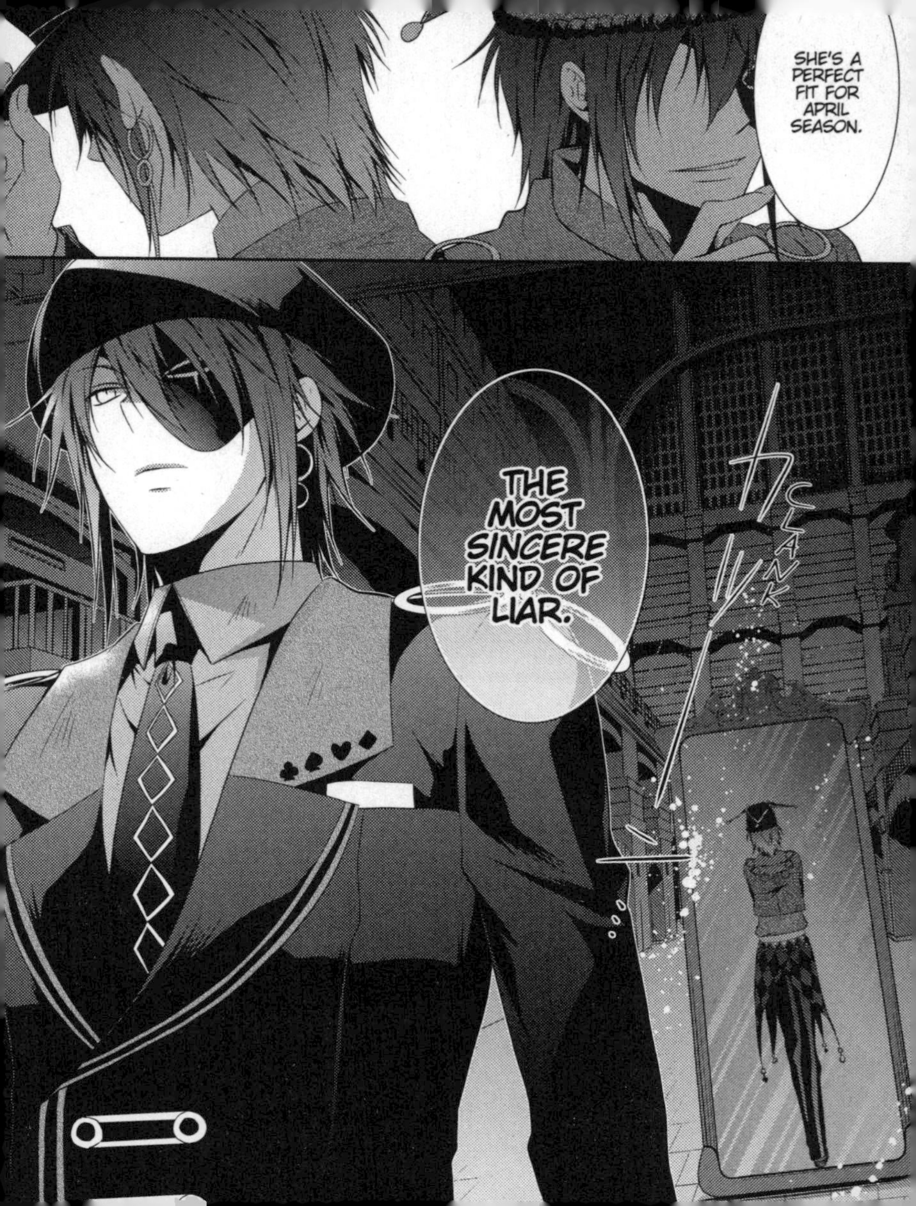
SHE'S A PERFECT FIT FOR APRIL SEASON.
THE MOST SINCERE KIND OF LIAR.
CLANK

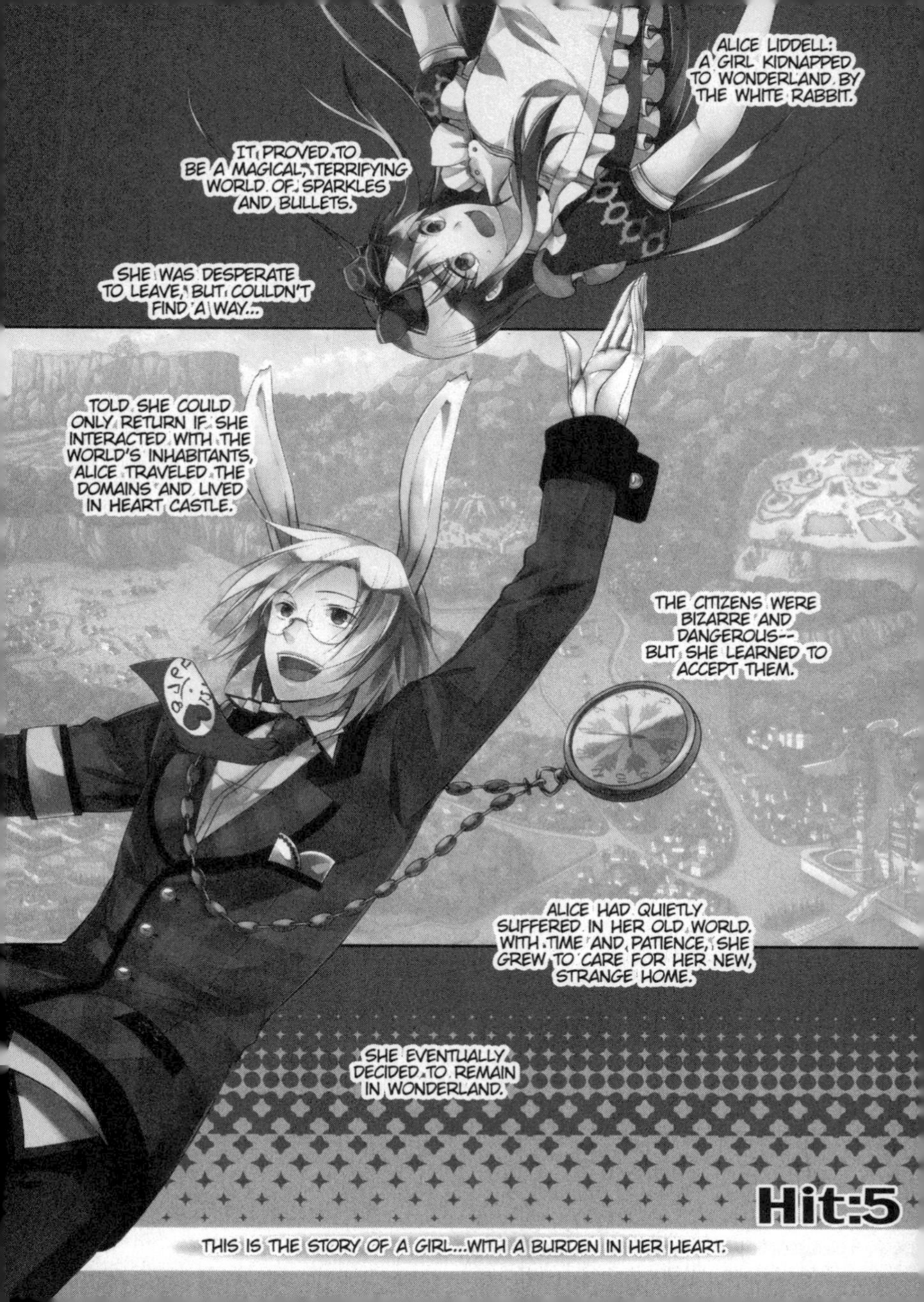
ALICE LIDDELL: A GIRL KIDNAPPED TO WONDERLAND BY THE WHITE RABBIT.
IT PROVED TO BE A MAGICAL, TERRIFYING WORLD OF SPARKLES AND BULLETS.
SHE WAS DESPERATE TO LEAVE, BUT COULDN'T FIND A WAY...
TOLD SHE COULD ONLY RETURN IF SHE INTERACTED WITH THE WORLD'S INHABITANTS, ALICE TRAVELED THE DOMAINS AND LIVED IN HEART CASTLE.
THE CITIZENS WERE BIZARRE AND DANGEROUS-- BUT SHE LEARNED TO ACCEPT THEM.
ALICE HAD QUIETLY SUFFERED IN HER OLD WORLD. WITH TIME AND PATIENCE, SHE GREW TO CARE FOR HER NEW, STRANGE HOME.
SHE EVENTUALLY DECIDED TO REMAIN IN WONDERLAND.
Hit:5
THIS IS THE STORY OF A GIRL...WITH A BURDEN IN HER HEART.

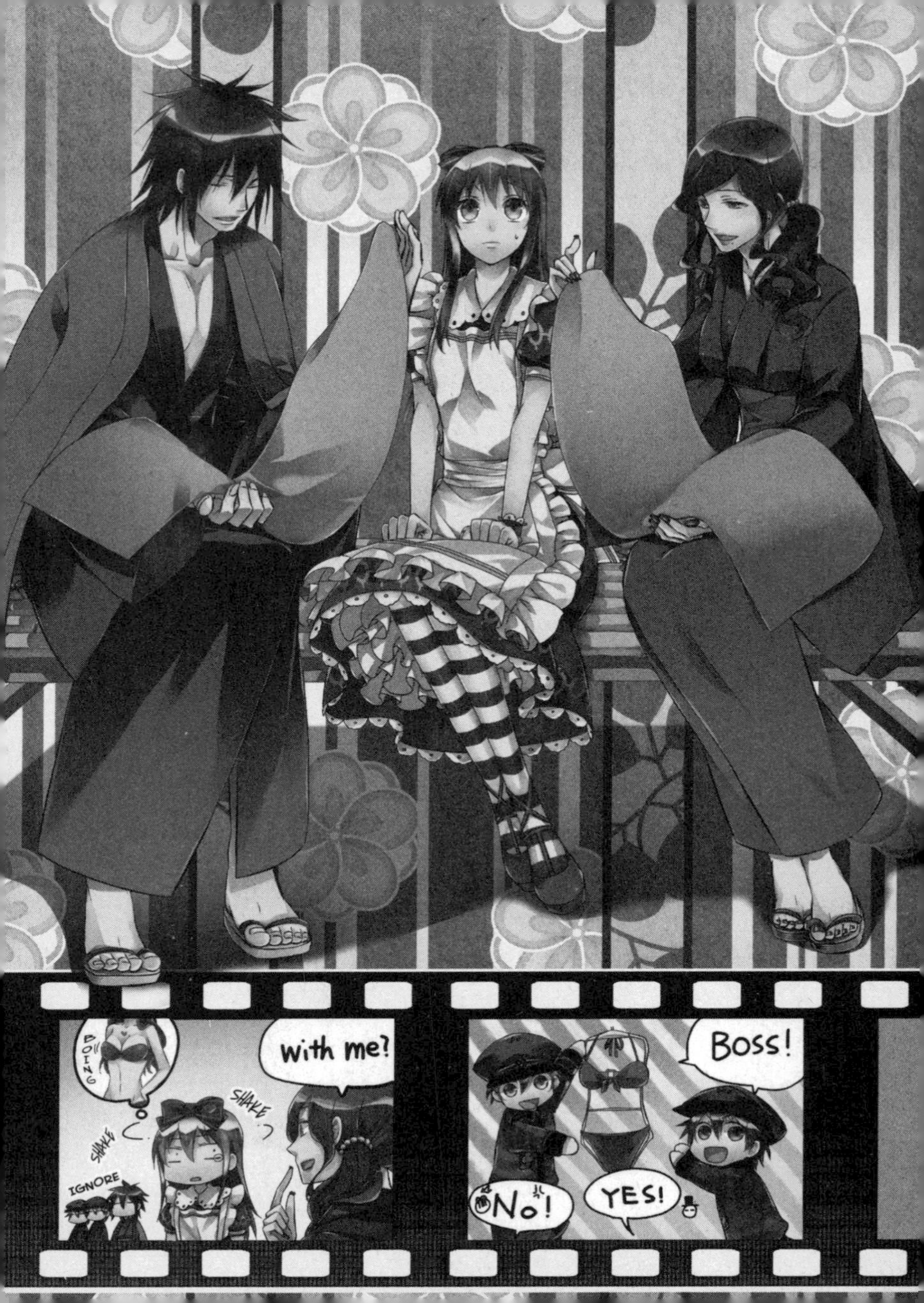
Boss!
YES!
No!
with me?
SHAKE
BOING
SHAKE
IGNORE

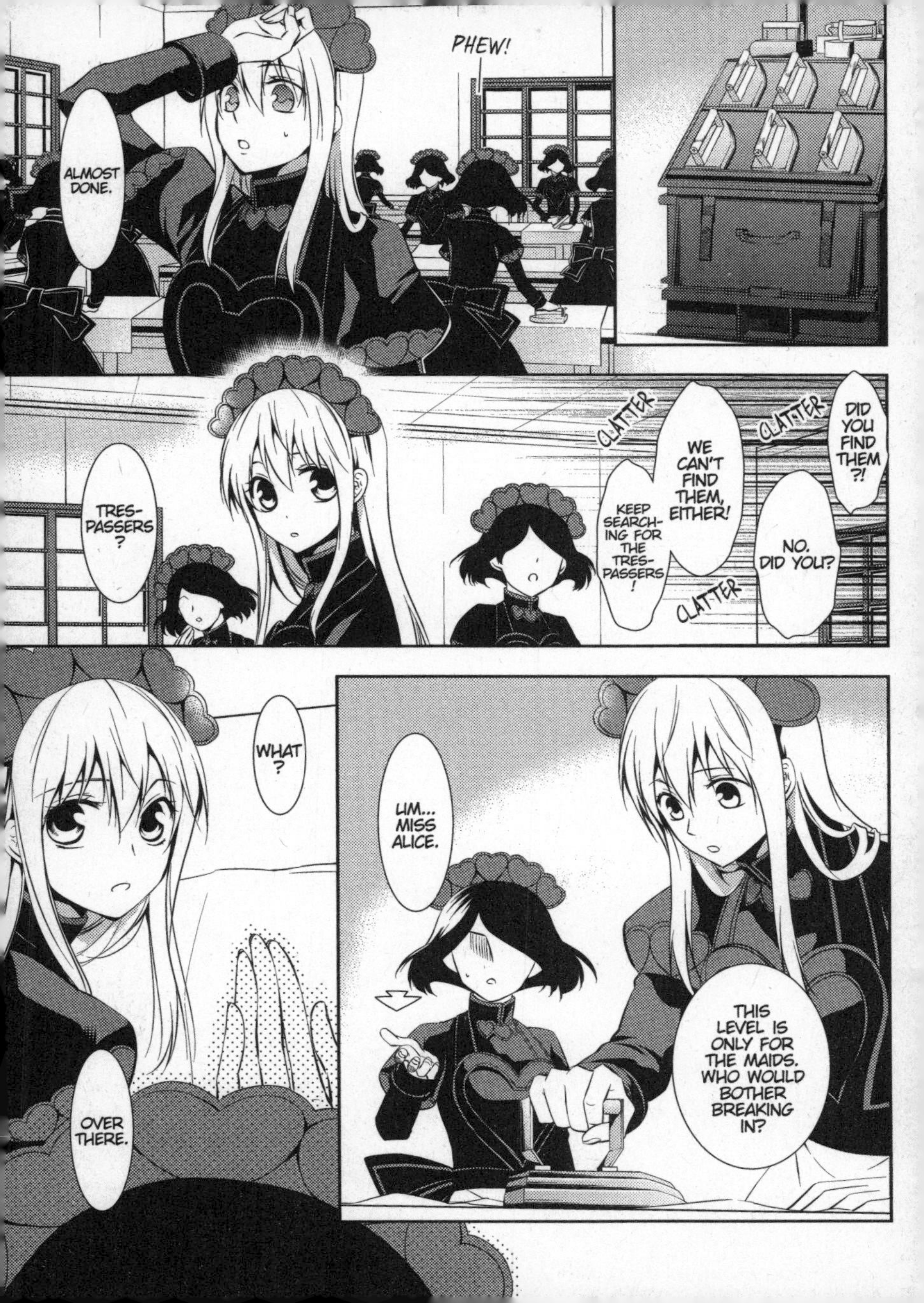
PHEW!
ALMOST DONE.
DID YOU FIND THEM?!
CLATTER
CLATTER
NO. DID YOU?
WE CAN'T FIND THEM, EITHER!
KEEP SEARCHING FOR THE TRES-PASSERS!
CLATTER
TRES-PASSERS?
THIS LEVEL IS ONLY FOR THE MAIDS. WHO WOULD BOTHER BREAKING IN?
UM... MISS ALICE.
WHAT?
OVER THERE.

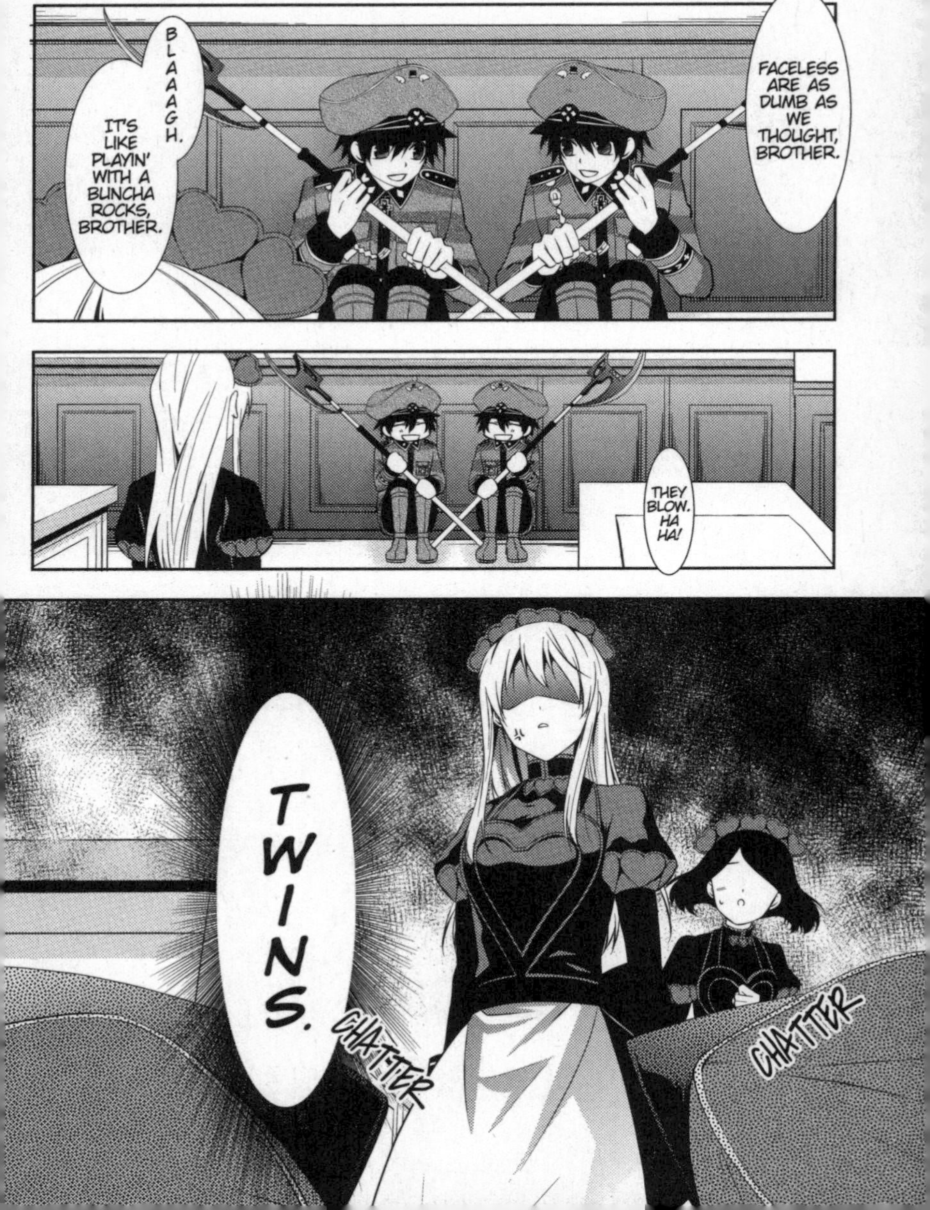
FACELESS ARE AS DUMB AS WE THOUGHT, BROTHER.
BLAAAAGH.
IT'S LIKE PLAYIN' WITH A BUNCHA ROCKS, BROTHER.
THEY BLOW. HA HA!
TWINS.
CHATTER
CHATTER

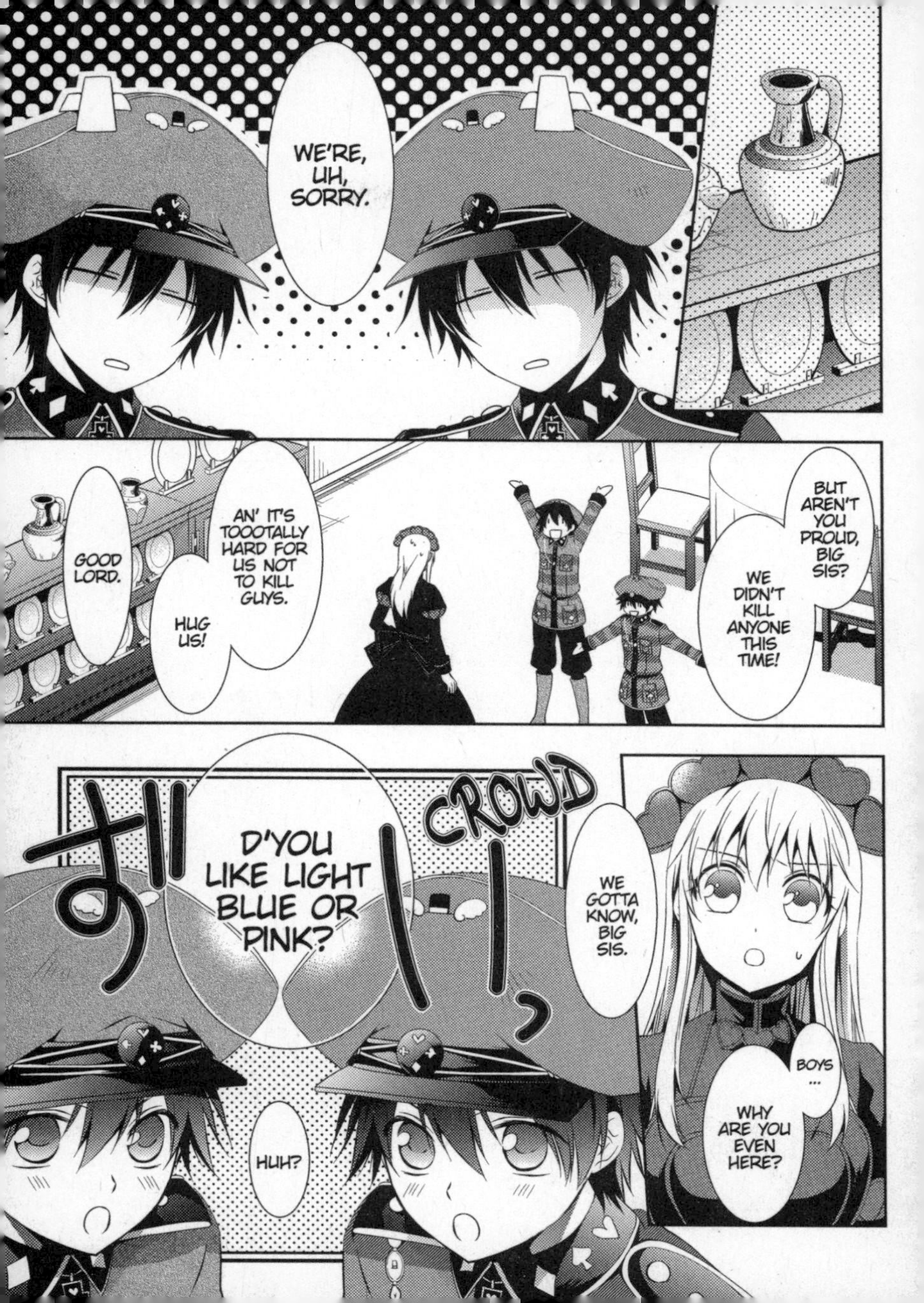
WE'RE, UH, SORRY.
BUT AREN'T YOU PROUD, BIG SIS?
WE DIDN'T KILL ANYONE THIS TIME!
AN' IT'S TOOOTALLY HARD FOR US NOT TO KILL GUYS.
HUG US!
GOOD LORD.
WE GOTTA KNOW, BIG SIS.
BOYS... WHY ARE YOU EVEN HERE?
CROWD
D'YOU LIKE LIGHT BLUE OR PINK?
HUH?

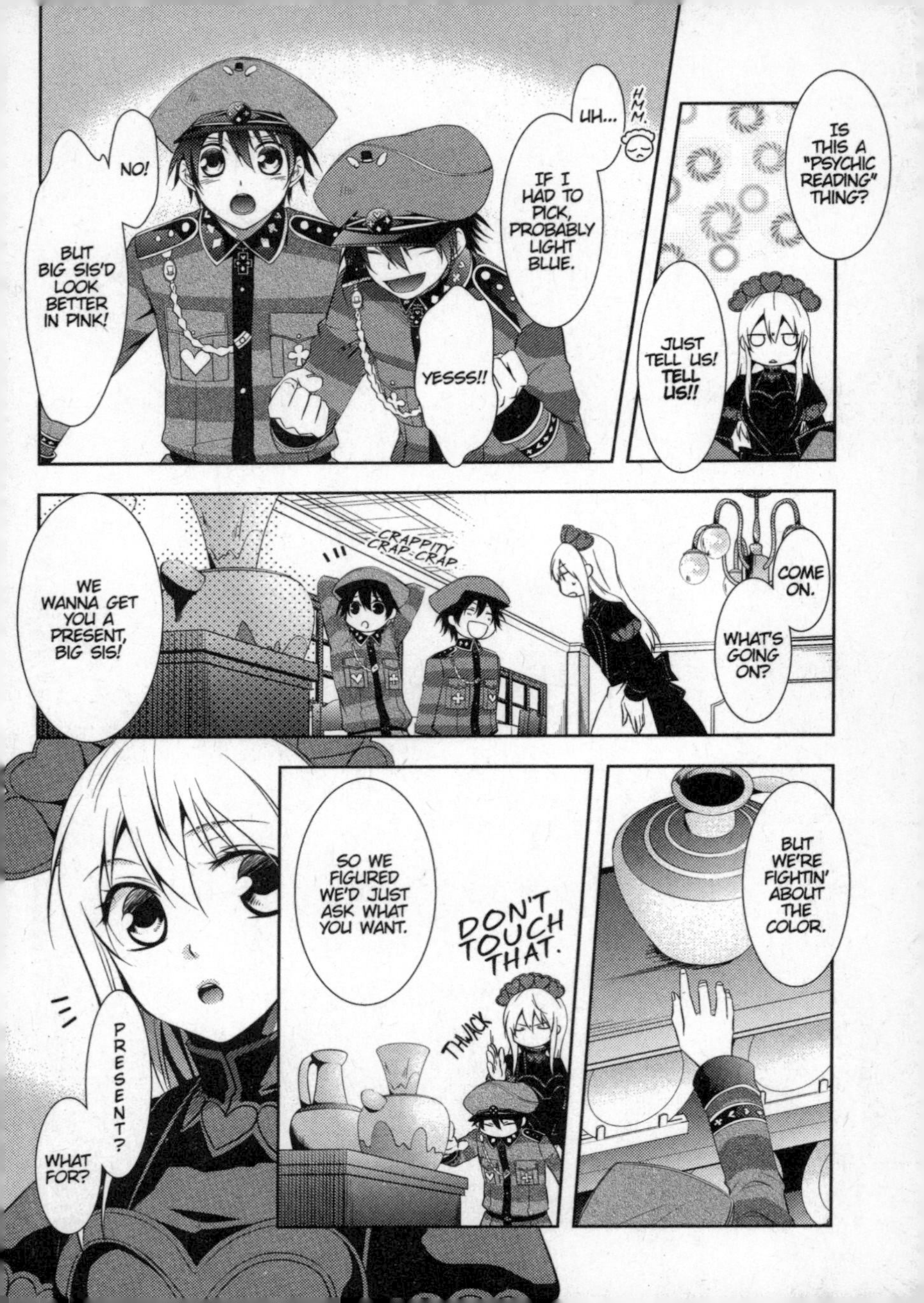
IS THIS A "PSYCHIC READING" THING?
JUST TELL US! TELL US!!
HMMM.
UH...
IF I HAD TO PICK, PROBABLY LIGHT BLUE.
YESSS!!
NO!
BUT BIG SIS'D LOOK BETTER IN PINK!
COME ON.
WHAT'S GOING ON?
CRAPPITY CRAP CRAP
WE WANNA GET YOU A PRESENT, BIG SIS!
BUT WE'RE FIGHTIN' ABOUT THE COLOR.
DON'T TOUCH THAT.
THWACK
SO WE FIGURED WE'D JUST ASK WHAT YOU WANT.
PRESENT? WHAT FOR?

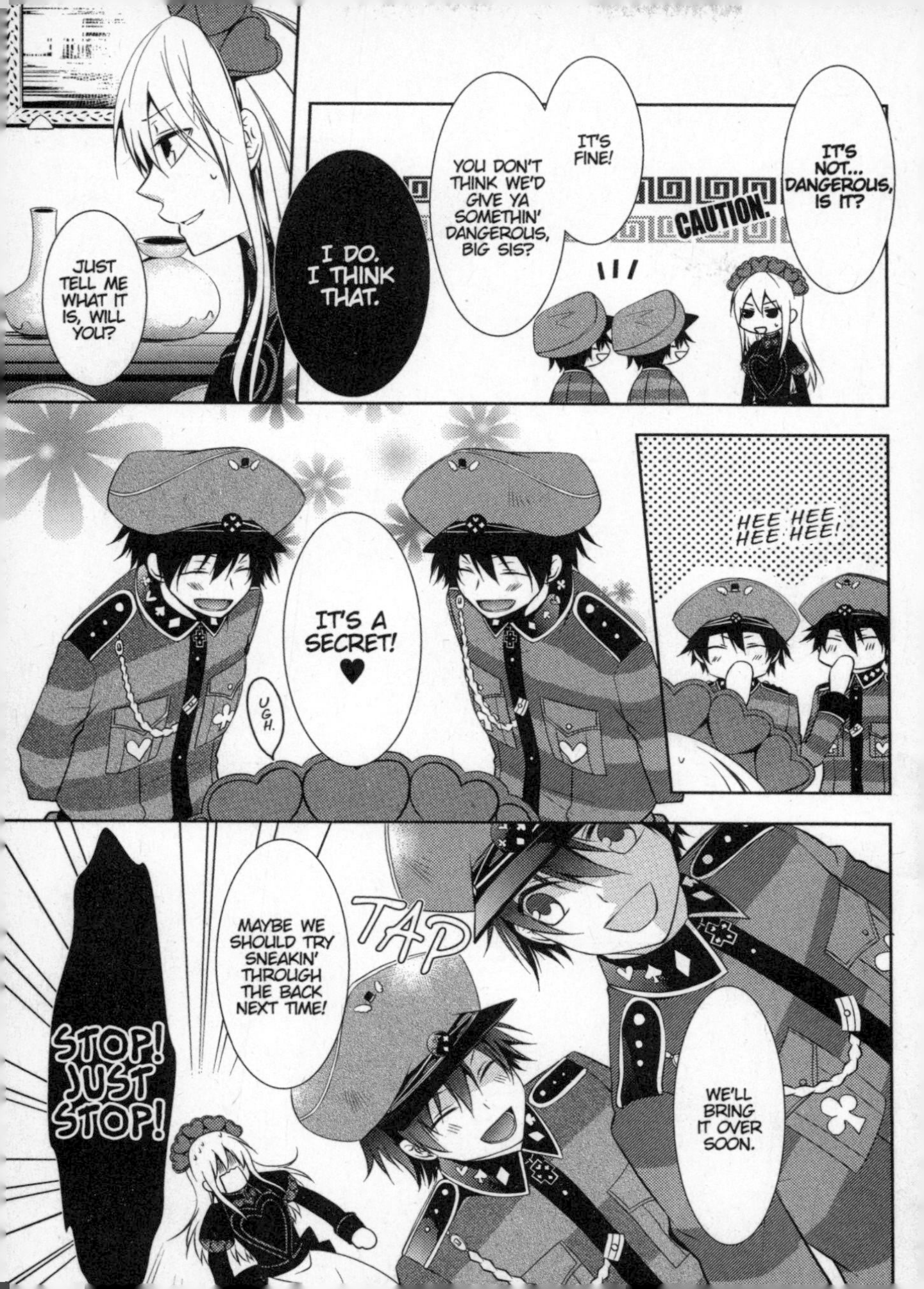
IT'S NOT... DANGEROUS, IS IT?
CAUTION!
IT'S FINE!
YOU DON'T THINK WE'D GIVE YA SOMETHIN' DANGEROUS, BIG SIS?
I DO. I THINK THAT.
JUST TELL ME WHAT IT IS, WILL YOU?
HEE HEE HEE HEE!
IT'S A SECRET! ♥
UGH.
WE'LL BRING IT OVER SOON.
TAP
MAYBE WE SHOULD TRY SNEAKIN' THROUGH THE BACK NEXT TIME!
STOP! JUST STOP!

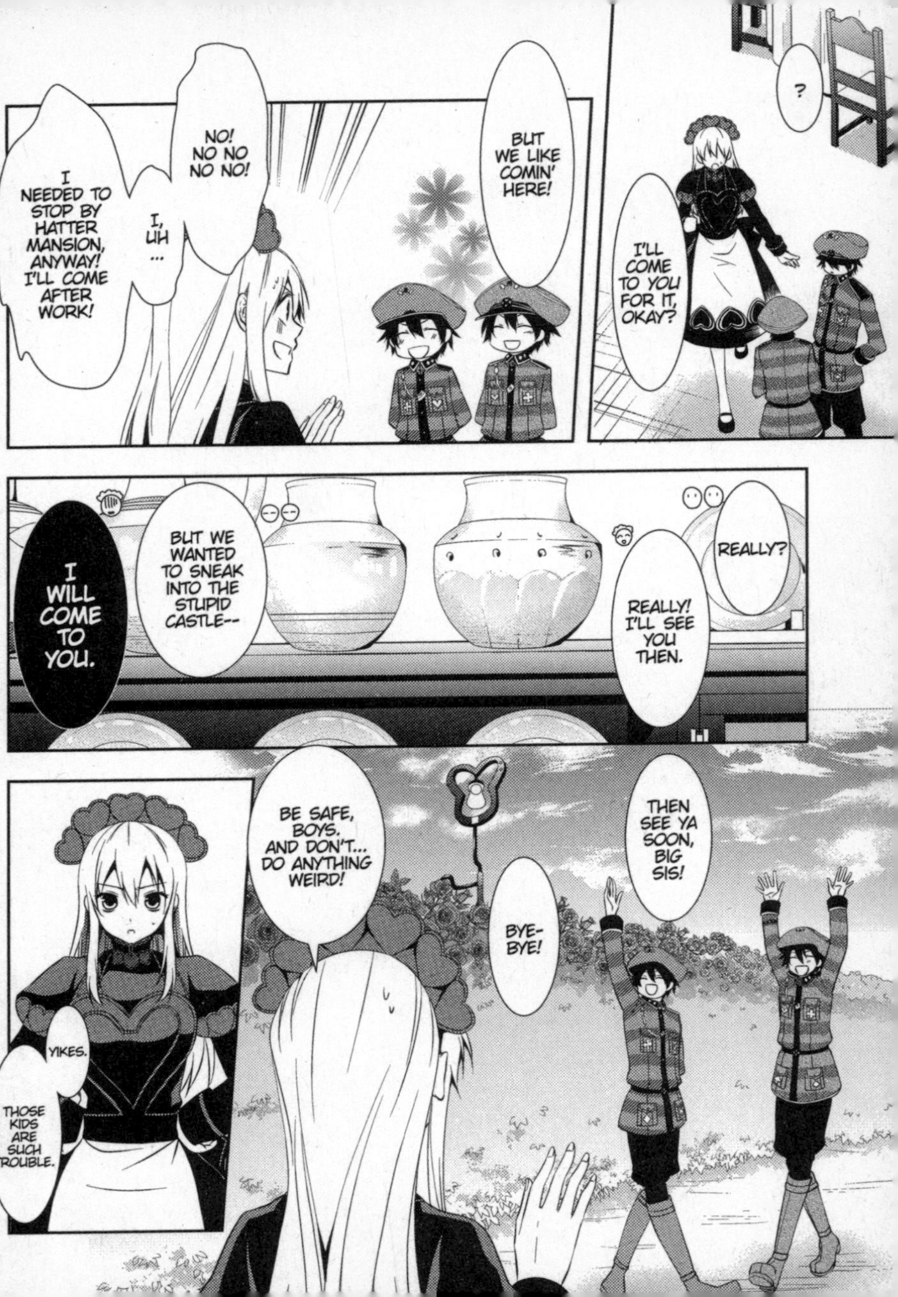
?
I'LL COME TO YOU FOR IT, OKAY?
BUT WE LIKE COMIN' HERE!
NO! NO NO NO NO!
I, UH ...
I NEEDED TO STOP BY HATTER MANSION, ANYWAY! I'LL COME AFTER WORK!
REALLY?
REALLY! I'LL SEE YOU THEN.
BUT WE WANTED TO SNEAK INTO THE STUPID CASTLE--
I WILL COME TO YOU.
THEN SEE YA SOON, BIG SIS!
BYE-BYE!
BE SAFE, BOYS. AND DON'T... DO ANYTHING WEIRD!
YIKES.
THOSE KIDS ARE SUCH TROUBLE.

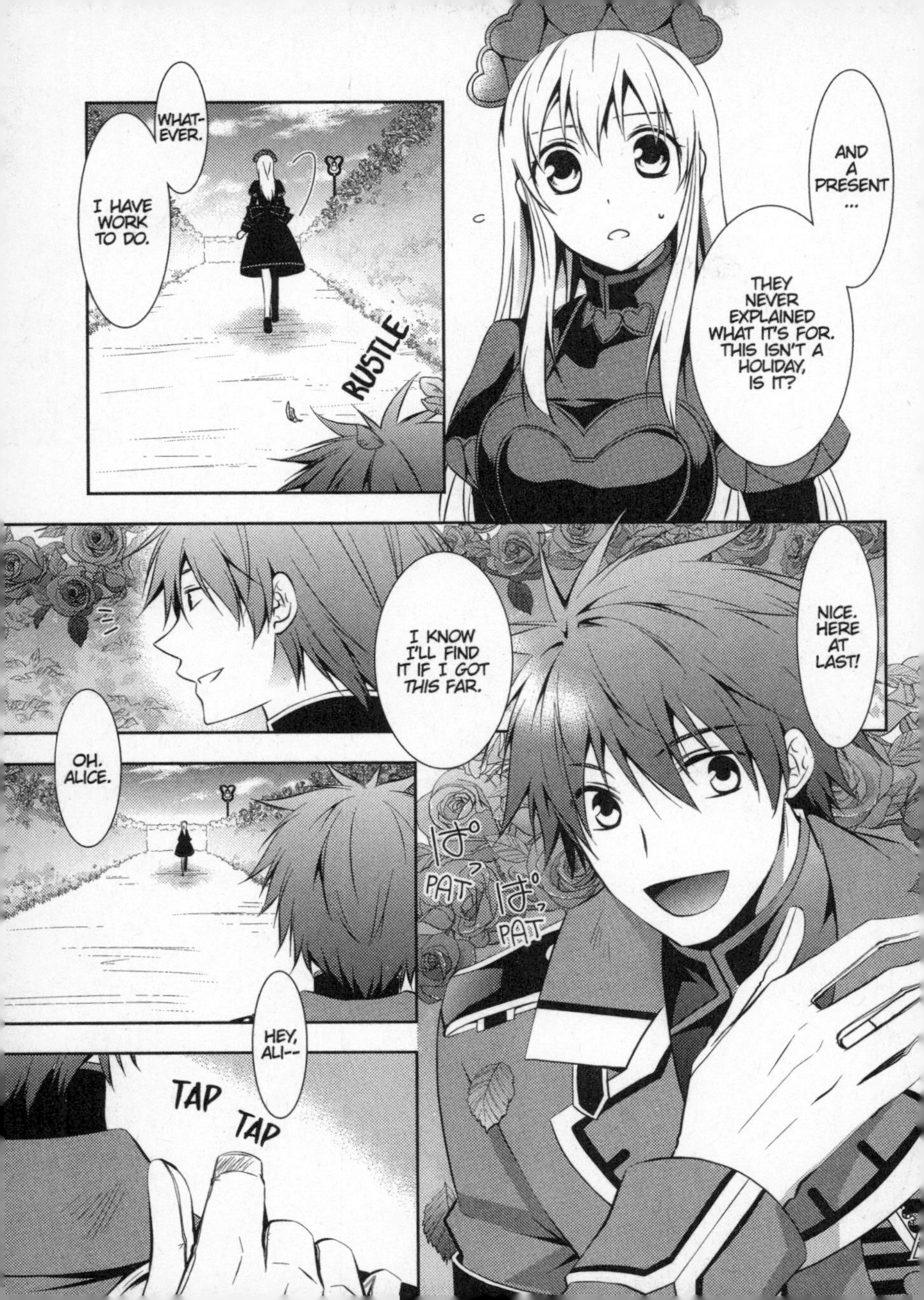
AND A PRESENT ...
THEY NEVER EXPLAINED WHAT IT'S FOR. THIS ISN'T A HOLIDAY, IS IT?
WHAT-EVER.
I HAVE WORK TO DO.
RUSTLE
NICE. HERE AT LAST!
ぱっ PAT ぱっ PAT
I KNOW I'LL FIND IT IF I GOT THIS FAR.
OH. ALICE.
HEY, ALI--
TAP TAP

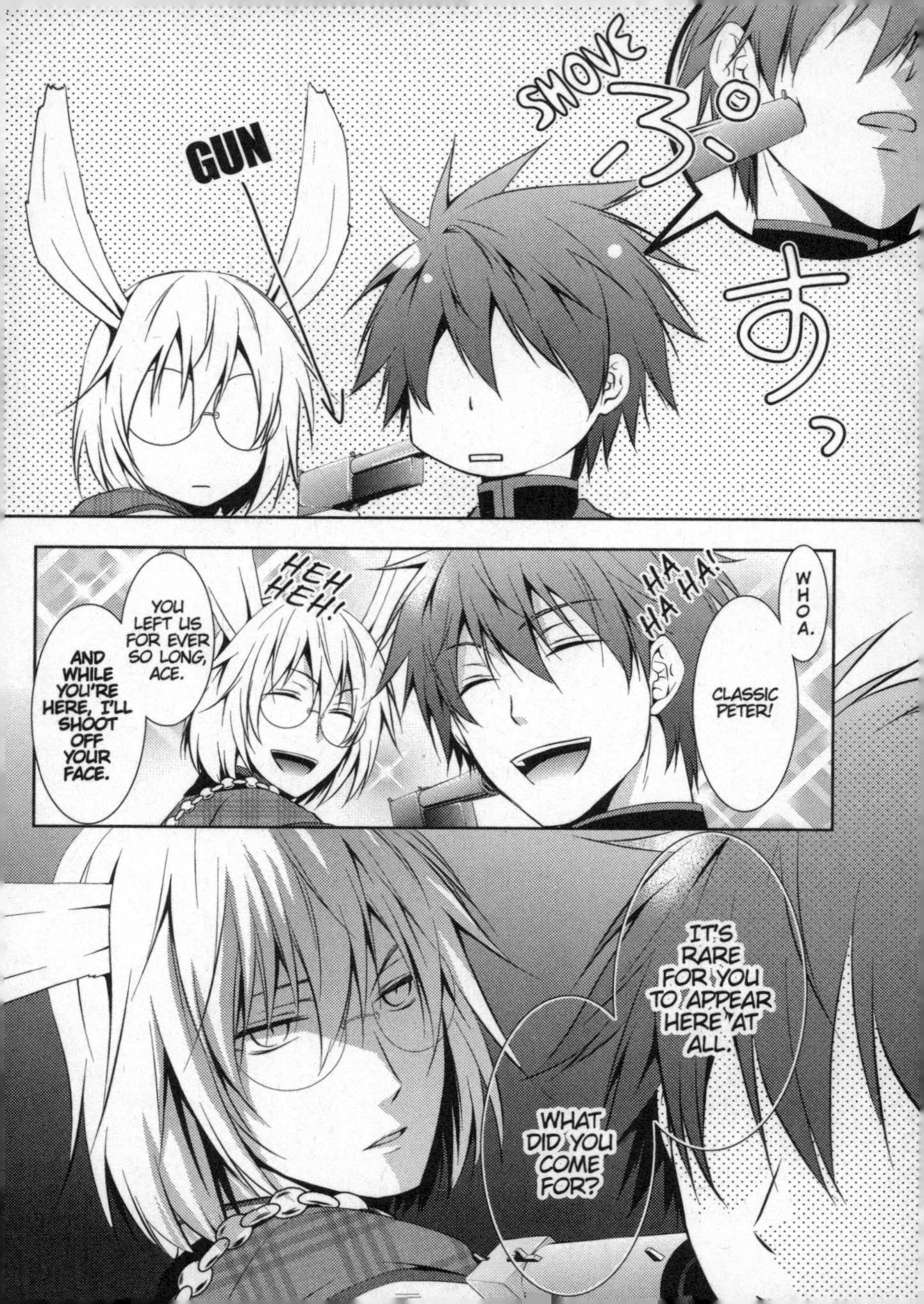
SHOVE
あっ
GUN
WHOA.
CLASSIC PETER!
HA HA HA!
HEH HEH!
YOU LEFT US FOR EVER SO LONG, ACE.
AND WHILE YOU'RE HERE, I'LL SHOOT OFF YOUR FACE.
IT'S RARE FOR YOU TO APPEAR HERE AT ALL.
WHAT DID YOU COME FOR?

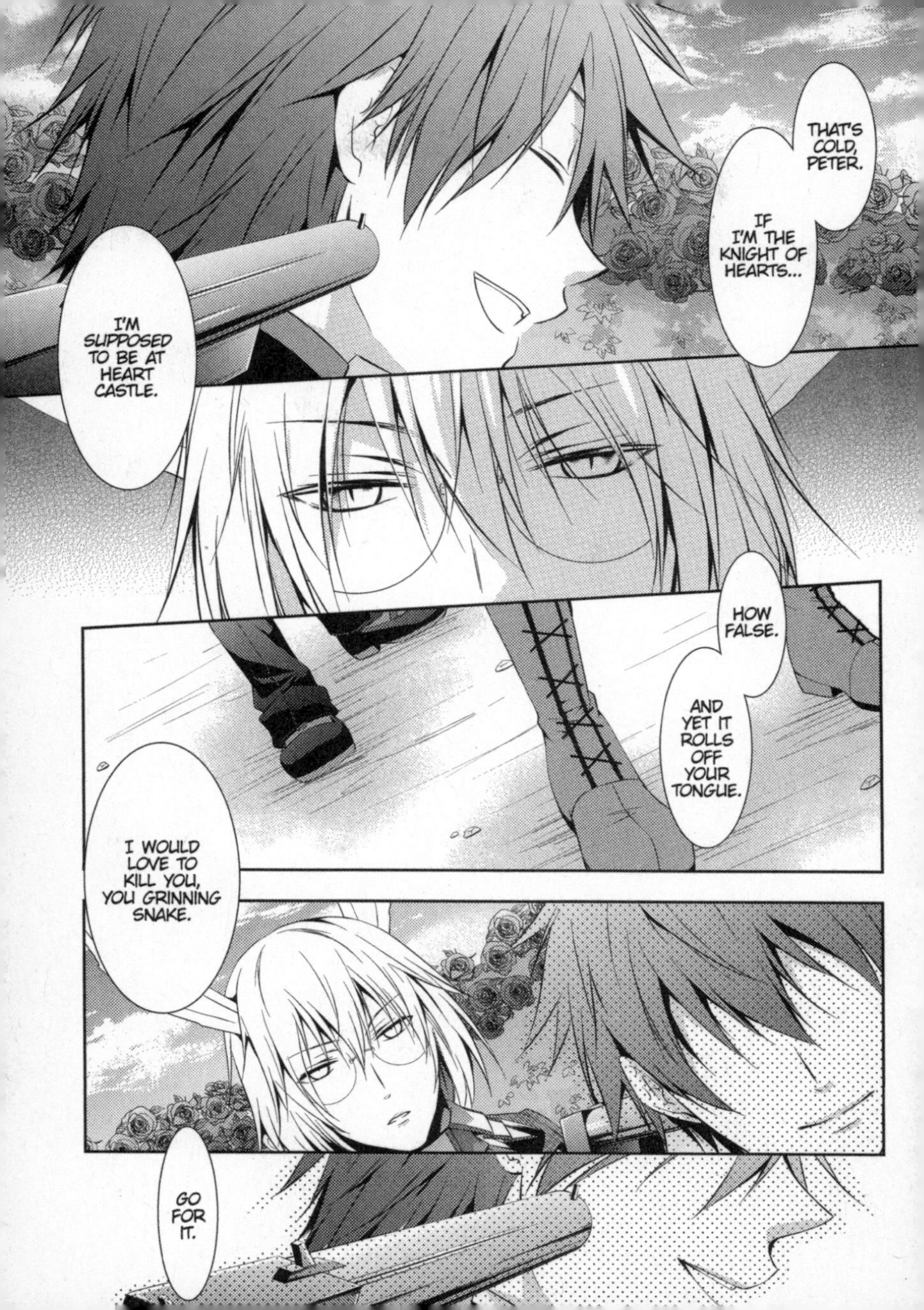
THAT'S COLD, PETER.
IF I'M THE KNIGHT OF HEARTS...
I'M SUPPOSED TO BE AT HEART CASTLE.
HOW FALSE.
AND YET IT ROLLS OFF YOUR TONGUE.
I WOULD LOVE TO KILL YOU, YOU GRINNING SNAKE.
GO FOR IT.

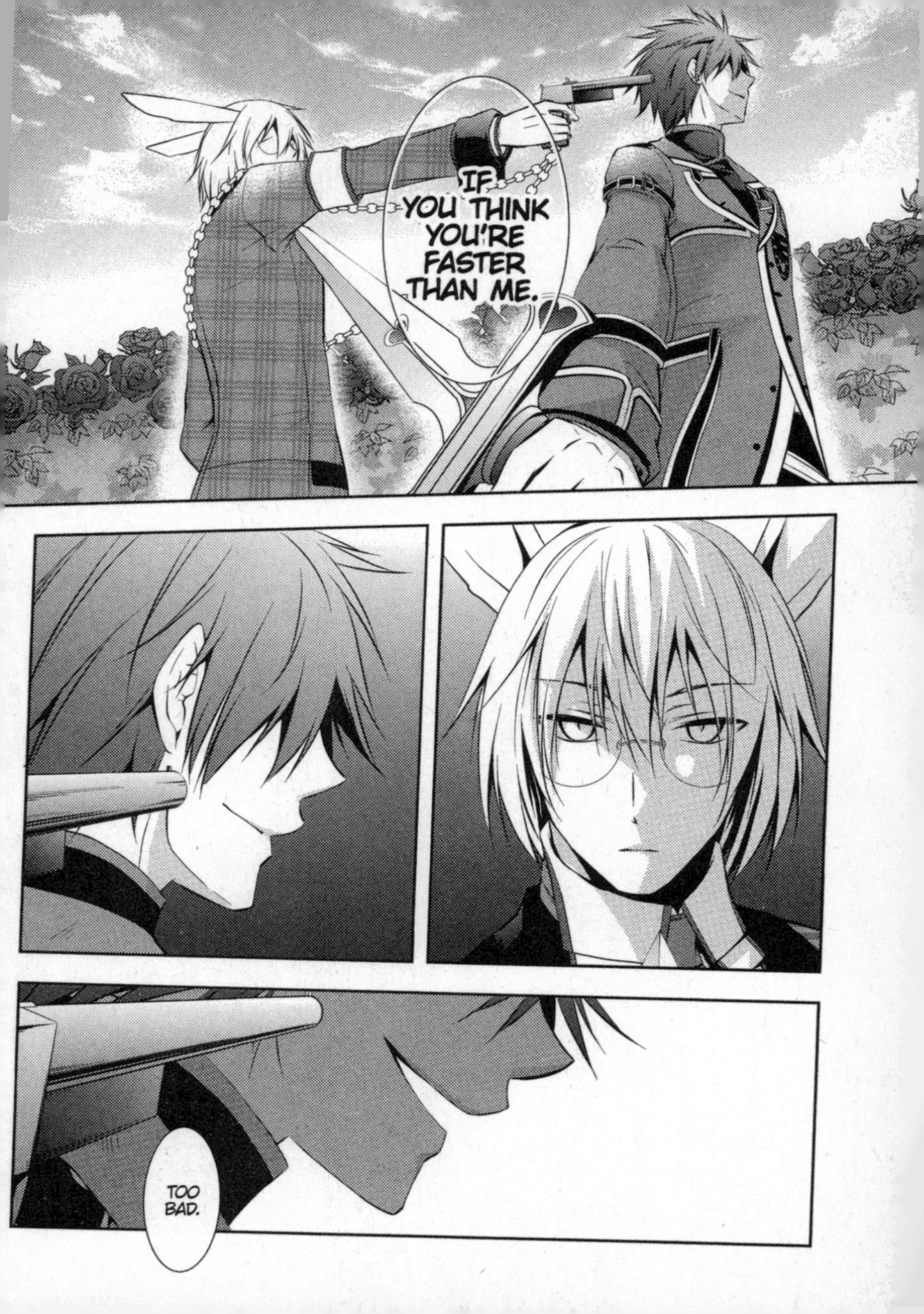
IF YOU THINK YOU'RE FASTER THAN ME.
TOO BAD.

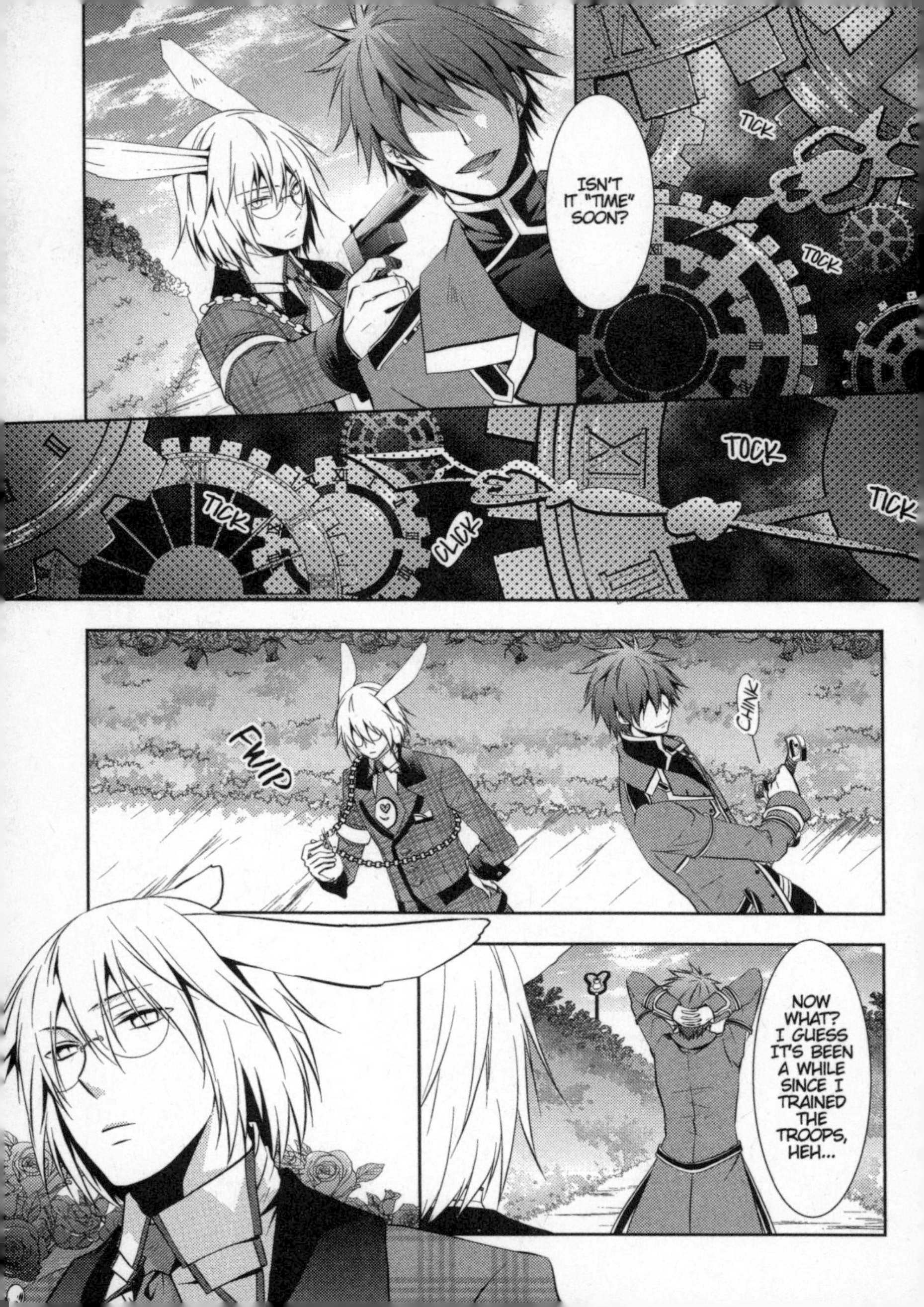
TICK
TOCK
ISN'T IT "TIME" SOON?
TICK
TOCK
CLICK
TICK
CHINK
FWIP
NOW WHAT? I GUESS IT'S BEEN A WHILE SINCE I TRAINED THE TROOPS, HEH...

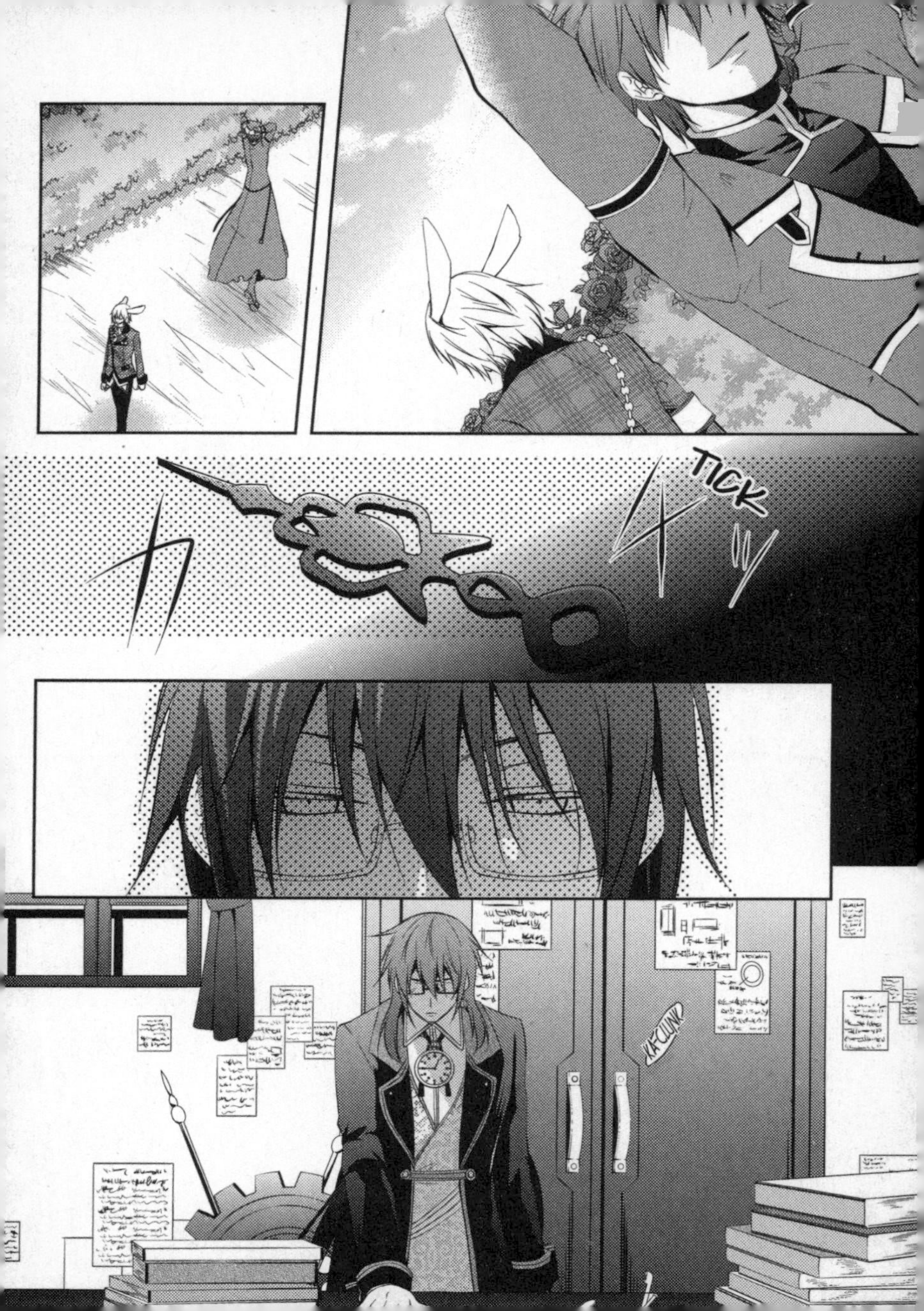
TICK
KA-CLUNK

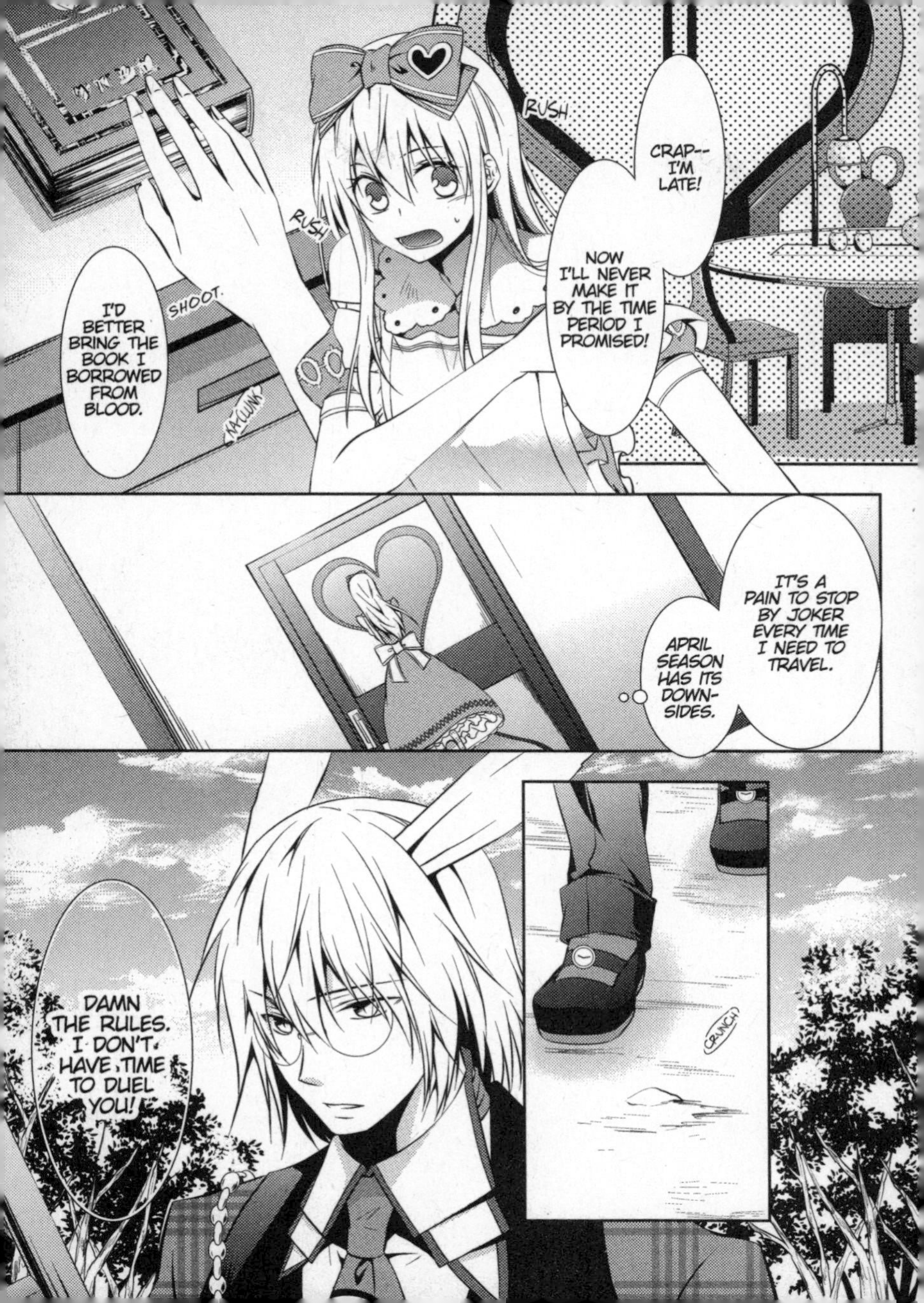
RUSH
CRAP-- I'M LATE!
NOW I'LL NEVER MAKE IT BY THE TIME PERIOD I PROMISED!
RUSH
SHOOT.
I'D BETTER BRING THE BOOK I BORROWED FROM BLOOD.
KA-CLUNK
IT'S A PAIN TO STOP BY JOKER EVERY TIME I NEED TO TRAVEL.
APRIL SEASON HAS ITS DOWN-SIDES.
CRUNCH
DAMN THE RULES. I DON'T HAVE TIME TO DUEL YOU!

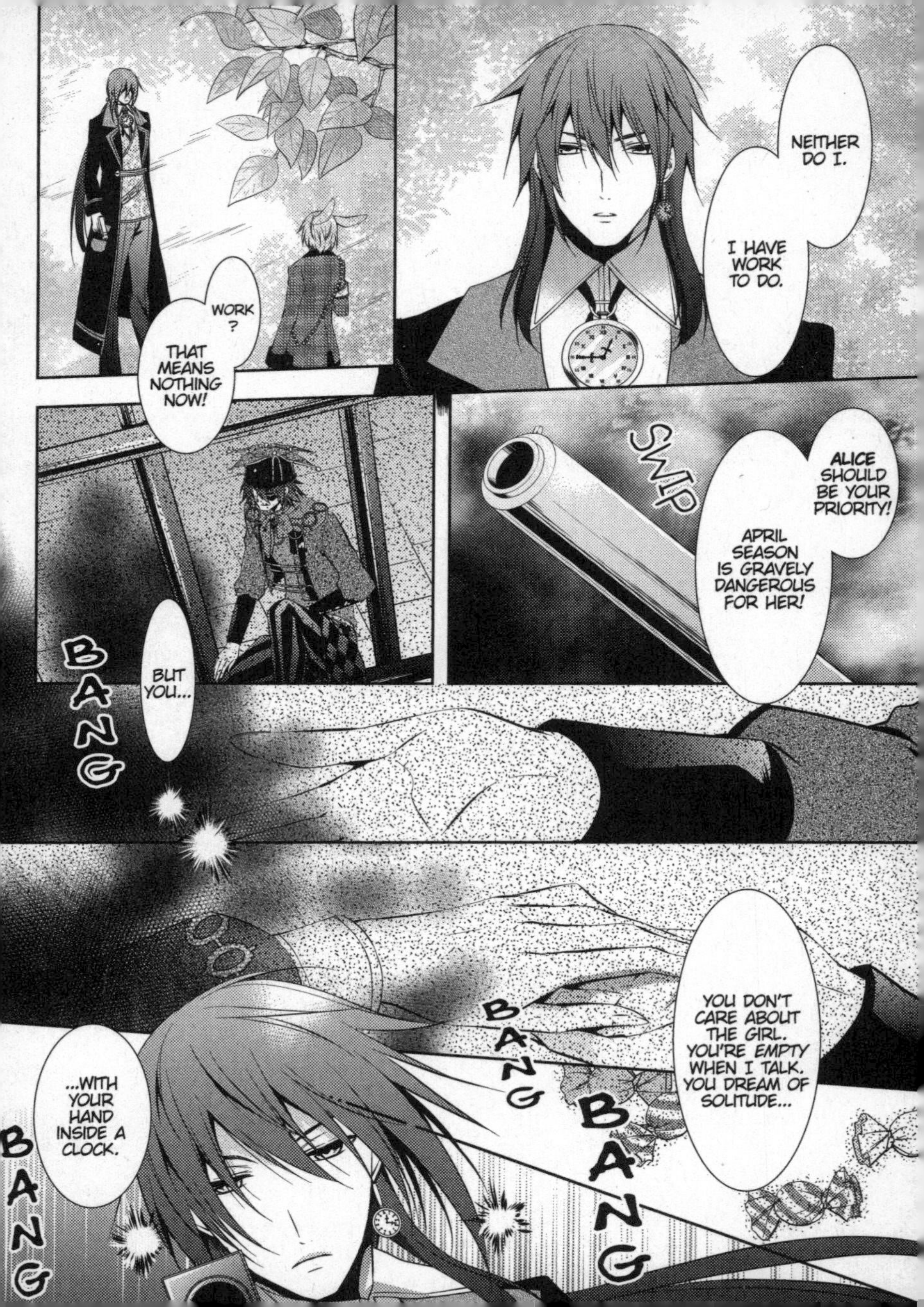
NEITHER DO I.
I HAVE WORK TO DO.
WORK ?
THAT MEANS NOTHING NOW!
SWIP
ALICE SHOULD BE YOUR PRIORITY!
APRIL SEASON IS GRAVELY DANGEROUS FOR HER!
BUT YOU...
BANG
YOU DON'T CARE ABOUT THE GIRL. YOU'RE EMPTY WHEN I TALK. YOU DREAM OF SOLITUDE...
BANG
BANG
...WITH YOUR HAND INSIDE A CLOCK.
BANG

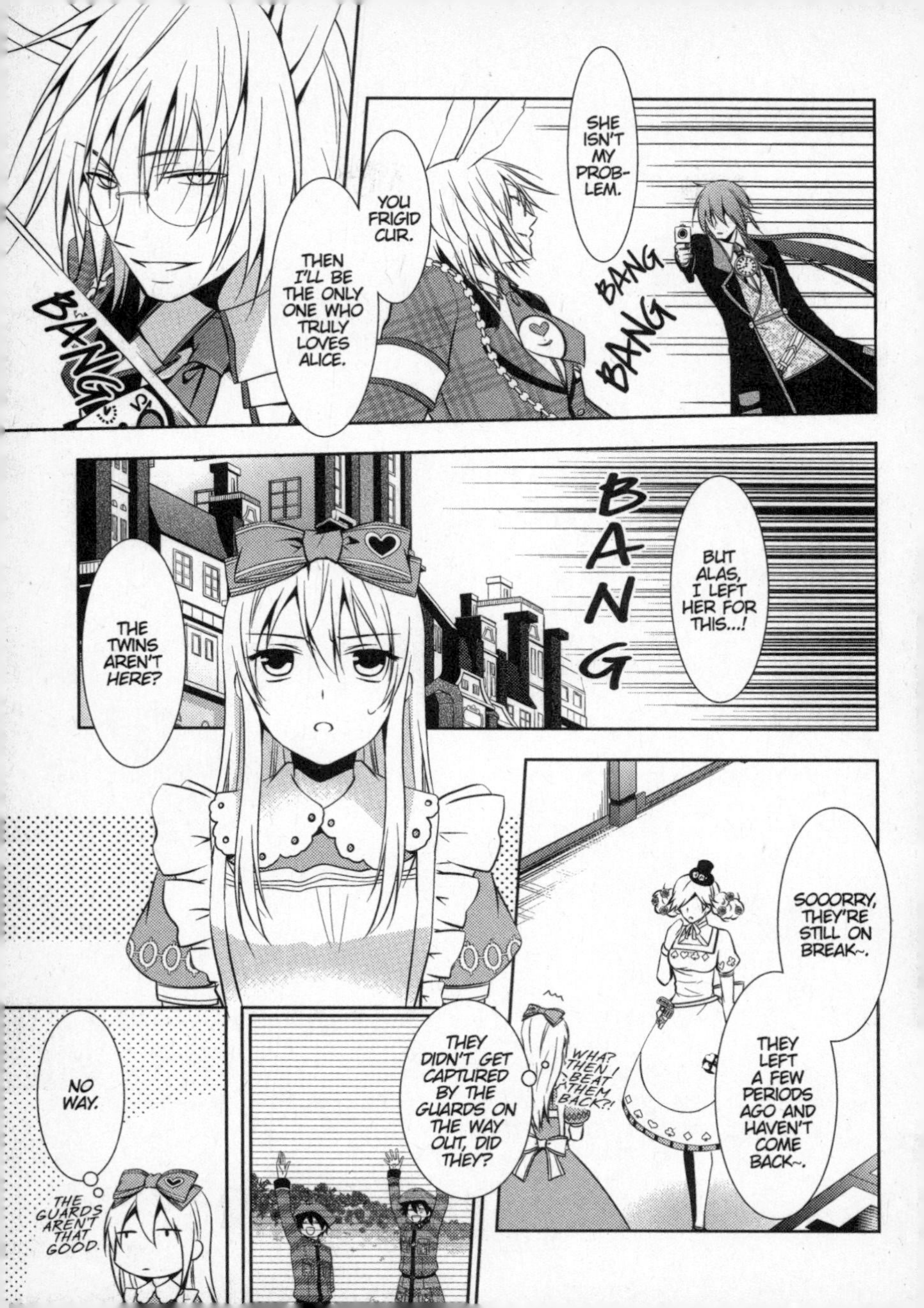
SHE ISN'T MY PROB-LEM.
BANG
BANG
YOU FRIGID CUR.
THEN I'LL BE THE ONLY ONE WHO TRULY LOVES ALICE.
BANG
BUT ALAS, I LEFT HER FOR THIS...!
BANG
THE TWINS AREN'T HERE?
SOOORRY, THEY'RE STILL ON BREAK~.
THEY LEFT A FEW PERIODS AGO AND HAVEN'T COME BACK~.
WHA? THEN I BEAT THEM BACK?!
THEY DIDN'T GET CAPTURED BY THE GUARDS ON THE WAY OUT, DID THEY?
NO WAY.
THE GUARDS AREN'T THAT GOOD.

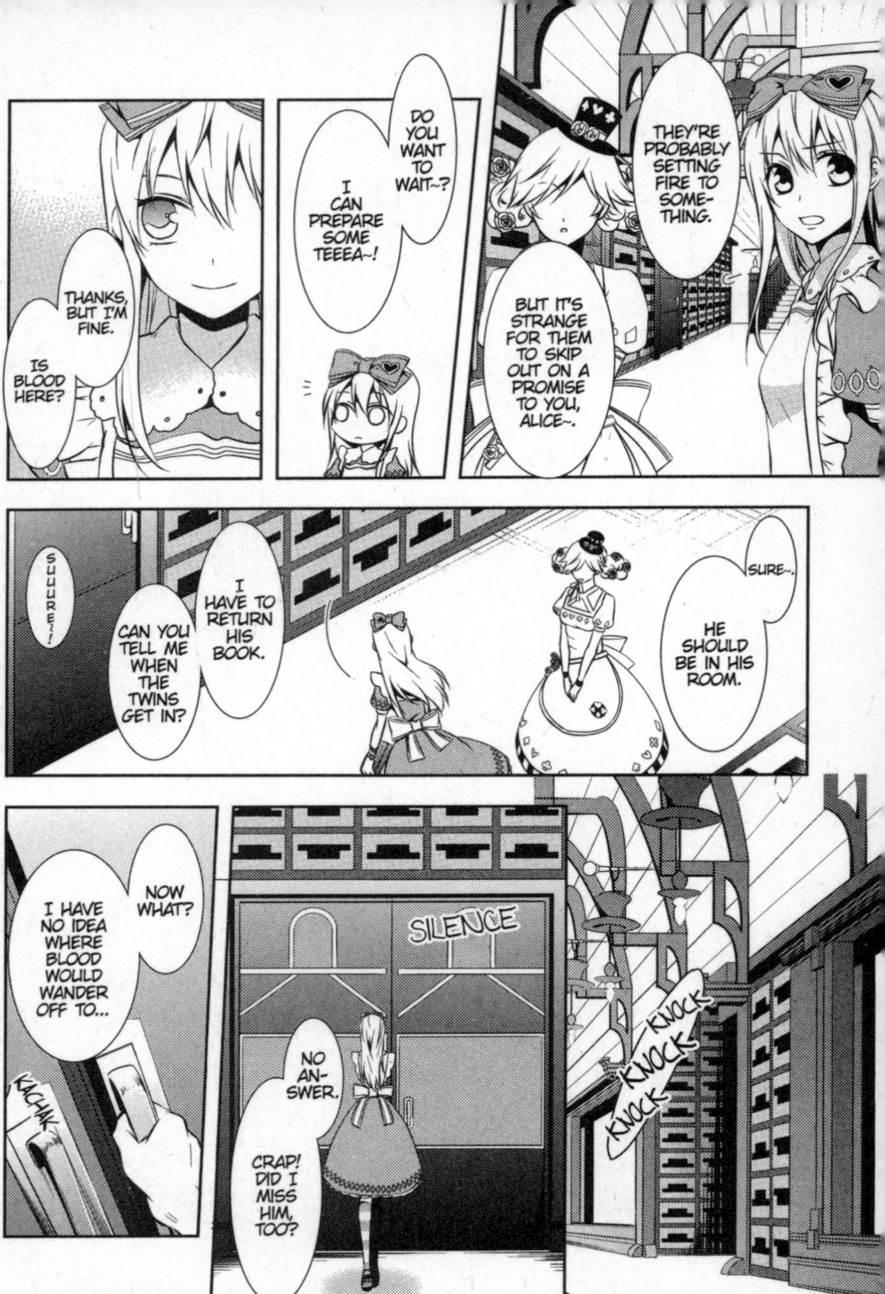
THEY'RE PROBABLY SETTING FIRE TO SOME-THING.
BUT IT'S STRANGE FOR THEM TO SKIP OUT ON A PROMISE TO YOU, ALICE~.
DO YOU WANT TO WAIT~?
I CAN PREPARE SOME TEEEA~!
THANKS, BUT I'M FINE.
IS BLOOD HERE?
SURE~.
HE SHOULD BE IN HIS ROOM.
I HAVE TO RETURN HIS BOOK.
CAN YOU TELL ME WHEN THE TWINS GET IN?
SUUURE~!
KNOCK KNOCK KNOCK
SILENCE
NO AN-SWER.
CRAP! DID I MISS HIM, TOO?
NOW WHAT?
I HAVE NO IDEA WHERE BLOOD WOULD WANDER OFF TO...
KACHAK

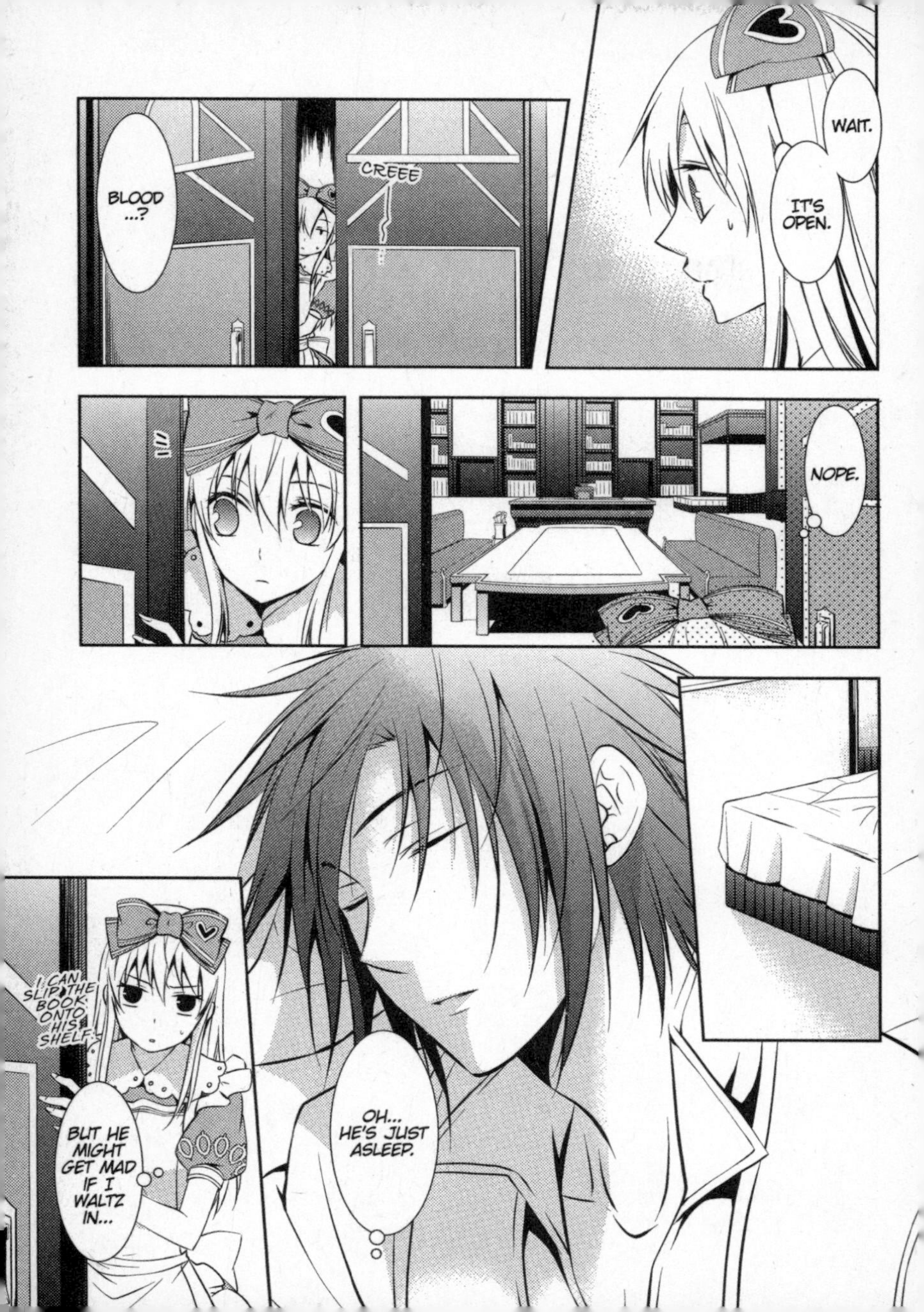
WAIT.
IT'S OPEN.
CREEE
BLOOD ...?
NOPE.
OH... HE'S JUST ASLEEP.
I CAN SLIP THE BOOK ONTO HIS SHELF.
BUT HE MIGHT GET MAD IF I WALTZ IN...

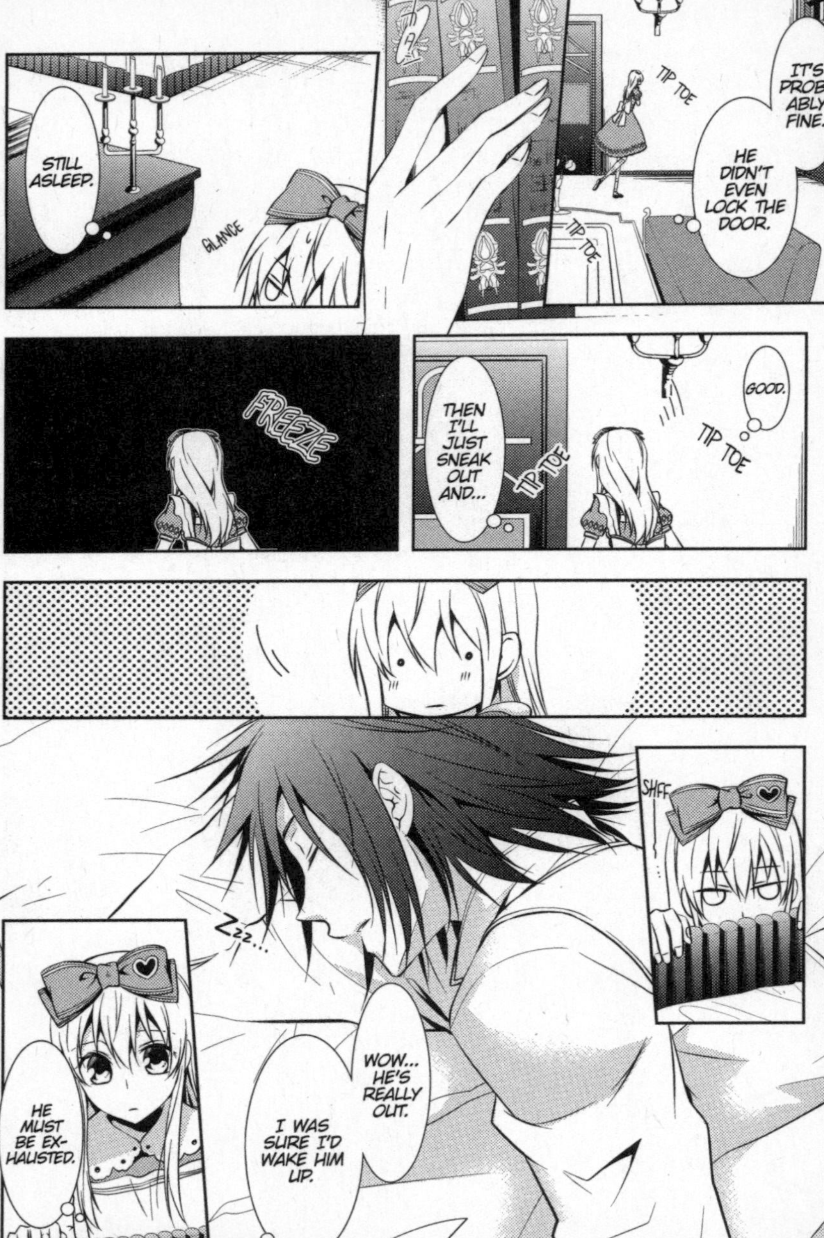
IT'S PROBABLY FINE.
HE DIDN'T EVEN LOCK THE DOOR.
TIP TOE
TIP TOE
GLANCE
STILL ASLEEP.
GOOD.
TIP TOE
THEN I'LL JUST SNEAK OUT AND...
TIP TOE
FREEZE
SHFF
Zzz...
WOW... HE'S REALLY OUT.
I WAS SURE I'D WAKE HIM UP.
HE MUST BE EXHAUSTED.

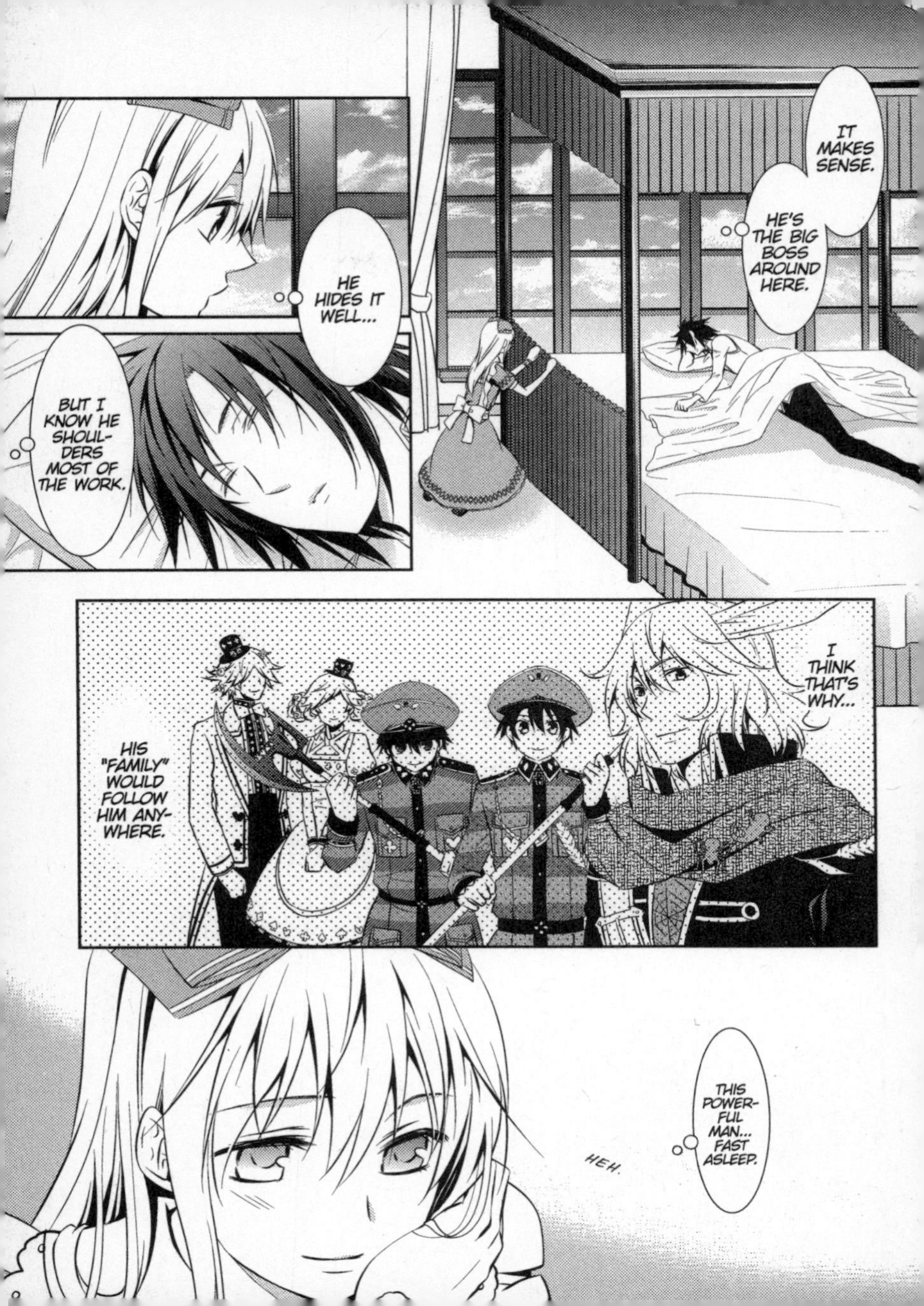
IT MAKES SENSE.
HE'S THE BIG BOSS AROUND HERE.
HE HIDES IT WELL...
BUT I KNOW HE SHOULDERS MOST OF THE WORK.
I THINK THAT'S WHY...
HIS "FAMILY" WOULD FOLLOW HIM ANYWHERE.
THIS POWERFUL MAN... FAST ASLEEP.
HEH.

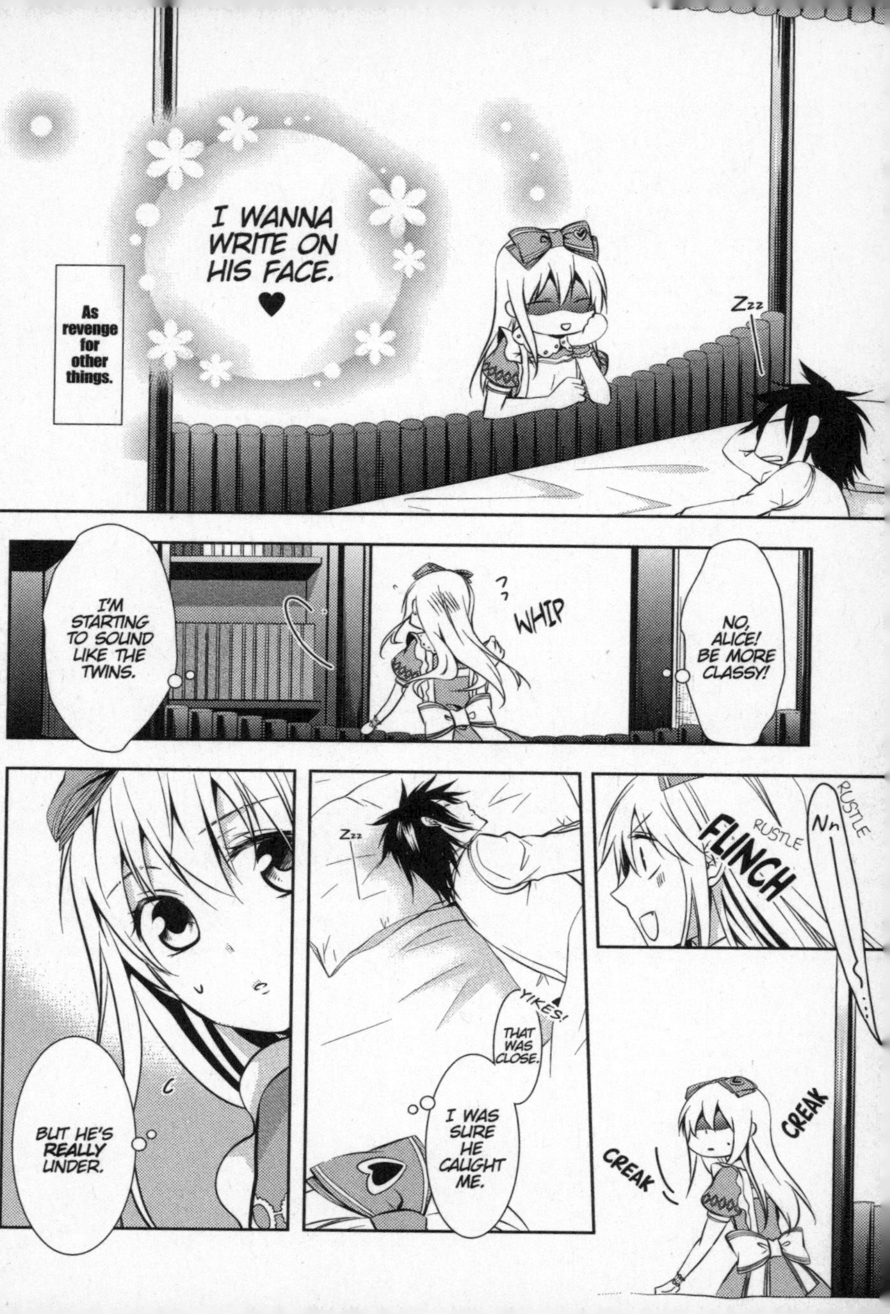
Zzz
I WANNA WRITE ON HIS FACE. ♥
As revenge for other things.
NO, ALICE! BE MORE CLASSY!
WHIP
I'M STARTING TO SOUND LIKE THE TWINS.
RUSTLE
Nn
RUSTLE
FLINCH
CREAK
CREAK
Zzz
YIKES!
THAT WAS CLOSE.
I WAS SURE HE CAUGHT ME.
BUT HE'S REALLY UNDER.

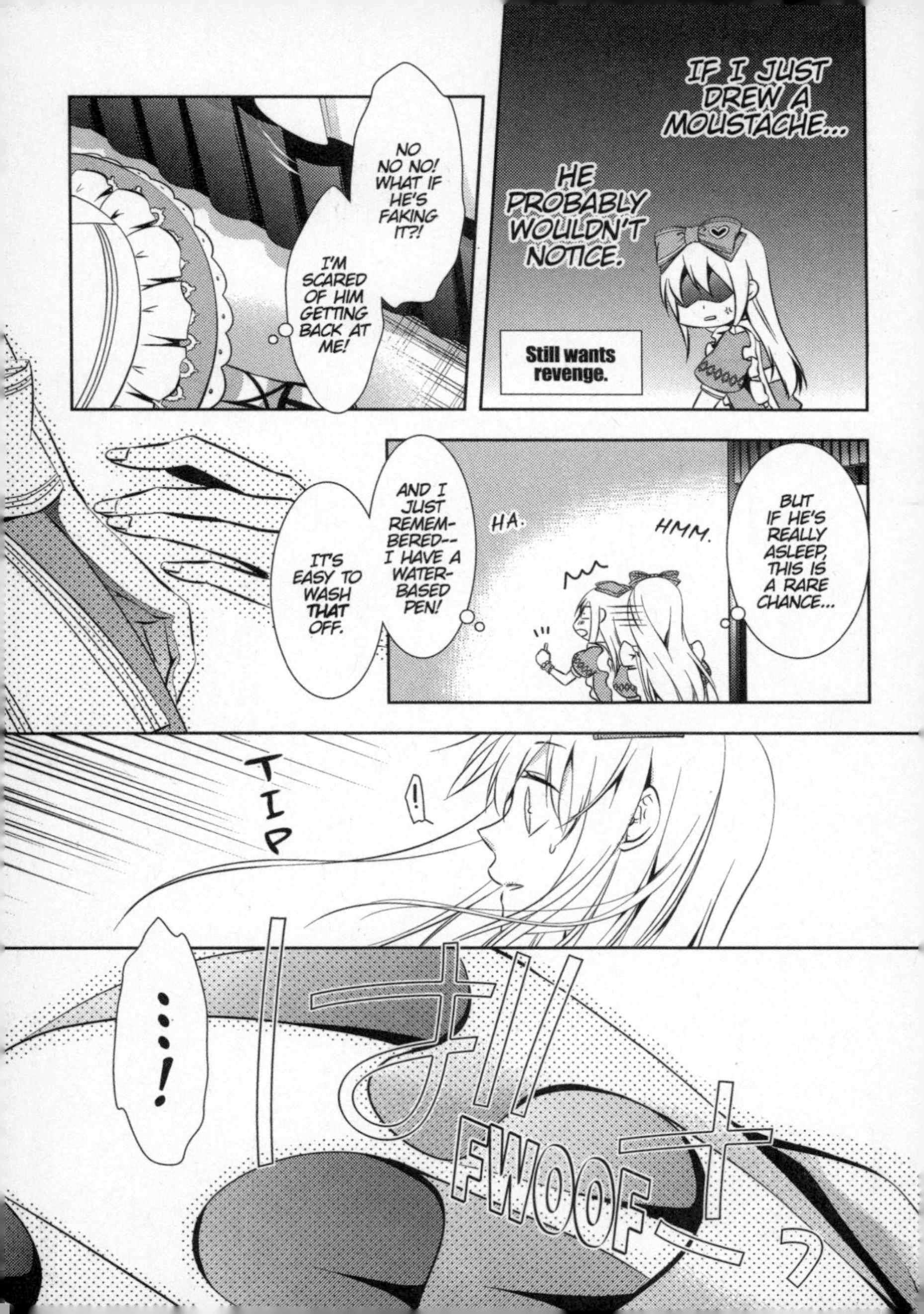
IF I JUST DREW A MOUSTACHE...
HE PROBABLY WOULDN'T NOTICE.
Still wants revenge.
NO NO NO! WHAT IF HE'S FAKING IT?!
I'M SCARED OF HIM GETTING BACK AT ME!
BUT IF HE'S REALLY ASLEEP, THIS IS A RARE CHANCE...
HMM.
HA.
AND I JUST REMEMBERED-- I HAVE A WATER-BASED PEN!
IT'S EASY TO WASH THAT OFF.
!
TIP
...!
FWOOF

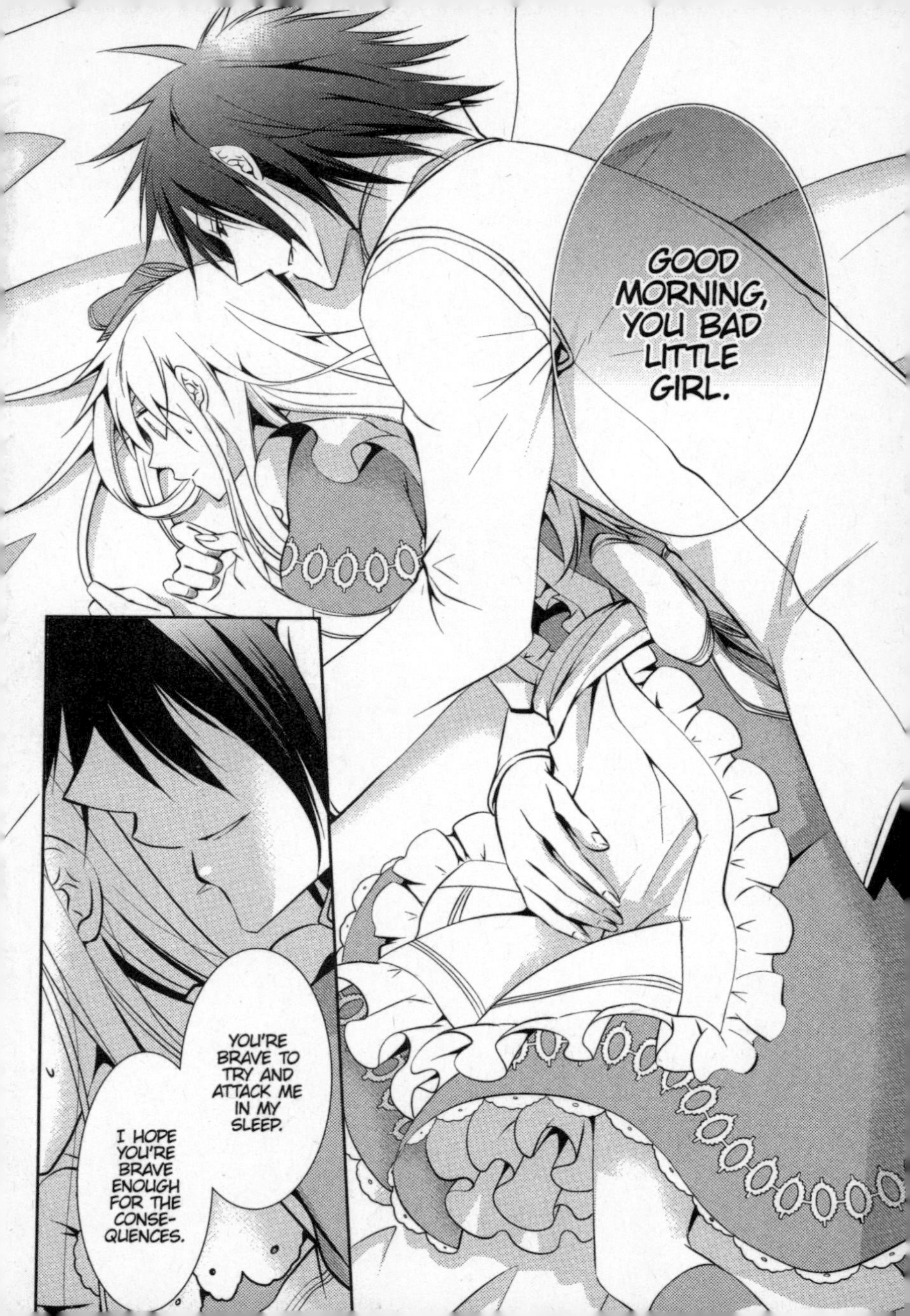
GOOD MORNING, YOU BAD LITTLE GIRL.
YOU'RE BRAVE TO TRY AND ATTACK ME IN MY SLEEP.
I HOPE YOU'RE BRAVE ENOUGH FOR THE CONSE-QUENCES.

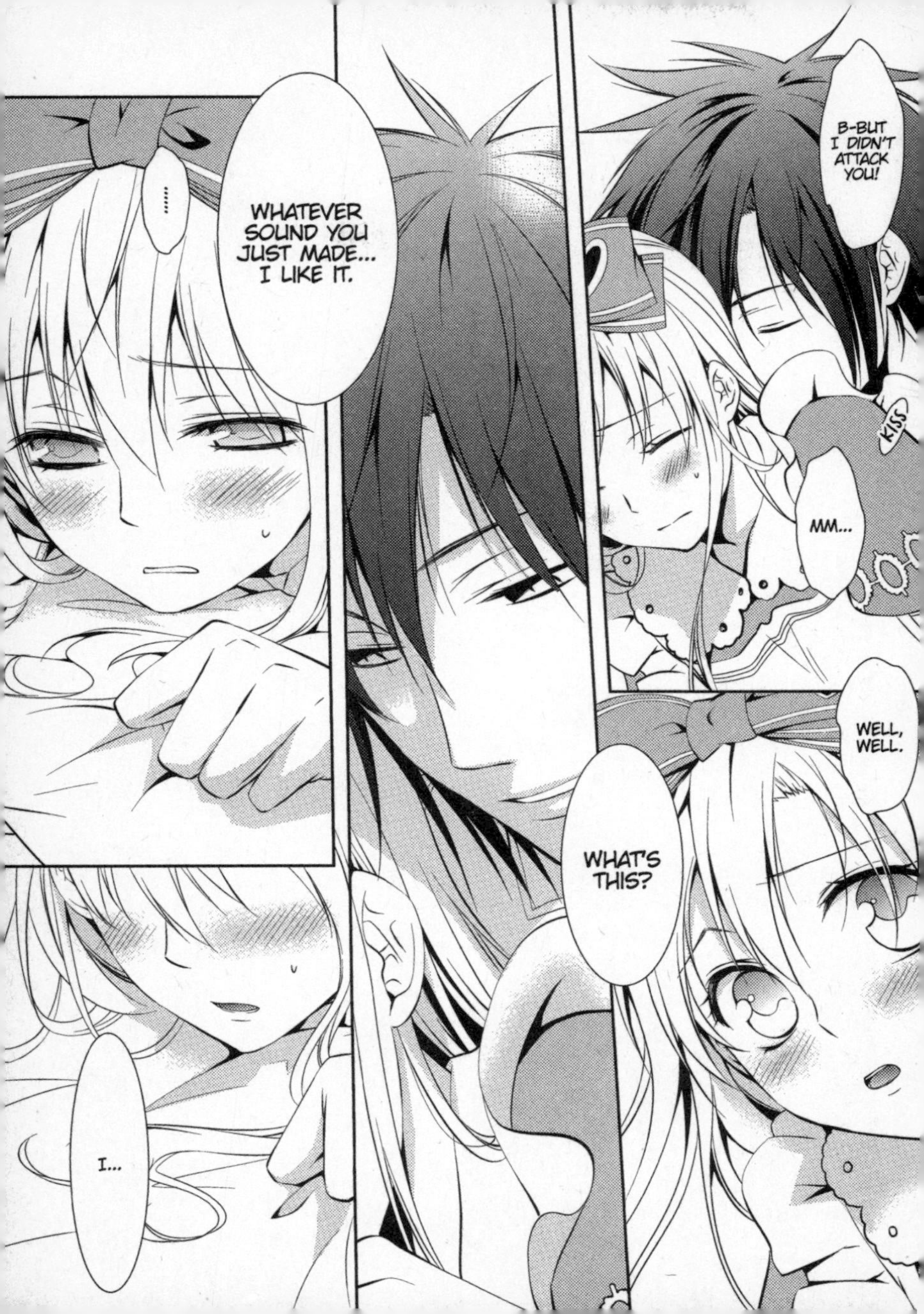
B-BUT I DIDN'T ATTACK YOU!
KISS
MM...
WELL, WELL.
WHAT'S THIS?
WHATEVER SOUND YOU JUST MADE... I LIKE IT.
......
I...

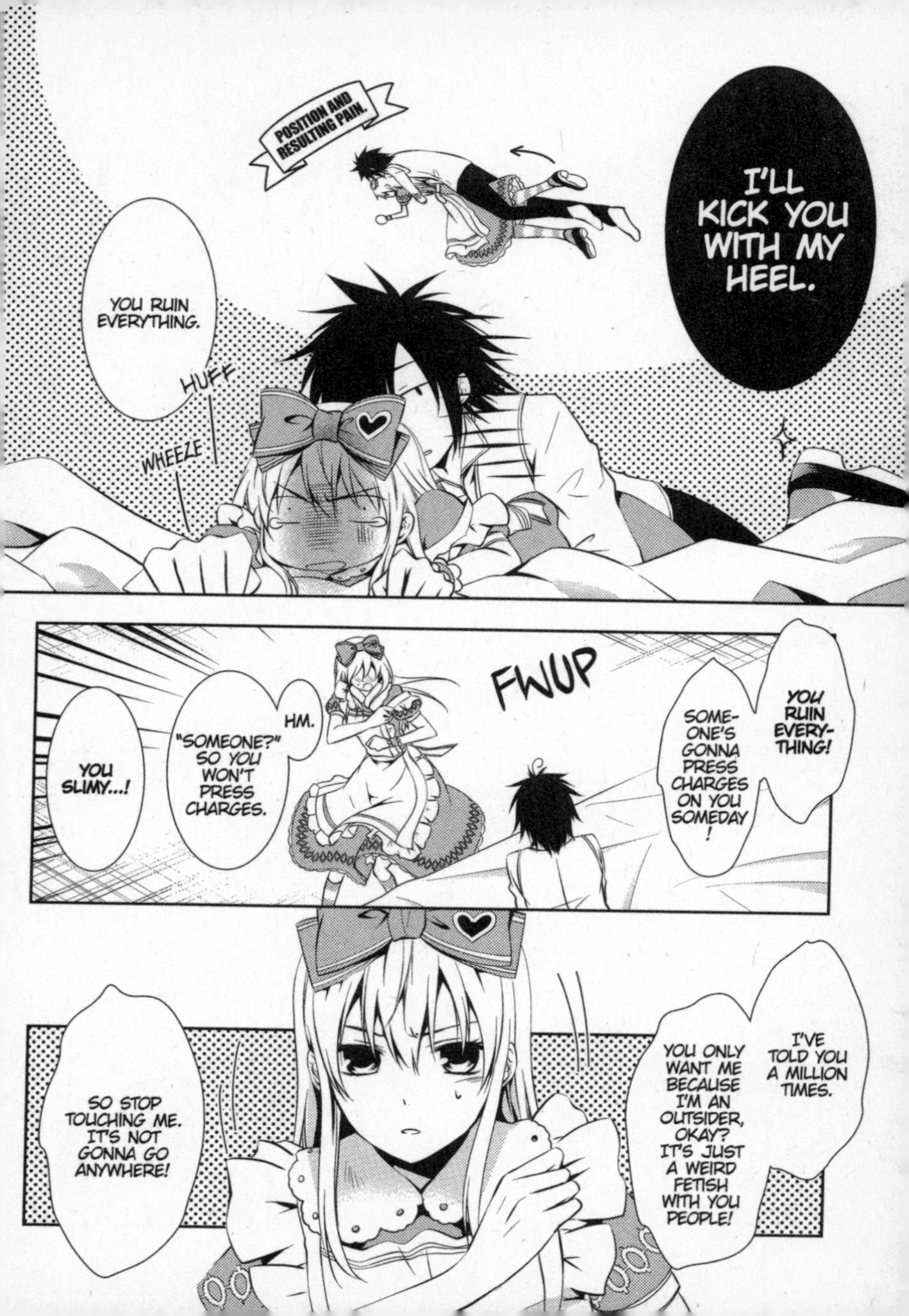
I'LL KICK YOU WITH MY HEEL.
POSITION AND RESULTING PAIN.
YOU RUIN EVERYTHING.
HUFF
WHEEZE
YOU RUIN EVERYTHING!
SOME-ONE'S GONNA PRESS CHARGES ON YOU SOMEDAY!
FWUP
HM.
"SOMEONE?" SO YOU WON'T PRESS CHARGES.
YOU SLIMY...!
I'VE TOLD YOU A MILLION TIMES.
YOU ONLY WANT ME BECAUSE I'M AN OUTSIDER, OKAY? IT'S JUST A WEIRD FETISH WITH YOU PEOPLE!
SO STOP TOUCHING ME. IT'S NOT GONNA GO ANYWHERE!

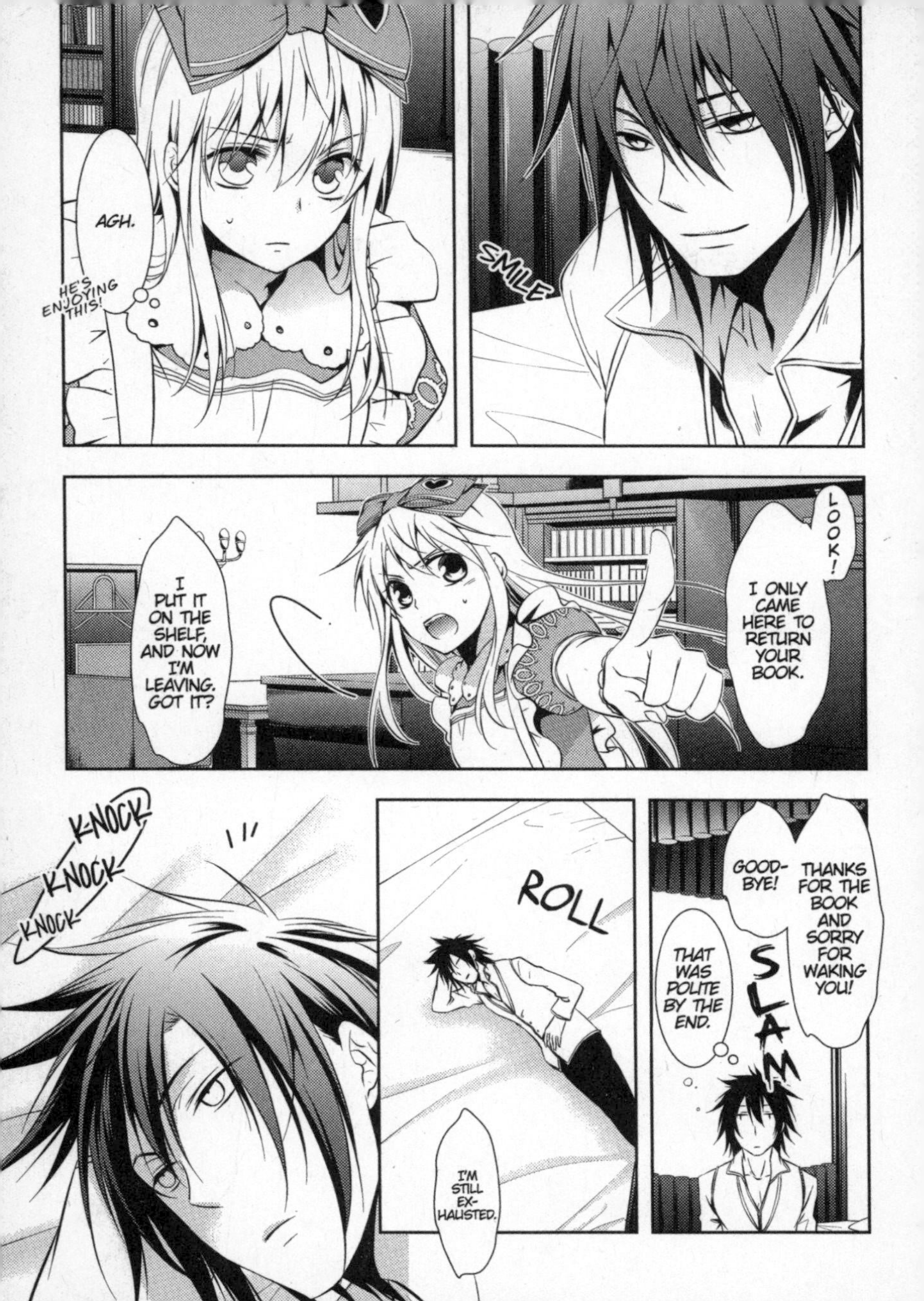
SMILE
AGH.
HE'S ENJOYING THIS!
LOOK!
I ONLY CAME HERE TO RETURN YOUR BOOK.
I PUT IT ON THE SHELF, AND NOW I'M LEAVING. GOT IT?
THANKS FOR THE BOOK AND SORRY FOR WAKING YOU!
GOOD-BYE!
SLAM
THAT WAS POLITE BY THE END.
ROLL
I'M STILL EX-HAUSTED.
K-NOCK
KNOCK
K-NOCK

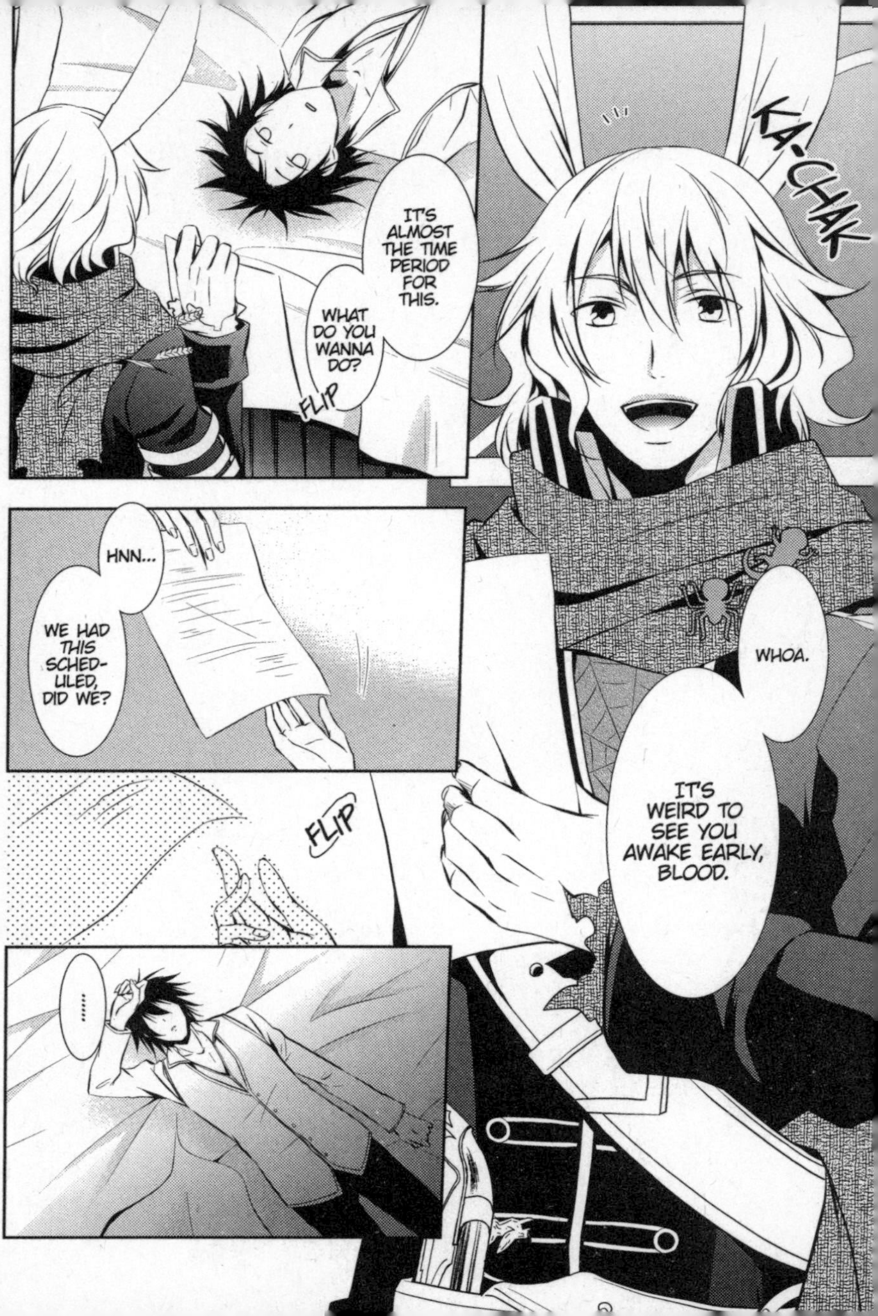
KA-CHAK
...
WHOA.
IT'S WEIRD TO SEE YOU AWAKE EARLY, BLOOD.
IT'S ALMOST THE TIME PERIOD FOR THIS.
WHAT DO YOU WANNA DO?
FLIP
HNN...
WE HAD THIS SCHED-ULED, DID WE?
FLIP
......

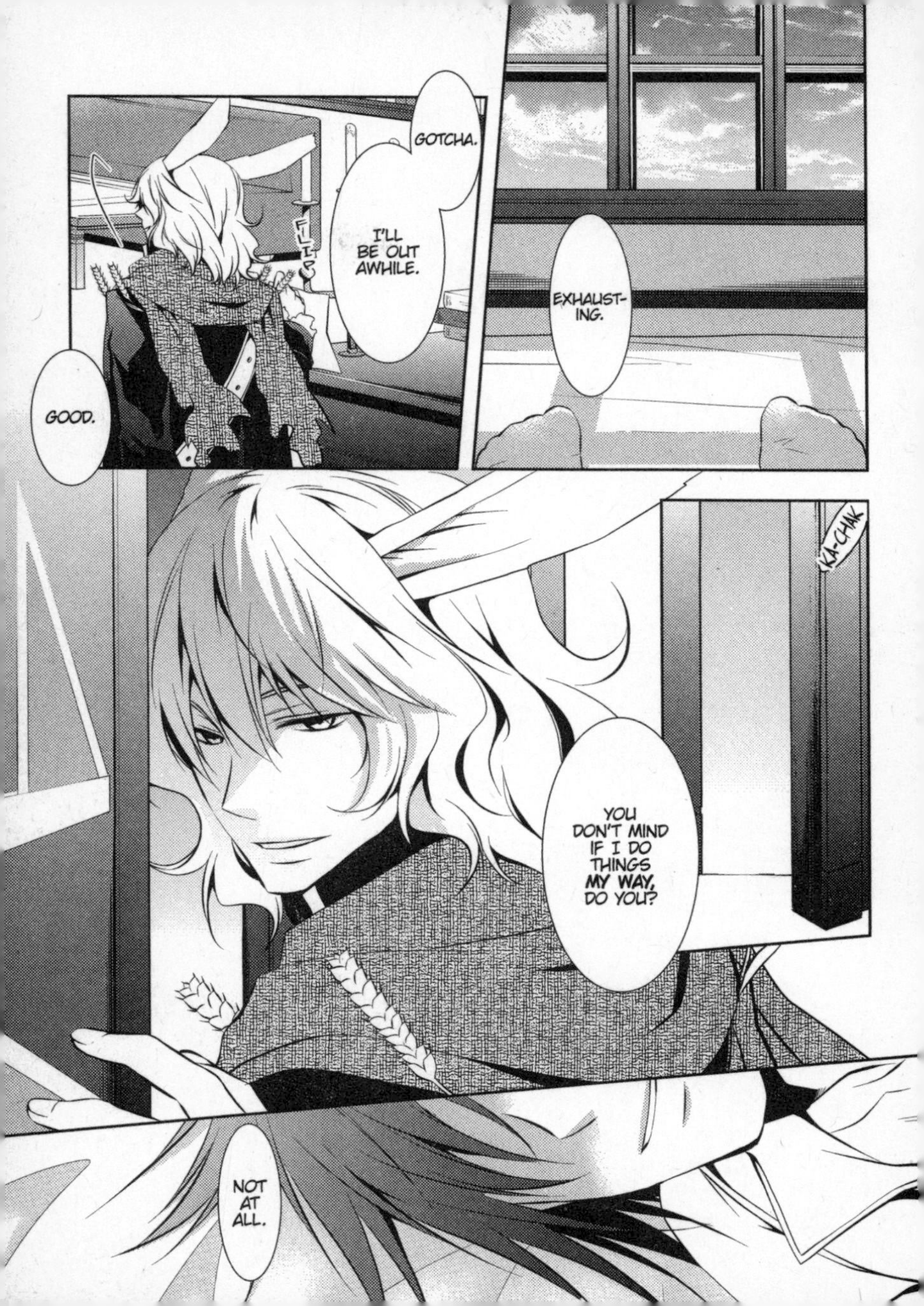
EXHAUST-ING.
GOTCHA.
I'LL BE OUT AWHILE.
FLIP
GOOD.
KA-CHAK
YOU DON'T MIND IF I DO THINGS MY WAY, DO YOU?
NOT AT ALL.

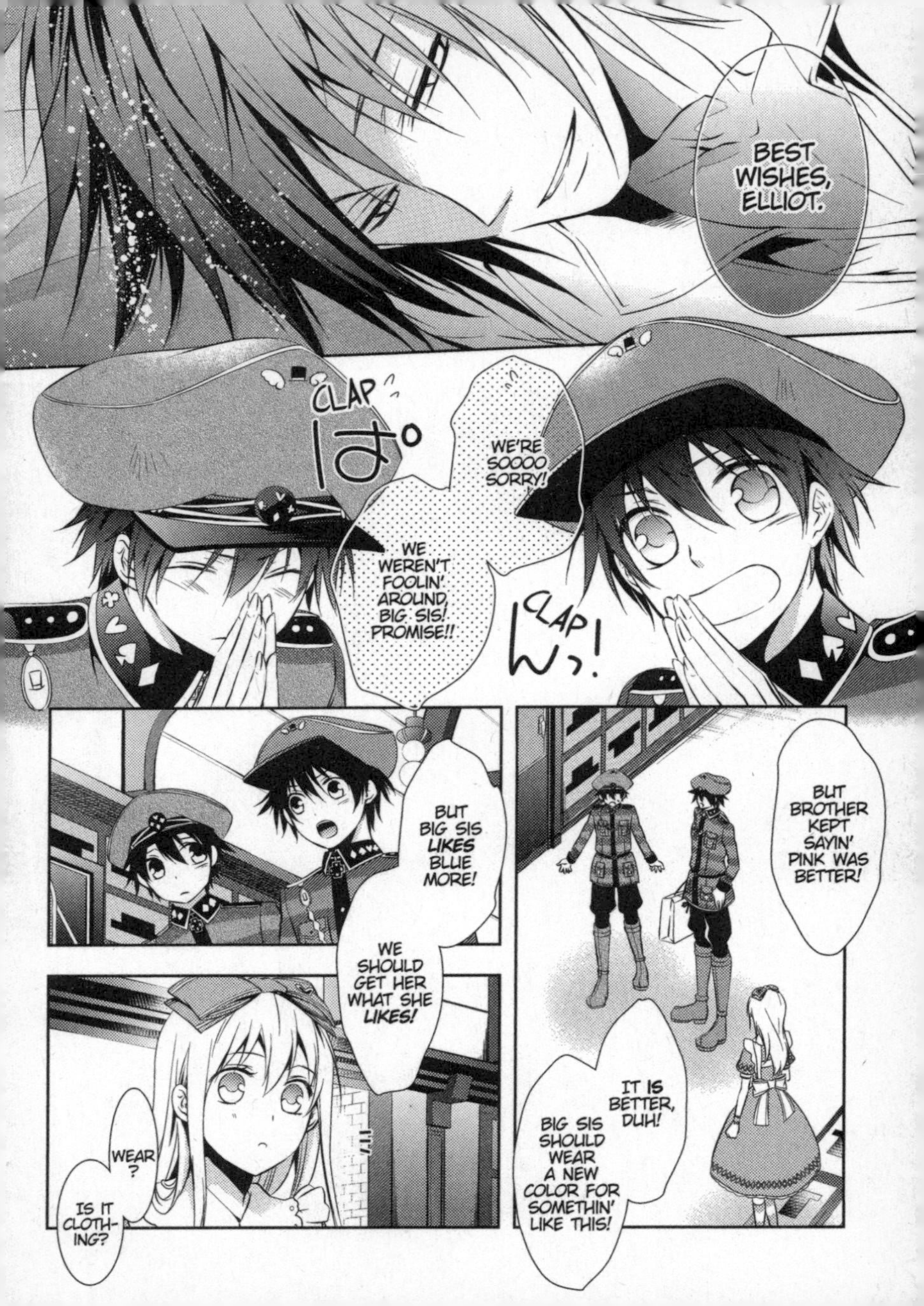
BEST WISHES, ELLIOT.
WE'RE SOOOO SORRY!
CLAP
WE WEREN'T FOOLIN' AROUND, BIG SIS! PROMISE!!
CLAP
BUT BROTHER KEPT SAYIN' PINK WAS BETTER!
IT IS BETTER, DUH!
BIG SIS SHOULD WEAR A NEW COLOR FOR SOMETHIN' LIKE THIS!
BUT BIG SIS LIKES BLUE MORE!
WE SHOULD GET HER WHAT SHE LIKES!
WEAR?
IS IT CLOTHING?

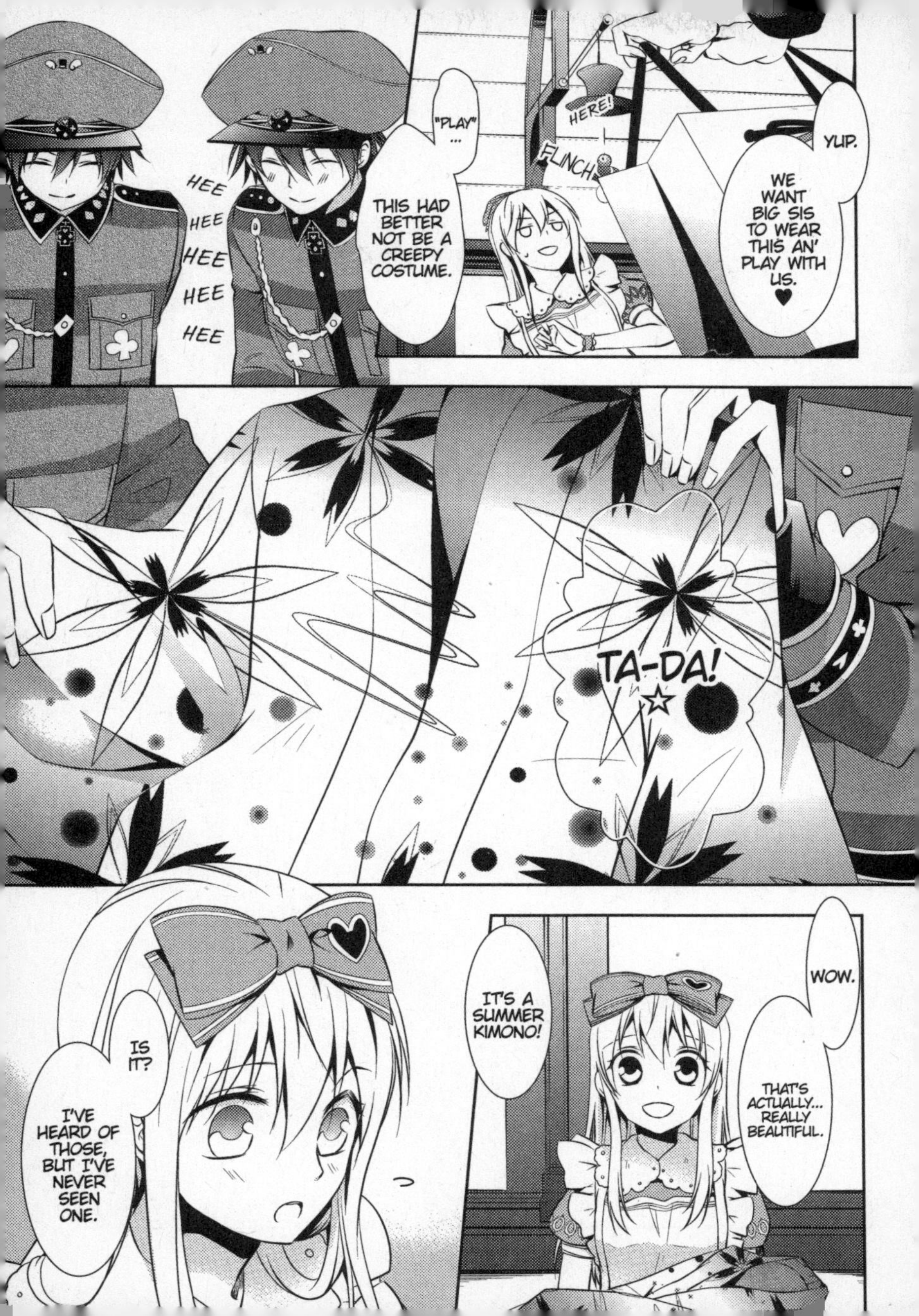
YUP.
WE WANT BIG SIS TO WEAR THIS AN' PLAY WITH US. ♥
HERE!
FLINCH
"PLAY" ...
THIS HAD BETTER NOT BE A CREEPY COSTUME.
HEE HEE HEE HEE HEE
TA-DA! ☆
WOW.
THAT'S ACTUALLY... REALLY BEAUTIFUL.
IT'S A SUMMER KIMONO!
IS IT?
I'VE HEARD OF THOSE, BUT I'VE NEVER SEEN ONE.

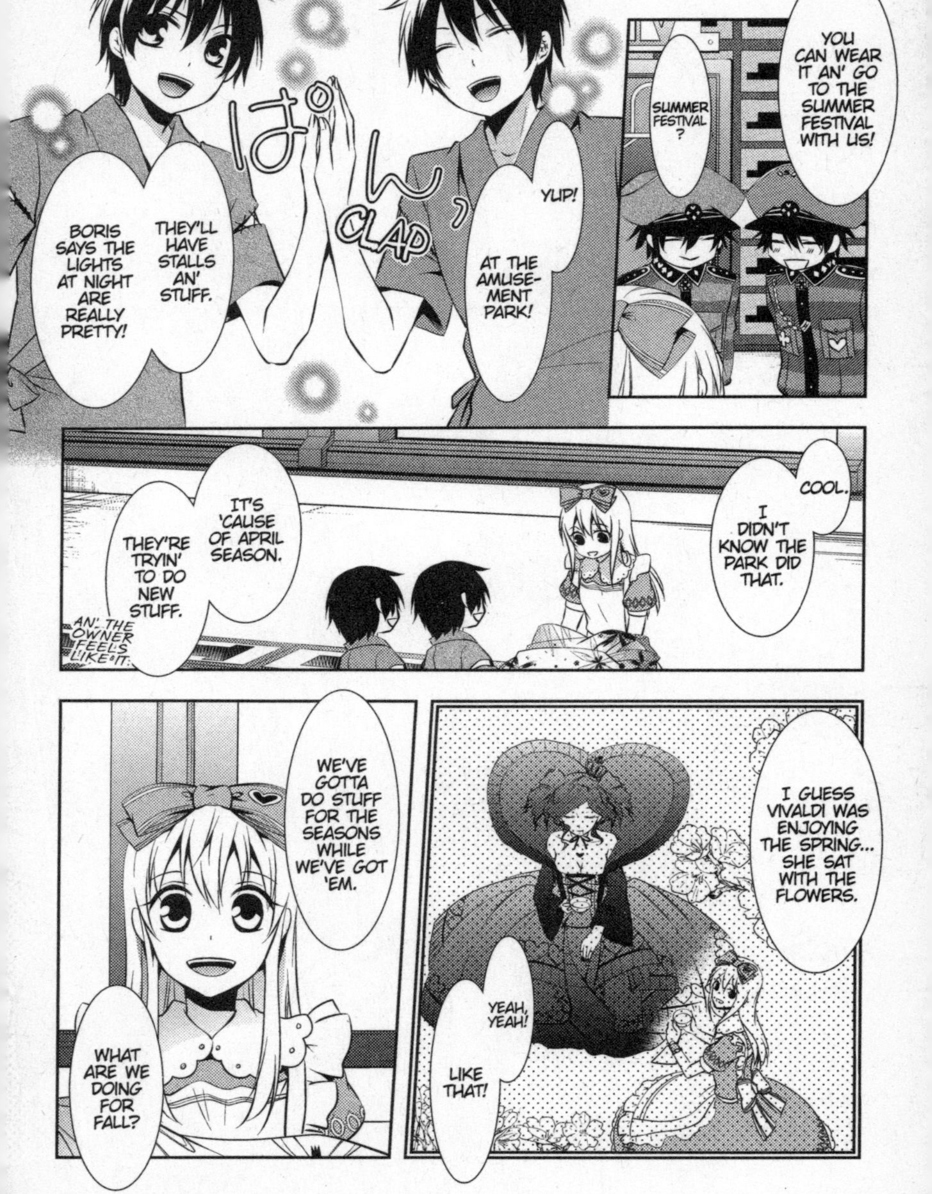
YOU CAN WEAR IT AN' GO TO THE SUMMER FESTIVAL WITH US!
SUMMER FESTIVAL?
YUP!
AT THE AMUSEMENT PARK!
ぱん, CLAP
THEY'LL HAVE STALLS AN' STUFF.
BORIS SAYS THE LIGHTS AT NIGHT ARE REALLY PRETTY!
COOL.
I DIDN'T KNOW THE PARK DID THAT.
IT'S 'CAUSE OF APRIL SEASON.
THEY'RE TRYIN' TO DO NEW STUFF.
AN' THE OWNER FEELS LIKE IT.
I GUESS VIVALDI WAS ENJOYING THE SPRING... SHE SAT WITH THE FLOWERS.
YEAH, YEAH!
LIKE THAT!
WE'VE GOTTA DO STUFF FOR THE SEASONS WHILE WE'VE GOT 'EM.
WHAT ARE WE DOING FOR FALL?

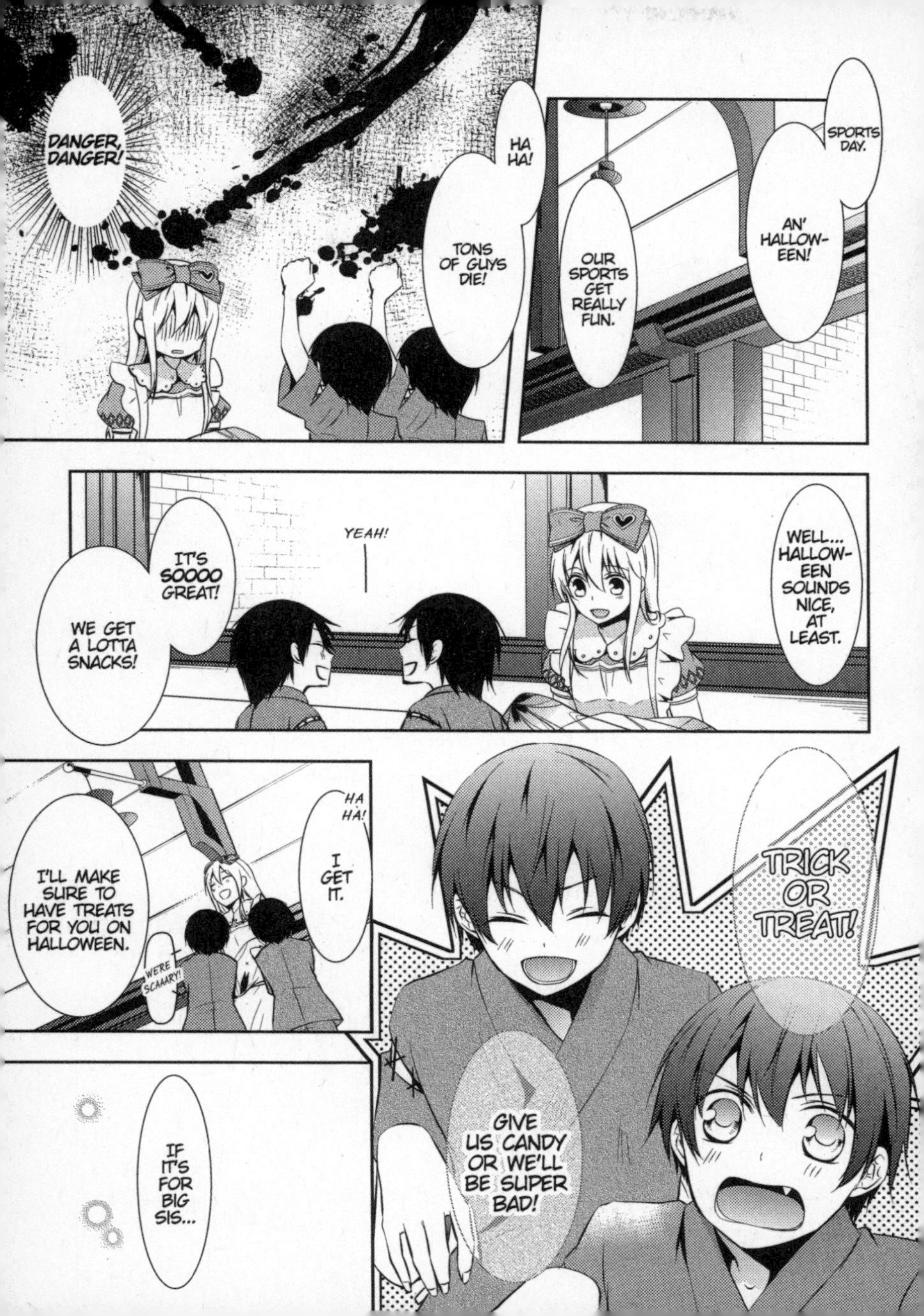
SPORTS DAY.
AN' HALLOWEEN!
OUR SPORTS GET REALLY FUN.
HA HA!
TONS OF GUYS DIE!
DANGER, DANGER!
WELL... HALLOWEEN SOUNDS NICE, AT LEAST.
YEAH!
IT'S SOOOO GREAT!
WE GET A LOTTA SNACKS!
TRICK OR TREAT!
GIVE US CANDY OR WE'LL BE SUPER BAD!
HA HA!
I GET IT.
I'LL MAKE SURE TO HAVE TREATS FOR YOU ON HALLOWEEN.
WE'RE SCAARY!
IF IT'S FOR BIG SIS...

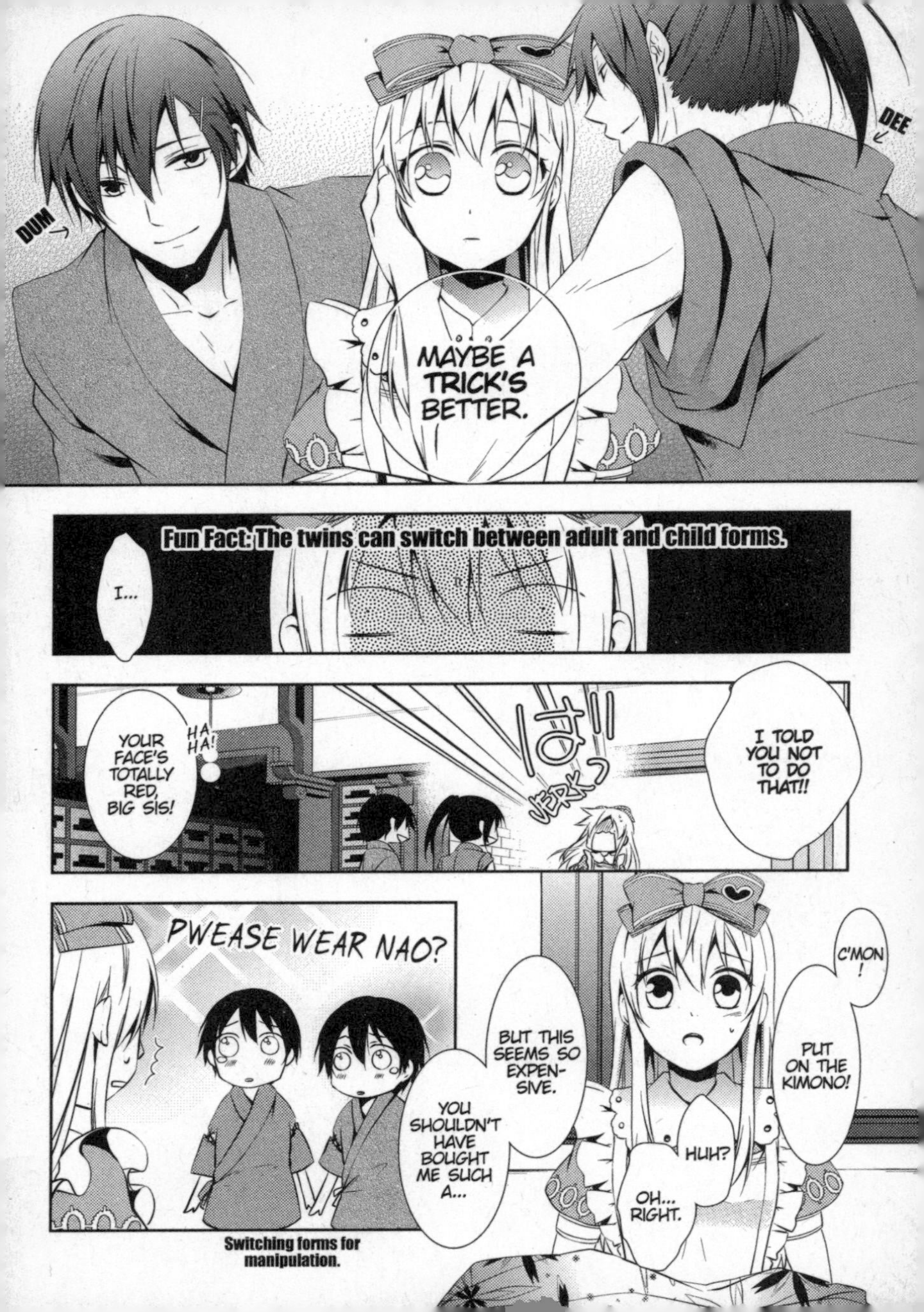
DEE
DUM
MAYBE A TRICK'S BETTER.
Fun Fact: The twins can switch between adult and child forms.
I...
I TOLD YOU NOT TO DO THAT!!
JERK
は!!
HA HA!
YOUR FACE'S TOTALLY RED, BIG SIS!
C'MON!
PUT ON THE KIMONO!
HUH?
OH... RIGHT.
BUT THIS SEEMS SO EXPEN-SIVE.
YOU SHOULDN'T HAVE BOUGHT ME SUCH A...
PWEASE WEAR NAO?

Switching forms for manipulation.

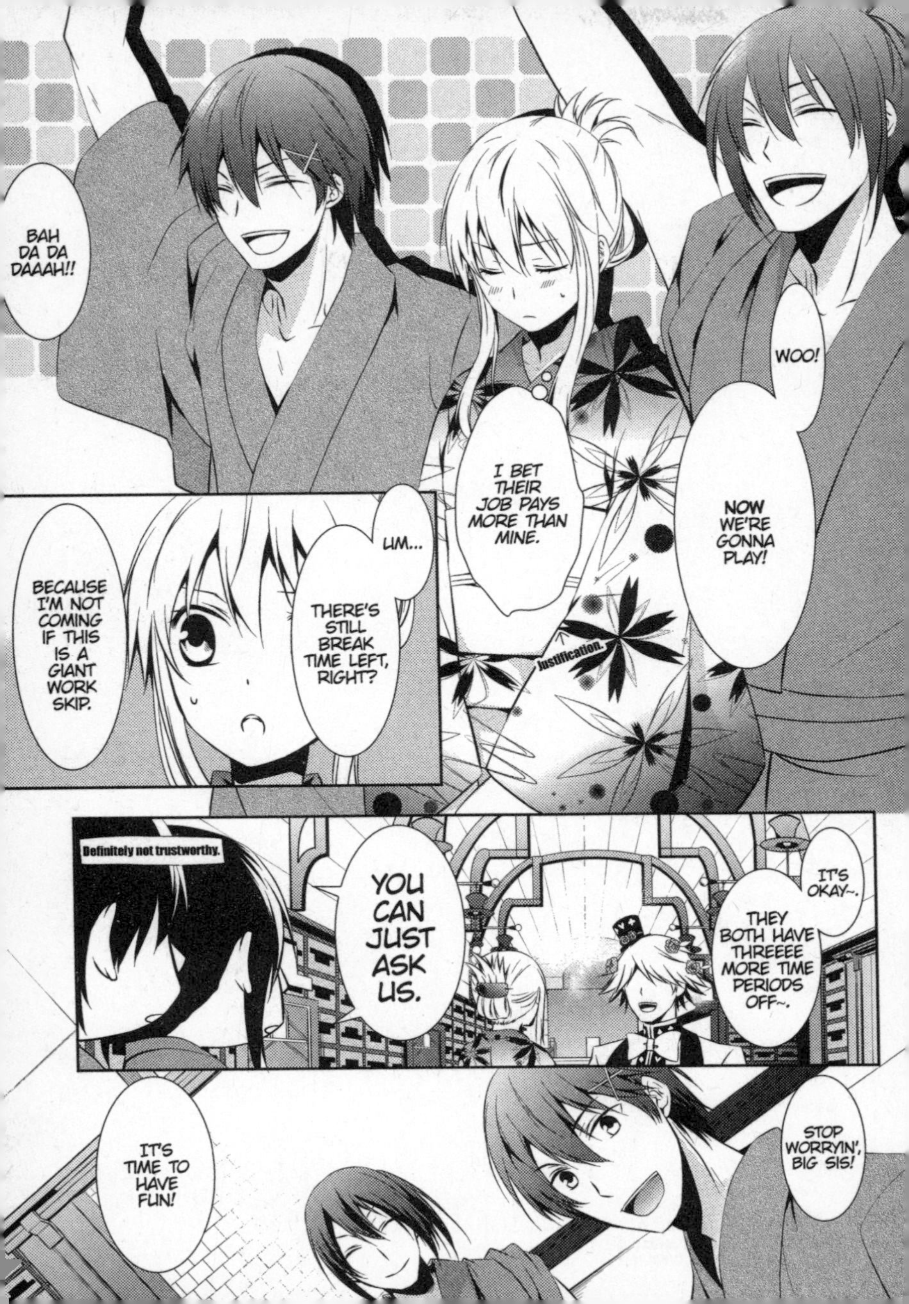
WOO!
BAH DA DA DAAAH!!
NOW WE'RE GONNA PLAY!
I BET THEIR JOB PAYS MORE THAN MINE.
Justification.
UM...
THERE'S STILL BREAK TIME LEFT, RIGHT?
BECAUSE I'M NOT COMING IF THIS IS A GIANT WORK SKIP.
IT'S OKAY~.
THEY BOTH HAVE THREEEE MORE TIME PERIODS OFF~.
YOU CAN JUST ASK US.
Definitely not trustworthy.
STOP WORRYIN', BIG SIS!
IT'S TIME TO HAVE FUN!

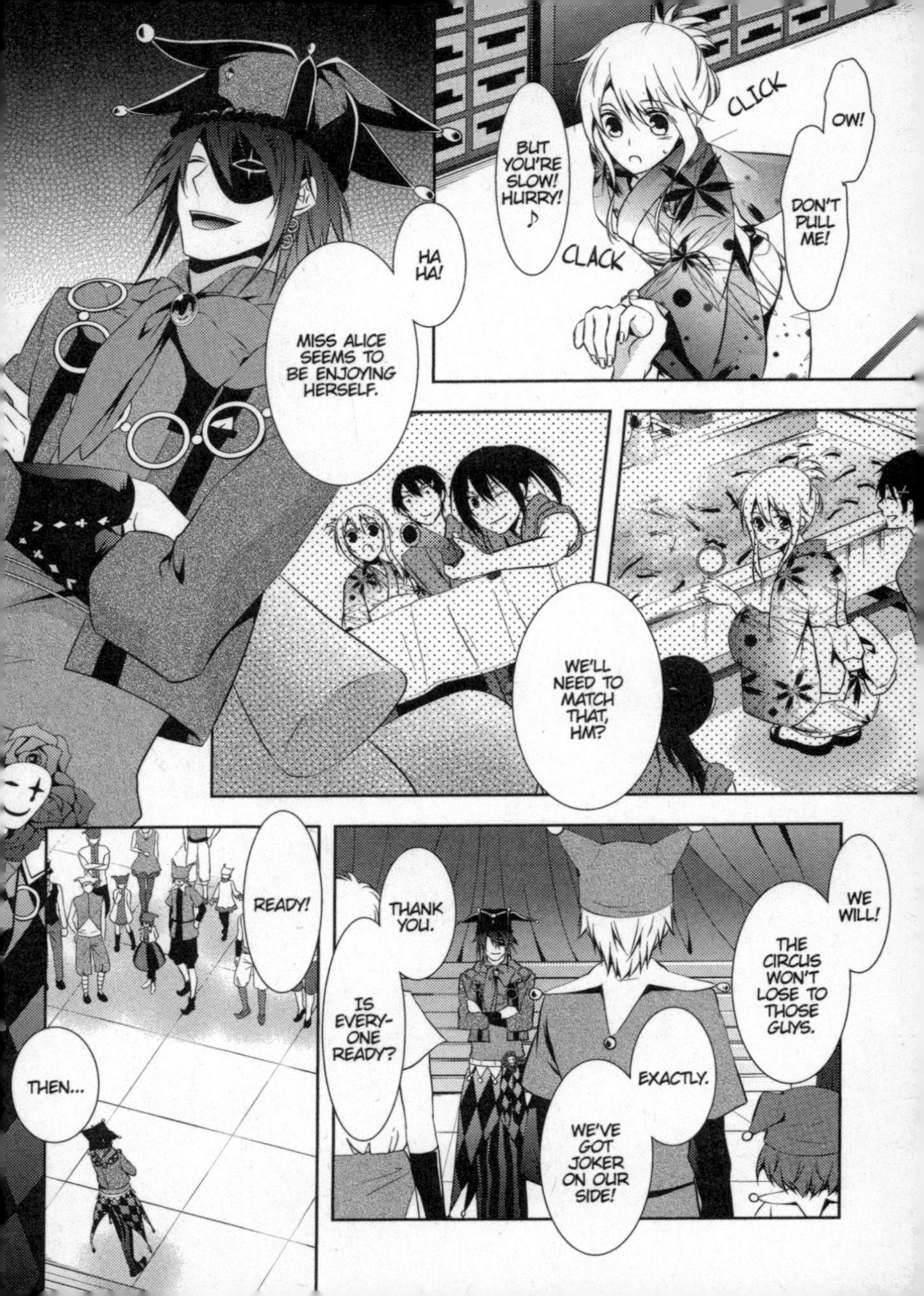
OW!
DON'T PULL ME!
CLICK
BUT YOU'RE SLOW! HURRY! ♪
CLACK
HA HA!
MISS ALICE SEEMS TO BE ENJOYING HERSELF.
WE'LL NEED TO MATCH THAT, HM?
WE WILL!
THE CIRCUS WON'T LOSE TO THOSE GUYS.
EXACTLY.
WE'VE GOT JOKER ON OUR SIDE!
THANK YOU.
IS EVERYONE READY?
READY!
THEN...

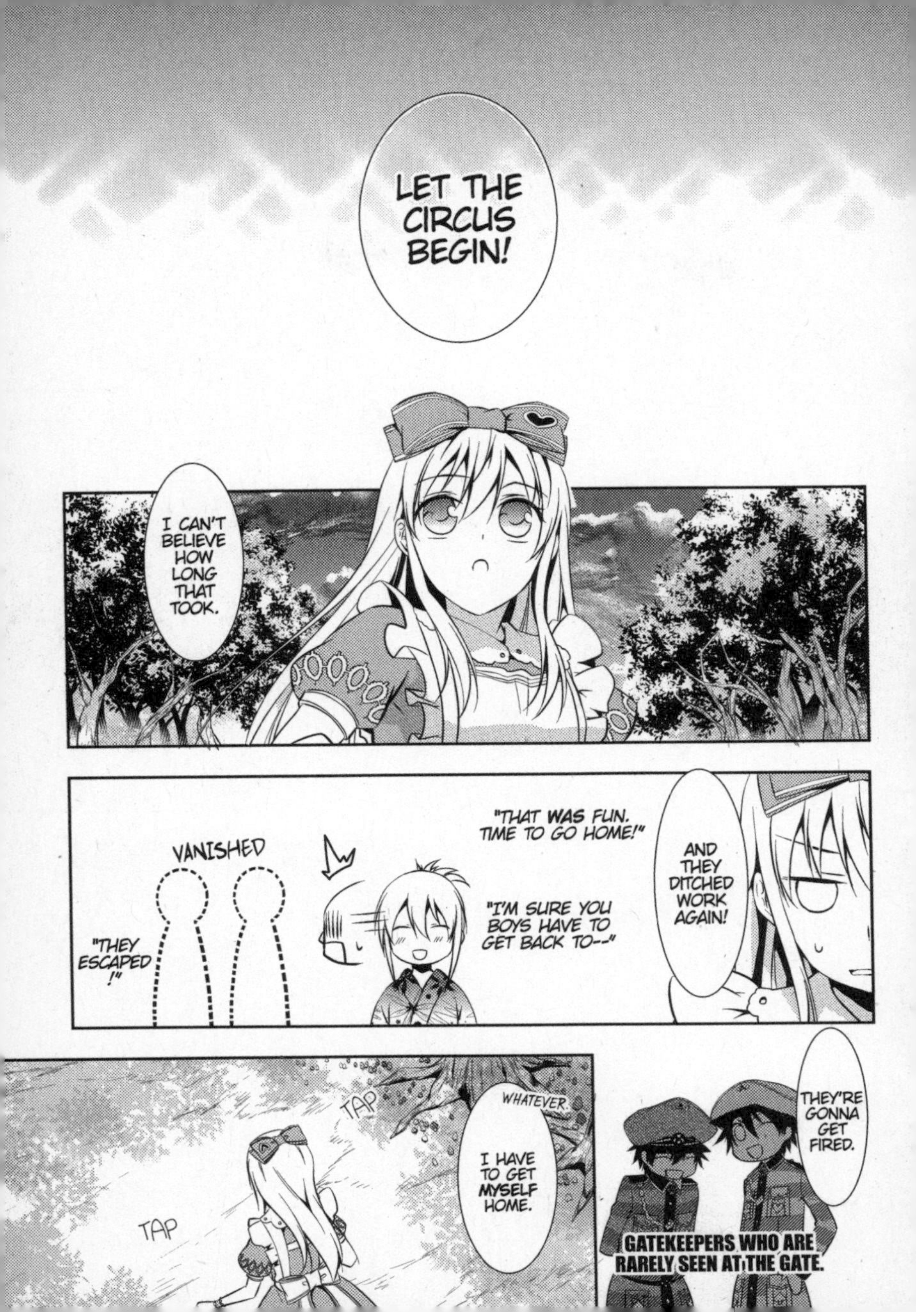
LET THE CIRCUS BEGIN!
I CAN'T BELIEVE HOW LONG THAT TOOK.
AND THEY DITCHED WORK AGAIN!
"THAT WAS FUN. TIME TO GO HOME!"
"I'M SURE YOU BOYS HAVE TO GET BACK TO--"
VANISHED
"THEY ESCAPED!"
THEY'RE GONNA GET FIRED.
GATEKEEPERS WHO ARE RARELY SEEN AT THE GATE.
WHATEVER.
I HAVE TO GET MYSELF HOME.
TAP
TAP

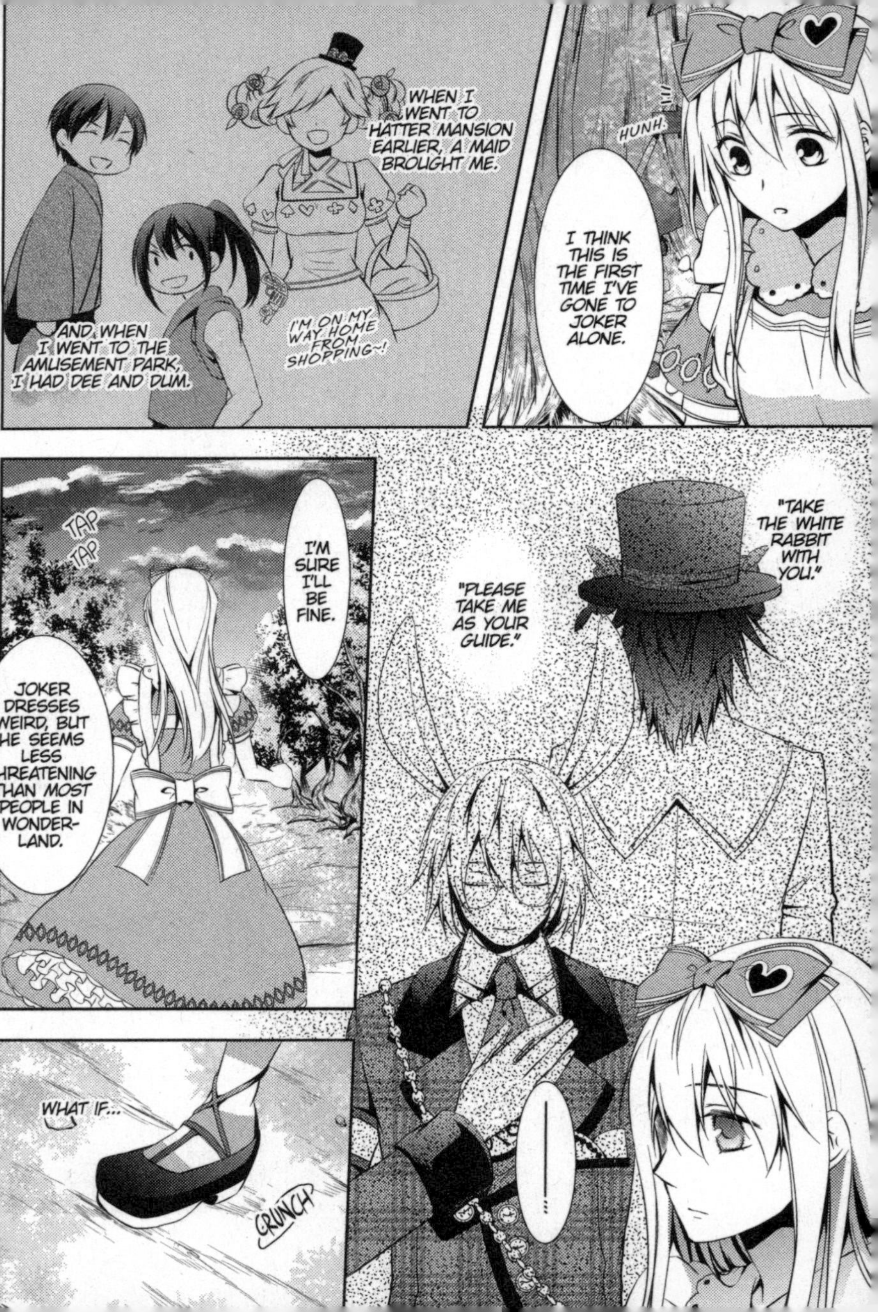
HUNH.
I THINK THIS IS THE FIRST TIME I'VE GONE TO JOKER ALONE.
WHEN I WENT TO HATTER MANSION EARLIER, A MAID BROUGHT ME.
I'M ON MY WAY HOME FROM SHOPPING~!
AND WHEN I WENT TO THE AMUSEMENT PARK, I HAD DEE AND DUM.
"TAKE THE WHITE RABBIT WITH YOU."
"PLEASE TAKE ME AS YOUR GUIDE."
......
TAP TAP
I'M SURE I'LL BE FINE.
JOKER DRESSES WEIRD, BUT HE SEEMS LESS THREATENING THAN MOST PEOPLE IN WONDER-LAND.
WHAT IF...
CRUNCH

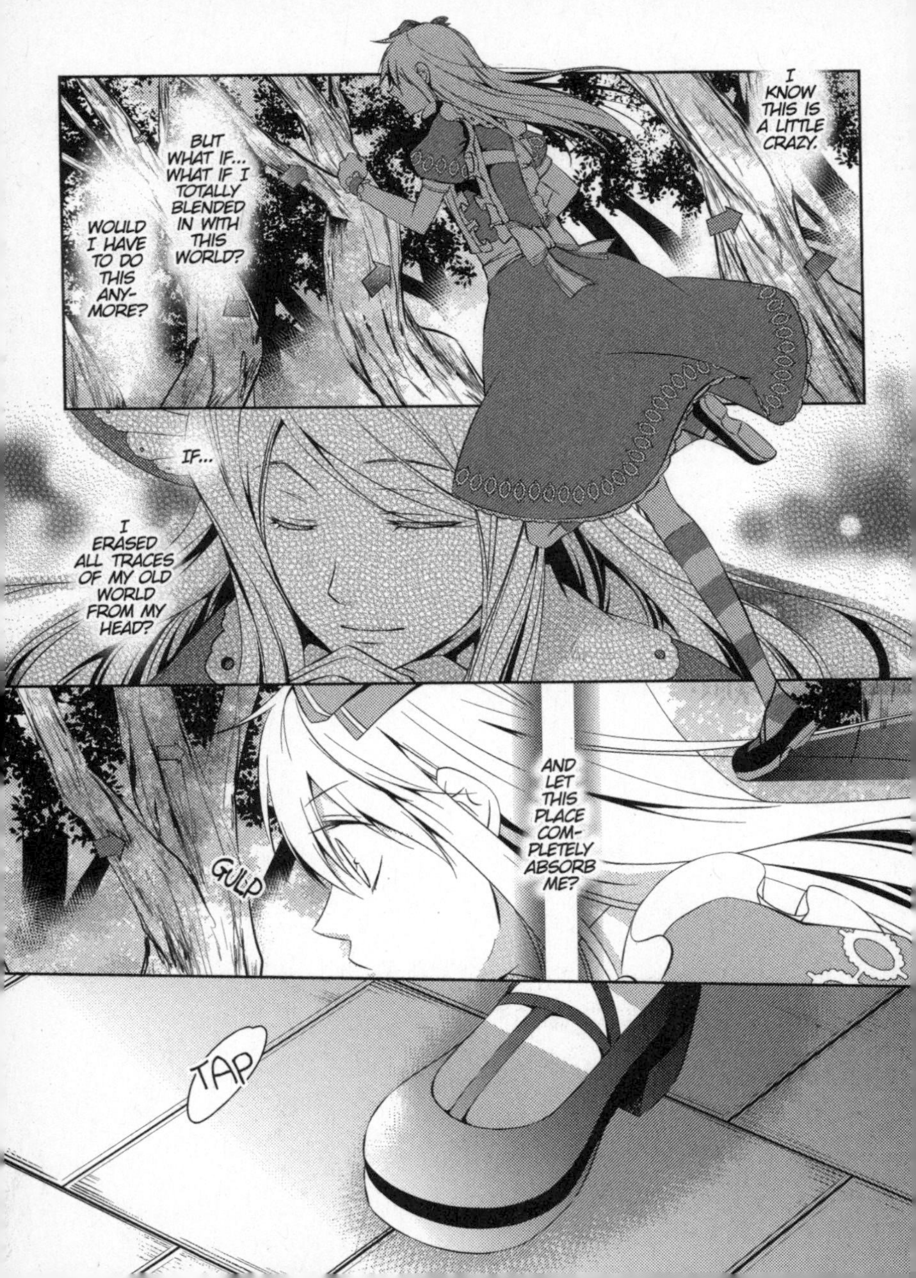
I KNOW THIS IS A LITTLE CRAZY.
BUT WHAT IF... WHAT IF I TOTALLY BLENDED IN WITH THIS WORLD?
WOULD I HAVE TO DO THIS ANYMORE?
IF...
I ERASED ALL TRACES OF MY OLD WORLD FROM MY HEAD?
AND LET THIS PLACE COMPLETELY ABSORB ME?
GULP
TAP

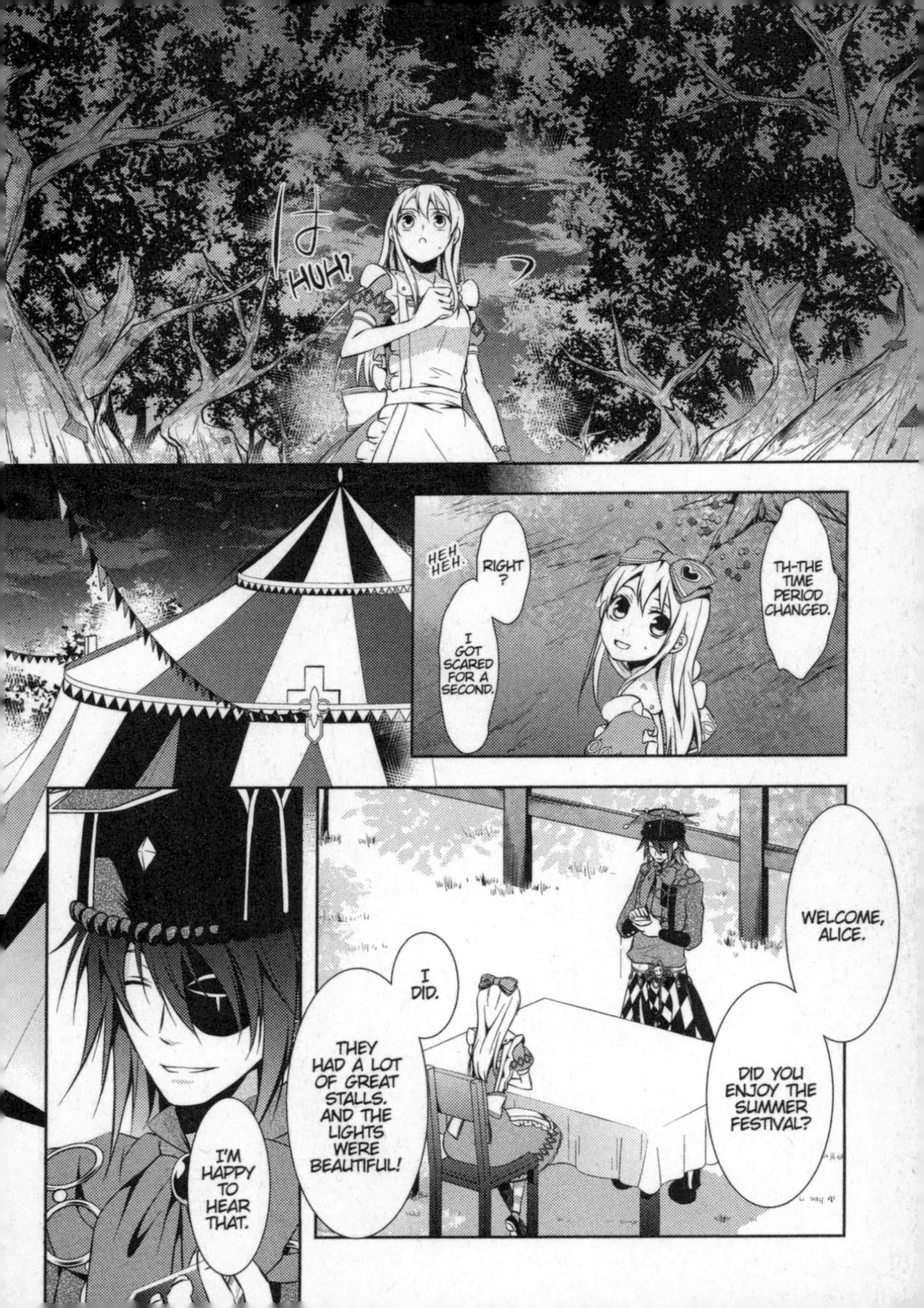
は
HUH?
TH-THE TIME PERIOD CHANGED.
RIGHT?
HEH HEH.
I GOT SCARED FOR A SECOND.
WELCOME, ALICE.
DID YOU ENJOY THE SUMMER FESTIVAL?
I DID.
THEY HAD A LOT OF GREAT STALLS. AND THE LIGHTS WERE BEAUTIFUL!
I'M HAPPY TO HEAR THAT.

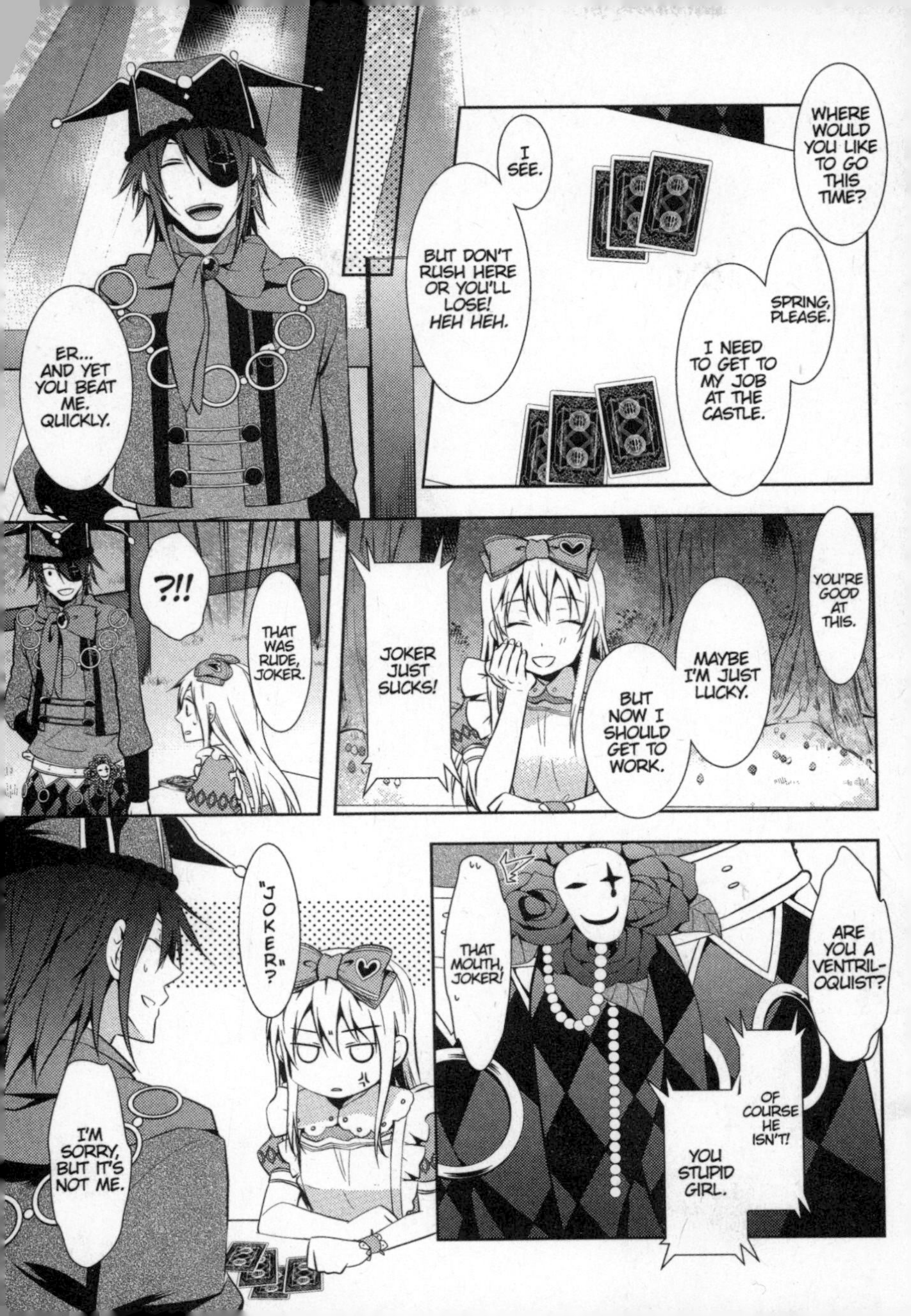
WHERE WOULD YOU LIKE TO GO THIS TIME?
SPRING, PLEASE.
I NEED TO GET TO MY JOB AT THE CASTLE.
I SEE.
BUT DON'T RUSH HERE OR YOU'LL LOSE! HEH HEH.
ER... AND YET YOU BEAT ME. QUICKLY.
YOU'RE GOOD AT THIS.
MAYBE I'M JUST LUCKY.
BUT NOW I SHOULD GET TO WORK.
JOKER JUST SUCKS!
?!!
THAT WAS RUDE, JOKER.
ARE YOU A VENTRIL-OQUIST?
OF COURSE HE ISN'T!
YOU STUPID GIRL.
THAT MOUTH, JOKER!
"JOKER"?
I'M SORRY, BUT IT'S NOT ME.

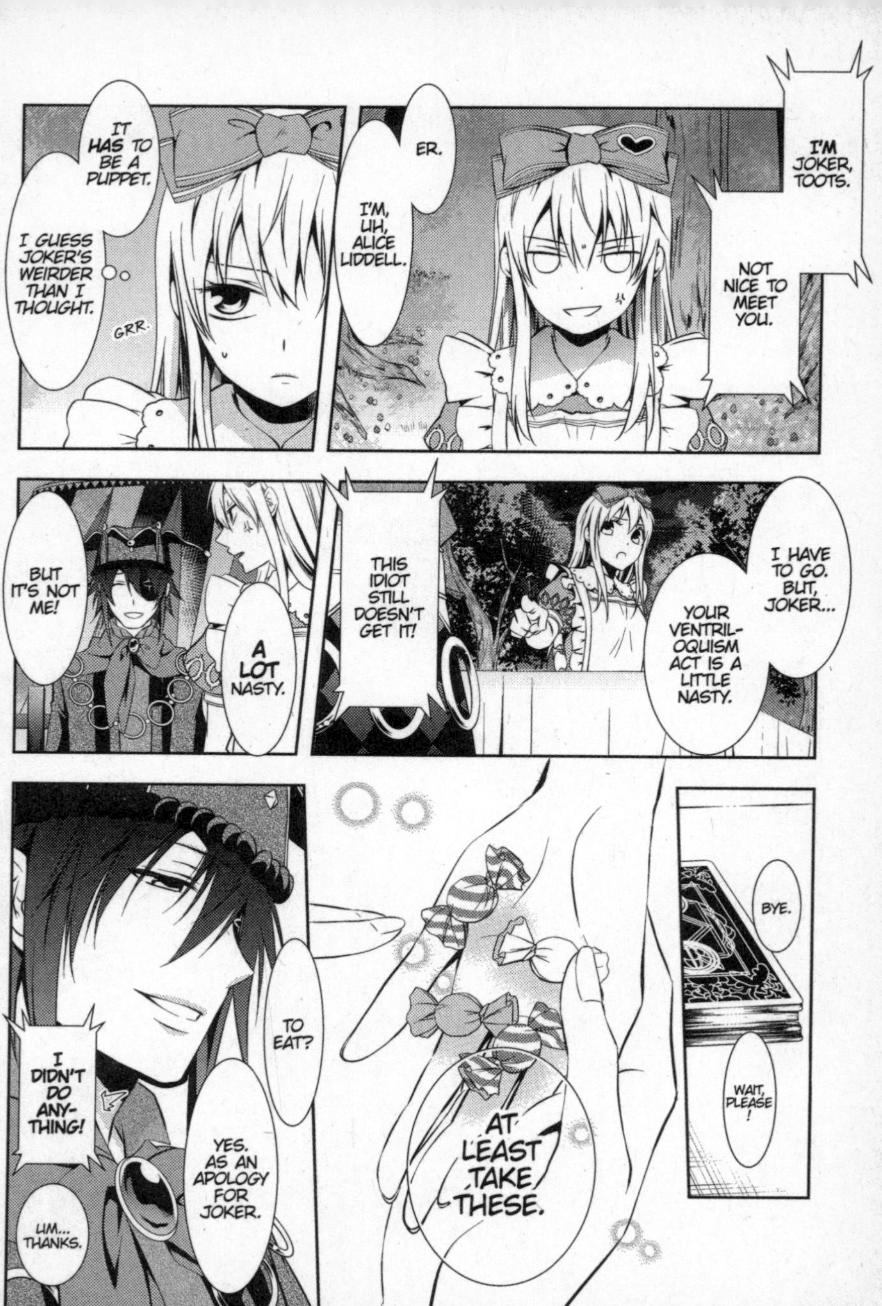
I'M JOKER, TOOTS.
NOT NICE TO MEET YOU.
ER.
I'M, UH, ALICE LIDDELL.
IT HAS TO BE A PUPPET.
I GUESS JOKER'S WEIRDER THAN I THOUGHT.
GRR.
I HAVE TO GO. BUT, JOKER...
YOUR VENTRILOQUISM ACT IS A LITTLE NASTY.
THIS IDIOT STILL DOESN'T GET IT!
A LOT NASTY.
BUT IT'S NOT ME!
BYE.
WAIT, PLEASE!
AT LEAST TAKE THESE.
TO EAT?
YES. AS AN APOLOGY FOR JOKER.
I DIDN'T DO ANYTHING!
UM... THANKS.

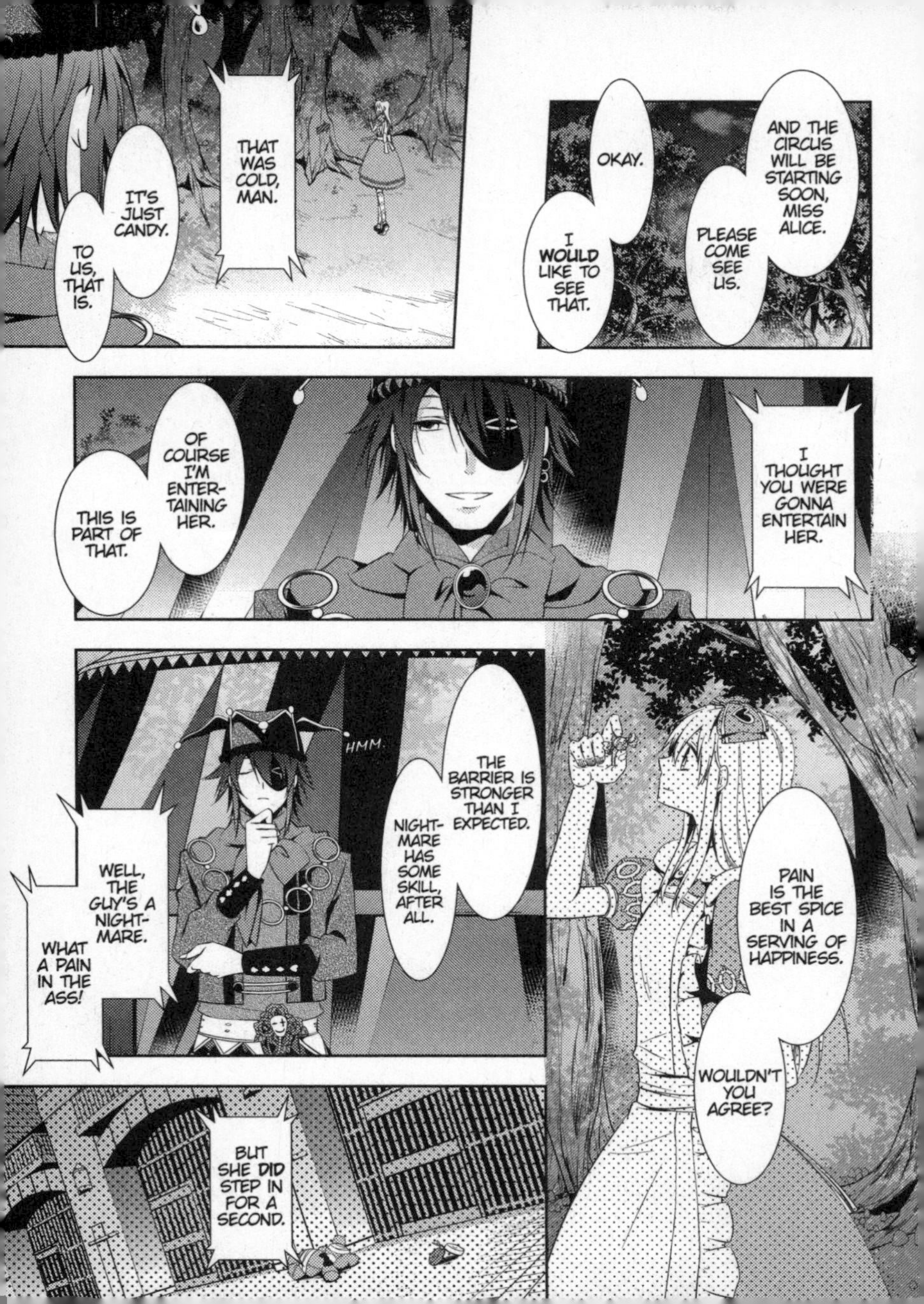
AND THE CIRCUS WILL BE STARTING SOON, MISS ALICE.
PLEASE COME SEE US.
OKAY.
I **WOULD** LIKE TO SEE THAT.
THAT WAS COLD, MAN.
IT'S JUST CANDY.
TO US, THAT IS.
I THOUGHT YOU WERE GONNA ENTERTAIN HER.
OF COURSE I'M ENTERTAINING HER.
THIS IS PART OF THAT.
PAIN IS THE BEST SPICE IN A SERVING OF HAPPINESS.
WOULDN'T YOU AGREE?
HMM.
THE BARRIER IS STRONGER THAN I EXPECTED.
NIGHTMARE HAS SOME SKILL, AFTER ALL.
WELL, THE GUY'S A NIGHTMARE.
WHAT A PAIN IN THE ASS!
BUT SHE **DID** STEP IN FOR A SECOND.

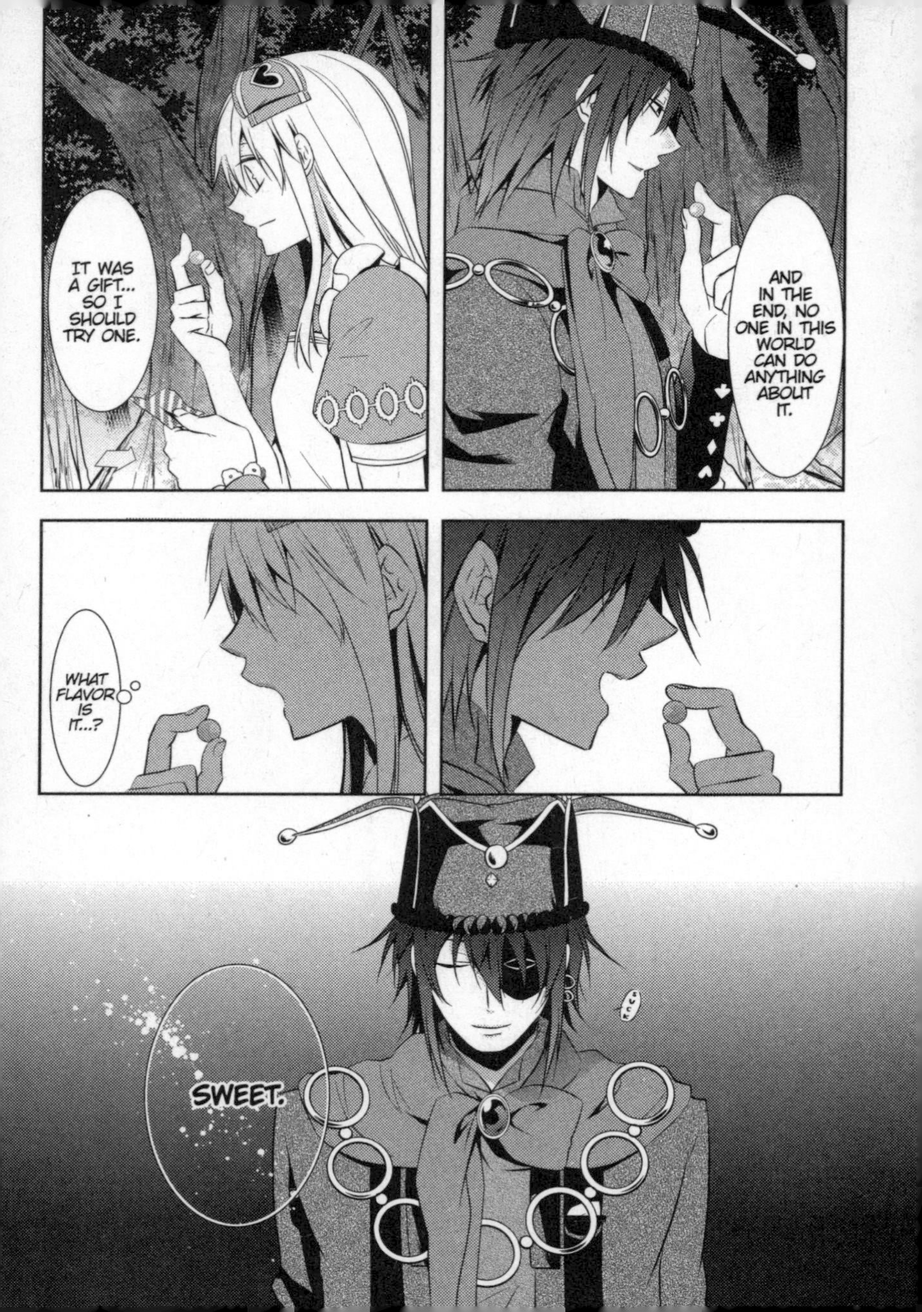
AND IN THE END, NO ONE IN THIS WORLD CAN DO ANYTHING ABOUT IT.
IT WAS A GIFT... SO I SHOULD TRY ONE.
WHAT FLAVOR IS IT...?
SUCK
SWEET.

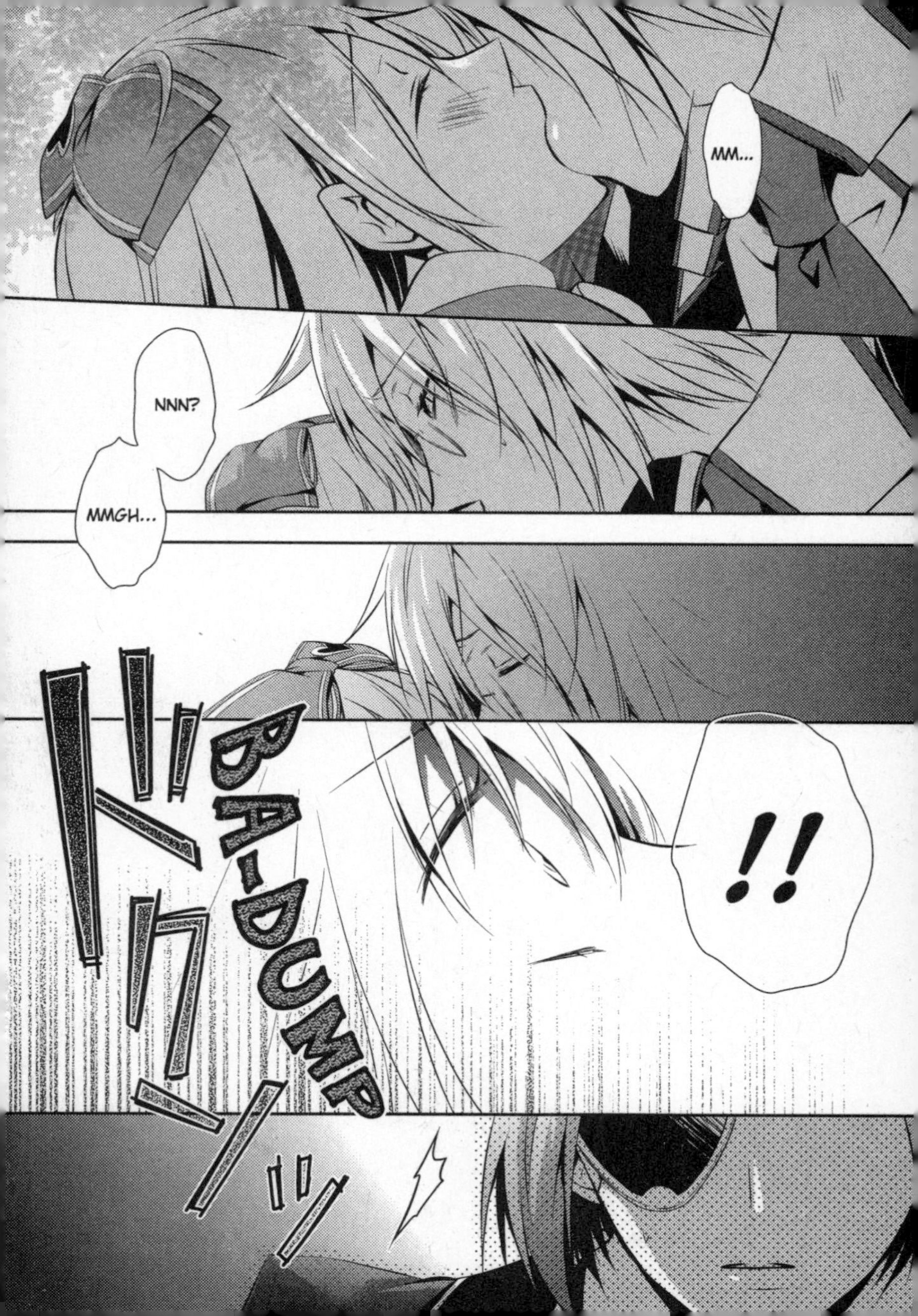
MM...
NNN?
MMGH...
!!
BA-DUMP

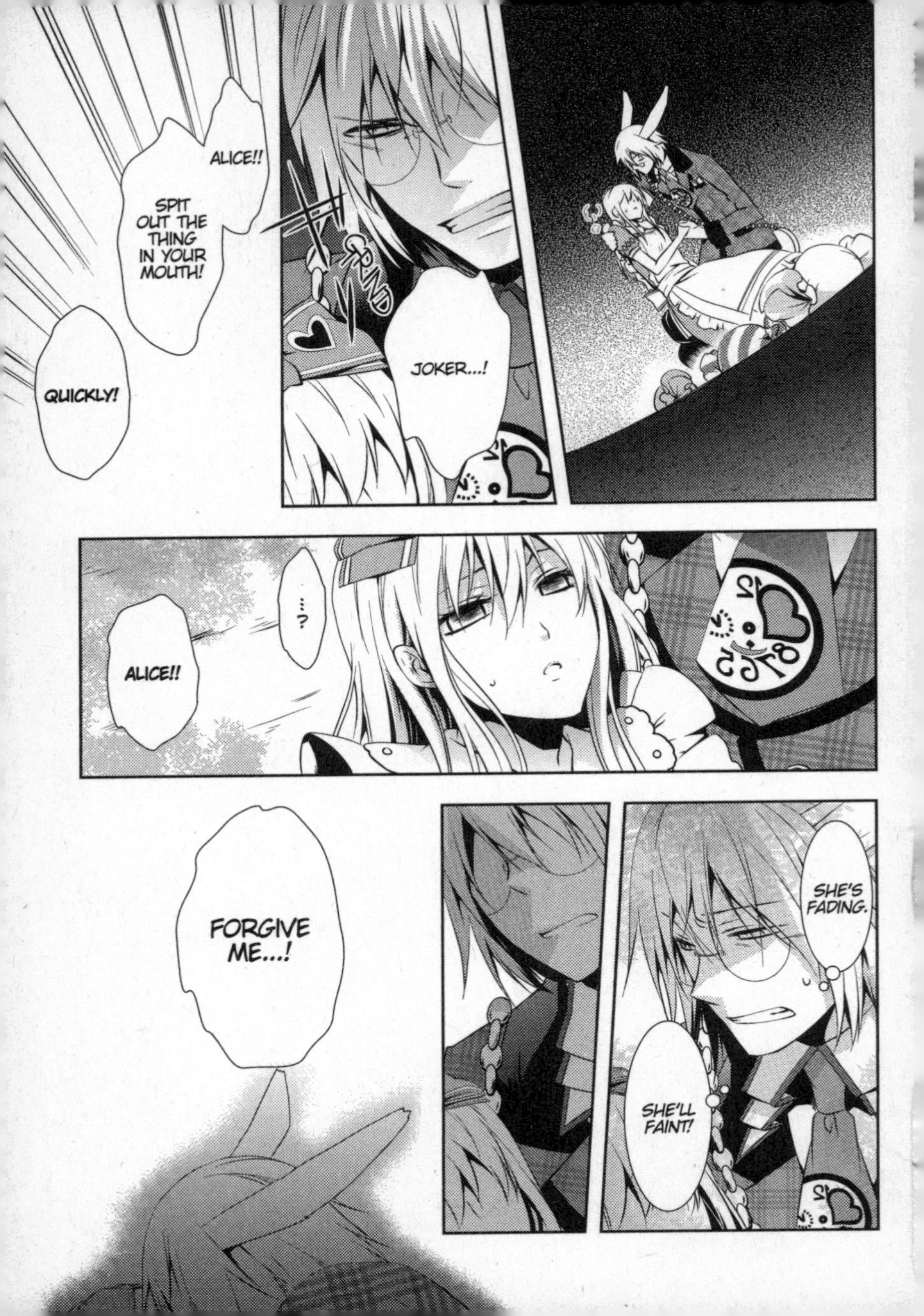
GRIND
JOKER...!
ALICE!!
SPIT OUT THE THING IN YOUR MOUTH!
QUICKLY!
...?
ALICE!!
SHE'S FADING.
SHE'LL FAINT!
FORGIVE ME...!

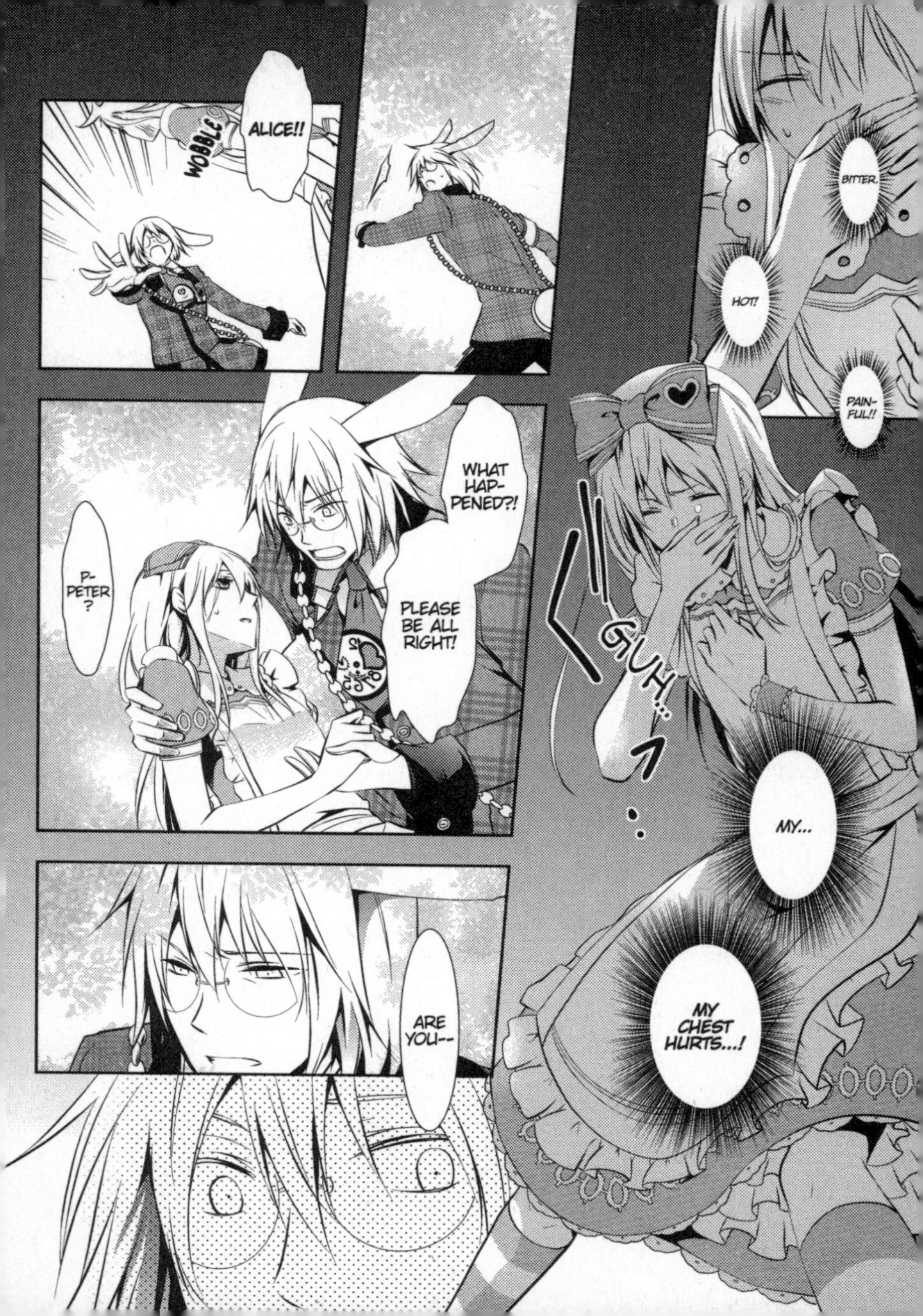
BITTER.
HOT!
PAINFUL!!
GUH...!
MY...
MY CHEST HURTS...!
ALICE!!
WOBBLE
WHAT HAPPENED?!
PLEASE BE ALL RIGHT!
P-PETER?
ARE YOU--

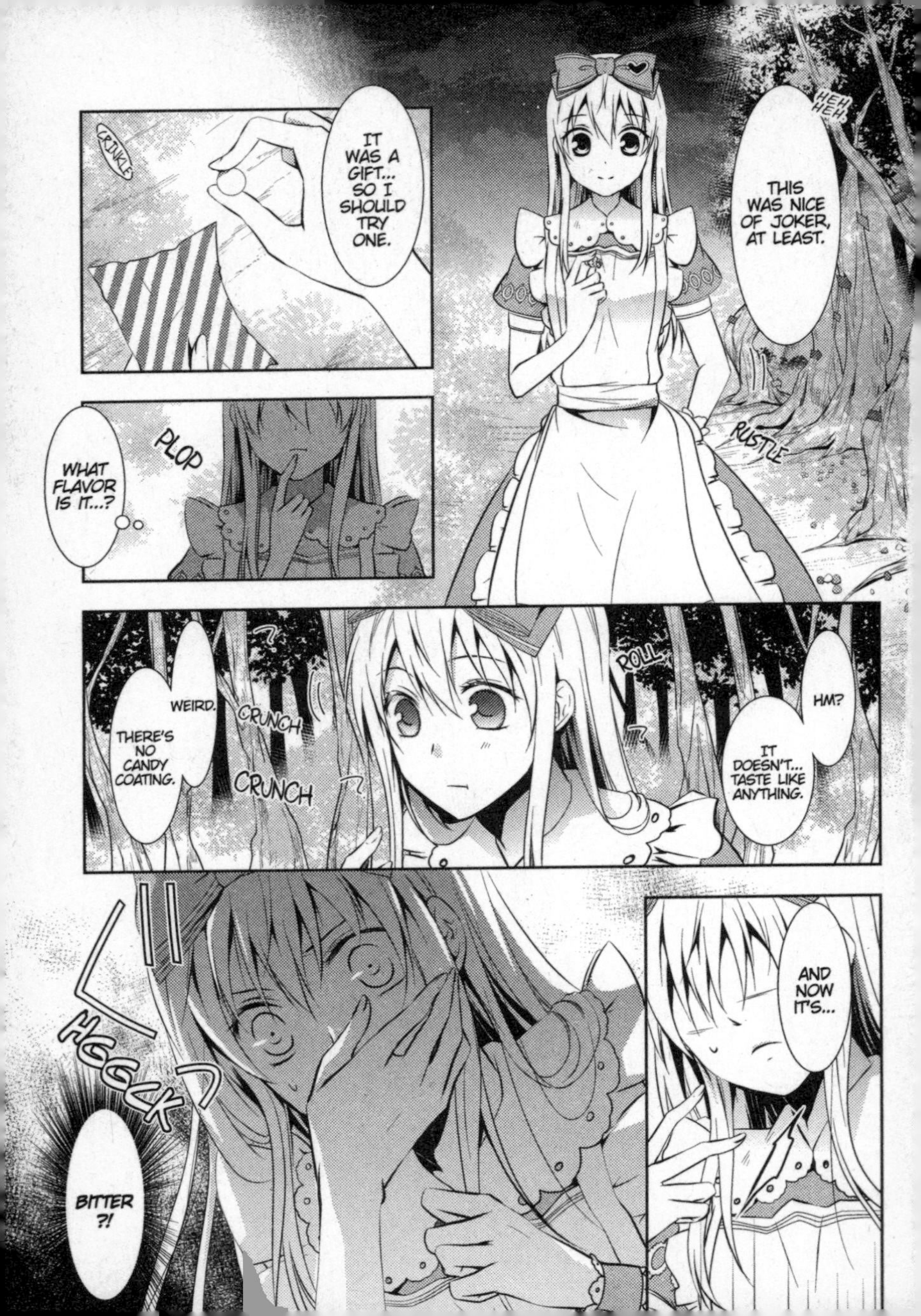
HEH HEH
THIS WAS NICE OF JOKER, AT LEAST.
RUSTLE
CRINKLE
IT WAS A GIFT... SO I SHOULD TRY ONE.
PLOP
WHAT FLAVOR IS IT...?
ROLL
HM?
IT DOESN'T... TASTE LIKE ANYTHING.
CRUNCH
CRUNCH
WEIRD.
THERE'S NO CANDY COATING.
AND NOW IT'S...
HGGCK
BITTER?!

Hit: 6

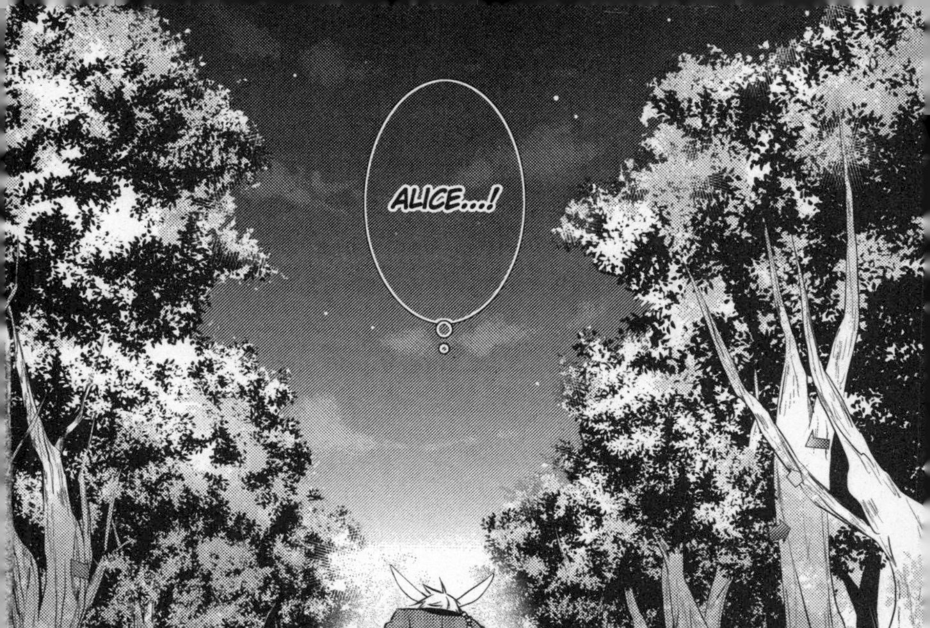
ALICE...!

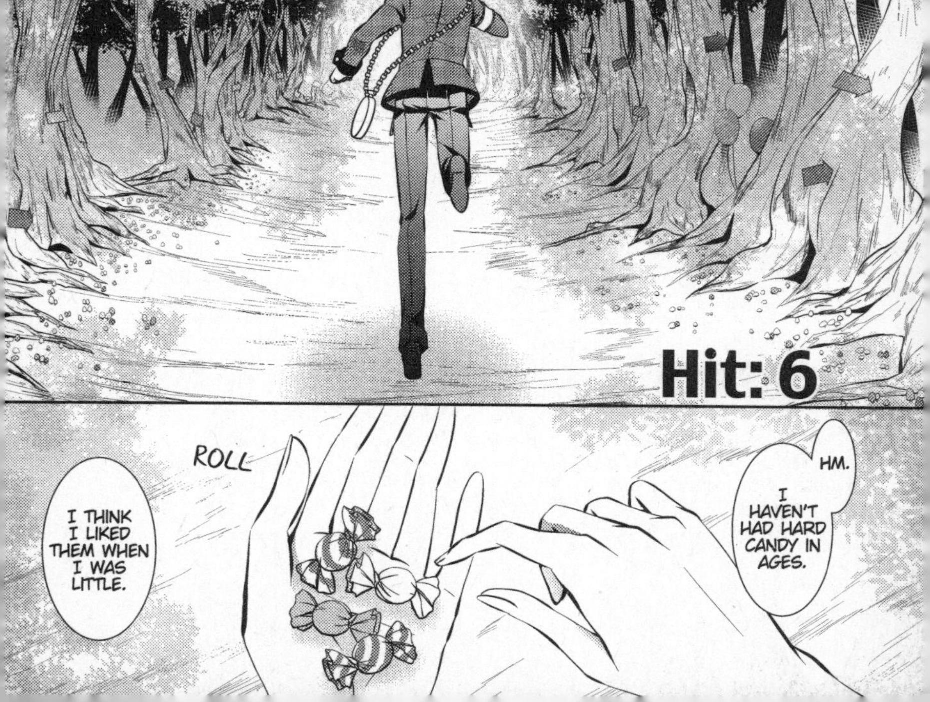
HM.
I HAVEN'T HAD HARD CANDY IN AGES.
ROLL
I THINK I LIKED THEM WHEN I WAS LITTLE.

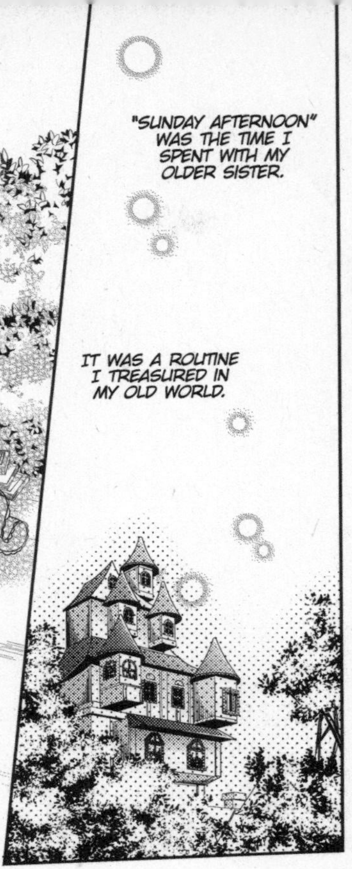
"SUNDAY AFTERNOON" WAS THE TIME I SPENT WITH MY OLDER SISTER.
IT WAS A ROUTINE I TREASURED IN MY OLD WORLD.

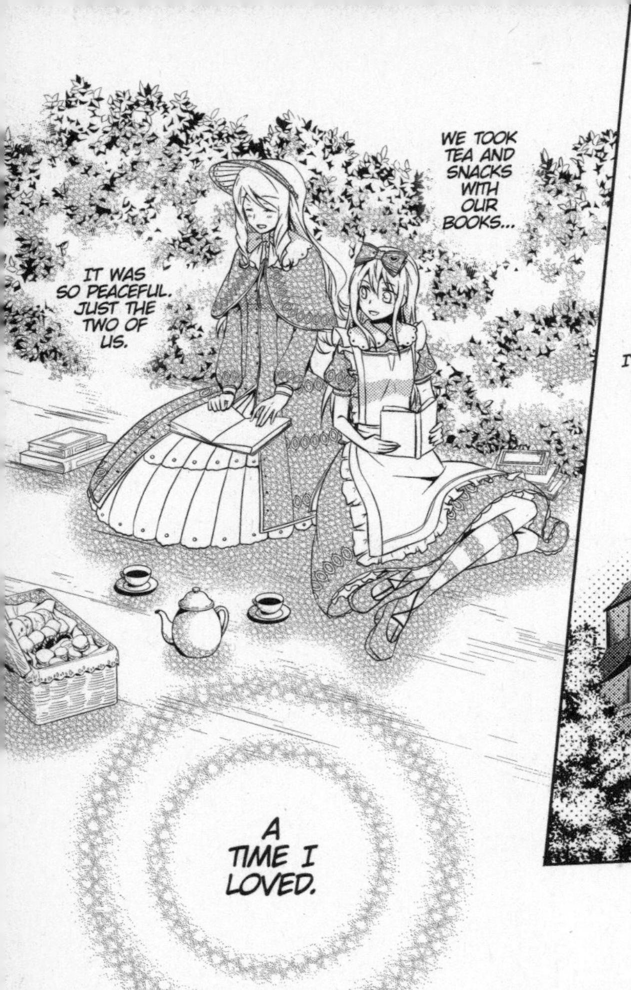
WE TOOK TEA AND SNACKS WITH OUR BOOKS...
IT WAS SO PEACEFUL. JUST THE TWO OF US.
A TIME I LOVED.

Hit: 6

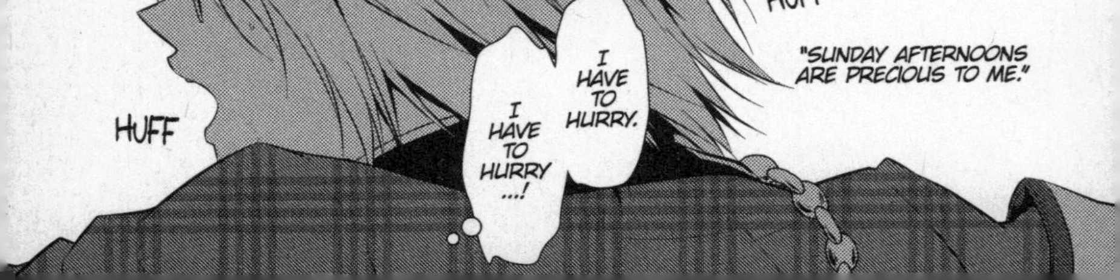
HUFF
"SUNDAY AFTERNOONS ARE PRECIOUS TO ME."
I HAVE TO HURRY.
I HAVE TO HURRY ...!
HUFF

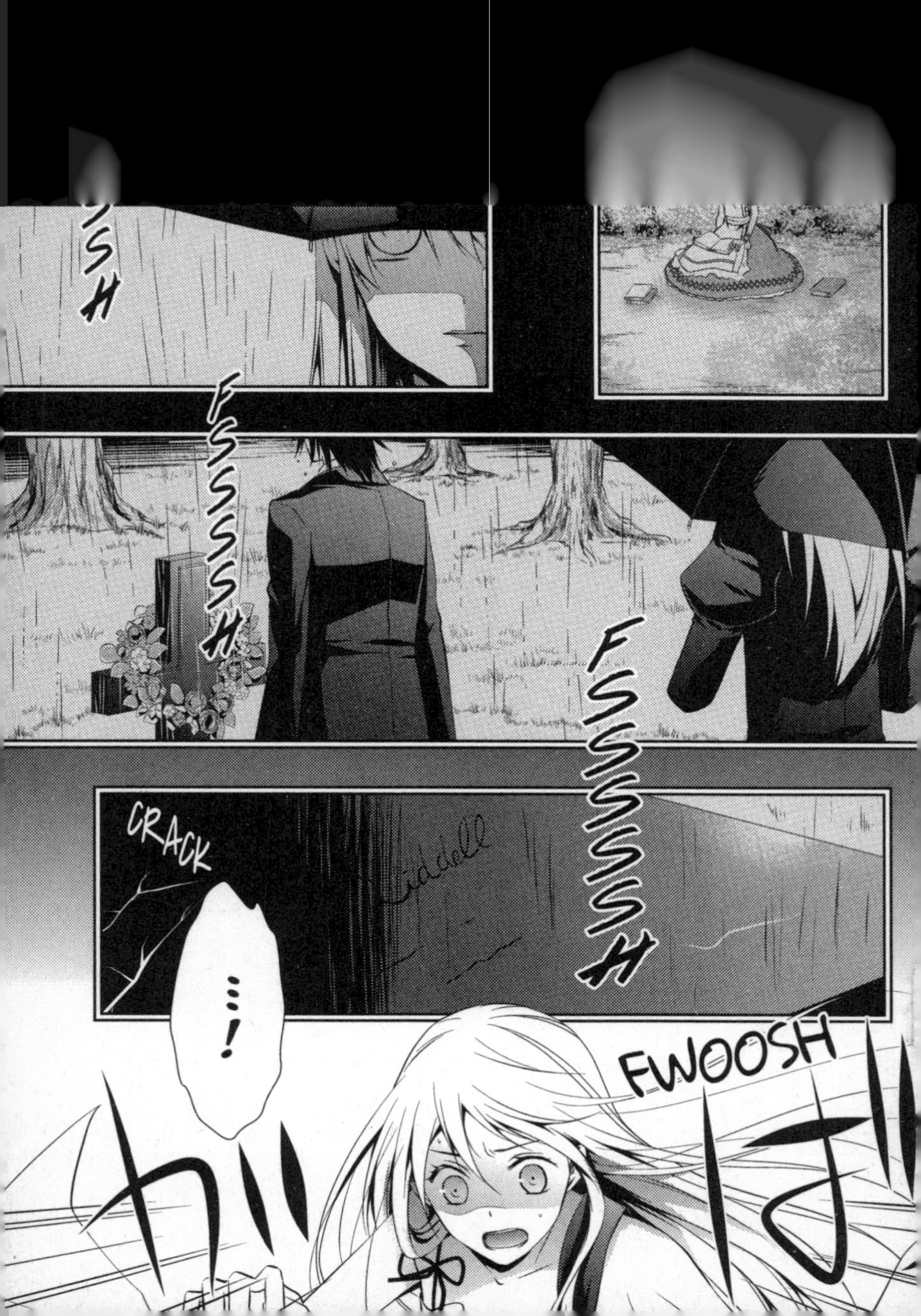
SH
FSSSSH
FSSSSSSH
CRACK
...!
FWOOSH

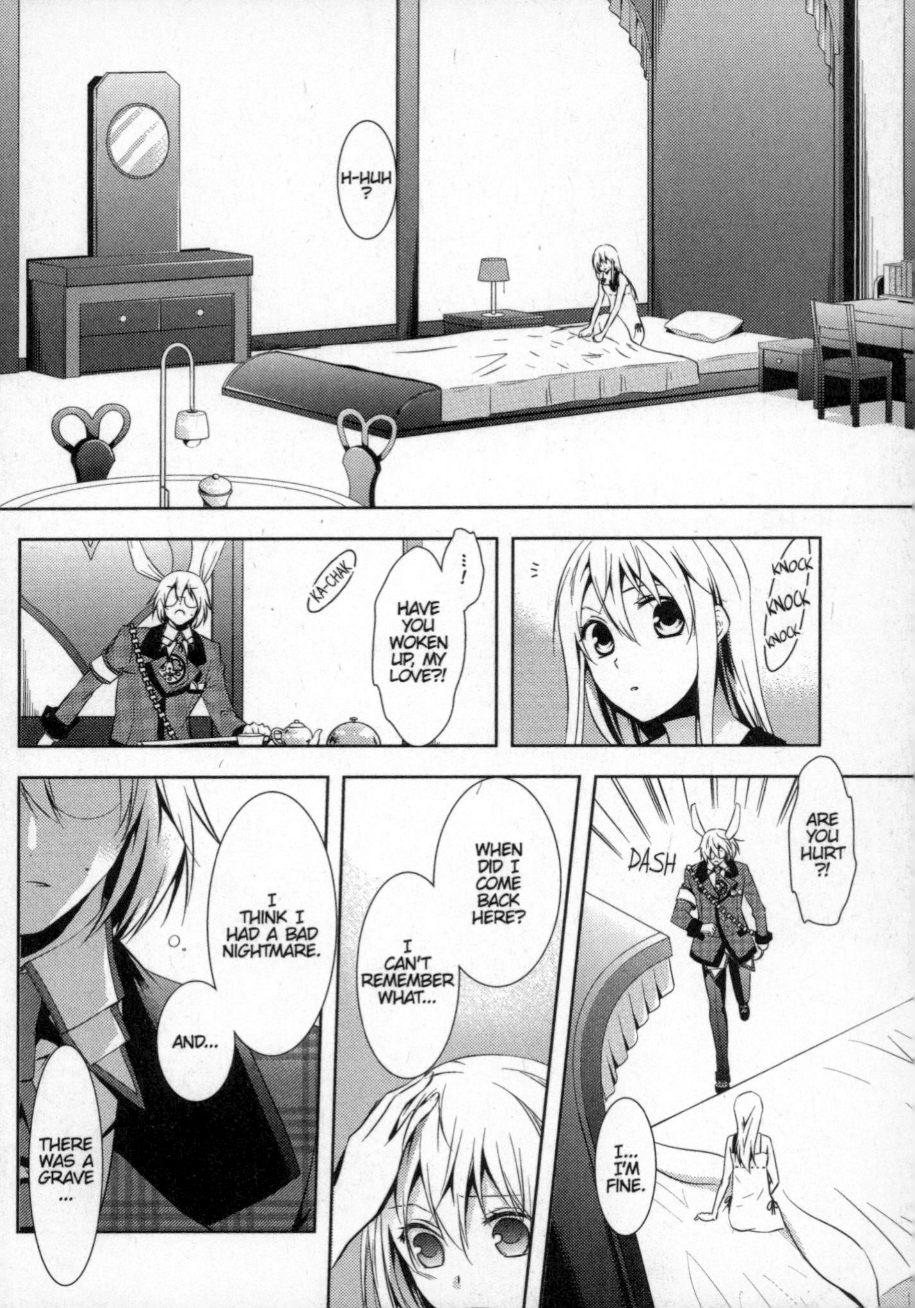
H-HUH?
KNOCK
KNOCK
KNOCK
...!
KA-CHAK
HAVE YOU WOKEN UP, MY LOVE?!
ARE YOU HURT?!
DASH
I... I'M FINE.
WHEN DID I COME BACK HERE?
I CAN'T REMEMBER WHAT...
I THINK I HAD A BAD NIGHTMARE.
AND...
THERE WAS A GRAVE...

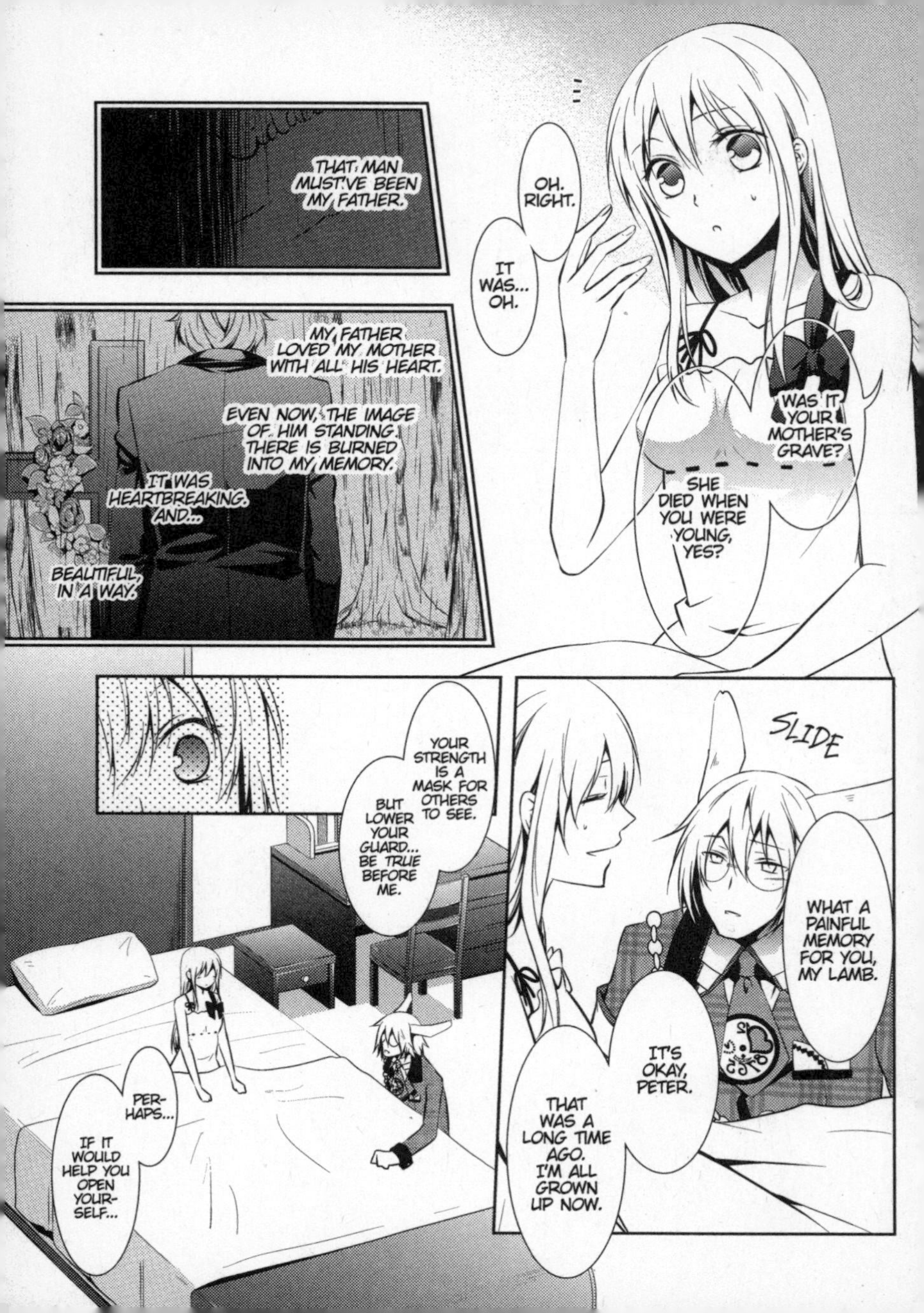
...
OH. RIGHT.
IT WAS... OH.
WAS IT YOUR MOTHER'S GRAVE?
SHE DIED WHEN YOU WERE YOUNG, YES?
THAT MAN MUST'VE BEEN MY FATHER.
MY FATHER LOVED MY MOTHER WITH ALL HIS HEART.
EVEN NOW, THE IMAGE OF HIM STANDING THERE IS BURNED INTO MY MEMORY.
IT WAS HEARTBREAKING. AND...
BEAUTIFUL, IN A WAY.
SLIDE
WHAT A PAINFUL MEMORY FOR YOU, MY LAMB.
IT'S OKAY, PETER.
THAT WAS A LONG TIME AGO. I'M ALL GROWN UP NOW.
YOUR STRENGTH IS A MASK FOR OTHERS TO SEE.
BUT LOWER YOUR GUARD... BE TRUE BEFORE ME.
PER-HAPS...
IF IT WOULD HELP YOU OPEN YOUR-SELF...

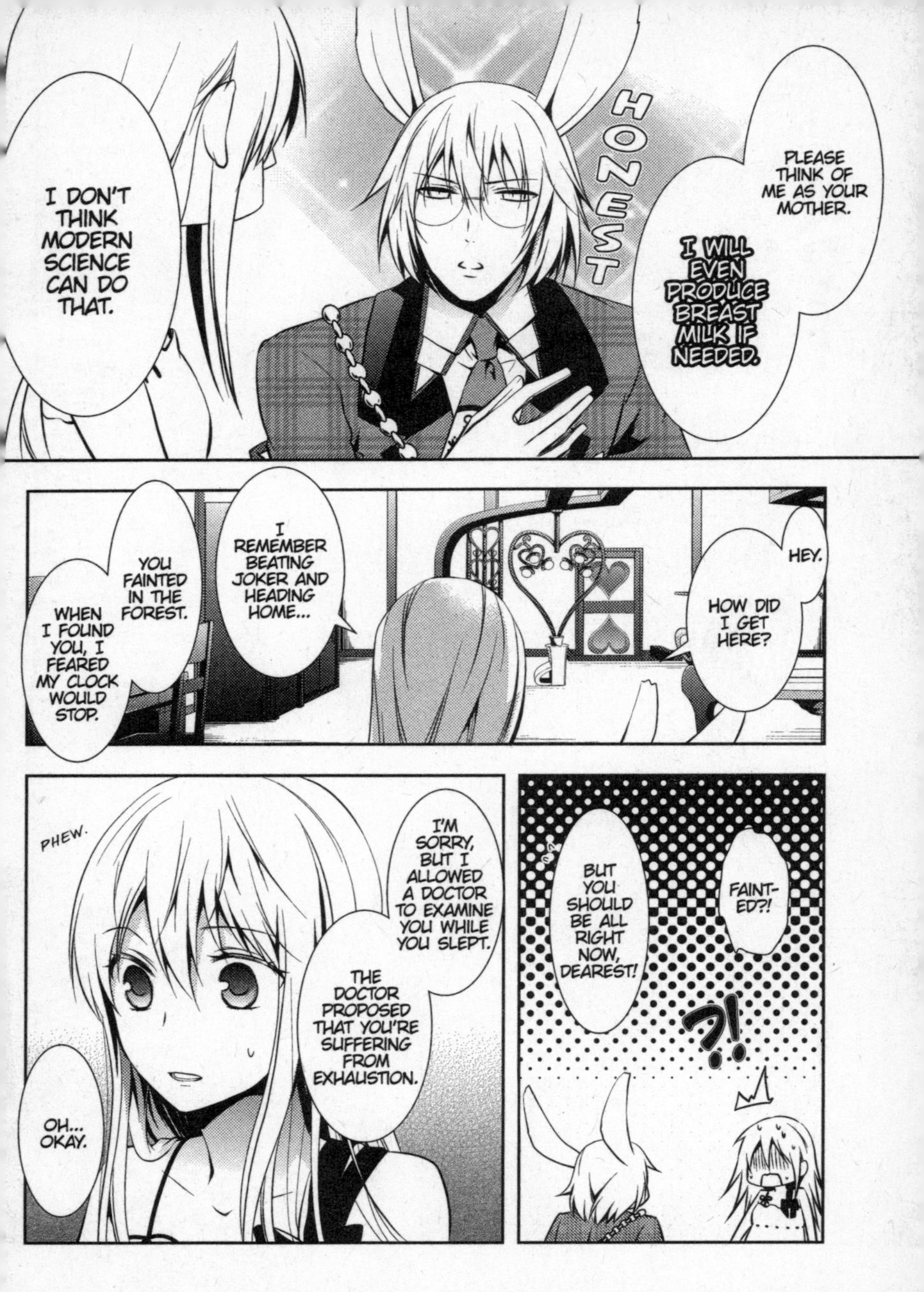
PLEASE THINK OF ME AS YOUR MOTHER.
I WILL EVEN PRODUCE BREAST MILK IF NEEDED.
HONEST
I DON'T THINK MODERN SCIENCE CAN DO THAT.
HEY.
HOW DID I GET HERE?
I REMEMBER BEATING JOKER AND HEADING HOME...
YOU FAINTED IN THE FOREST.
WHEN I FOUND YOU, I FEARED MY CLOCK WOULD STOP.
FAINT-ED?!
BUT YOU SHOULD BE ALL RIGHT NOW, DEAREST!
?!
I'M SORRY, BUT I ALLOWED A DOCTOR TO EXAMINE YOU WHILE YOU SLEPT.
THE DOCTOR PROPOSED THAT YOU'RE SUFFERING FROM EXHAUSTION.
PHEW.
OH... OKAY.

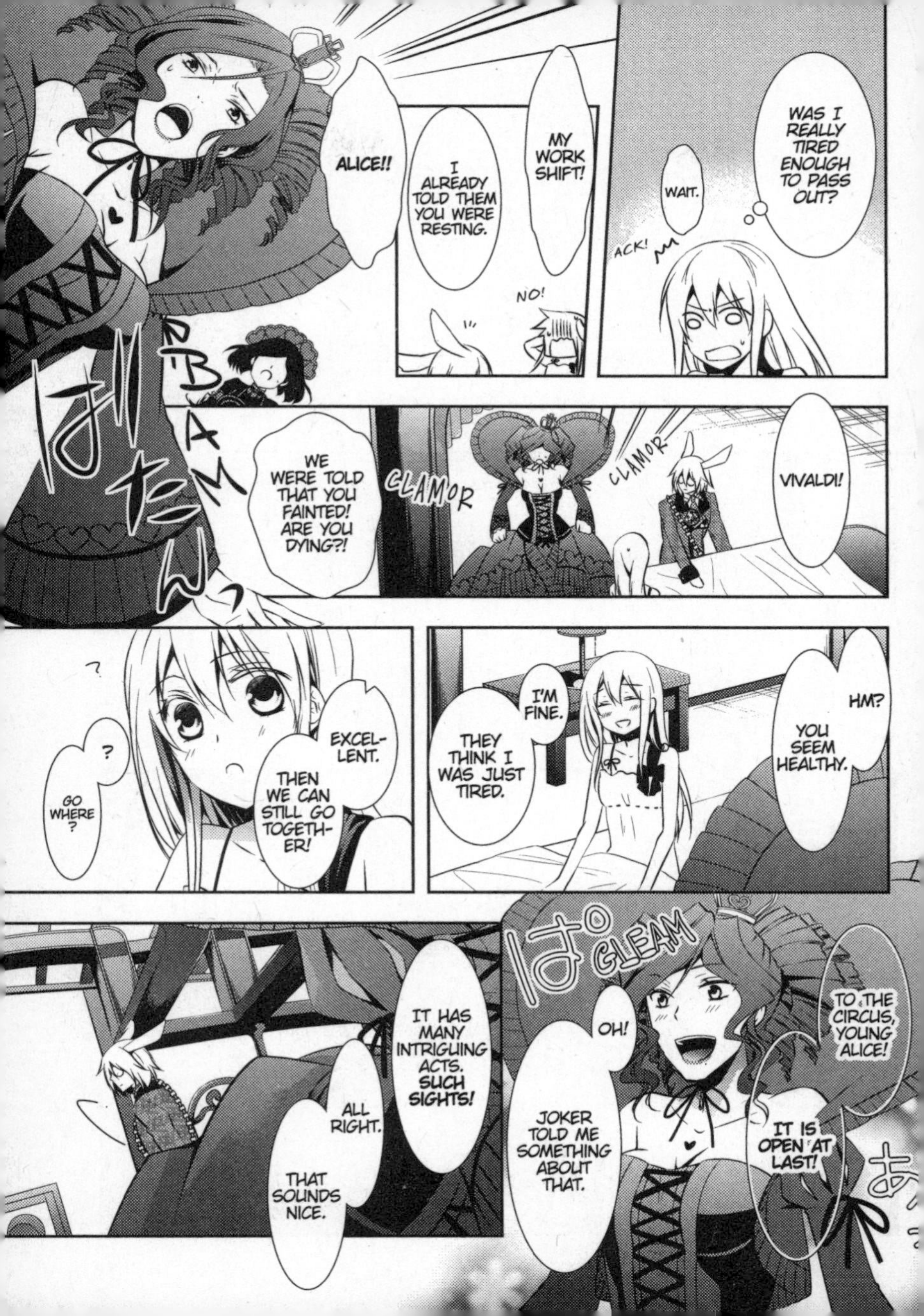
WAS I REALLY TIRED ENOUGH TO PASS OUT?
WAIT.
ACK!
MY WORK SHIFT!
I ALREADY TOLD THEM YOU WERE RESTING.
NO!
VIVALDI!
CLAMOR
CLAMOR
WE WERE TOLD THAT YOU FAINTED! ARE YOU DYING?!
ALICE!!
BAM
HM?
YOU SEEM HEALTHY.
I'M FINE.
THEY THINK I WAS JUST TIRED.
EXCEL-LENT.
THEN WE CAN STILL GO TOGETH-ER!
?
?
GO WHERE?
TO THE CIRCUS, YOUNG ALICE!
IT IS OPEN AT LAST!
GLEAM
OH!
JOKER TOLD ME SOMETHING ABOUT THAT.
IT HAS MANY INTRIGUING ACTS. SUCH SIGHTS!
ALL RIGHT.
THAT SOUNDS NICE.

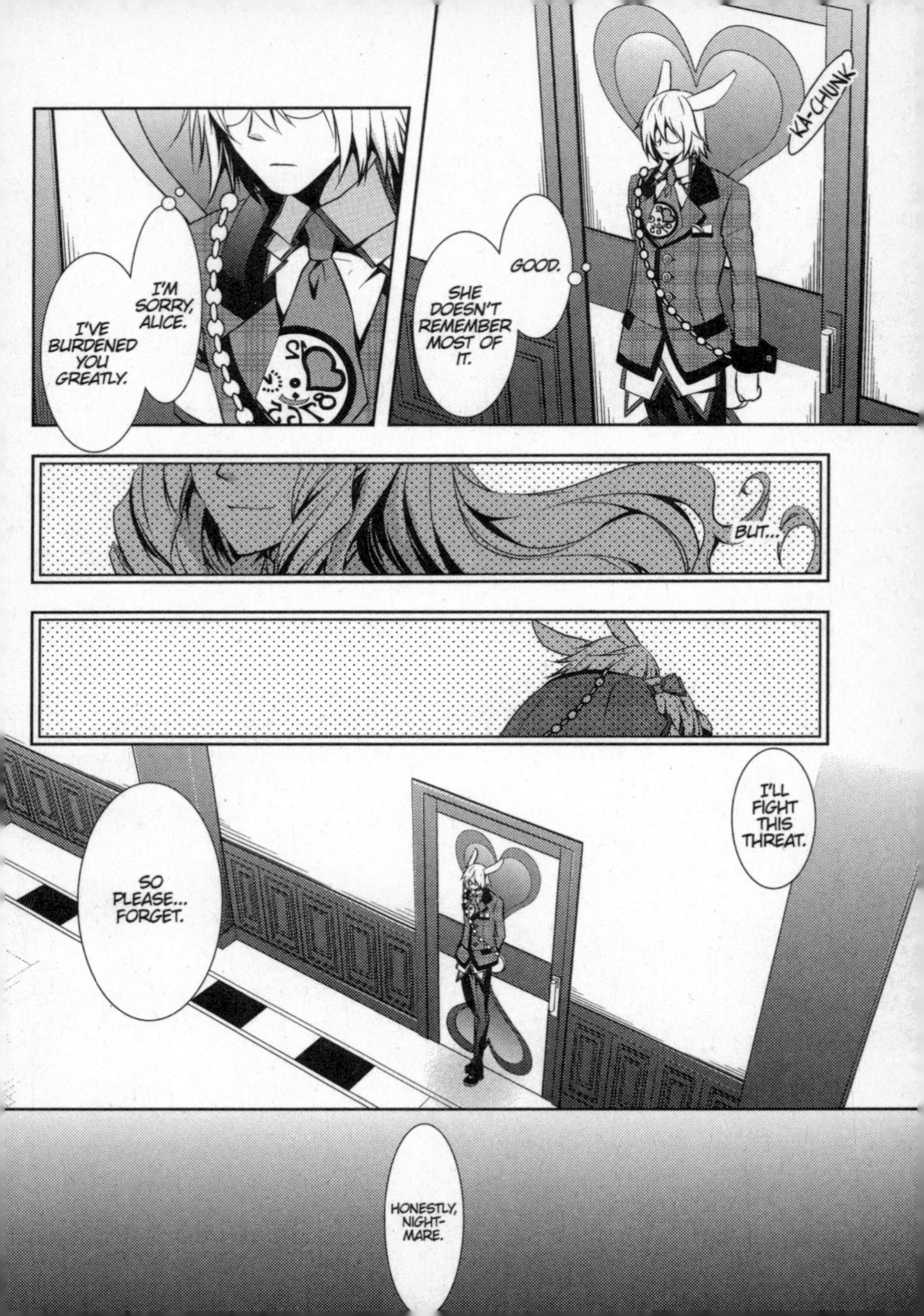
KA-CHUNK
GOOD.
SHE DOESN'T REMEMBER MOST OF IT.
I'M SORRY, ALICE.
I'VE BURDENED YOU GREATLY.
BUT...
I'LL FIGHT THIS THREAT.
SO PLEASE... FORGET.
HONESTLY, NIGHT-MARE.

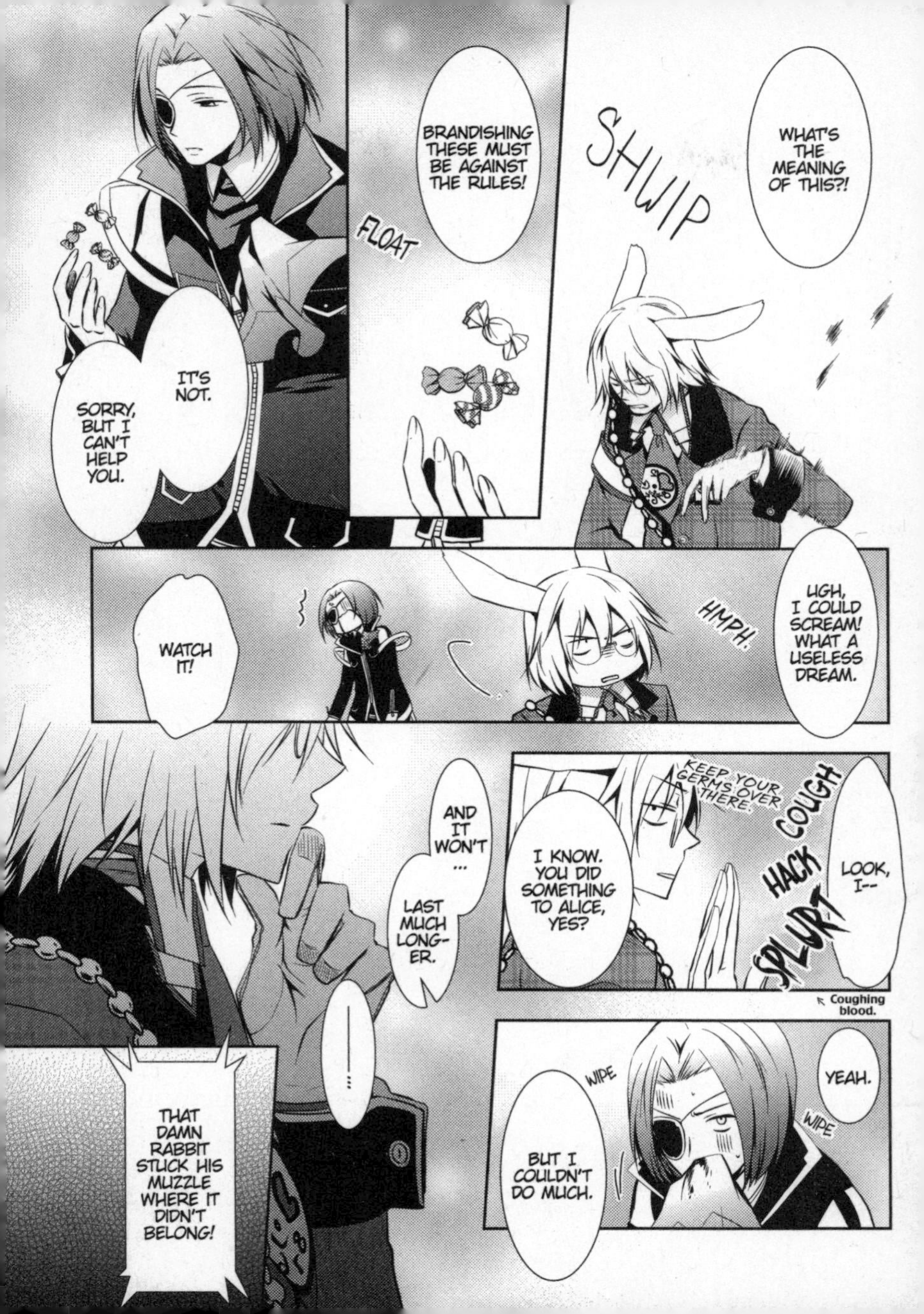
WHAT'S THE MEANING OF THIS?!
SHWIP
BRANDISHING THESE MUST BE AGAINST THE RULES!
FLOAT
IT'S NOT.
SORRY, BUT I CAN'T HELP YOU.
UGH, I COULD SCREAM! WHAT A USELESS DREAM.
HMPH.
WATCH IT!
LOOK, I--
COUGH
HACK
SPLURT
KEEP YOUR GERMS OVER THERE.
I KNOW. YOU DID SOMETHING TO ALICE, YES?
Coughing blood.
YEAH.
WIPE
WIPE
BUT I COULDN'T DO MUCH.
AND IT WON'T ...
LAST MUCH LONGER.
......!!
THAT DAMN RABBIT STUCK HIS MUZZLE WHERE IT DIDN'T BELONG!

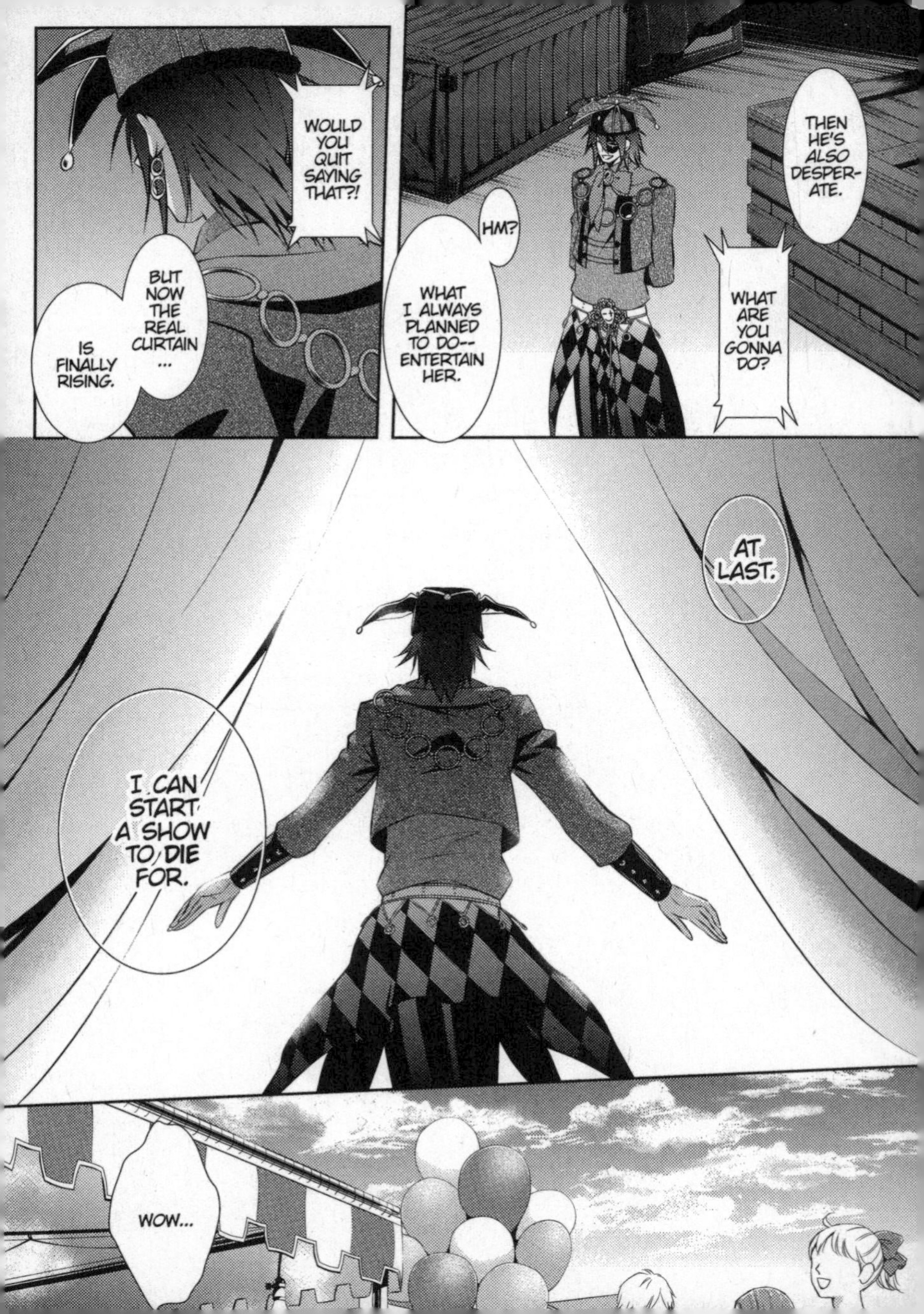
THEN HE'S ALSO DESPERATE.
WHAT ARE YOU GONNA DO?
HM?
WHAT I ALWAYS PLANNED TO DO-- ENTERTAIN HER.
WOULD YOU QUIT SAYING THAT?!
BUT NOW THE REAL CURTAIN ...
IS FINALLY RISING.
AT LAST.
I CAN START A SHOW TO DIE FOR.
WOW...

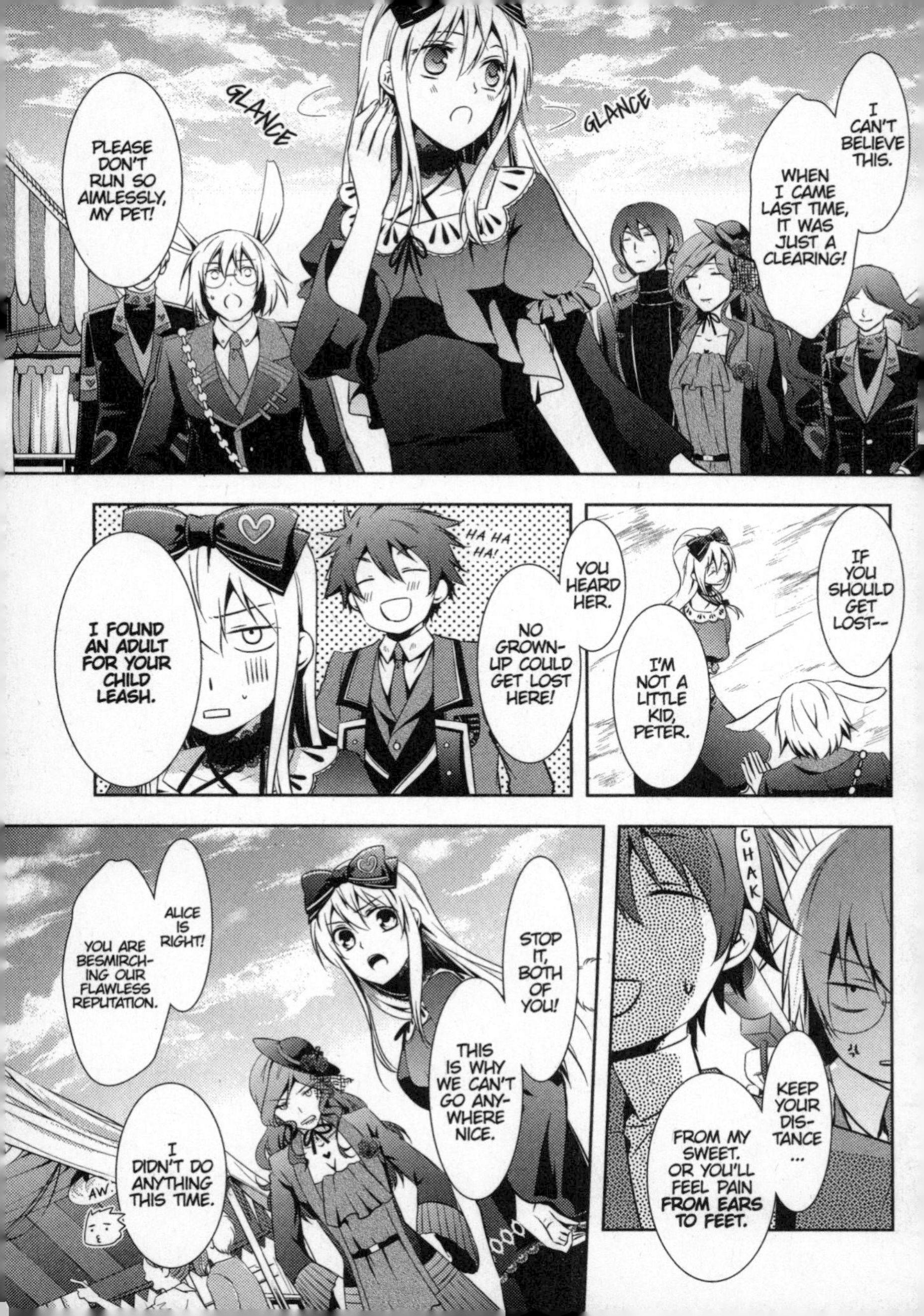
I CAN'T BELIEVE THIS.
WHEN I CAME LAST TIME, IT WAS JUST A CLEARING!
GLANCE
GLANCE
PLEASE DON'T RUN SO AIMLESSLY, MY PET!
IF YOU SHOULD GET LOST--
I'M NOT A LITTLE KID, PETER.
YOU HEARD HER.
NO GROWN-UP COULD GET LOST HERE!
HA HA HA!
I FOUND AN ADULT FOR YOUR CHILD LEASH.
CHAK
KEEP YOUR DISTANCE...
FROM MY SWEET. OR YOU'LL FEEL PAIN FROM EARS TO FEET.
STOP IT, BOTH OF YOU!
THIS IS WHY WE CAN'T GO ANYWHERE NICE.
ALICE IS RIGHT!
YOU ARE BESMIRCHING OUR FLAWLESS REPUTATION.
I DIDN'T DO ANYTHING THIS TIME.
AW.

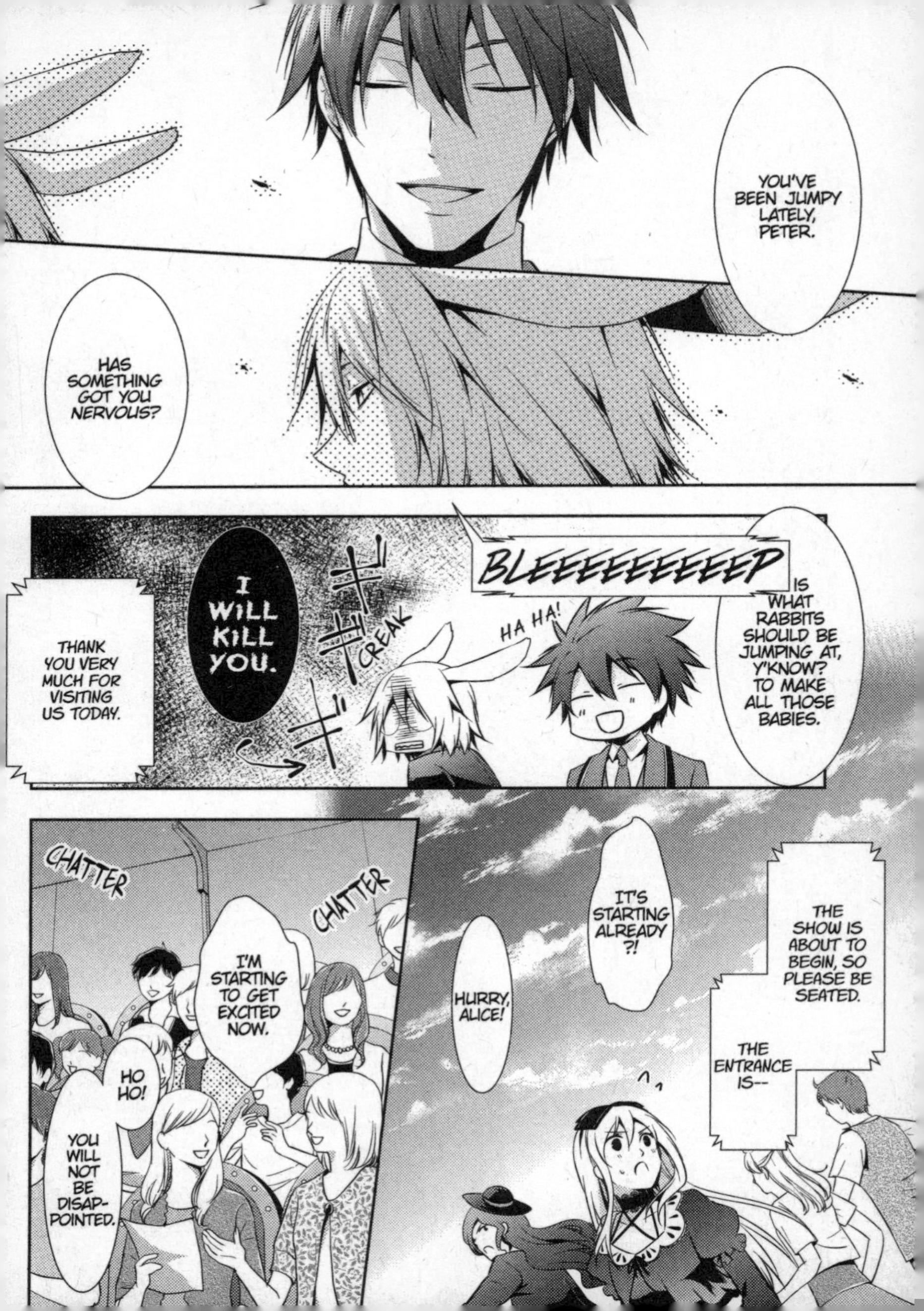
YOU'VE BEEN JUMPY LATELY, PETER.
HAS SOMETHING GOT YOU NERVOUS?
BLEEEEEEEEEP
IS WHAT RABBITS SHOULD BE JUMPING AT, Y'KNOW? TO MAKE ALL THOSE BABIES.
HA HA!
CREAK
I WILL KILL YOU.
THANK YOU VERY MUCH FOR VISITING US TODAY.
THE SHOW IS ABOUT TO BEGIN, SO PLEASE BE SEATED.
THE ENTRANCE IS--
IT'S STARTING ALREADY?!
HURRY, ALICE!
CHATTER
CHATTER
I'M STARTING TO GET EXCITED NOW.
HO HO!
YOU WILL NOT BE DISAPPOINTED.

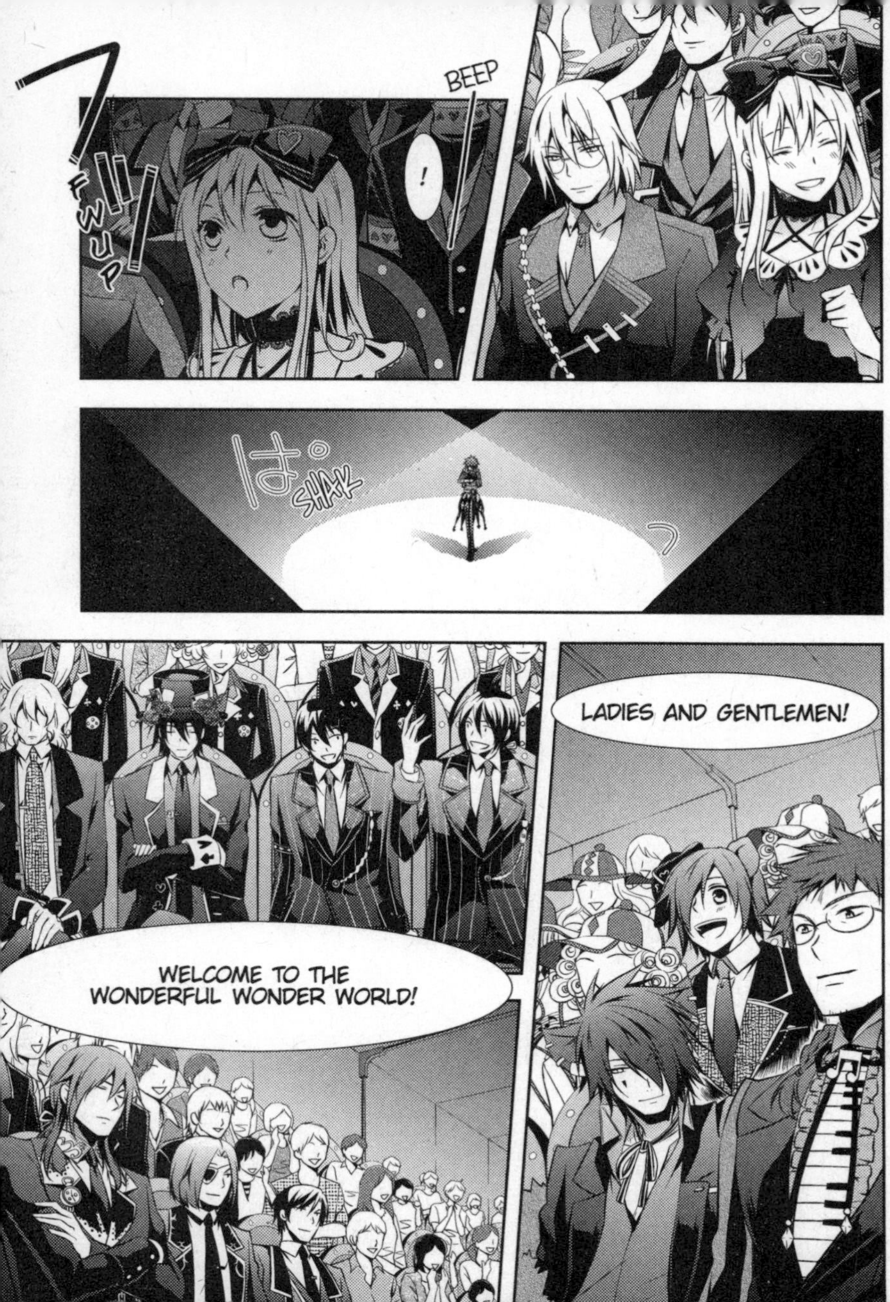
BEEP
!
FWUP
ぱっ
SHAK
LADIES AND GENTLEMEN!
WELCOME TO THE WONDERFUL WONDER WORLD!

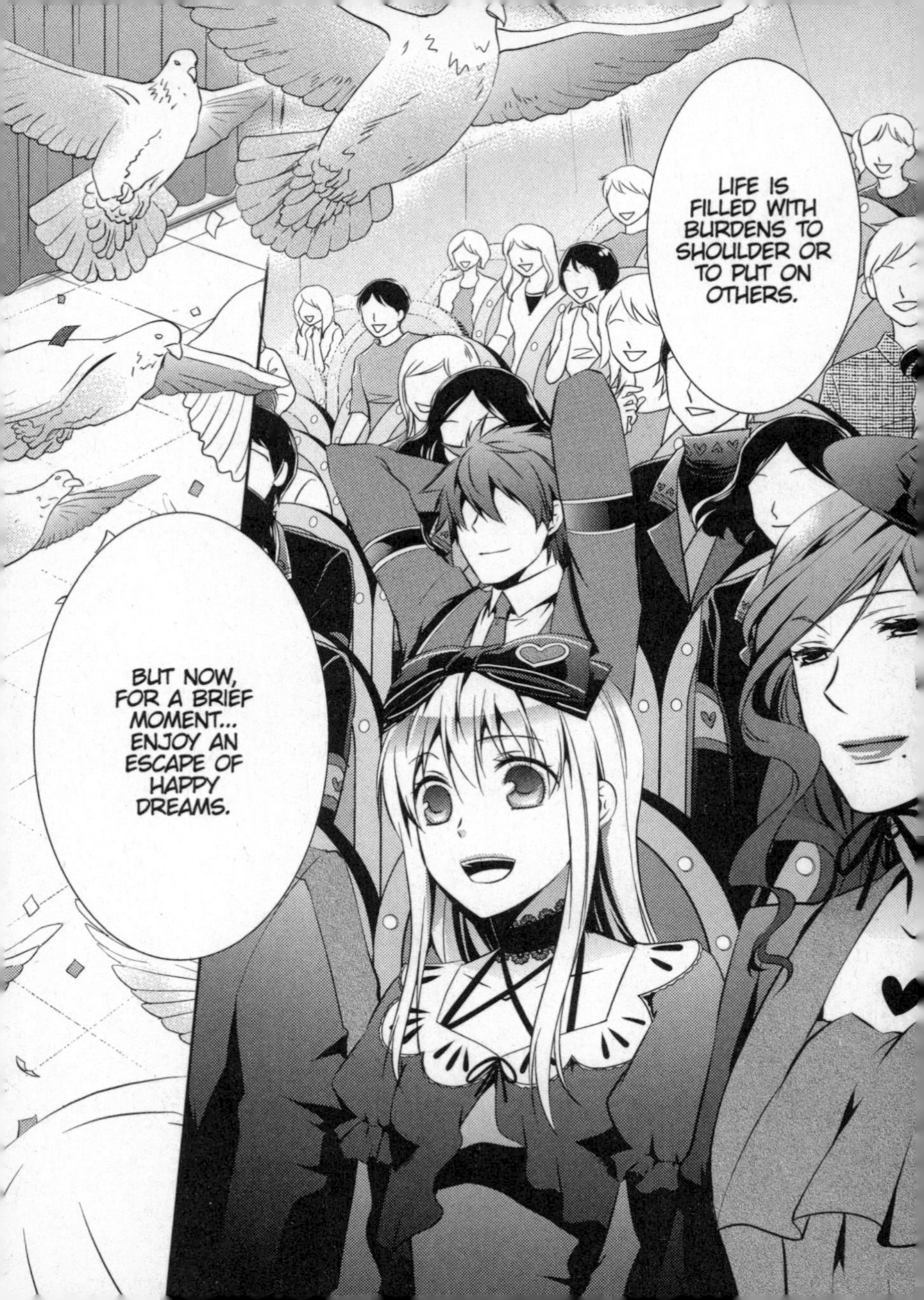
LIFE IS FILLED WITH BURDENS TO SHOULDER OR TO PUT ON OTHERS.
BUT NOW, FOR A BRIEF MOMENT... ENJOY AN ESCAPE OF HAPPY DREAMS.

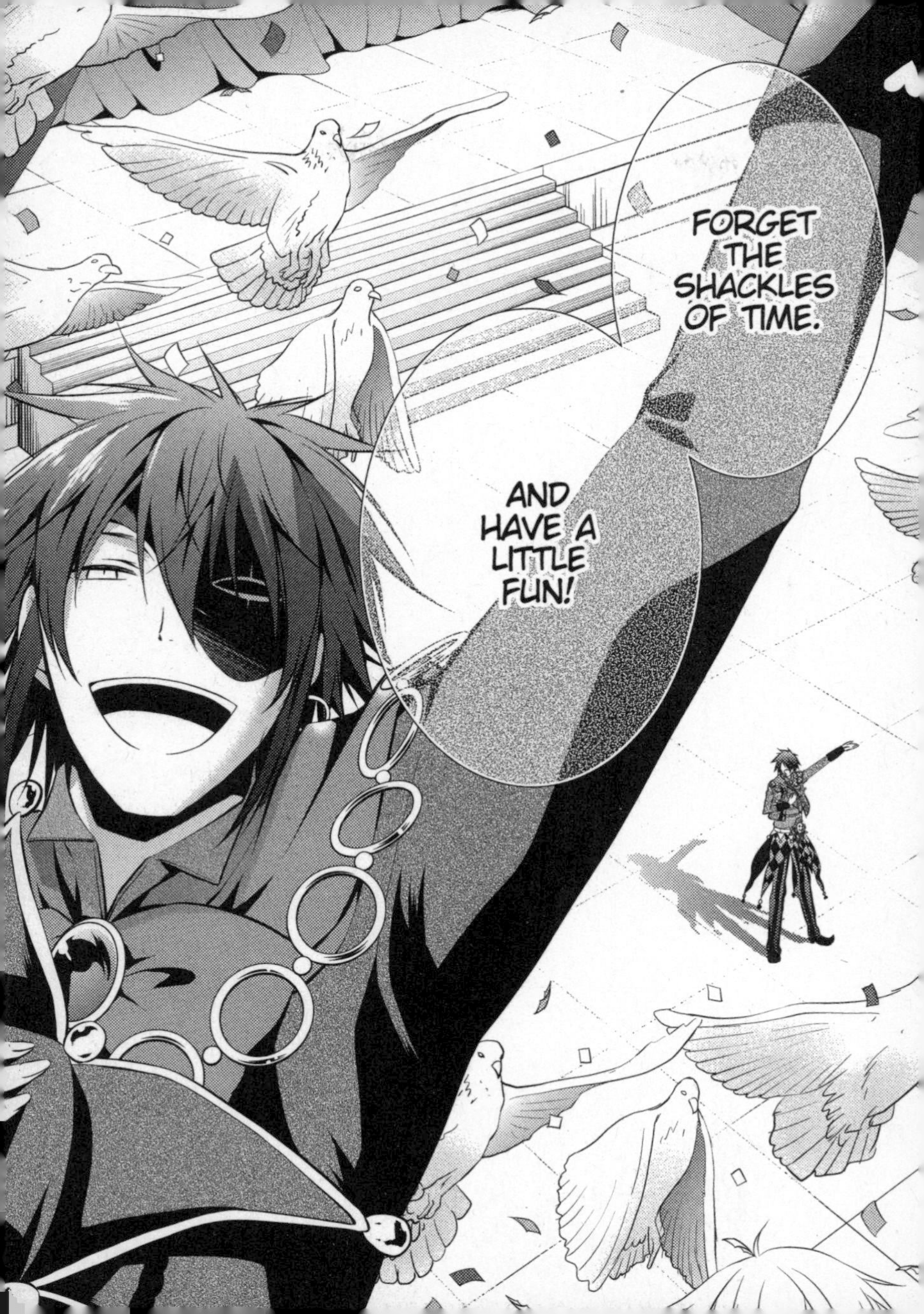
FORGET THE SHACKLES OF TIME.
AND HAVE A LITTLE FUN!

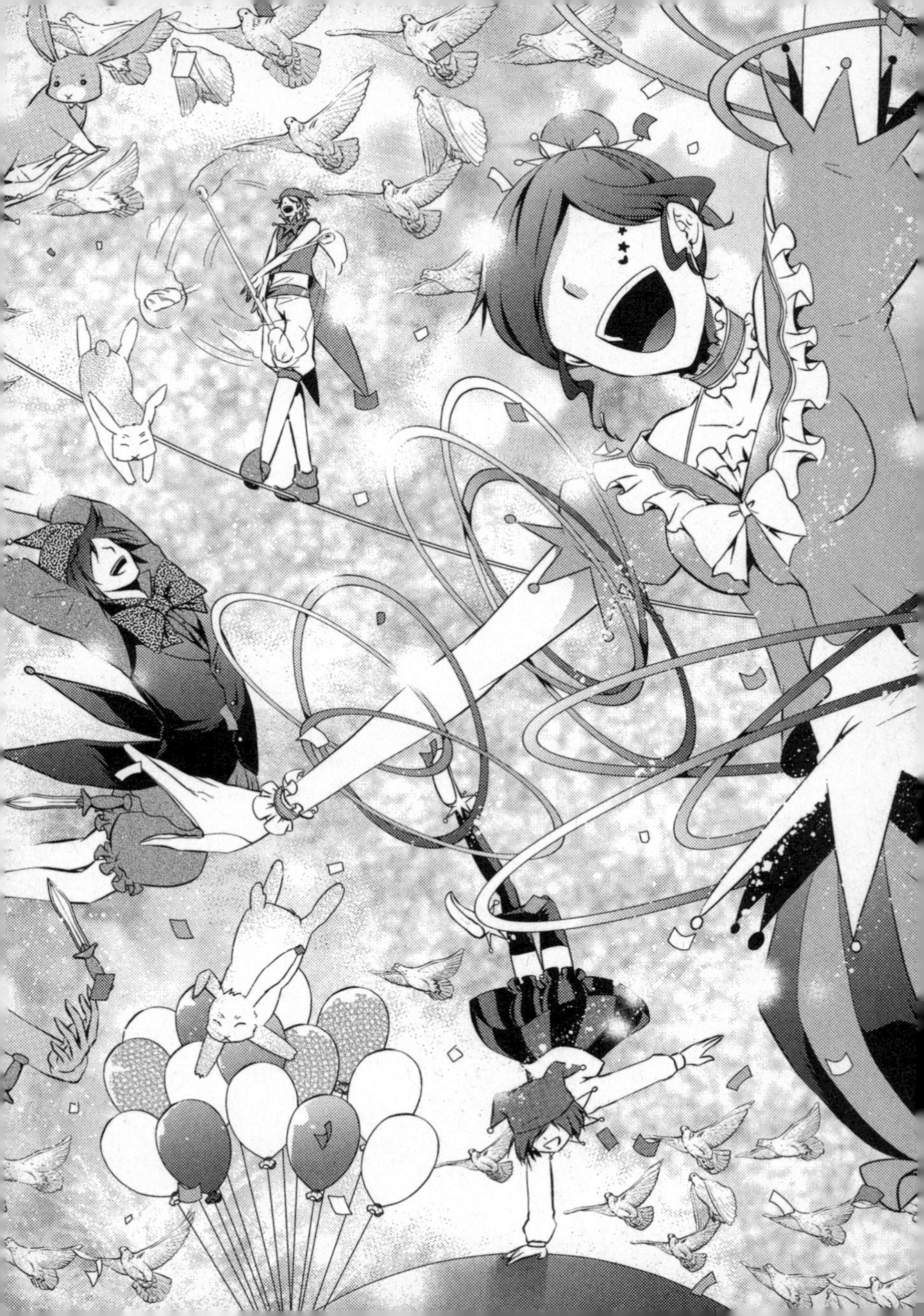

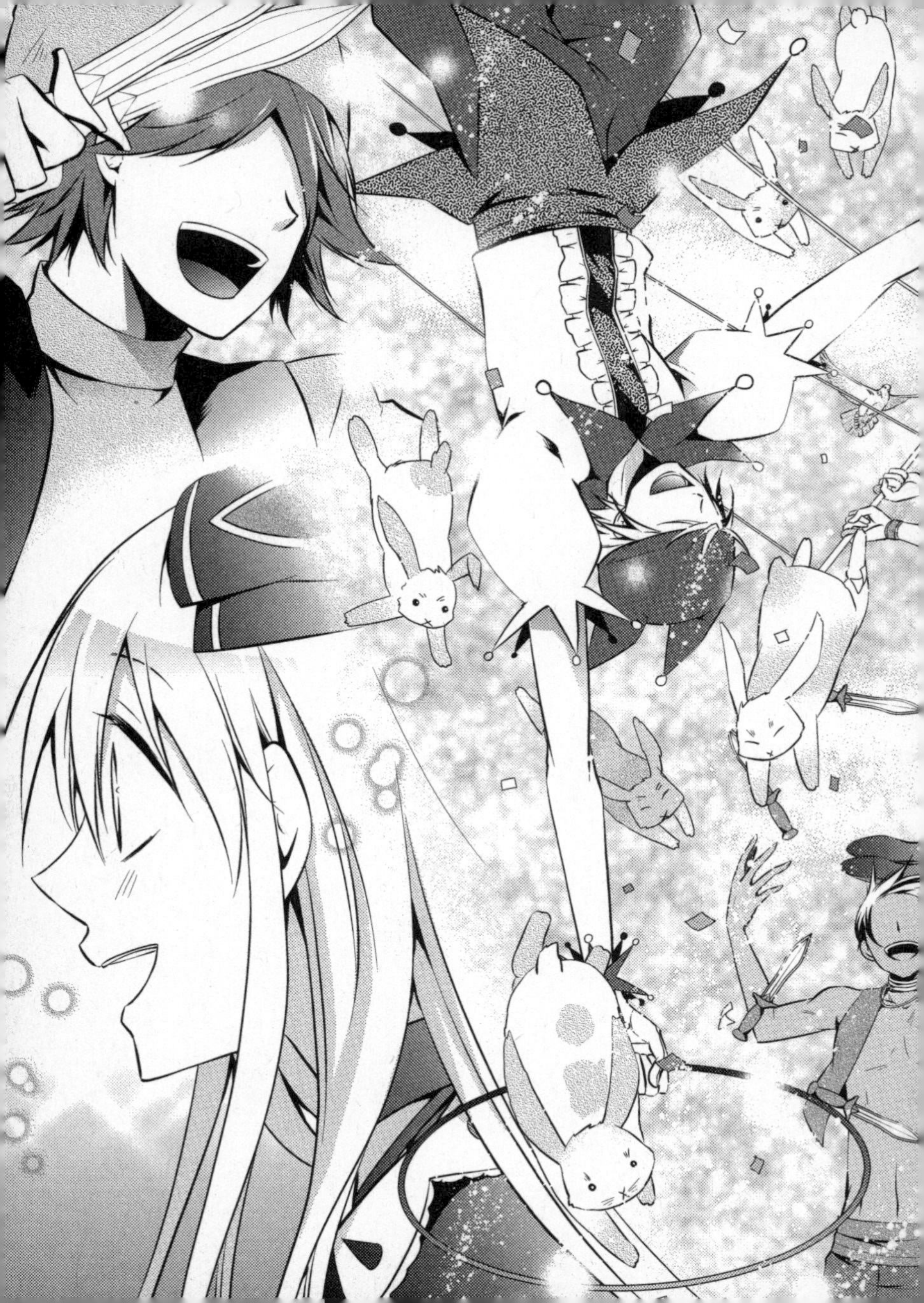

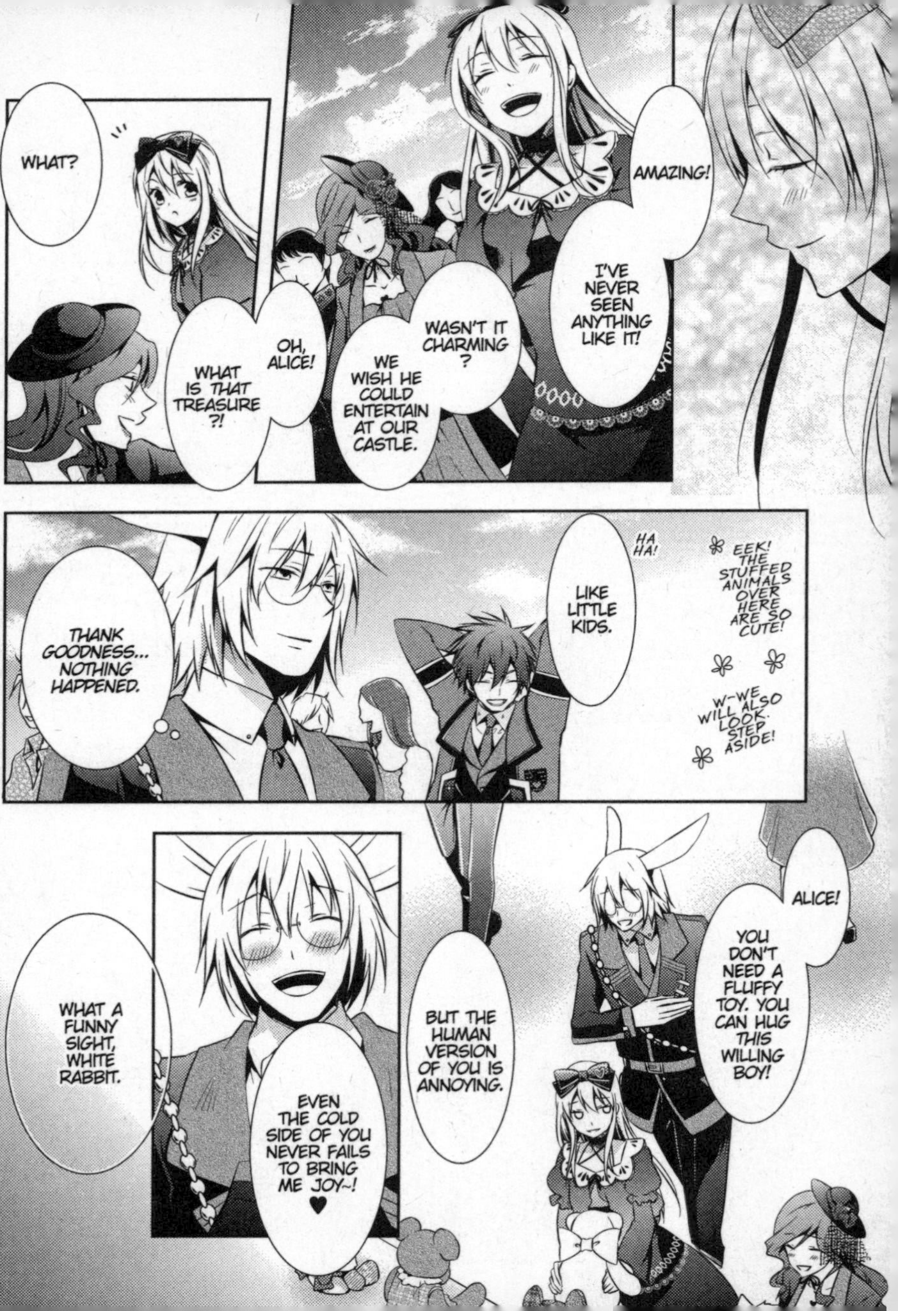
AMAZING!
I'VE NEVER SEEN ANYTHING LIKE IT!
WASN'T IT CHARMING?
WE WISH HE COULD ENTERTAIN AT OUR CASTLE.
OH, ALICE!
WHAT IS THAT TREASURE?!
WHAT?
EEK! THE STUFFED ANIMALS OVER HERE ARE SO CUTE!
W-WE WILL ALSO LOOK. STEP ASIDE!
HA HA!
LIKE LITTLE KIDS.
THANK GOODNESS... NOTHING HAPPENED.
ALICE!
YOU DON'T NEED A FLUFFY TOY. YOU CAN HUG THIS WILLING BOY!
BUT THE HUMAN VERSION OF YOU IS ANNOYING.
WHAT A FUNNY SIGHT, WHITE RABBIT.
EVEN THE COLD SIDE OF YOU NEVER FAILS TO BRING ME JOY~! ♥

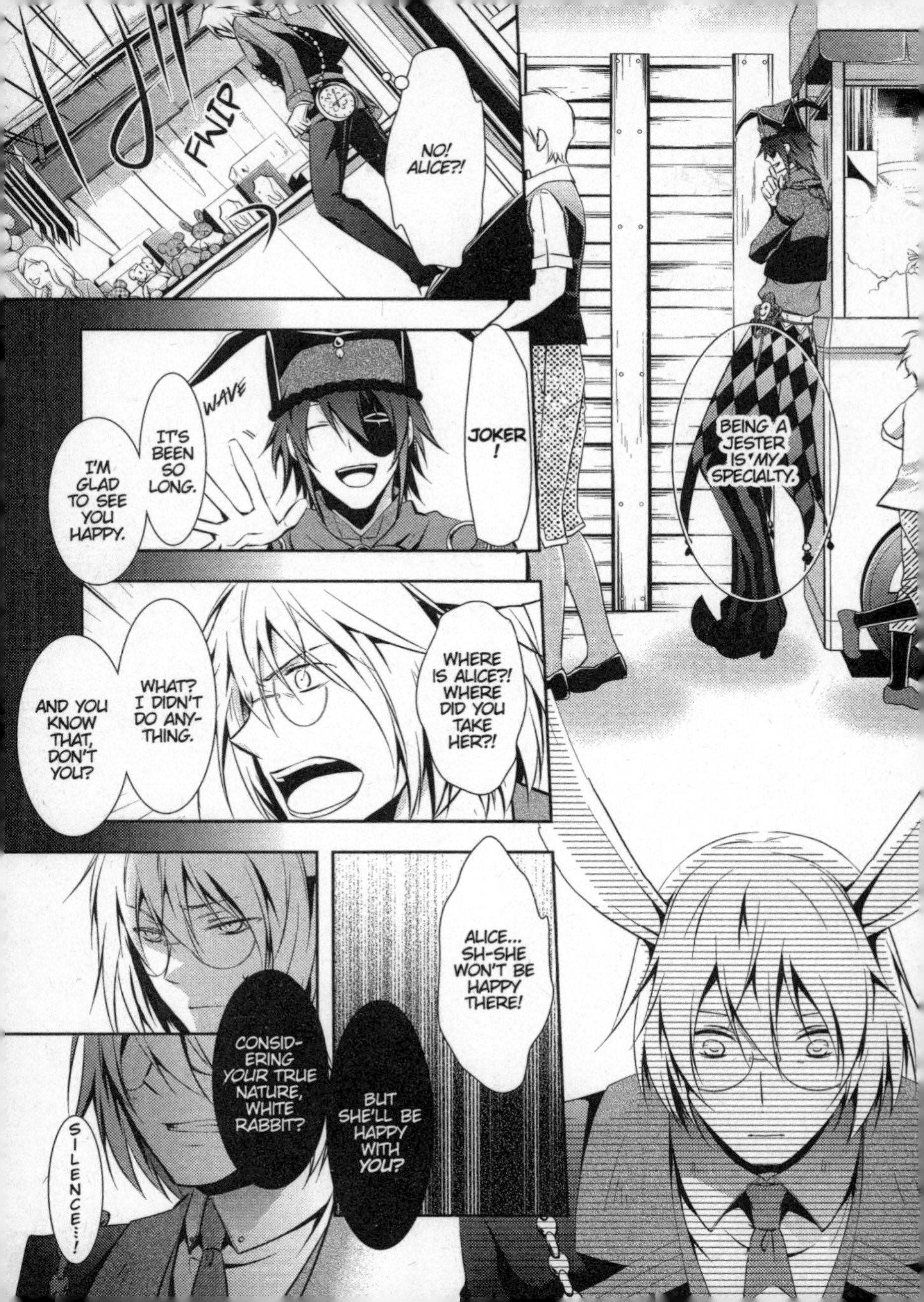

BEING A JESTER IS MY SPECIALTY.
NO! ALICE?!
FWIP
JOKER!
WAVE
IT'S BEEN SO LONG.
I'M GLAD TO SEE YOU HAPPY.
WHERE IS ALICE?! WHERE DID YOU TAKE HER?!
WHAT? I DIDN'T DO ANYTHING.
AND YOU KNOW THAT, DON'T YOU?
ALICE... SH-SHE WON'T BE HAPPY THERE!
BUT SHE'LL BE HAPPY WITH YOU?
CONSIDERING YOUR TRUE NATURE, WHITE RABBIT?
SILENCE...!

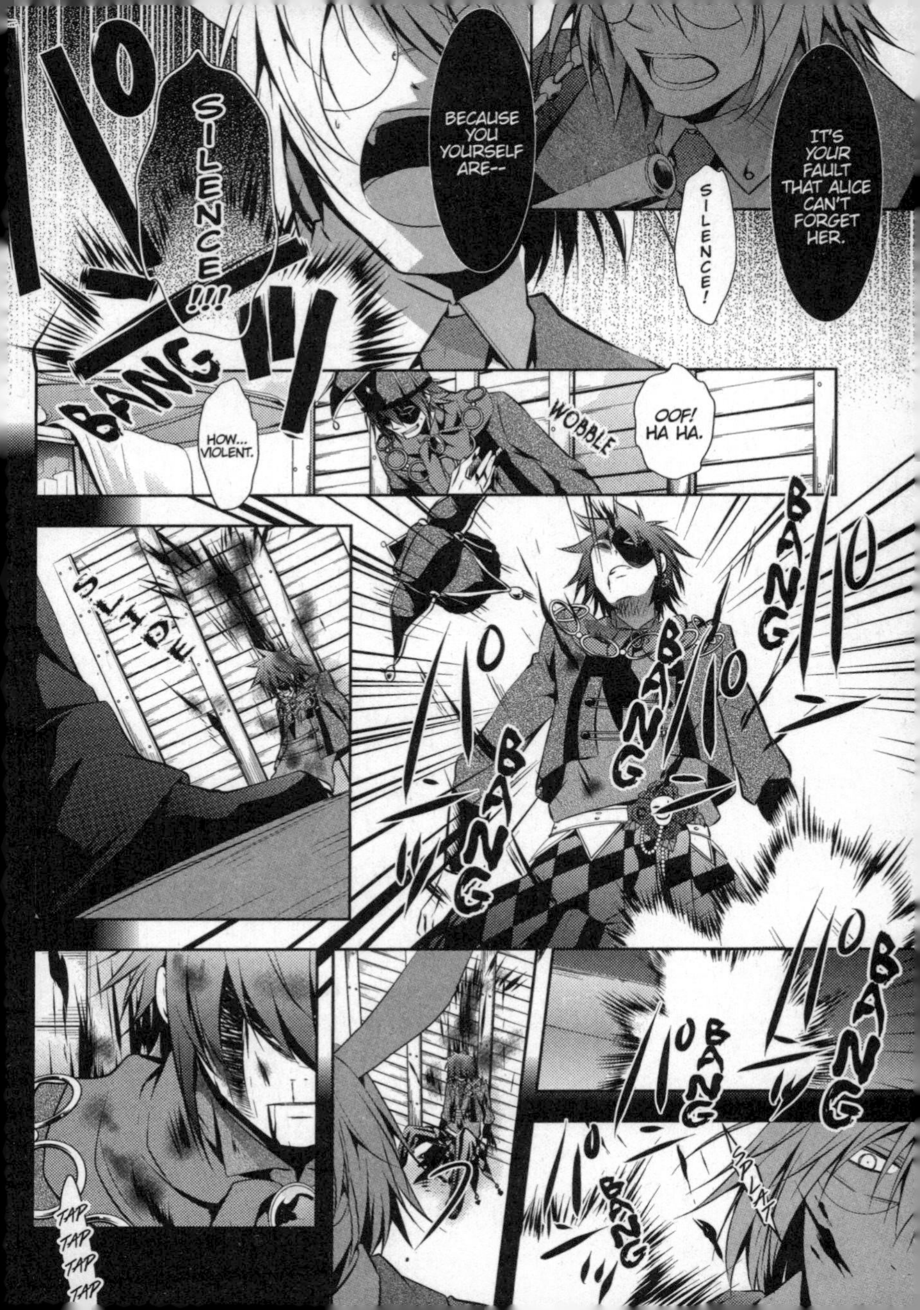
IT'S YOUR FAULT THAT ALICE CAN'T FORGET HER.
SILENCE!
BECAUSE YOU YOURSELF ARE--
SILENCE!!!
BANG!!!
OOF! HA HA.
WOBBLE
HOW... VIOLENT.
BANG
BANG
BANG
BANG
SLIDE
BANG
BANG
BANG
SPLAT
BANG
TAP
TAP
TAP
TAP

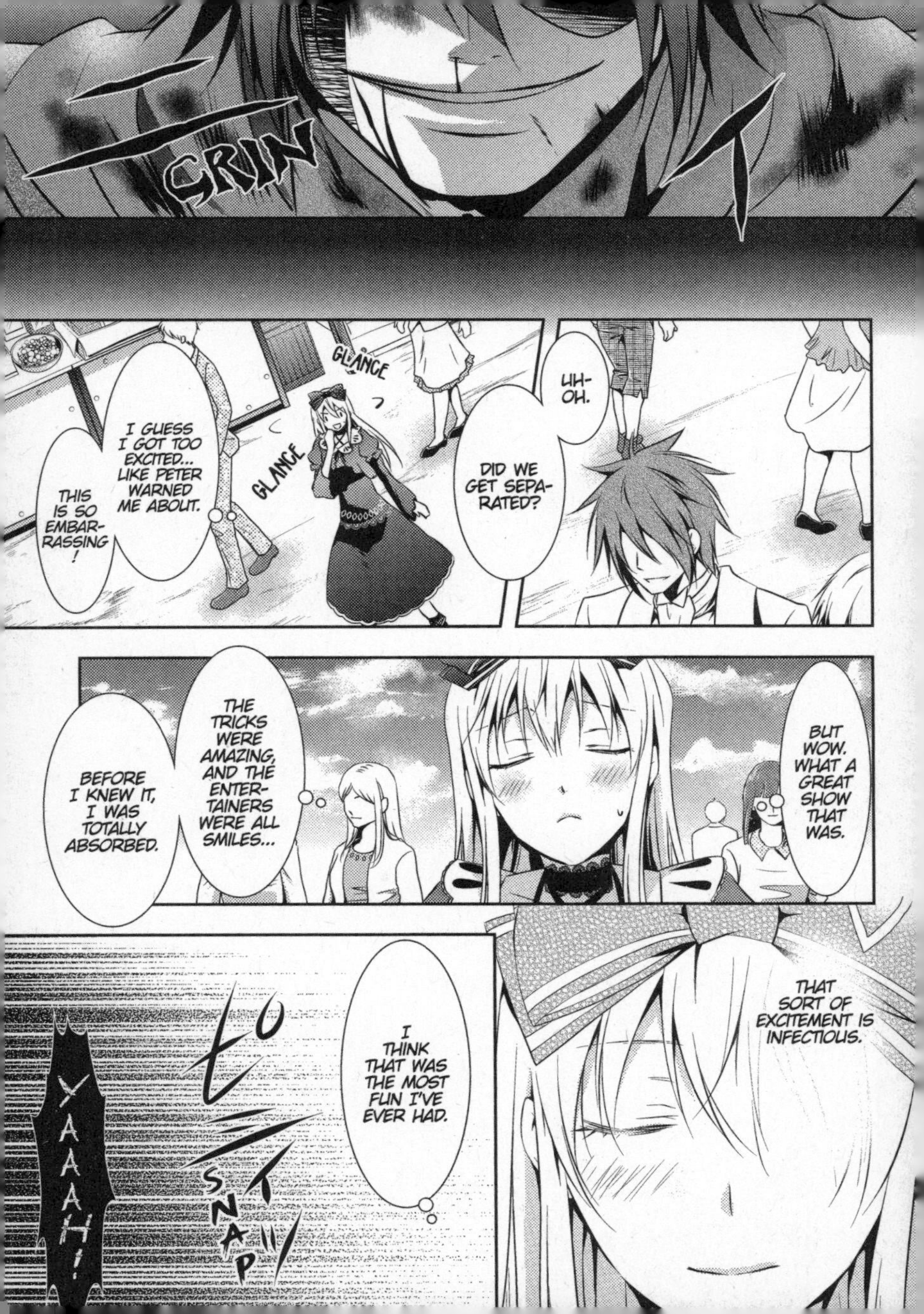
GRIN
UH-OH.
DID WE GET SEPA-RATED?
GLANCE
GLANCE
I GUESS I GOT TOO EXCITED... LIKE PETER WARNED ME ABOUT.
THIS IS SO EMBAR-RASSING!
BUT WOW. WHAT A GREAT SHOW THAT WAS.
THE TRICKS WERE AMAZING, AND THE ENTER-TAINERS WERE ALL SMILES...
BEFORE I KNEW IT, I WAS TOTALLY ABSORBED.
THAT SORT OF EXCITEMENT IS INFECTIOUS.
I THINK THAT WAS THE MOST FUN I'VE EVER HAD.
SNAP!!
YAAAH!

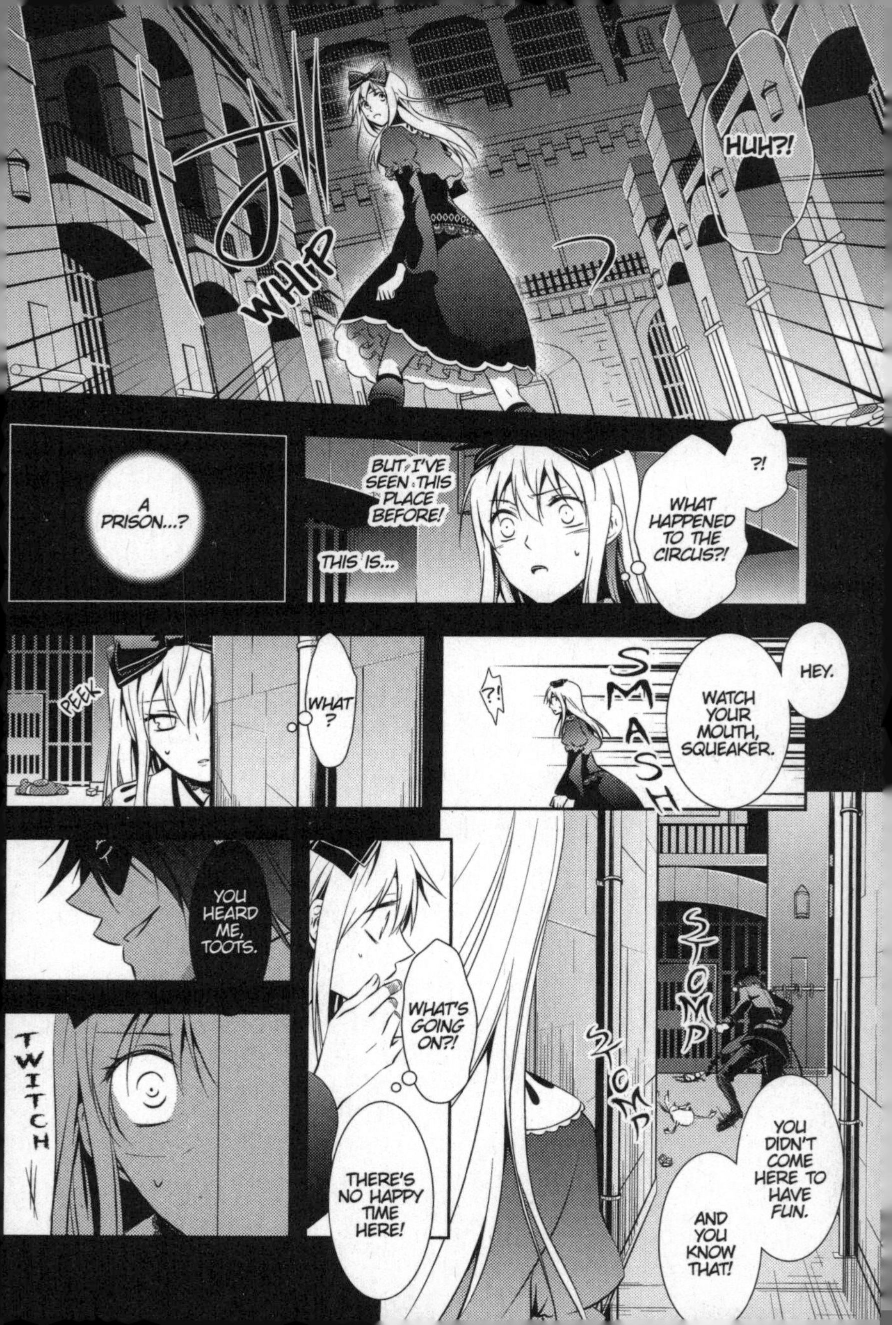
HUH?!
?
WHIP
?!
WHAT HAPPENED TO THE CIRCUS?!
BUT I'VE SEEN THIS PLACE BEFORE!
THIS IS...
A PRISON...?
HEY.
WATCH YOUR MOUTH, SQUEAKER.
SMASH
?!
WHAT?
PEEK
STOMP
STOMP
YOU DIDN'T COME HERE TO HAVE FUN.
AND YOU KNOW THAT!
WHAT'S GOING ON?!
THERE'S NO HAPPY TIME HERE!
YOU HEARD ME, TOOTS.
TWITCH

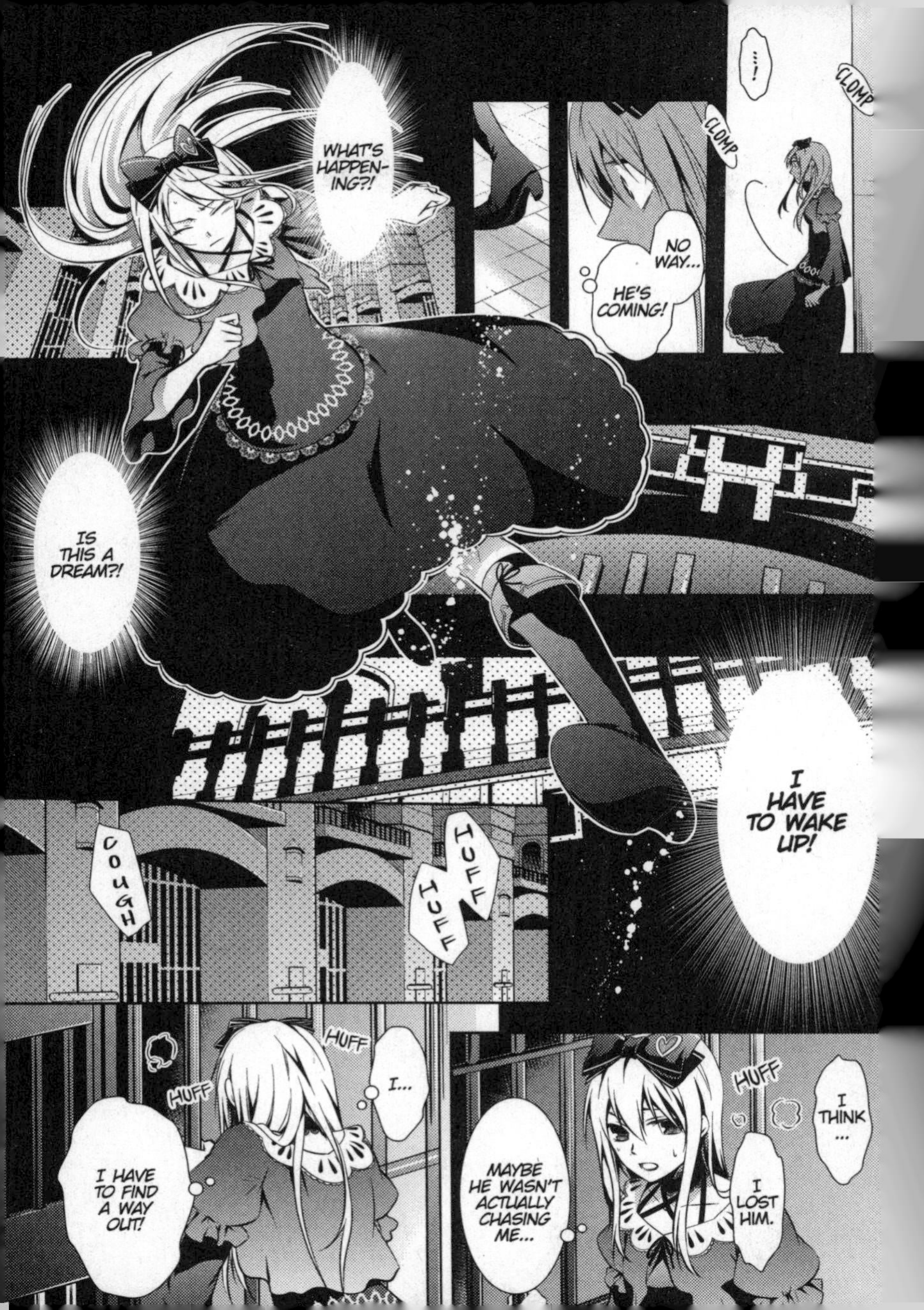
...!
CLOMP
CLOMP
NO WAY...
HE'S COMING!
WHAT'S HAPPEN-ING?!
IS THIS A DREAM?!
I HAVE TO WAKE UP!
HUFF HUFF
COUGH
HUFF
I THINK...
I LOST HIM.
MAYBE HE WASN'T ACTUALLY CHASING ME...
HUFF
HUFF
I...
I HAVE TO FIND A WAY OUT!

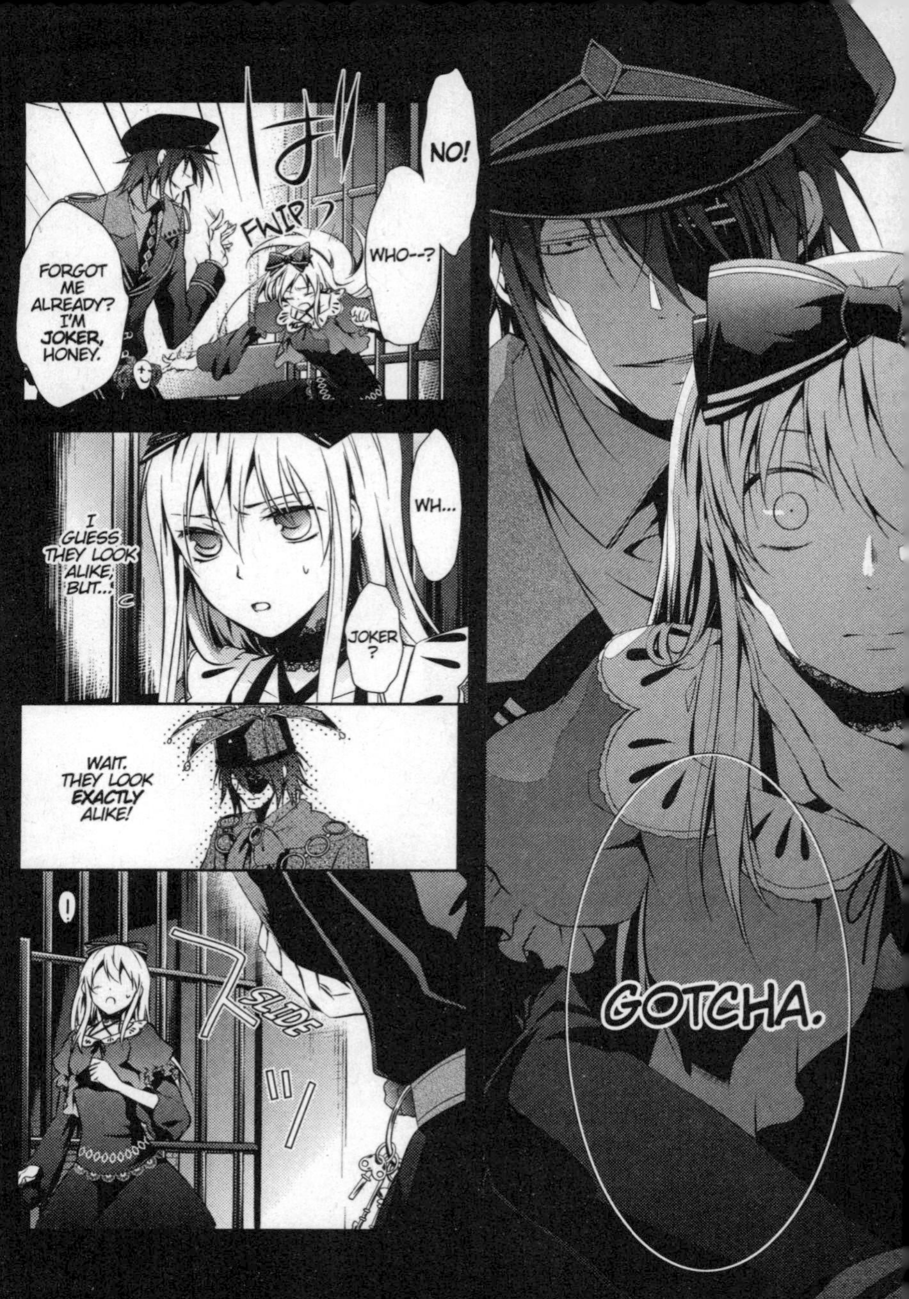
GOTCHA.
NO!
FWIP
WHO--?
FORGOT ME ALREADY? I'M JOKER, HONEY.
WH...
JOKER?
I GUESS THEY LOOK ALIKE, BUT...
WAIT. THEY LOOK EXACTLY ALIKE!
!
SLIDE

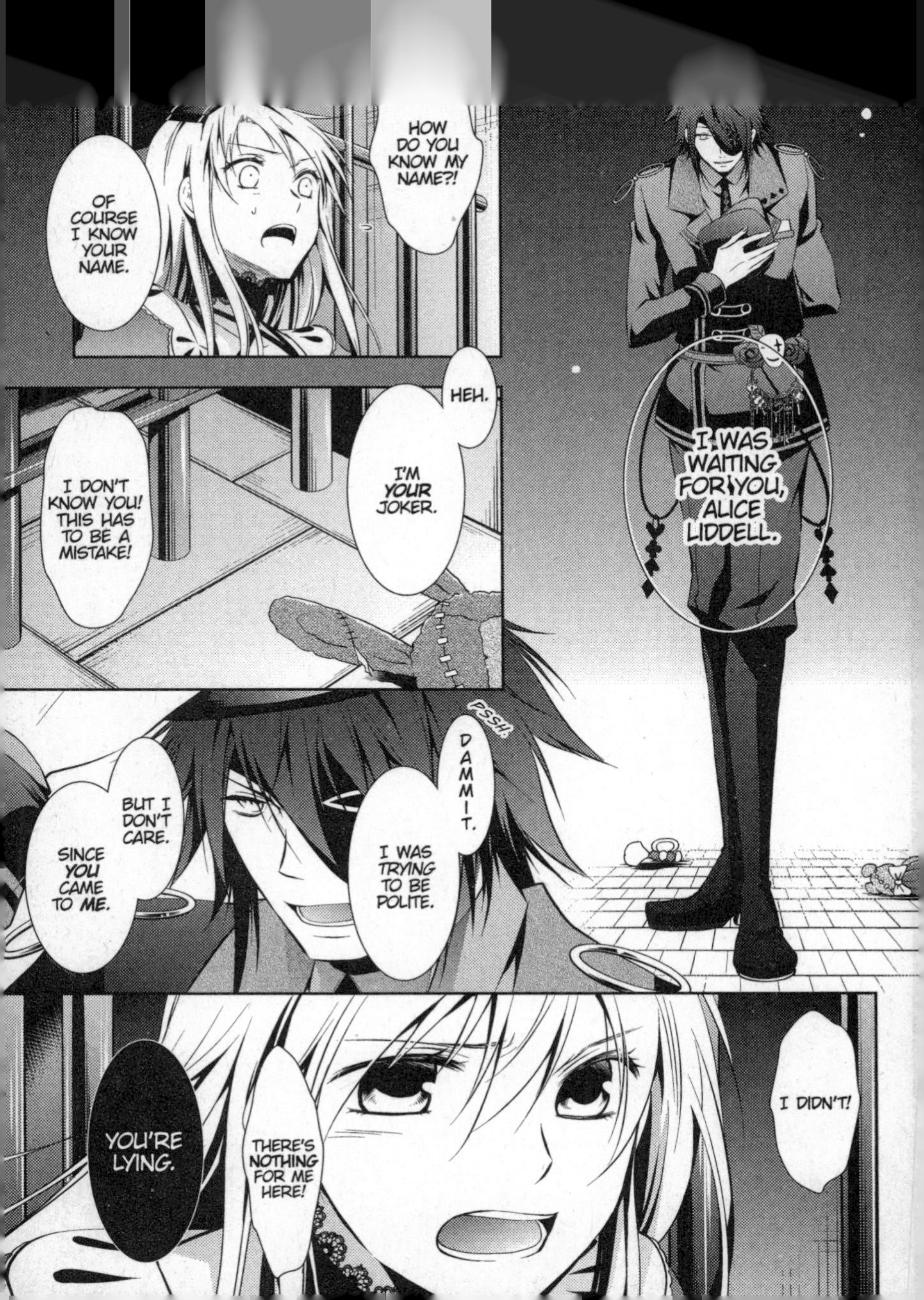
I WAS WAITING FOR YOU, ALICE LIDDELL.
HOW DO YOU KNOW MY NAME?!
OF COURSE I KNOW YOUR NAME.
HEH.
I'M YOUR JOKER.
I DON'T KNOW YOU! THIS HAS TO BE A MISTAKE!
PSSH.
DAMMIT.
I WAS TRYING TO BE POLITE.
BUT I DON'T CARE.
SINCE YOU CAME TO ME.
I DIDN'T!
THERE'S NOTHING FOR ME HERE!
YOU'RE LYING.

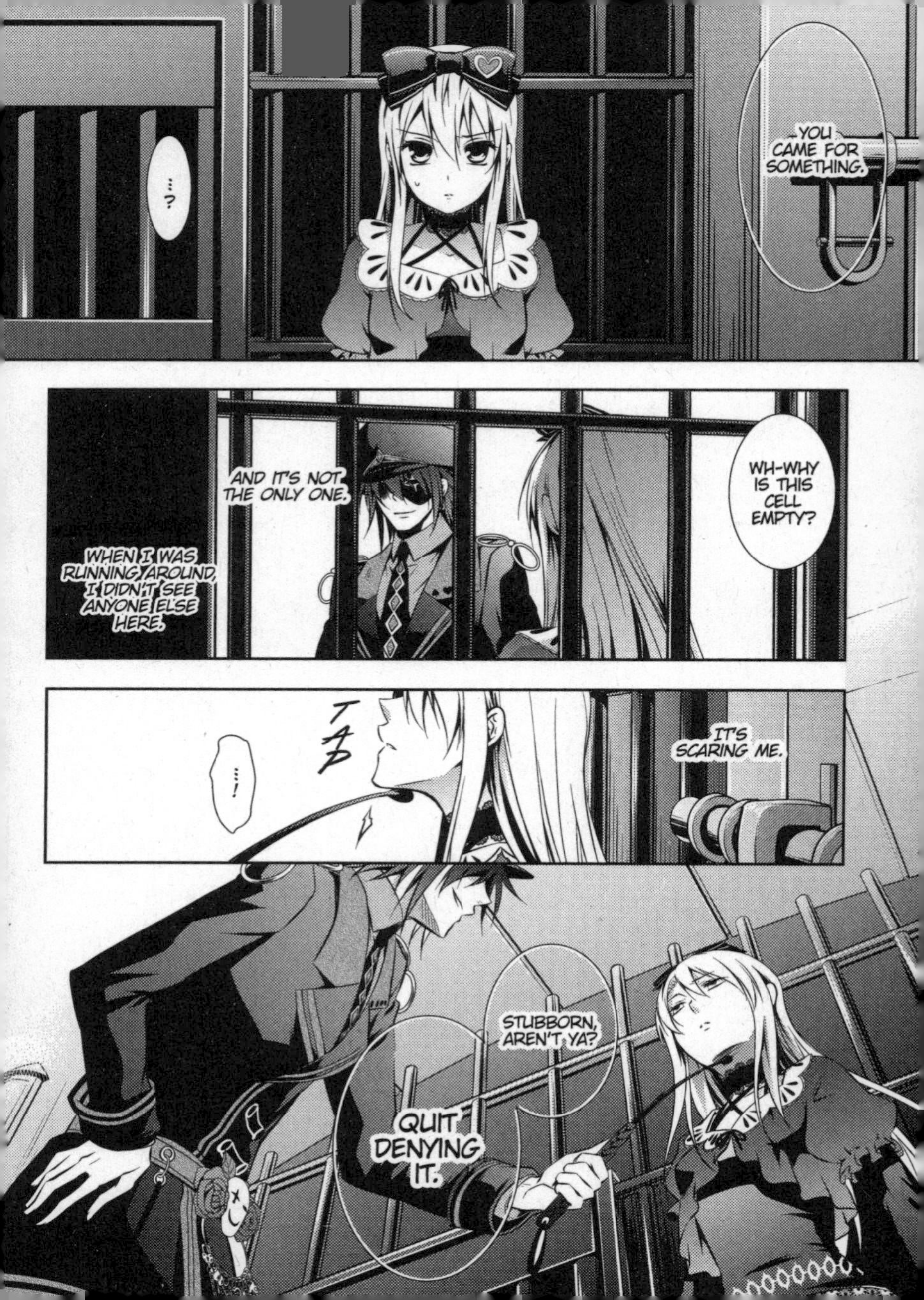
...YOU CAME FOR SOMETHING.
...?
WH-WHY IS THIS CELL EMPTY?
AND IT'S NOT THE ONLY ONE.
WHEN I WAS RUNNING AROUND, I DIDN'T SEE ANYONE ELSE HERE.
IT'S SCARING ME.
TAP
...!
STUBBORN, AREN'T YA?
QUIT DENYING IT.

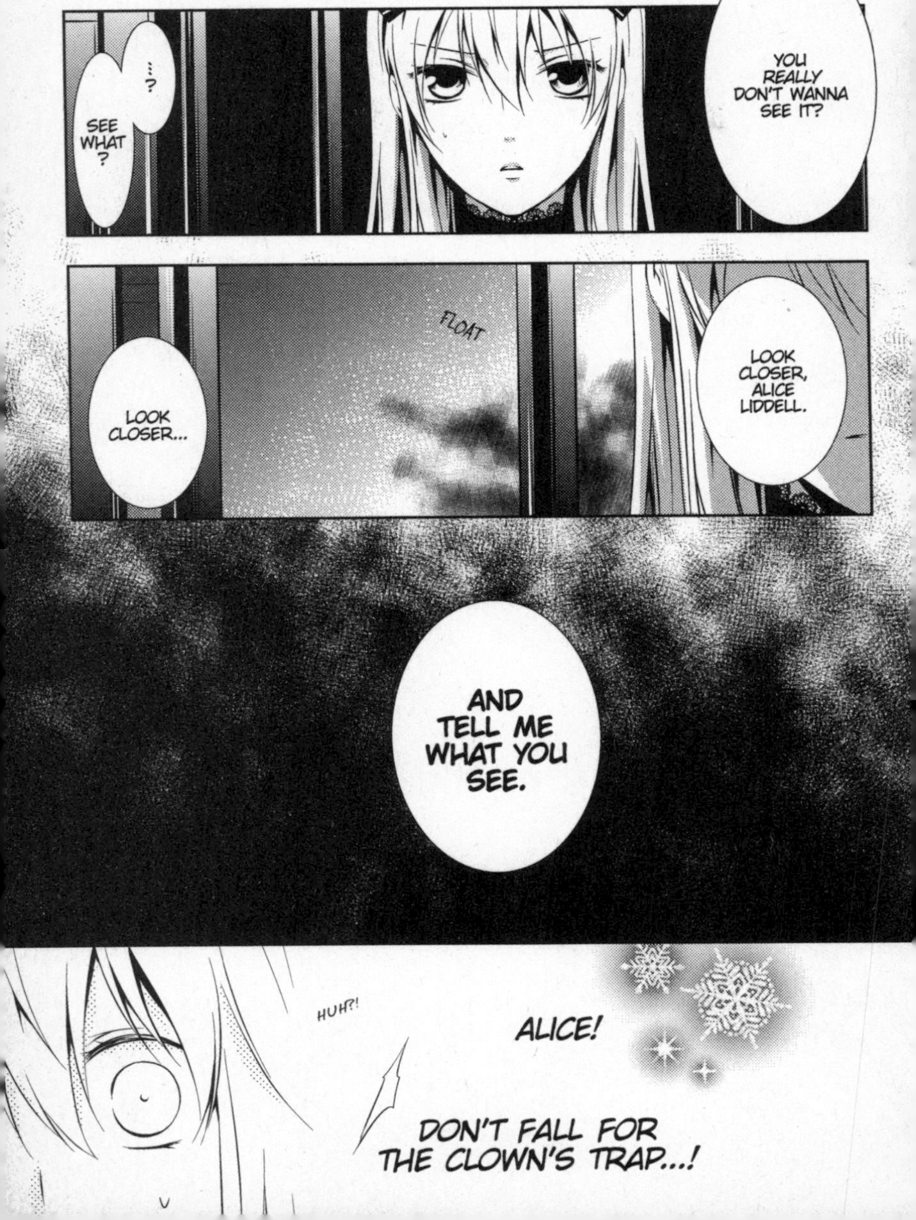
YOU REALLY DON'T WANNA SEE IT?
...?
SEE WHAT?
LOOK CLOSER, ALICE LIDDELL.
FLOAT
LOOK CLOSER...
AND TELL ME WHAT YOU SEE.
ALICE!
HUH?!
DON'T FALL FOR THE CLOWN'S TRAP...!

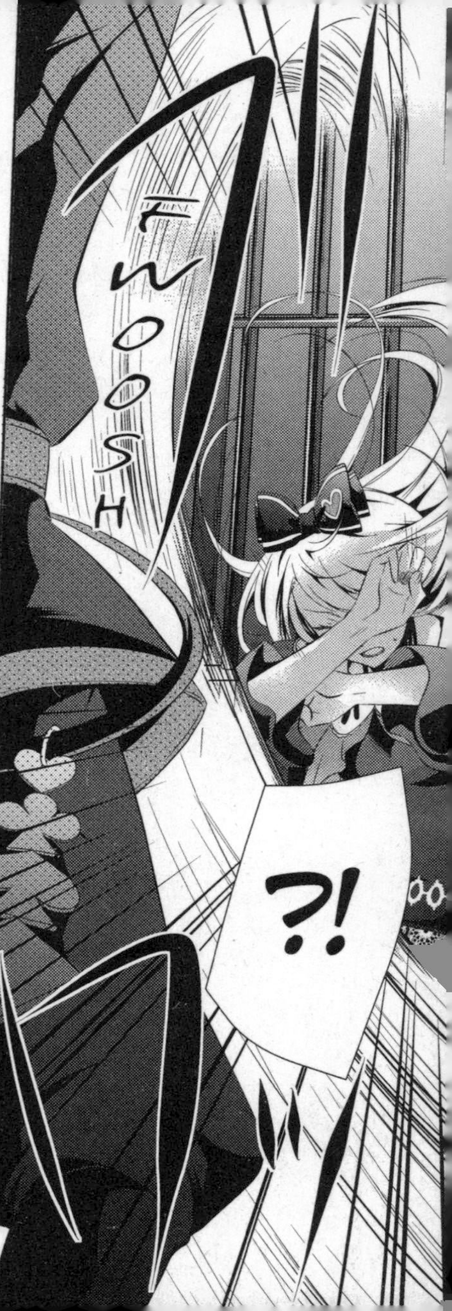
FWOOSH
?!
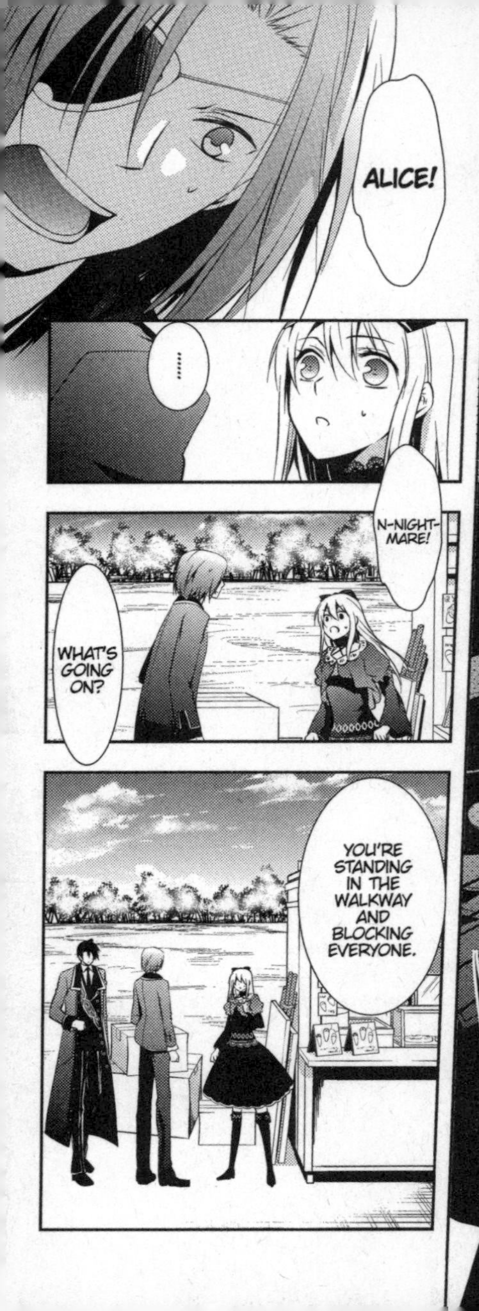
ALICE!
......
N-NIGHT-MARE!
WHAT'S GOING ON?
YOU'RE STANDING IN THE WALKWAY AND BLOCKING EVERYONE.

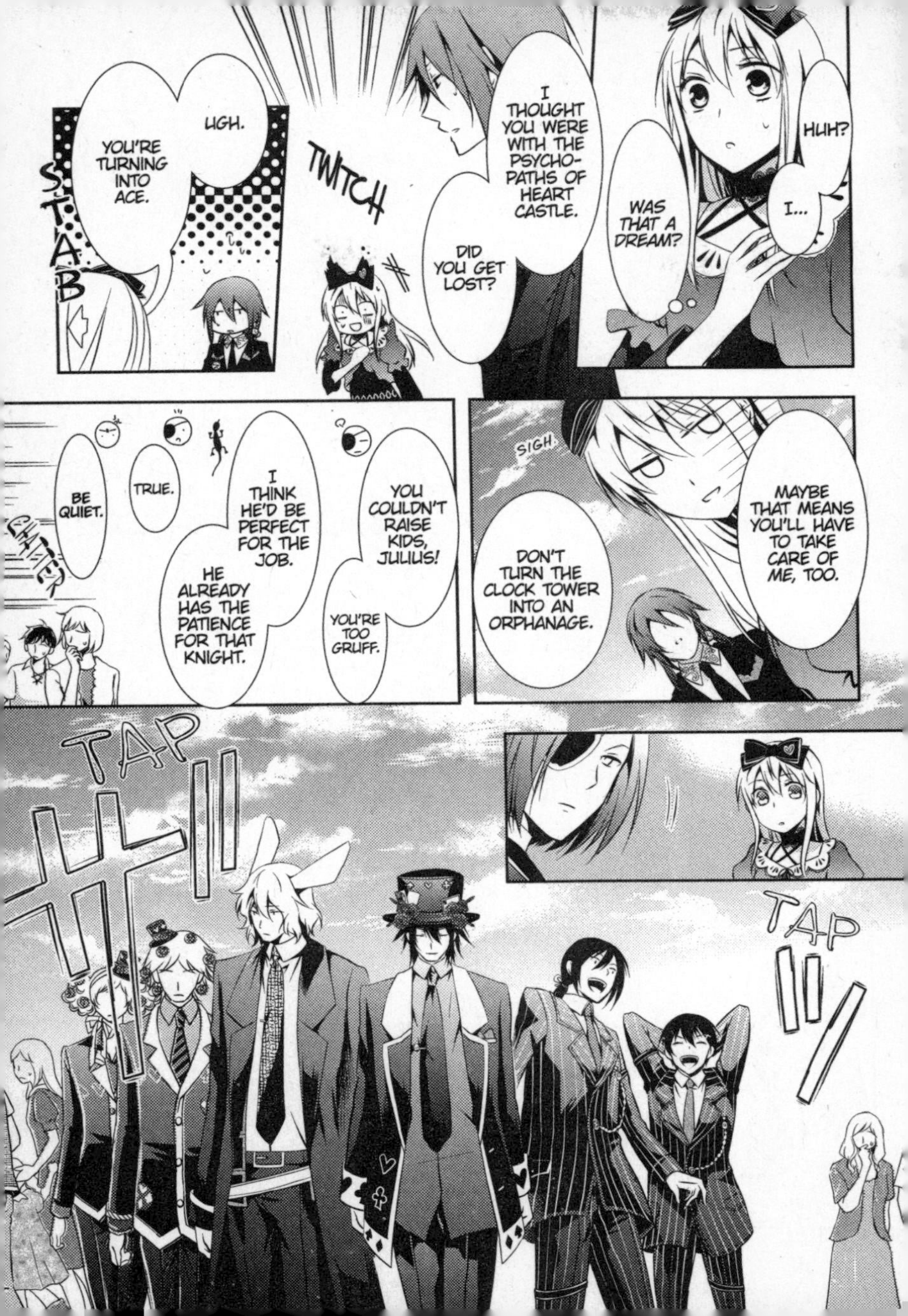
HUH?
I...
WAS THAT A DREAM?
I THOUGHT YOU WERE WITH THE PSYCHO-PATHS OF HEART CASTLE.
DID YOU GET LOST?
TWITCH
UGH.
YOU'RE TURNING INTO ACE.
STAB
SIGH.
MAYBE THAT MEANS YOU'LL HAVE TO TAKE CARE OF ME, TOO.
DON'T TURN THE CLOCK TOWER INTO AN ORPHANAGE.
YOU COULDN'T RAISE KIDS, JULIUS!
YOU'RE TOO GRUFF.
I THINK HE'D BE PERFECT FOR THE JOB.
HE ALREADY HAS THE PATIENCE FOR THAT KNIGHT.
TRUE.
BE QUIET.
CHATTER
TAP
TAP

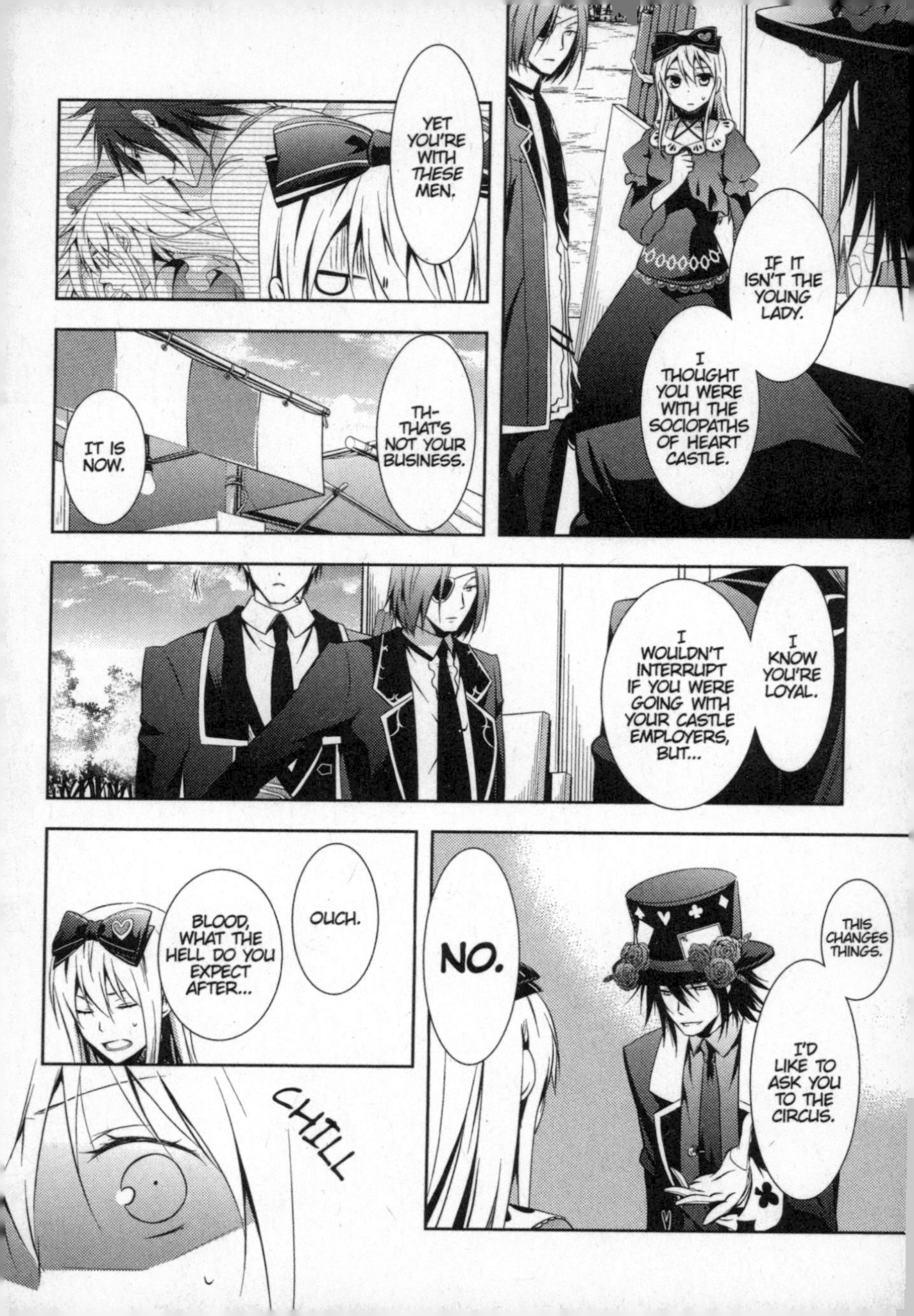

IF IT ISN'T THE YOUNG LADY.
I THOUGHT YOU WERE WITH THE SOCIOPATHS OF HEART CASTLE.
YET YOU'RE WITH THESE MEN.
TH-THAT'S NOT YOUR BUSINESS.
IT IS NOW.
I KNOW YOU'RE LOYAL.
I WOULDN'T INTERRUPT IF YOU WERE GOING WITH YOUR CASTLE EMPLOYERS, BUT...
THIS CHANGES THINGS.
I'D LIKE TO ASK YOU TO THE CIRCUS.
NO.
OUCH.
BLOOD, WHAT THE HELL DO YOU EXPECT AFTER...
CHILL

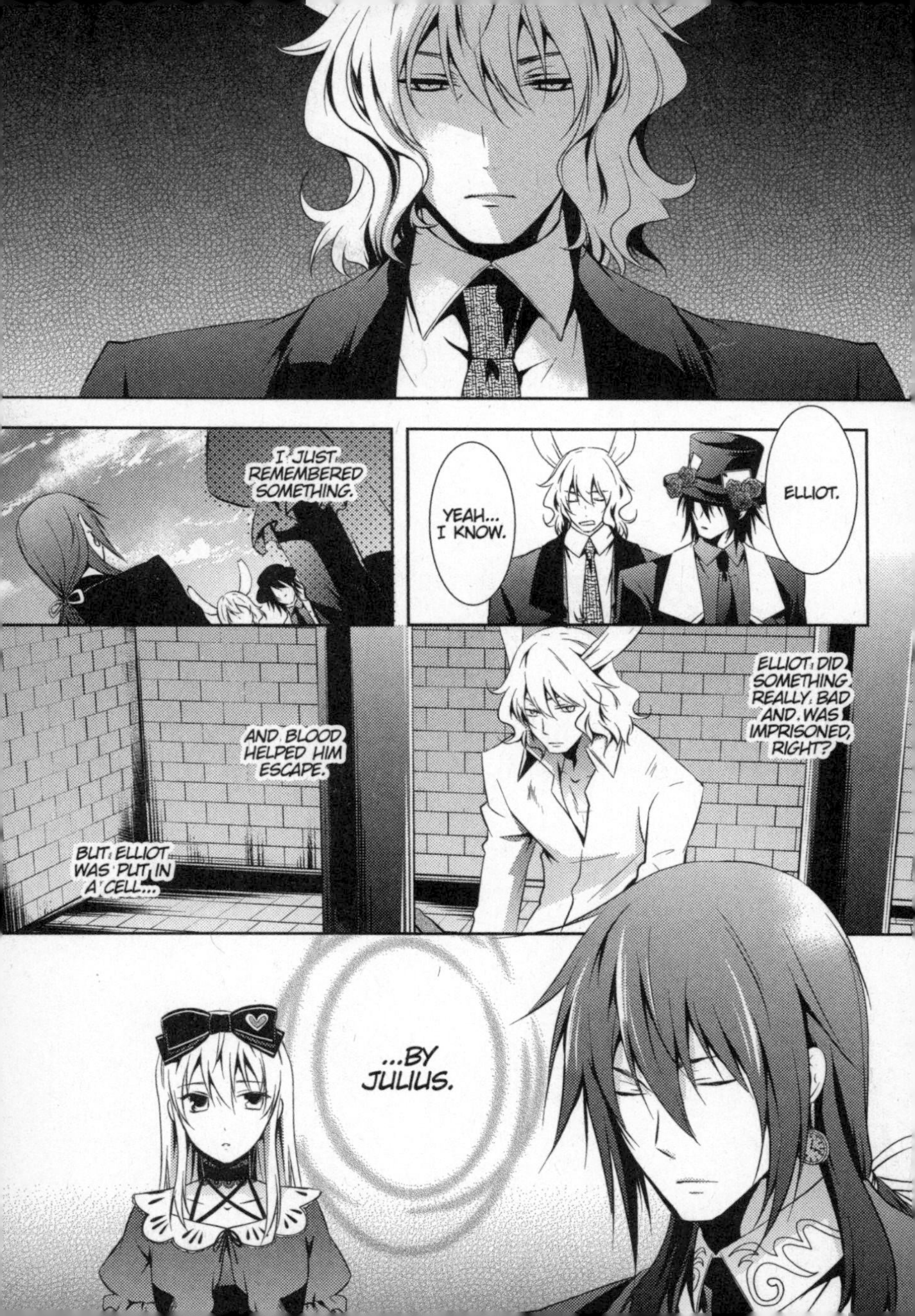
ELLIOT.
YEAH... I KNOW.
I JUST REMEMBERED SOMETHING.
ELLIOT DID SOMETHING REALLY BAD AND WAS IMPRISONED, RIGHT?
AND BLOOD HELPED HIM ESCAPE.
BUT ELLIOT WAS PUT IN A CELL...
...BY JULIUS.

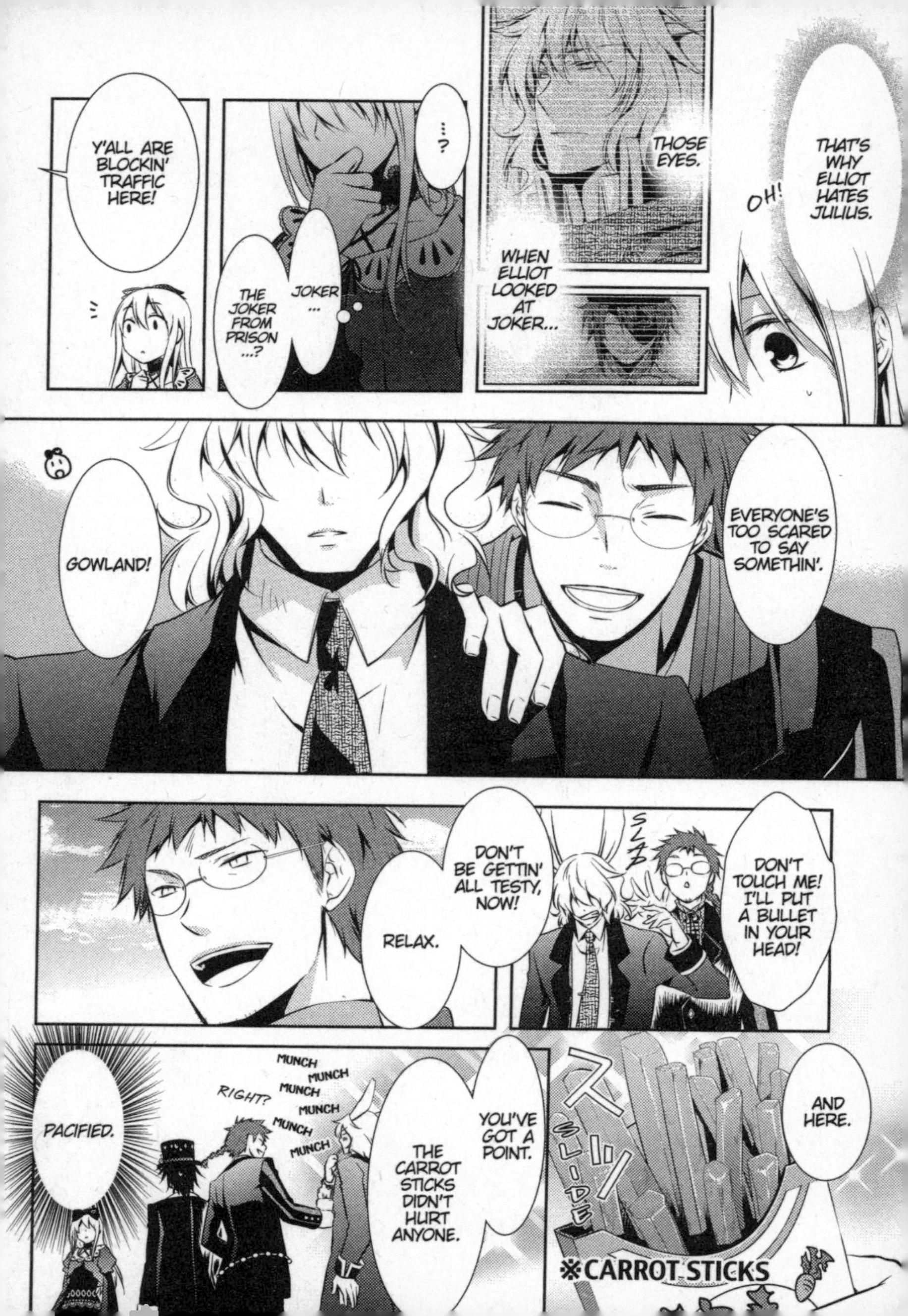
THAT'S WHY ELLIOT HATES JULIUS.
OH!
THOSE EYES.
WHEN ELLIOT LOOKED AT JOKER...
...?
JOKER...
THE JOKER FROM PRISON...?
Y'ALL ARE BLOCKIN' TRAFFIC HERE!
EVERYONE'S TOO SCARED TO SAY SOMETHIN'.
GOWLAND!
DON'T TOUCH ME! I'LL PUT A BULLET IN YOUR HEAD!
SLAP
DON'T BE GETTIN' ALL TESTY, NOW!
RELAX.
AND HERE.
SLI-DE
※CARROT STICKS
YOU'VE GOT A POINT.
THE CARROT STICKS DIDN'T HURT ANYONE.
RIGHT?
MUNCH
MUNCH
MUNCH
MUNCH
MUNCH
MUNCH
PACIFIED.

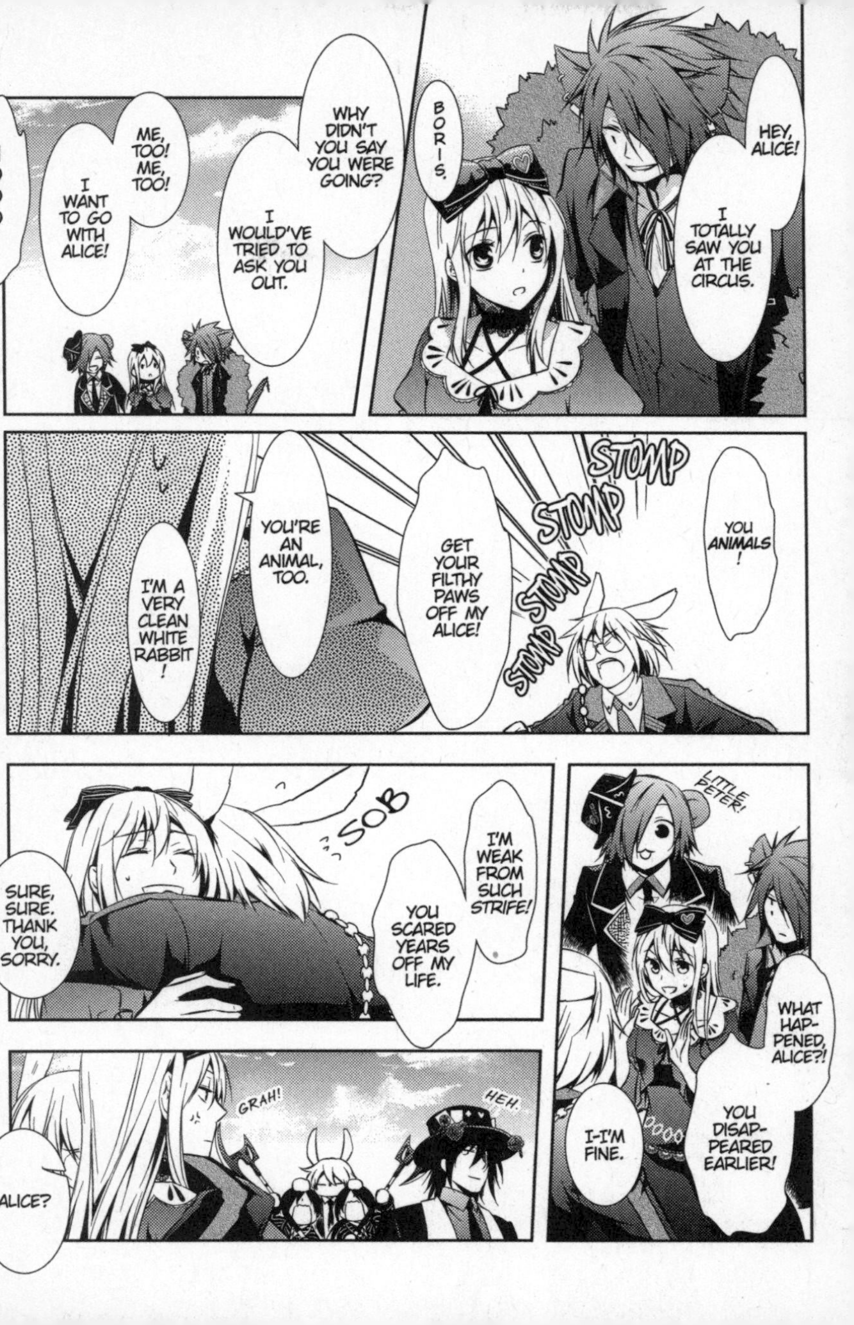
HEY, ALICE!
I TOTALLY SAW YOU AT THE CIRCUS.
BORIS.
WHY DIDN'T YOU SAY YOU WERE GOING?
I WOULD'VE TRIED TO ASK YOU OUT.
ME, TOO! ME, TOO!
I WANT TO GO WITH ALICE!
NOOOO!
YOU ANIMALS!
STOMP
STOMP
STOMP
STOMP
STOMP
GET YOUR FILTHY PAWS OFF MY ALICE!
YOU'RE AN ANIMAL, TOO.
I'M A VERY CLEAN WHITE RABBIT!
LITTLE PETER!
WHAT HAPPENED, ALICE?!
YOU DISAPPEARED EARLIER!
I-I'M FINE.
SOB
I'M WEAK FROM SUCH STRIFE!
YOU SCARED YEARS OFF MY LIFE.
SURE, SURE. THANK YOU, SORRY.
HEH.
GRAH!
ALICE?

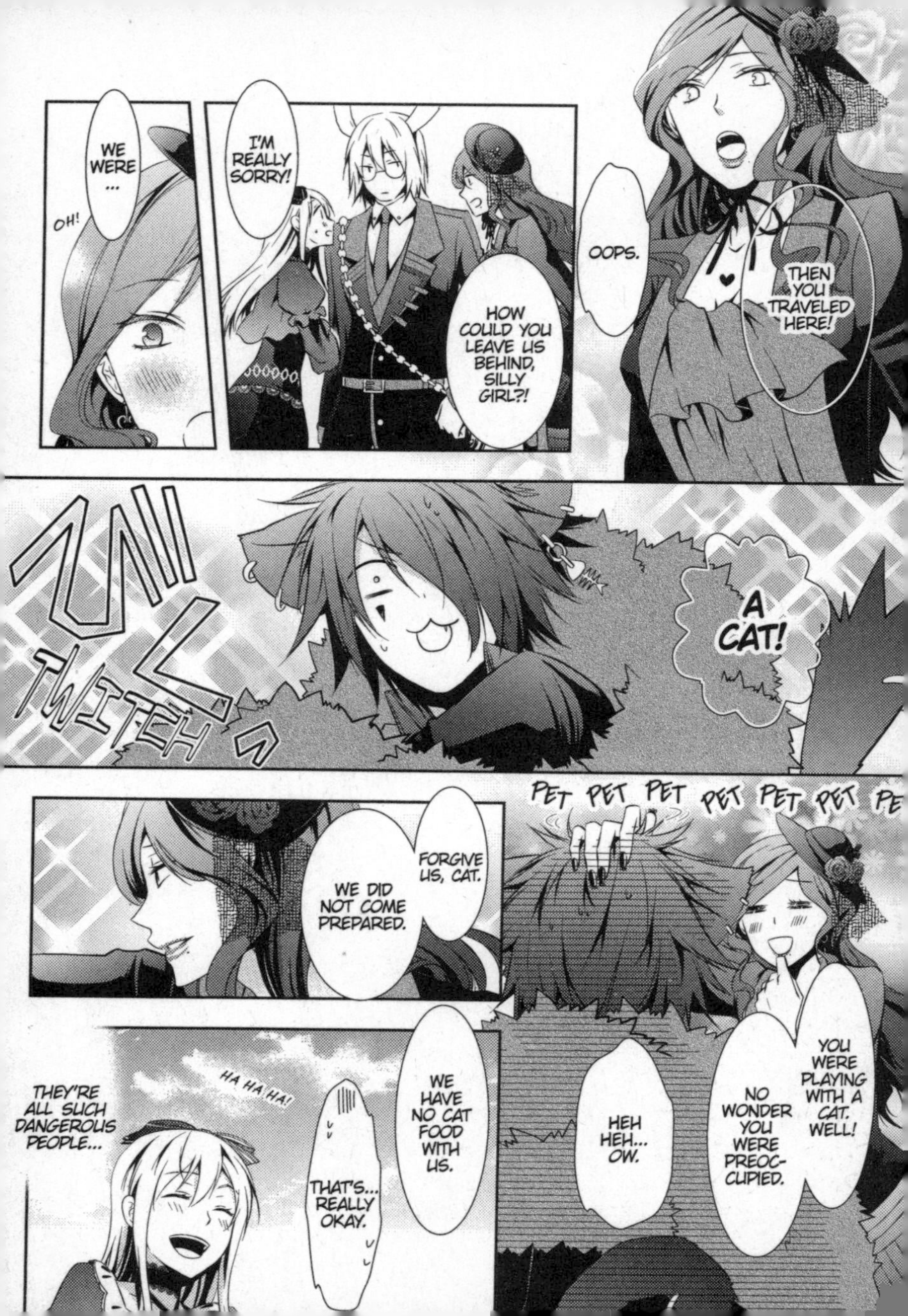
OOPS.
THEN YOU TRAVELED HERE!
HOW COULD YOU LEAVE US BEHIND, SILLY GIRL?!
I'M REALLY SORRY!
WE WERE...
OH!
A CAT!
TWITCH
PET PET PET PET PET PET PE
YOU WERE PLAYING WITH A CAT. WELL!
NO WONDER YOU WERE PREOCCUPIED.
HEH HEH... OW.
FORGIVE US, CAT.
WE DID NOT COME PREPARED.
WE HAVE NO CAT FOOD WITH US.
THAT'S... REALLY OKAY.
HA HA HA!
THEY'RE ALL SUCH DANGEROUS PEOPLE...

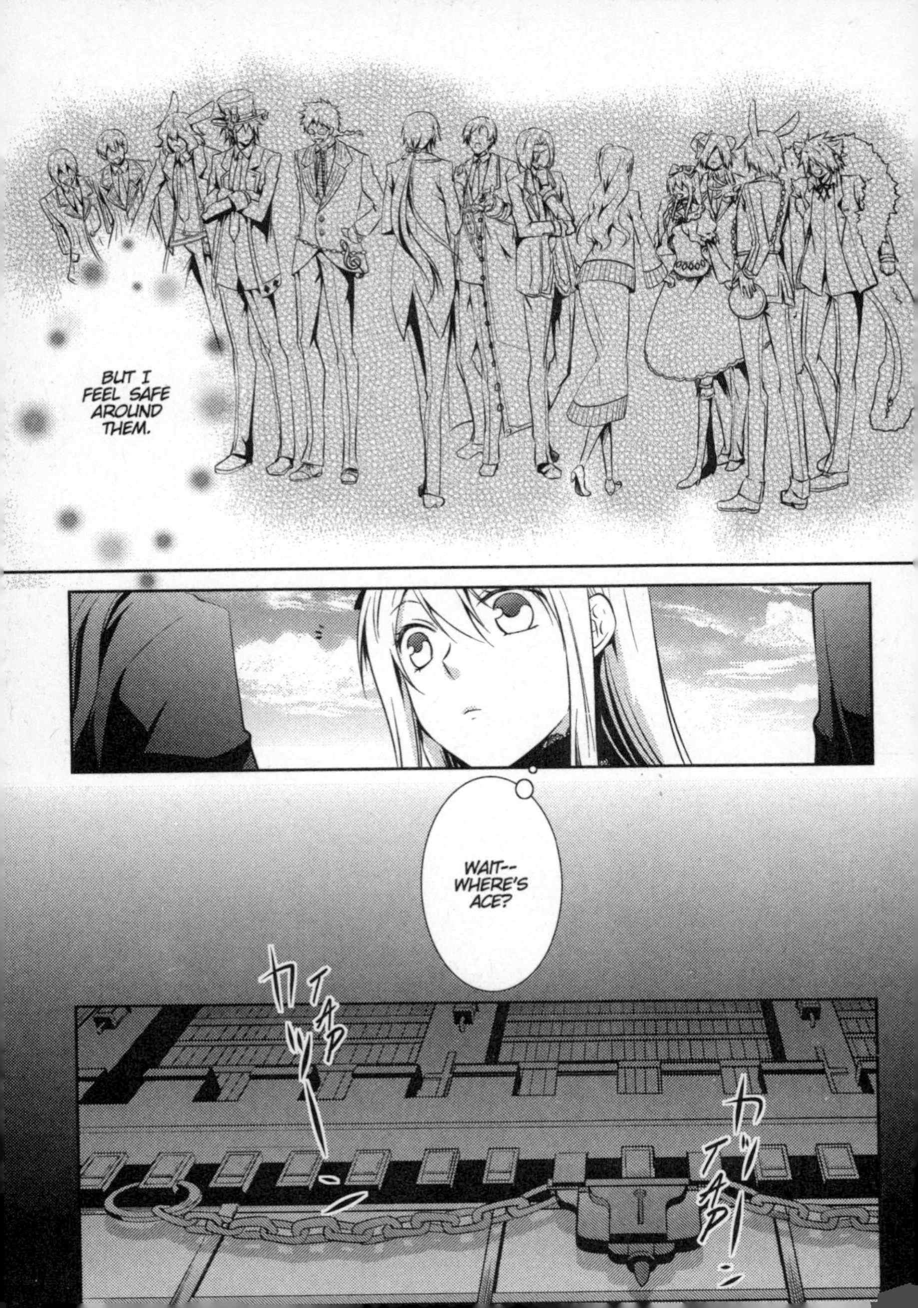
BUT I FEEL SAFE AROUND THEM.
WAIT-- WHERE'S ACE?

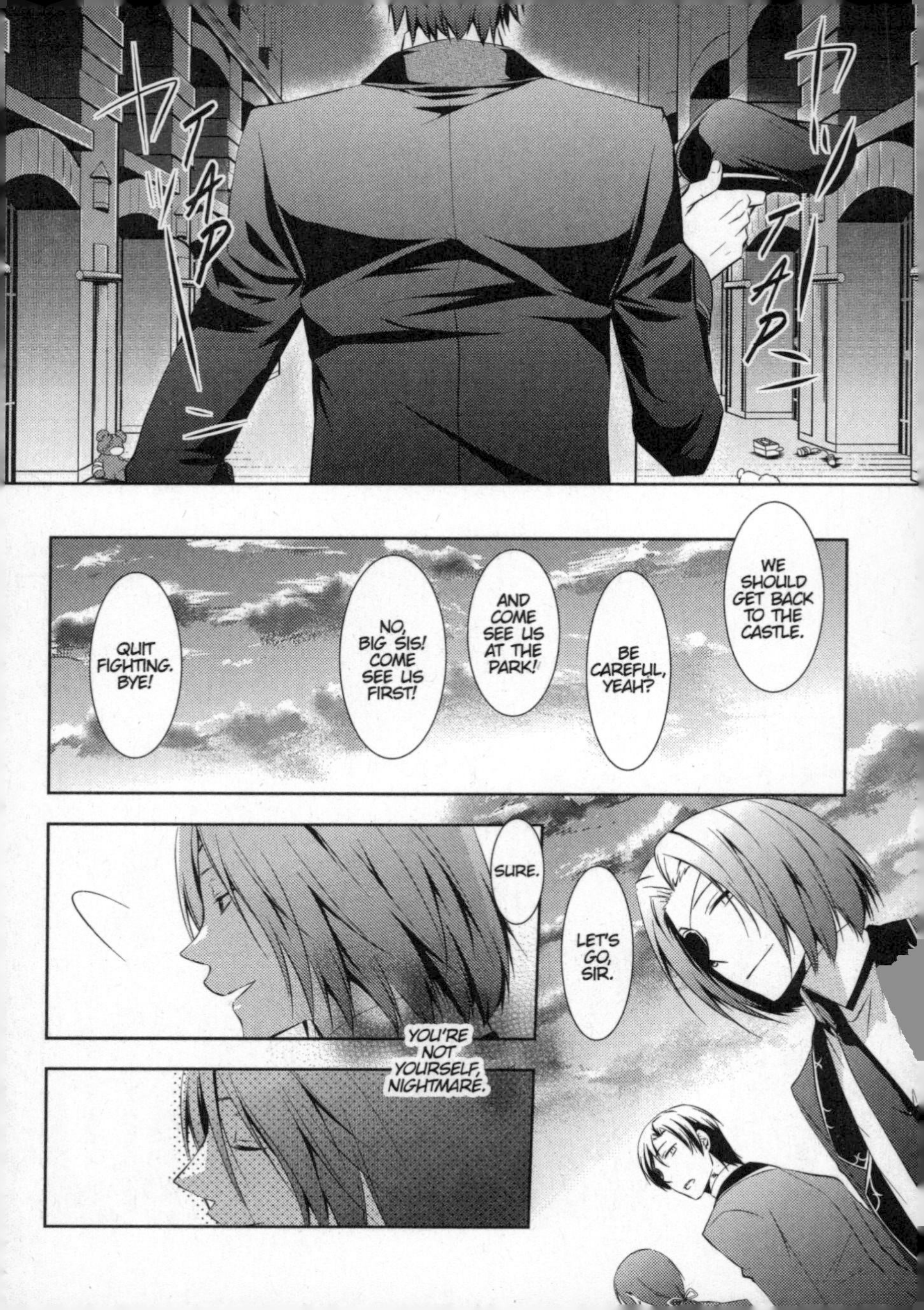
TAP
TAP
WE SHOULD GET BACK TO THE CASTLE.
BE CAREFUL, YEAH?
AND COME SEE US AT THE PARK!
NO, BIG SIS! COME SEE US FIRST!
QUIT FIGHTING. BYE!
LET'S GO, SIR.
SURE.
YOU'RE NOT YOURSELF, NIGHTMARE.

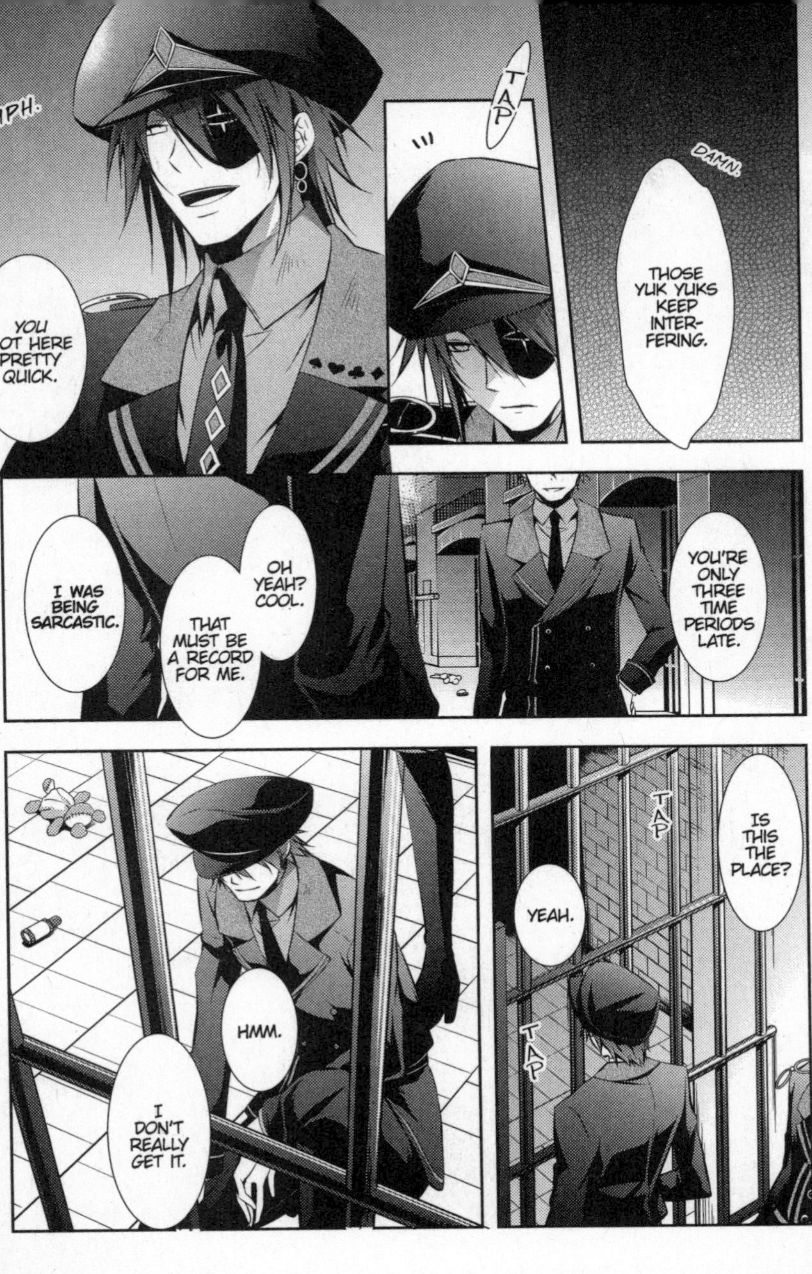
DAMN.
THOSE YUK YUKS KEEP INTER-FERING.
TAP
HMPH.
YOU GOT HERE PRETTY QUICK.
YOU'RE ONLY THREE TIME PERIODS LATE.
OH YEAH? COOL.
THAT MUST BE A RECORD FOR ME.
I WAS BEING SARCASTIC.
IS THIS THE PLACE?
TAP
YEAH.
TAP
HMM.
I DON'T REALLY GET IT.

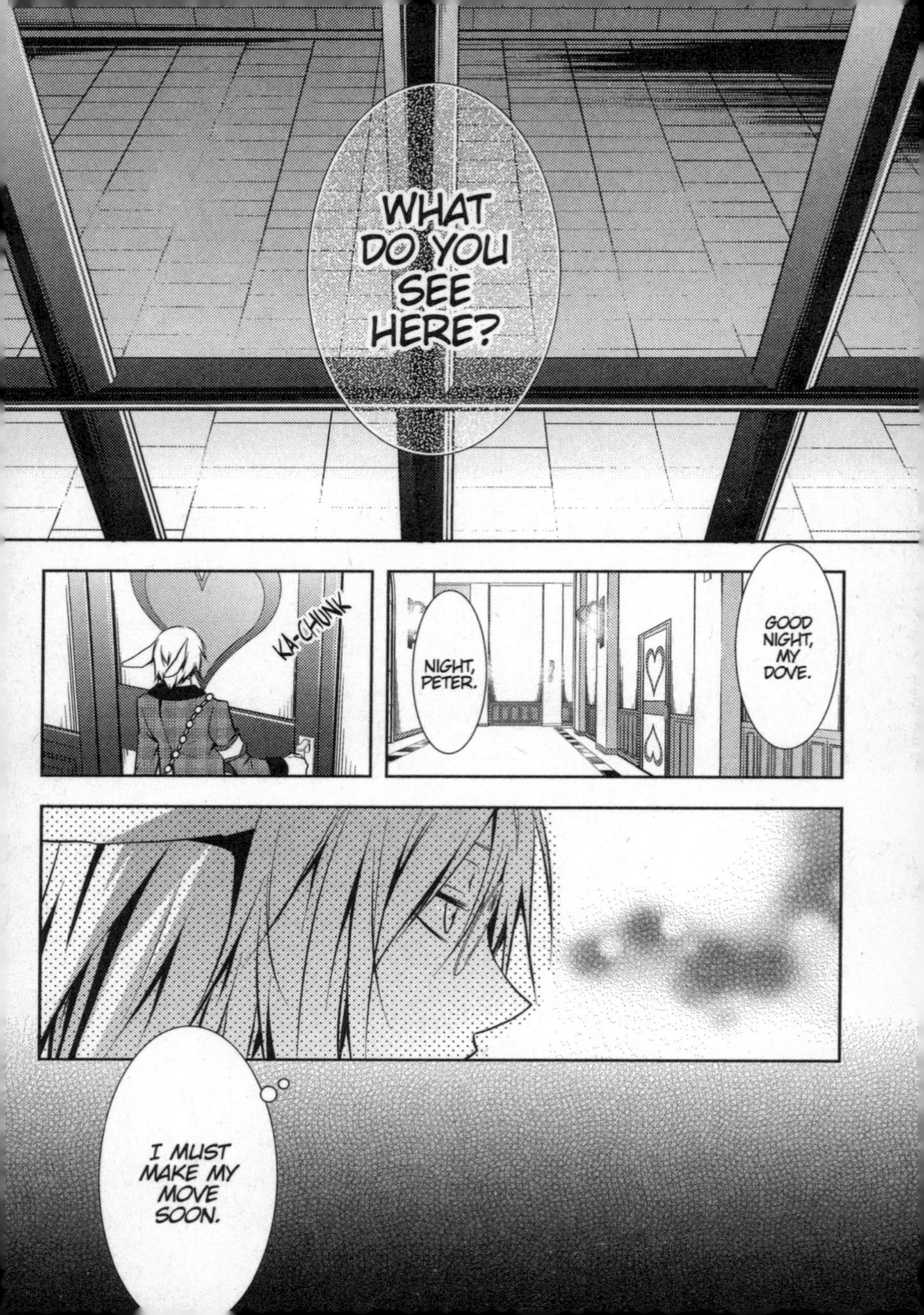
WHAT DO YOU SEE HERE?
GOOD NIGHT, MY DOVE.
NIGHT, PETER.
KA-CHUNK
I MUST MAKE MY MOVE SOON.

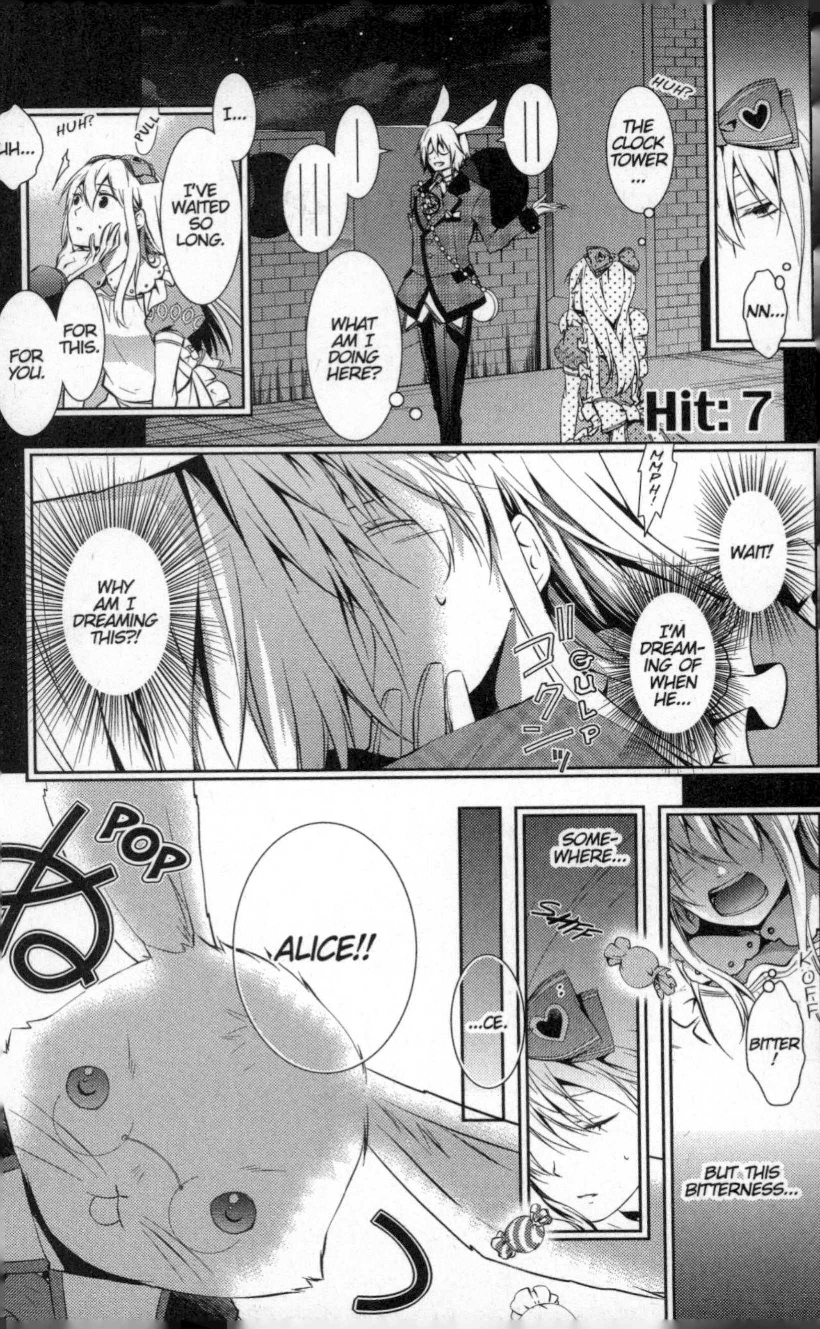
NN...
HUH?
THE CLOCK TOWER ...
WHAT AM I DOING HERE?
Hit: 7
I...
I'VE WAITED SO LONG.
PULL
HUH?
UH...
FOR THIS.
FOR YOU.
MMPH!
WAIT!
I'M DREAMING OF WHEN HE...
GULP
WHY AM I DREAMING THIS?!
KOFF
BITTER!
SOME-WHERE...
SNIFF
...CE.
BUT THIS BITTERNESS...
ALICE!!
POP

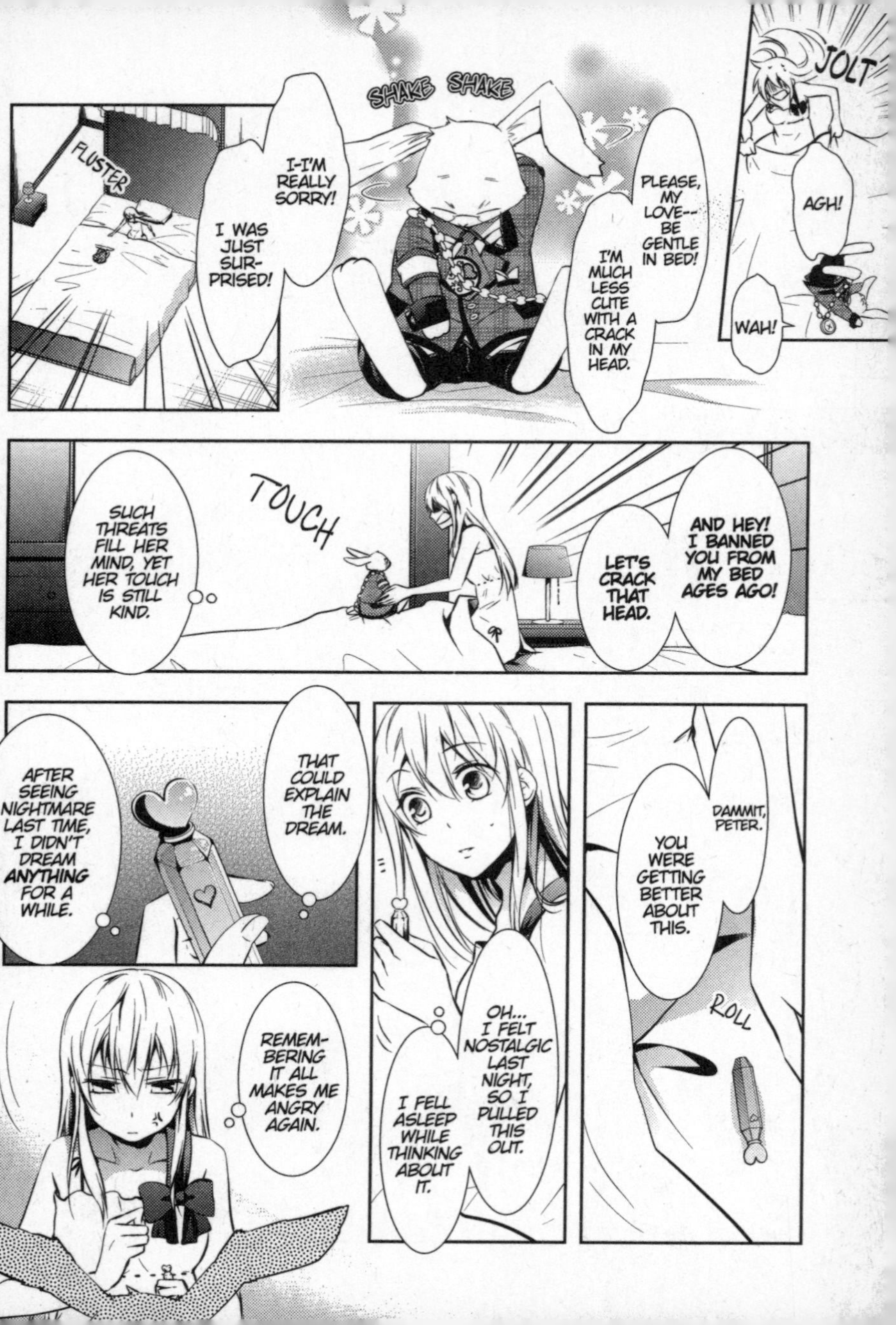
JOLT
AGH!
WAH!
SHAKE SHAKE
PLEASE, MY LOVE-- BE GENTLE IN BED!
I'M MUCH LESS CUTE WITH A CRACK IN MY HEAD.
I-I'M REALLY SORRY!
I WAS JUST SUR-PRISED!
FLUSTER
AND HEY! I BANNED YOU FROM MY BED AGES AGO!
LET'S CRACK THAT HEAD.
TOUCH
SUCH THREATS FILL HER MIND, YET HER TOUCH IS STILL KIND.
DAMMIT, PETER.
YOU WERE GETTING BETTER ABOUT THIS.
ROLL
OH... I FELT NOSTALGIC LAST NIGHT, SO I PULLED THIS OUT.
I FELL ASLEEP WHILE THINKING ABOUT IT.
THAT COULD EXPLAIN THE DREAM.
AFTER SEEING NIGHTMARE LAST TIME, I DIDN'T DREAM **ANYTHING** FOR A WHILE.
REMEMB-BERING IT ALL MAKES ME ANGRY AGAIN.

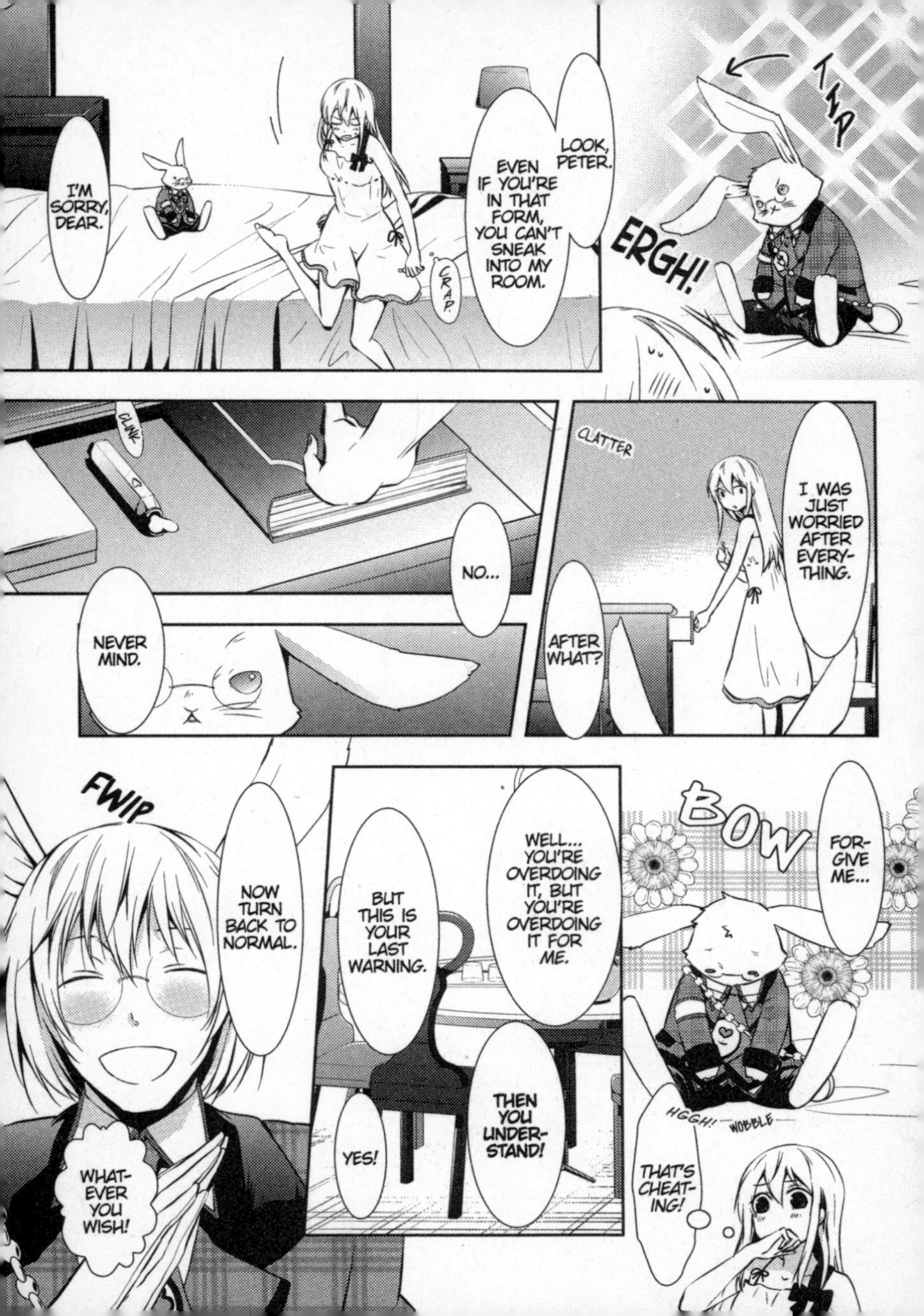
TMP
ERGH!
LOOK, PETER.
EVEN IF YOU'RE IN THAT FORM, YOU CAN'T SNEAK INTO MY ROOM.
CRAP.
I'M SORRY, DEAR.
CLATTER
I WAS JUST WORRIED AFTER EVERY-THING.
AFTER WHAT?
CLINK
NO...
NEVER MIND.
BOW
FOR-GIVE ME...
WELL... YOU'RE OVERDOING IT, BUT YOU'RE OVERDOING IT FOR ME.
BUT THIS IS YOUR LAST WARNING.
THEN YOU UNDER-STAND!
YES!
HGGH!
WOBBLE
THAT'S CHEAT-ING!
FWIP
NOW TURN BACK TO NORMAL.
WHAT-EVER YOU WISH!

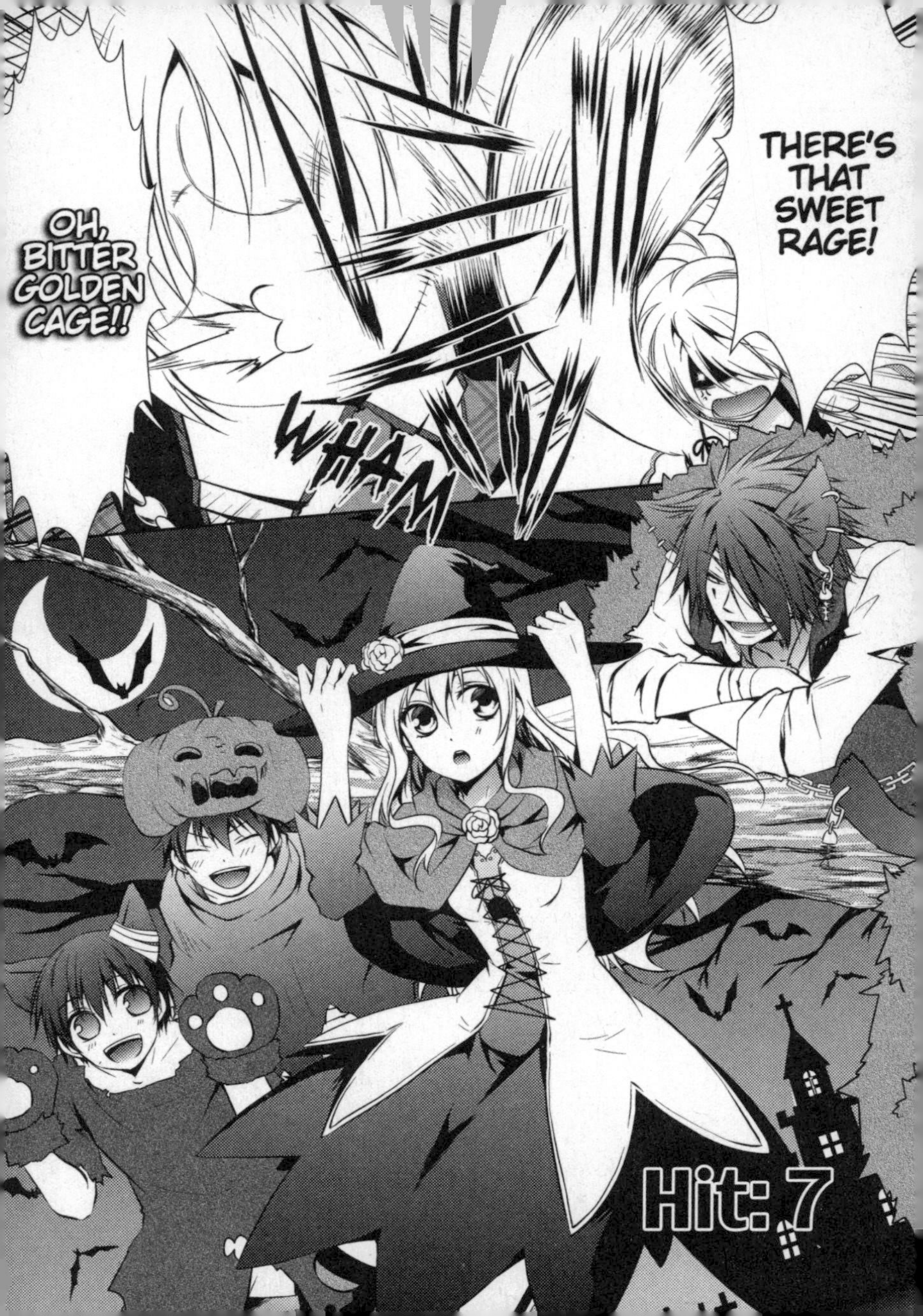
THERE'S THAT SWEET RAGE!
OH, BITTER GOLDEN CAGE!!
WHAM
Hit: 7

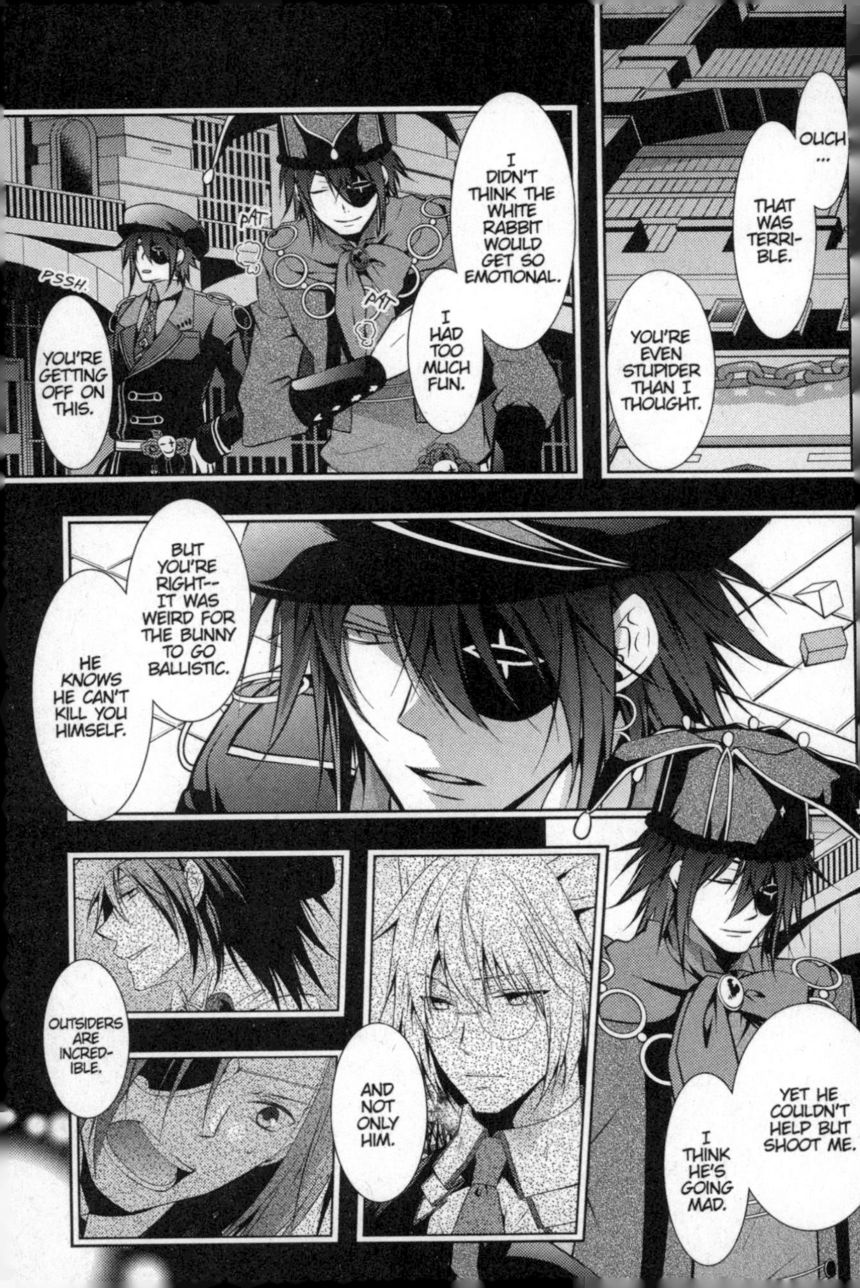
OUCH ...
THAT WAS TERRIBLE.
YOU'RE EVEN STUPIDER THAN I THOUGHT.
I DIDN'T THINK THE WHITE RABBIT WOULD GET SO EMOTIONAL.
PAT
I HAD TOO MUCH FUN.
PAT
PSSH.
YOU'RE GETTING OFF ON THIS.
BUT YOU'RE RIGHT-- IT WAS WEIRD FOR THE BUNNY TO GO BALLISTIC.
HE KNOWS HE CAN'T KILL YOU HIMSELF.
YET HE COULDN'T HELP BUT SHOOT ME.
I THINK HE'S GOING MAD.
AND NOT ONLY HIM.
OUTSIDERS ARE INCREDIBLE.

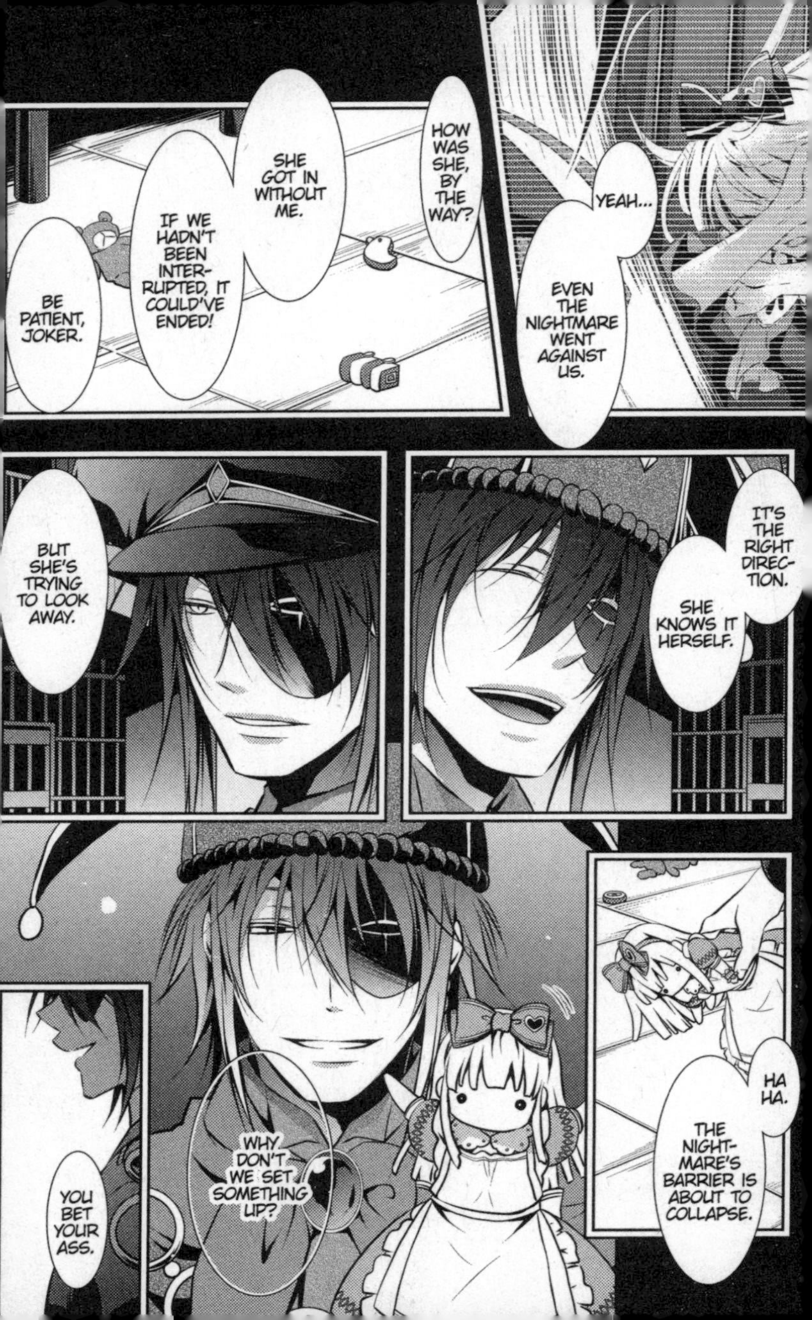
YEAH...
EVEN THE NIGHTMARE WENT AGAINST US.
HOW WAS SHE, BY THE WAY?
SHE GOT IN WITHOUT ME.
IF WE HADN'T BEEN INTER-RUPTED, IT COULD'VE ENDED!
BE PATIENT, JOKER.
IT'S THE RIGHT DIREC-TION.
SHE KNOWS IT HERSELF.
BUT SHE'S TRYING TO LOOK AWAY.
HA HA.
THE NIGHT-MARE'S BARRIER IS ABOUT TO COLLAPSE.
WHY DON'T WE SET SOMETHING UP?
YOU BET YOUR ASS.

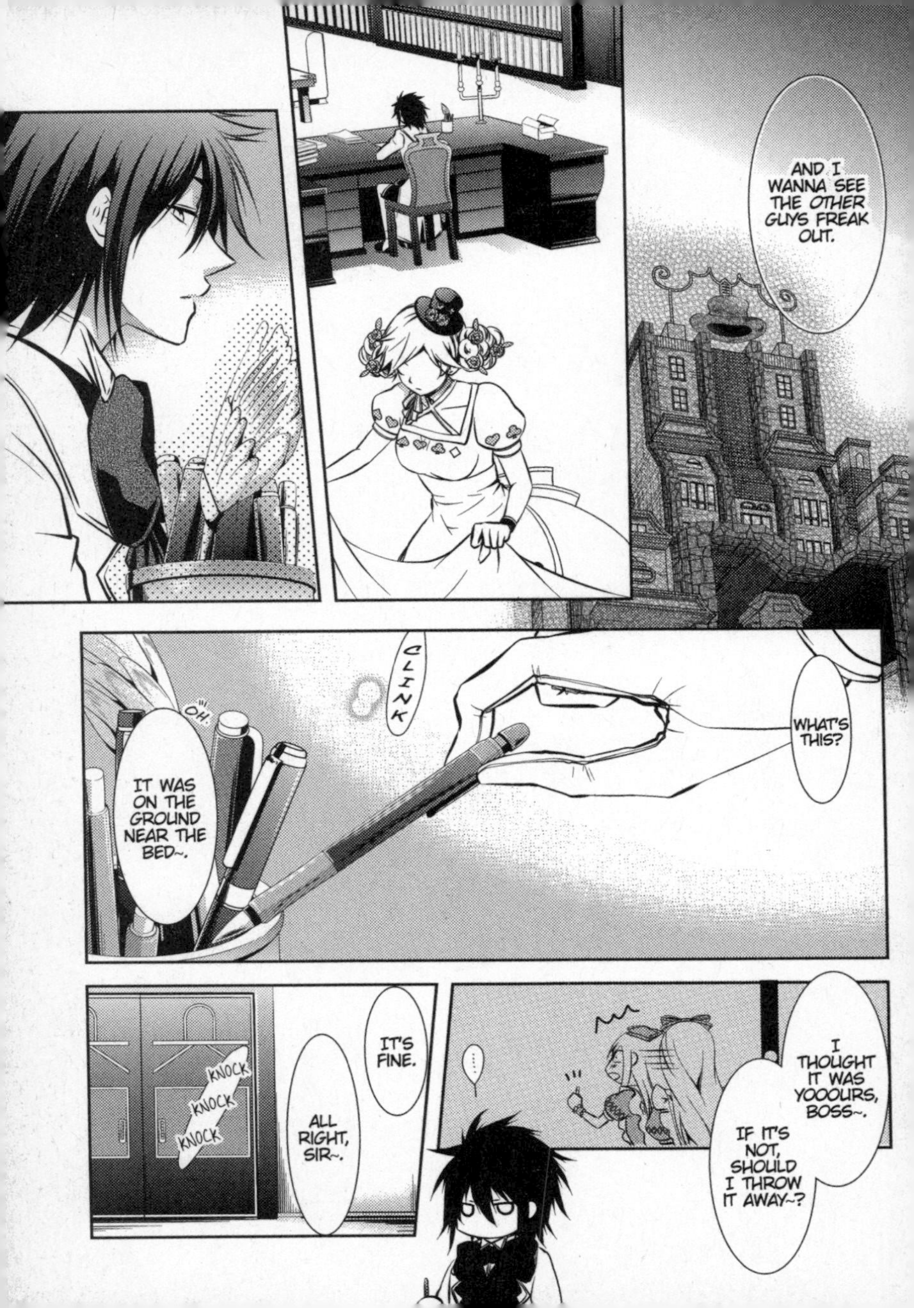
AND I WANNA SEE THE OTHER GUYS FREAK OUT.
WHAT'S THIS?
CLINK
OH.
IT WAS ON THE GROUND NEAR THE BED~.
I THOUGHT IT WAS YOOOURS, BOSS~.
IF IT'S NOT, SHOULD I THROW IT AWAY~?
...
IT'S FINE.
ALL RIGHT, SIR~.
KNOCK
KNOCK
KNOCK

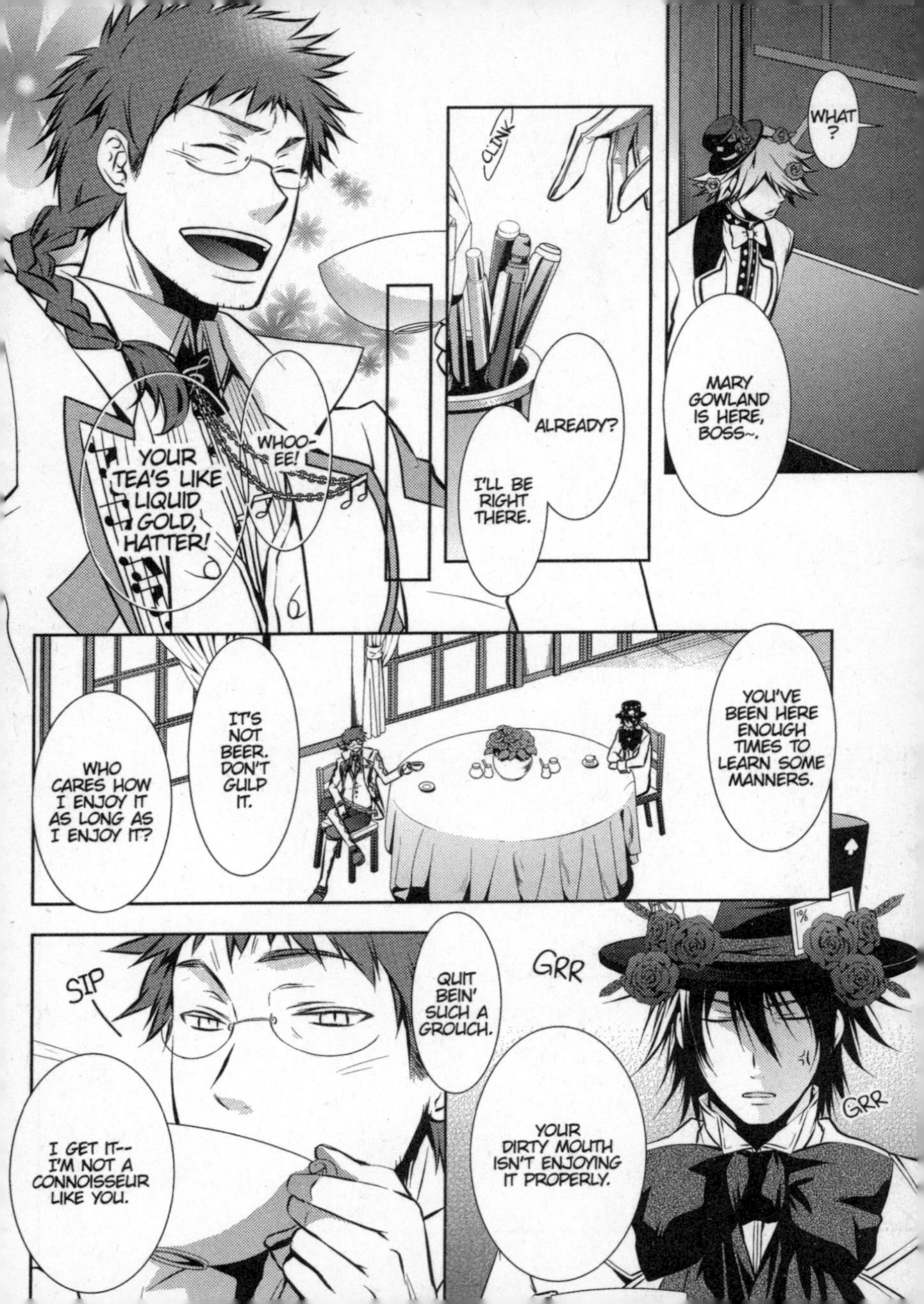

WHAT?
MARY GOWLAND IS HERE, BOSS~.
CLINK
ALREADY?
I'LL BE RIGHT THERE.
WHOOO-EE!
YOUR TEA'S LIKE LIQUID GOLD, HATTER!
YOU'VE BEEN HERE ENOUGH TIMES TO LEARN SOME MANNERS.
IT'S NOT BEER. DON'T GULP IT.
WHO CARES HOW I ENJOY IT AS LONG AS I ENJOY IT?
GRR
GRR
YOUR DIRTY MOUTH ISN'T ENJOYING IT PROPERLY.
QUIT BEIN' SUCH A GROUCH.
SIP
I GET IT-- I'M NOT A CONNOISSEUR LIKE YOU.

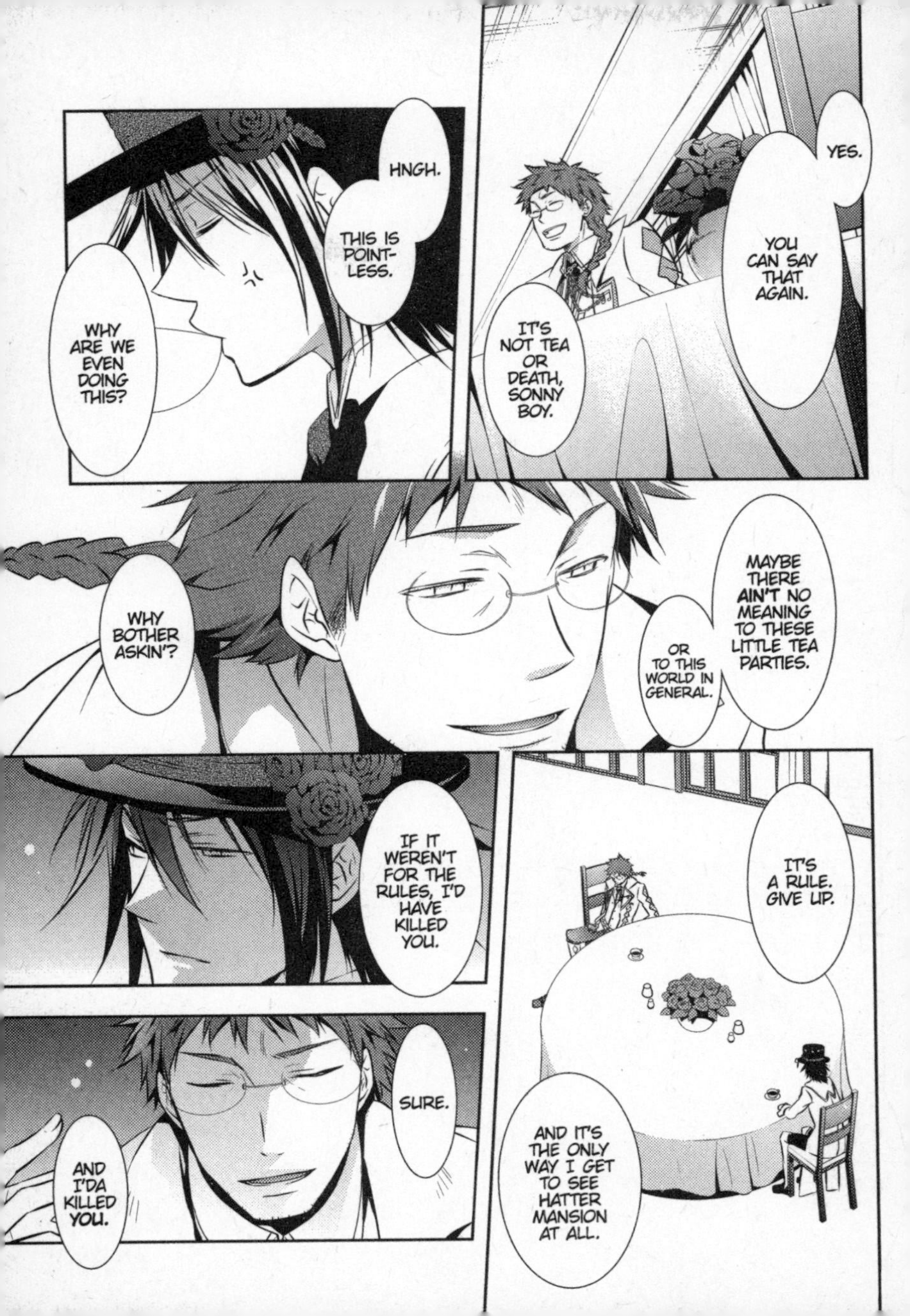
YES.
YOU CAN SAY THAT AGAIN.
IT'S NOT TEA OR DEATH, SONNY BOY.
HNGH.
THIS IS POINT-LESS.
WHY ARE WE EVEN DOING THIS?
MAYBE THERE AIN'T NO MEANING TO THESE LITTLE TEA PARTIES.
OR TO THIS WORLD IN GENERAL.
WHY BOTHER ASKIN'?
IT'S A RULE. GIVE UP.
AND IT'S THE ONLY WAY I GET TO SEE HATTER MANSION AT ALL.
IF IT WEREN'T FOR THE RULES, I'D HAVE KILLED YOU.
SURE.
AND I'DA KILLED YOU.

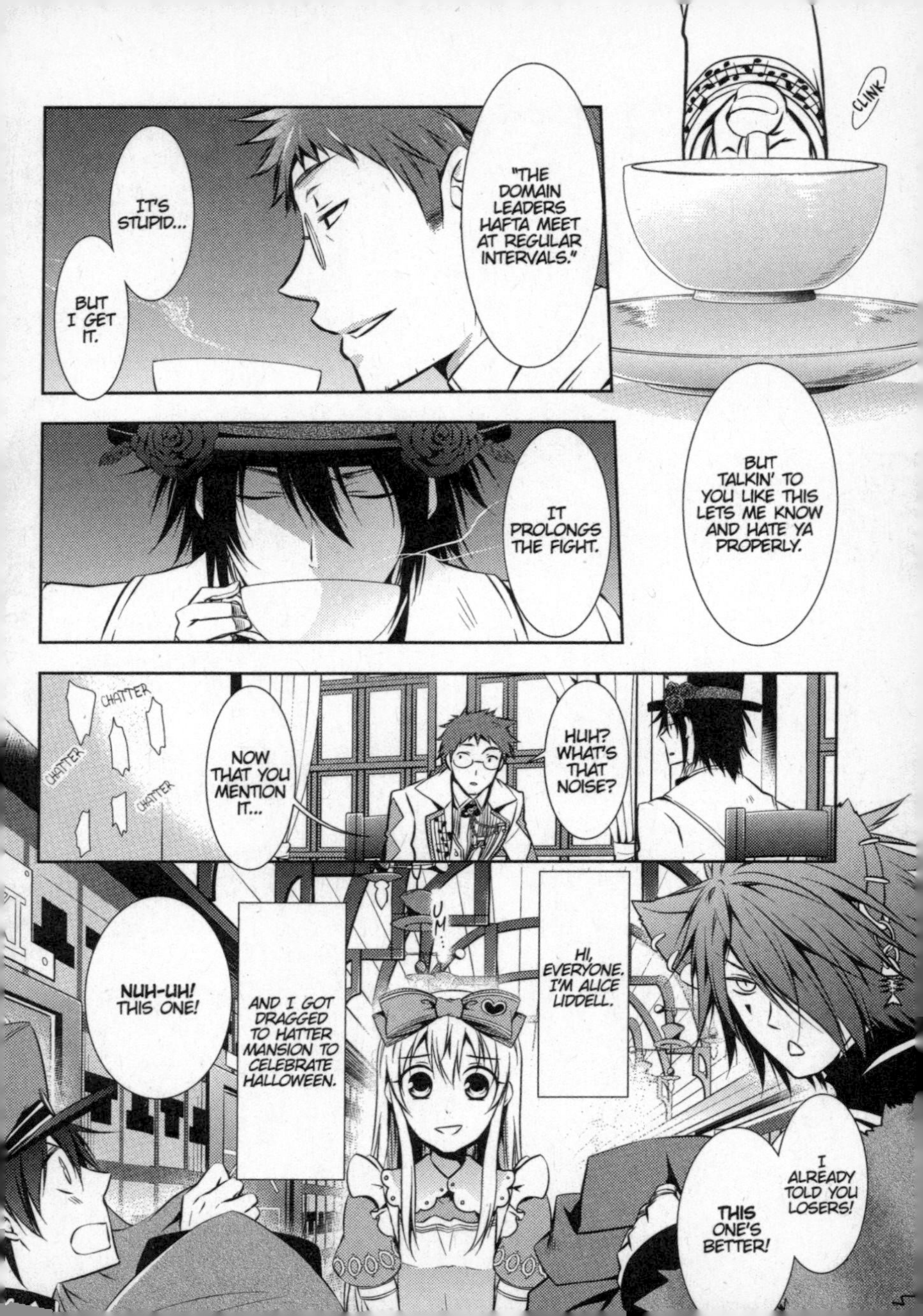
CLINK
BUT TALKIN' TO YOU LIKE THIS LETS ME KNOW AND HATE YA PROPERLY.
"THE DOMAIN LEADERS HAFTA MEET AT REGULAR INTERVALS."
IT'S STUPID...
BUT I GET IT.
IT PROLONGS THE FIGHT.
HUH? WHAT'S THAT NOISE?
NOW THAT YOU MENTION IT...
CHATTER
CHATTER
CHATTER
I ALREADY TOLD YOU LOSERS!
THIS ONE'S BETTER!
HI, EVERYONE. I'M ALICE LIDDELL.
UM...
AND I GOT DRAGGED TO HATTER MANSION TO CELEBRATE HALLOWEEN.
NUH-UH! THIS ONE!

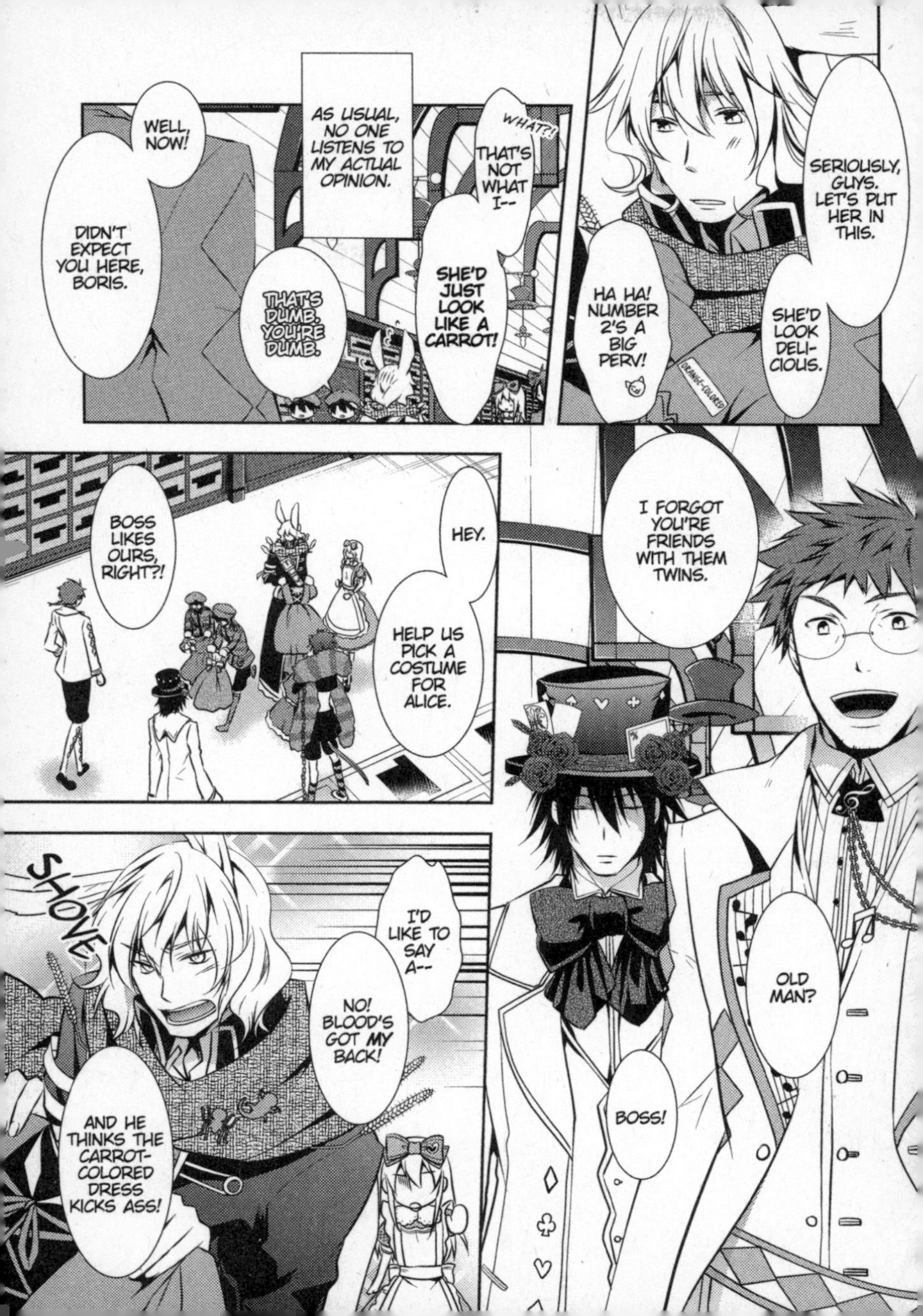
SERIOUSLY, GUYS. LET'S PUT HER IN THIS.
SHE'D LOOK DELICIOUS.
HA HA! NUMBER 2'S A BIG PERV!
ORANGE-COLORED
WHAT?!
THAT'S NOT WHAT I--
SHE'D JUST LOOK LIKE A CARROT!
AS USUAL, NO ONE LISTENS TO MY ACTUAL OPINION.
THAT'S DUMB. YOU'RE DUMB.
WELL, NOW!
DIDN'T EXPECT YOU HERE, BORIS.
I FORGOT YOU'RE FRIENDS WITH THEM TWINS.
HEY.
HELP US PICK A COSTUME FOR ALICE.
BOSS LIKES OURS, RIGHT?!
OLD MAN?
BOSS!
I'D LIKE TO SAY A--
SHOVE
NO! BLOOD'S GOT MY BACK!
AND HE THINKS THE CARROT-COLORED DRESS KICKS ASS!

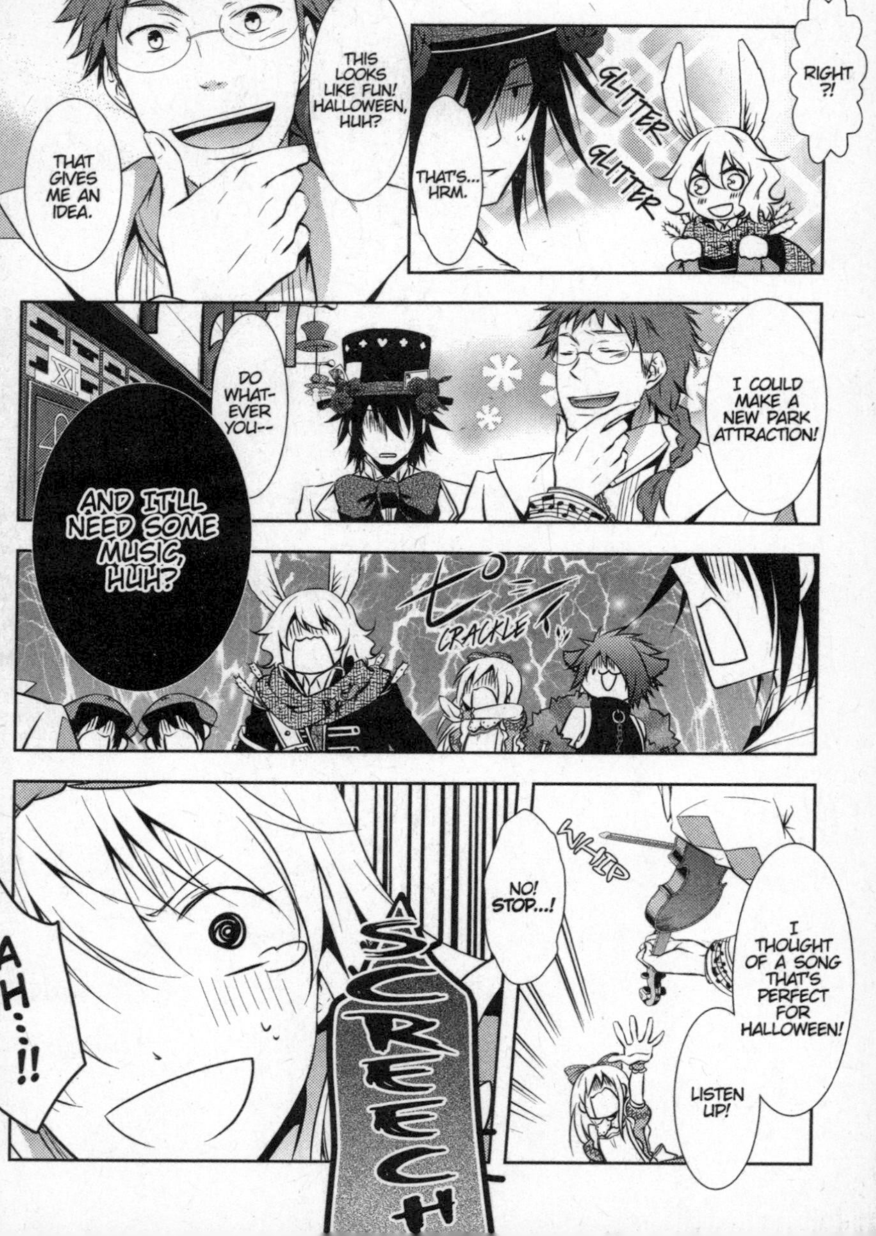
RIGHT ?!
GLITTER GLITTER
THAT'S... HRM.
THIS LOOKS LIKE FUN! HALLOWEEN, HUH?
THAT GIVES ME AN IDEA.
I COULD MAKE A NEW PARK ATTRACTION!
DO WHAT-EVER YOU--
AND IT'LL NEED SOME MUSIC, HUH?
CRACKLE
I THOUGHT OF A SONG THAT'S PERFECT FOR HALLOWEEN!
LISTEN UP!
WHIP
NO! STOP...!
SCREECH
AH...!!

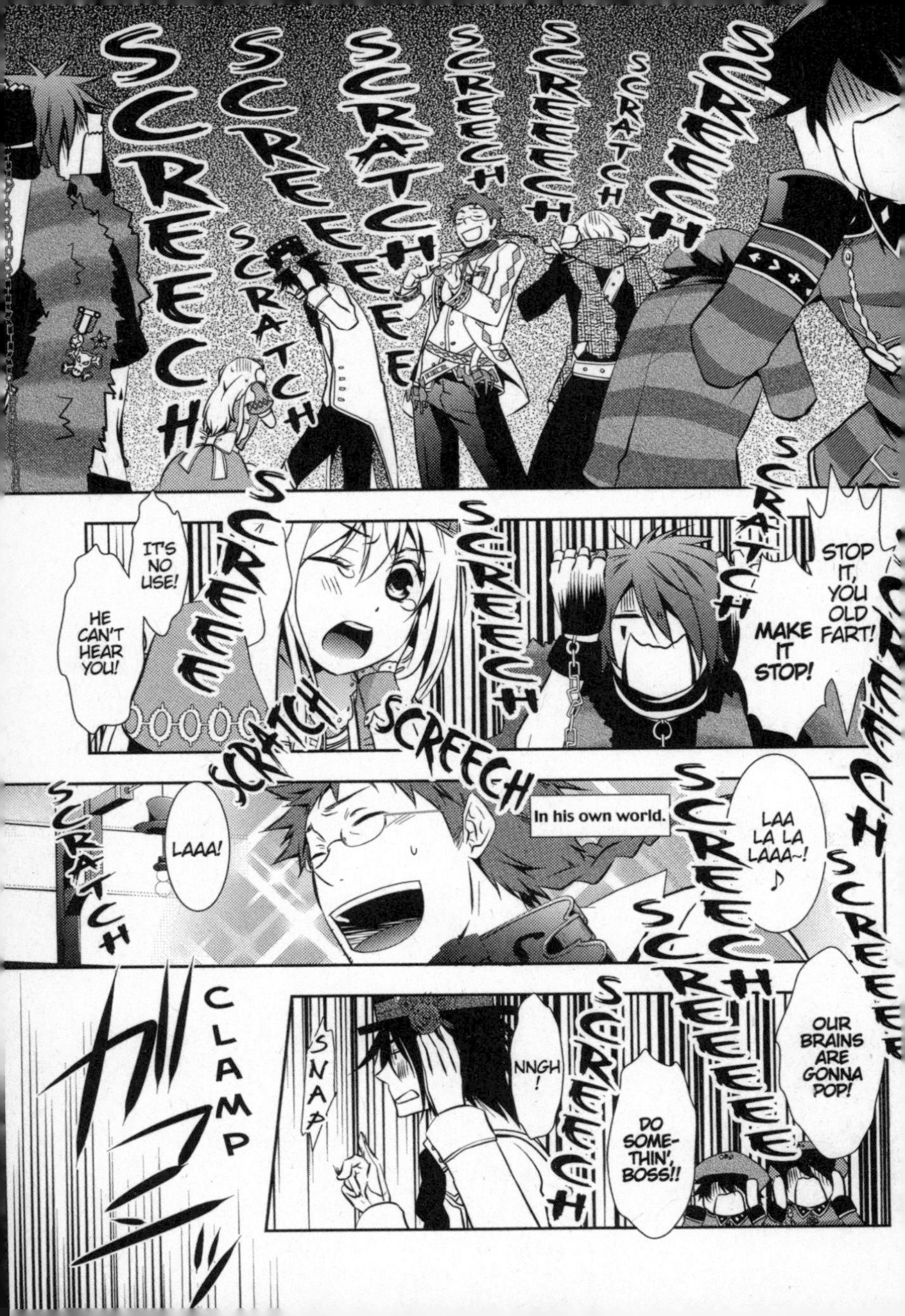
SCREECH
SCRATCH
SCREECH
SCREECH
SCRATCH
SCREEE
SCREECH
SCRATCH
SCREECH
SCRATCH
SCREECH
STOP IT, YOU OLD FART!
MAKE IT STOP!
SCREECH
SCREEE
IT'S NO USE!
HE CAN'T HEAR YOU!
SCREECH
SCRATCH
SCREECH
SCREEE
LAA LA LA LAAA~! ♪
In his own world.
LAAA!
SCRATCH
SCREEEE
SCREECH
OUR BRAINS ARE GONNA POP!
DO SOMETHIN', BOSS!!
NNGH!
SNAP
CLAMP

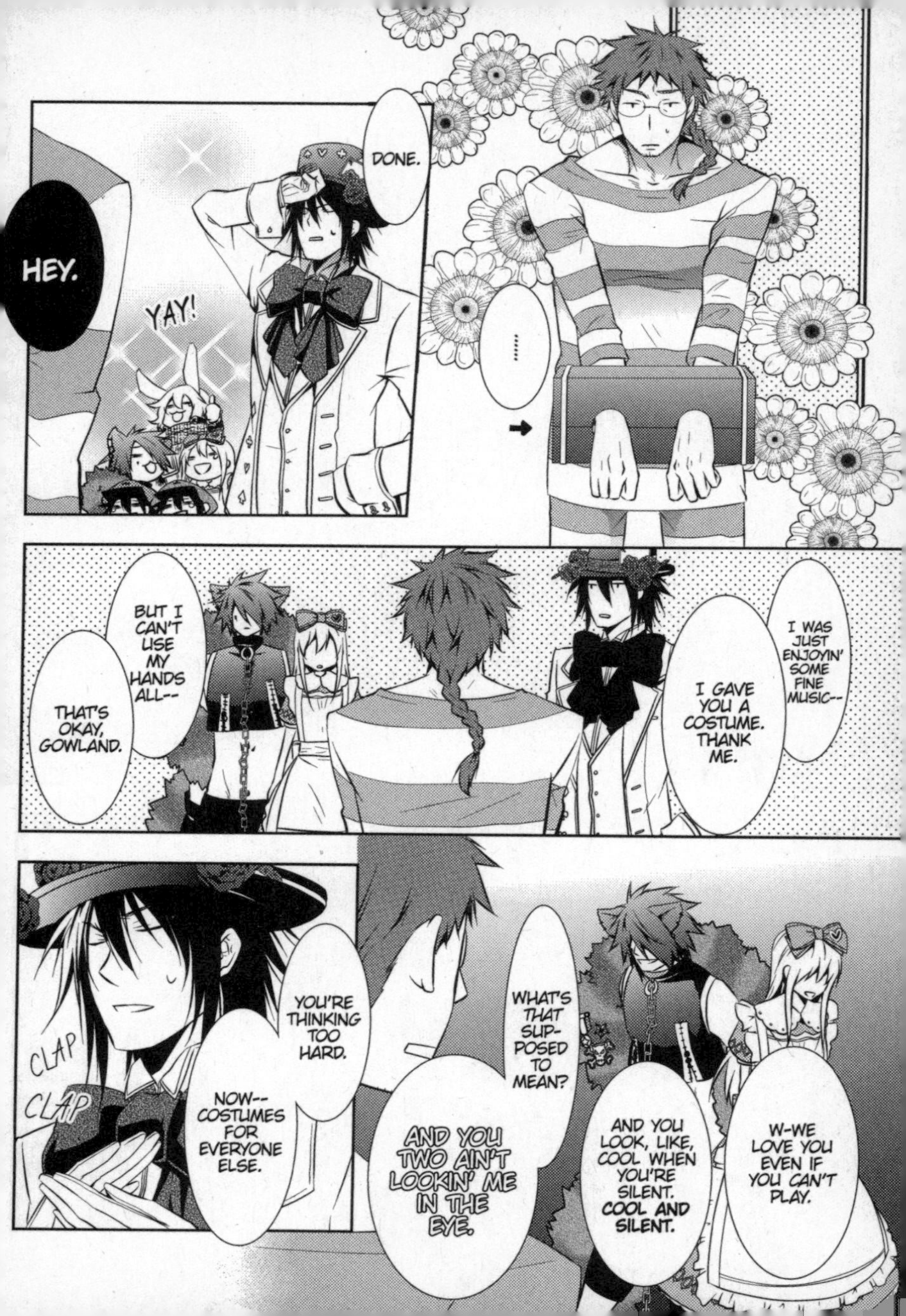
......
DONE.
HEY.
YAY!
I WAS JUST ENJOYIN' SOME FINE MUSIC--
I GAVE YOU A COSTUME. THANK ME.
BUT I CAN'T USE MY HANDS ALL--
THAT'S OKAY, GOWLAND.
W-WE LOVE YOU EVEN IF YOU CAN'T PLAY.
AND YOU LOOK, LIKE, COOL WHEN YOU'RE SILENT. COOL AND SILENT.
WHAT'S THAT SUP-POSED TO MEAN?
AND YOU TWO AIN'T LOOKIN' ME IN THE EYE.
YOU'RE THINKING TOO HARD.
NOW-- COSTUMES FOR EVERYONE ELSE.
CLAP
CLAP

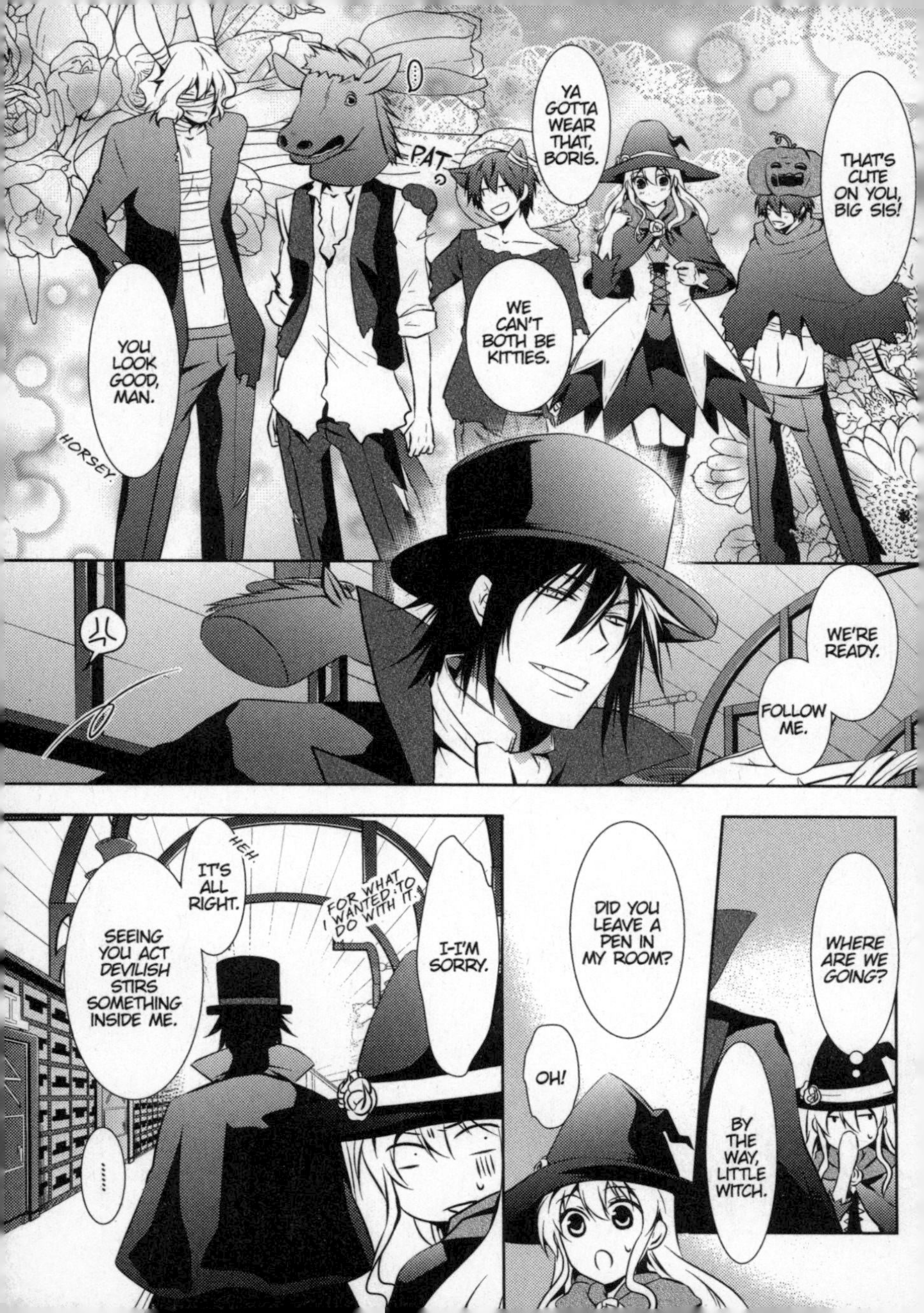
THAT'S CUTE ON YOU, BIG SIS!
YA GOTTA WEAR THAT, BORIS.
...
PAT
WE CAN'T BOTH BE KITTIES.
YOU LOOK GOOD, MAN.
HORSEY.
WE'RE READY.
FOLLOW ME.
WHERE ARE WE GOING?
BY THE WAY, LITTLE WITCH.
DID YOU LEAVE A PEN IN MY ROOM?
OH!
I-I'M SORRY.
FOR WHAT I WANTED TO DO WITH IT.
HEH.
IT'S ALL RIGHT.
SEEING YOU ACT DEVILISH STIRS SOMETHING INSIDE ME.
......

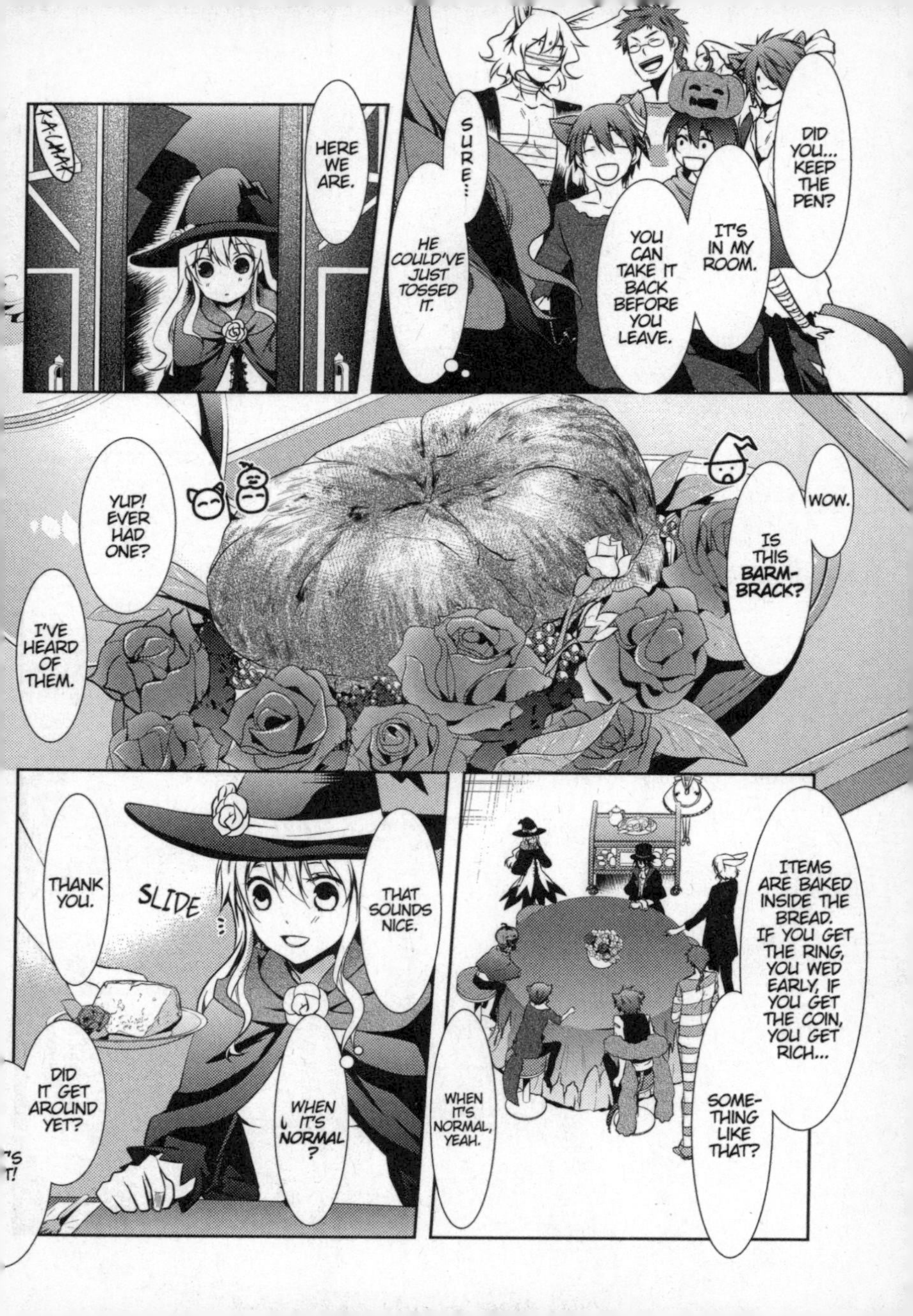
DID YOU... KEEP THE PEN?
IT'S IN MY ROOM.
YOU CAN TAKE IT BACK BEFORE YOU LEAVE.
SURE...
HE COULD'VE JUST TOSSED IT.
HERE WE ARE.
KA-CHAK
WOW.
IS THIS BARMBRACK?
YUP! EVER HAD ONE?
I'VE HEARD OF THEM.
ITEMS ARE BAKED INSIDE THE BREAD. IF YOU GET THE RING, YOU WED EARLY, IF YOU GET THE COIN, YOU GET RICH...
SOMETHING LIKE THAT?
WHEN IT'S NORMAL, YEAH.
THAT SOUNDS NICE.
THANK YOU.
SLIDE
WHEN IT'S NORMAL?
DID IT GET AROUND YET?

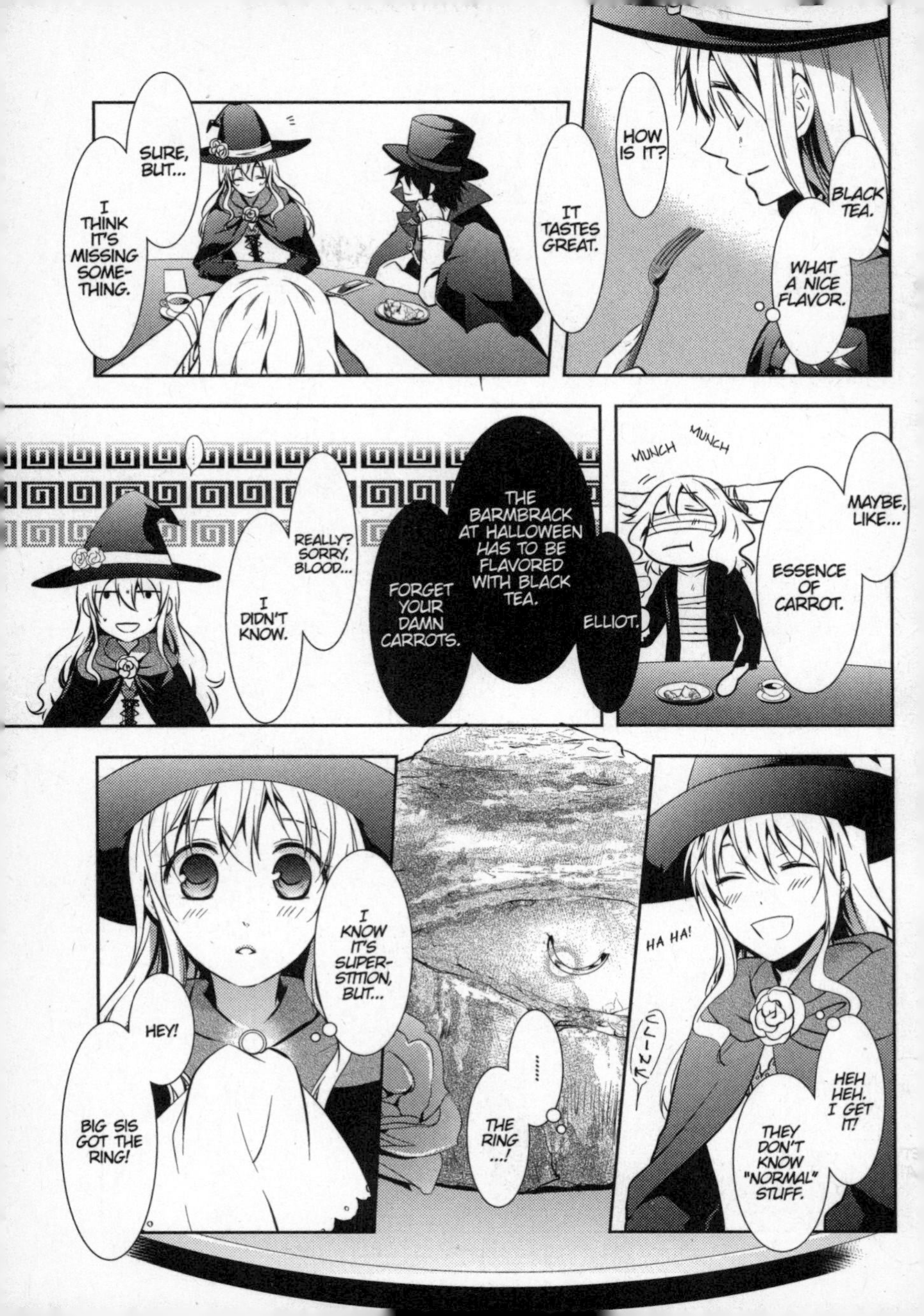
HOW IS IT?
BLACK TEA.
WHAT A NICE FLAVOR.
IT TASTES GREAT.
SURE, BUT...
I THINK IT'S MISSING SOMETHING.
MUNCH MUNCH
MAYBE, LIKE...
ESSENCE OF CARROT.
ELLIOT.
THE BARMBRACK AT HALLOWEEN HAS TO BE FLAVORED WITH BLACK TEA.
FORGET YOUR DAMN CARROTS.
......
REALLY? SORRY, BLOOD...
I DIDN'T KNOW.
HA HA!
HEH HEH. I GET IT!
THEY DON'T KNOW "NORMAL" STUFF.
CLINK
......
THE RING...!
I KNOW IT'S SUPERSTITION, BUT...
HEY!
BIG SIS GOT THE RING!

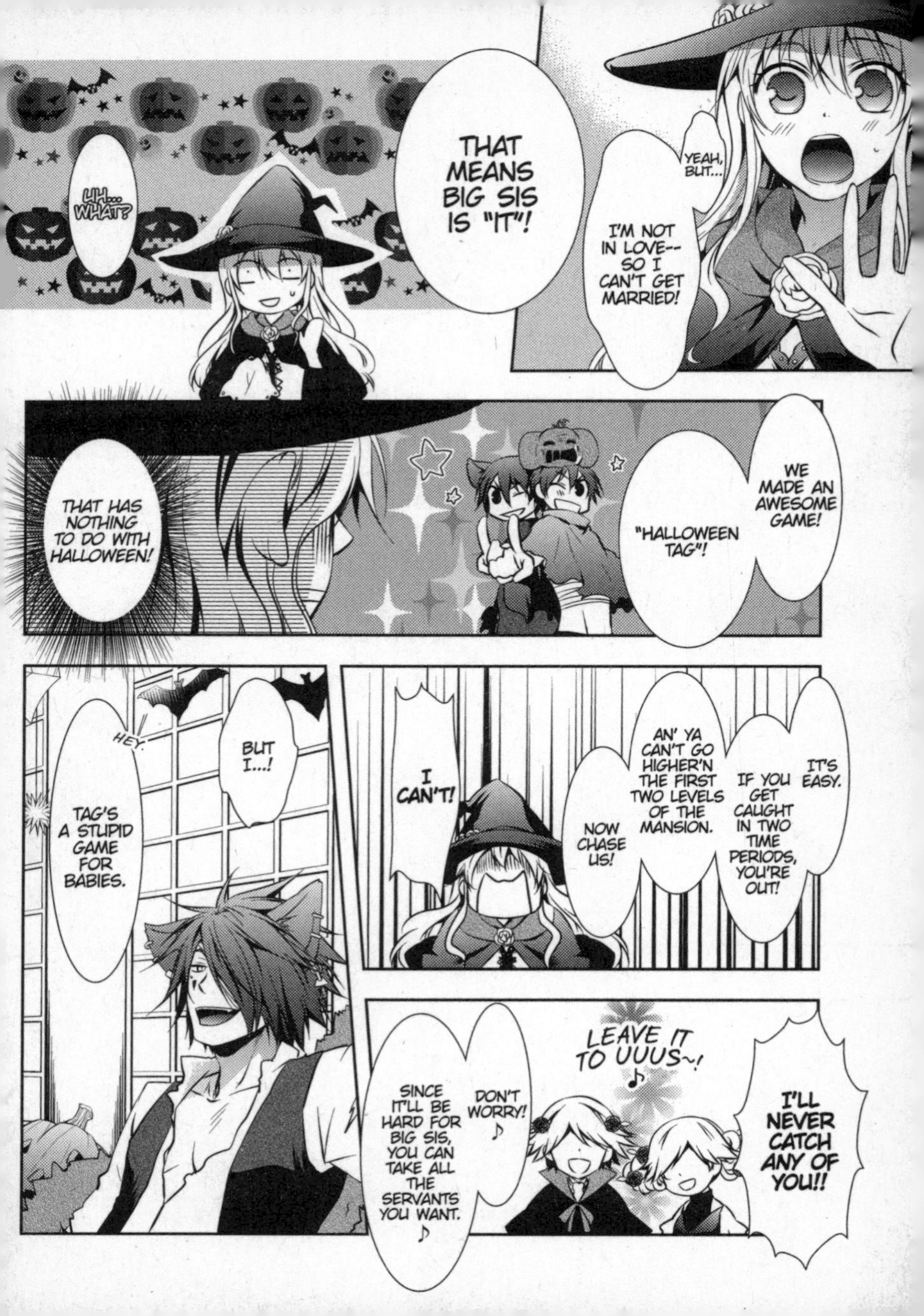
YEAH, BUT...
I'M NOT IN LOVE-- SO I CAN'T GET MARRIED!
THAT MEANS BIG SIS IS "IT"!
UH... WHAT?
WE MADE AN AWESOME GAME!
"HALLOWEEN TAG"!
THAT HAS NOTHING TO DO WITH HALLOWEEN!
IT'S EASY.
IF YOU GET CAUGHT IN TWO TIME PERIODS, YOU'RE OUT!
AN' YA CAN'T GO HIGHER'N THE FIRST TWO LEVELS OF THE MANSION.
NOW CHASE US!
I CAN'T!
I'LL NEVER CATCH ANY OF YOU!!
LEAVE IT TO UUUS~! ♪
DON'T WORRY! ♪
SINCE IT'LL BE HARD FOR BIG SIS, YOU CAN TAKE ALL THE SERVANTS YOU WANT. ♪
BUT I...!
HEY.
TAG'S A STUPID GAME FOR BABIES.

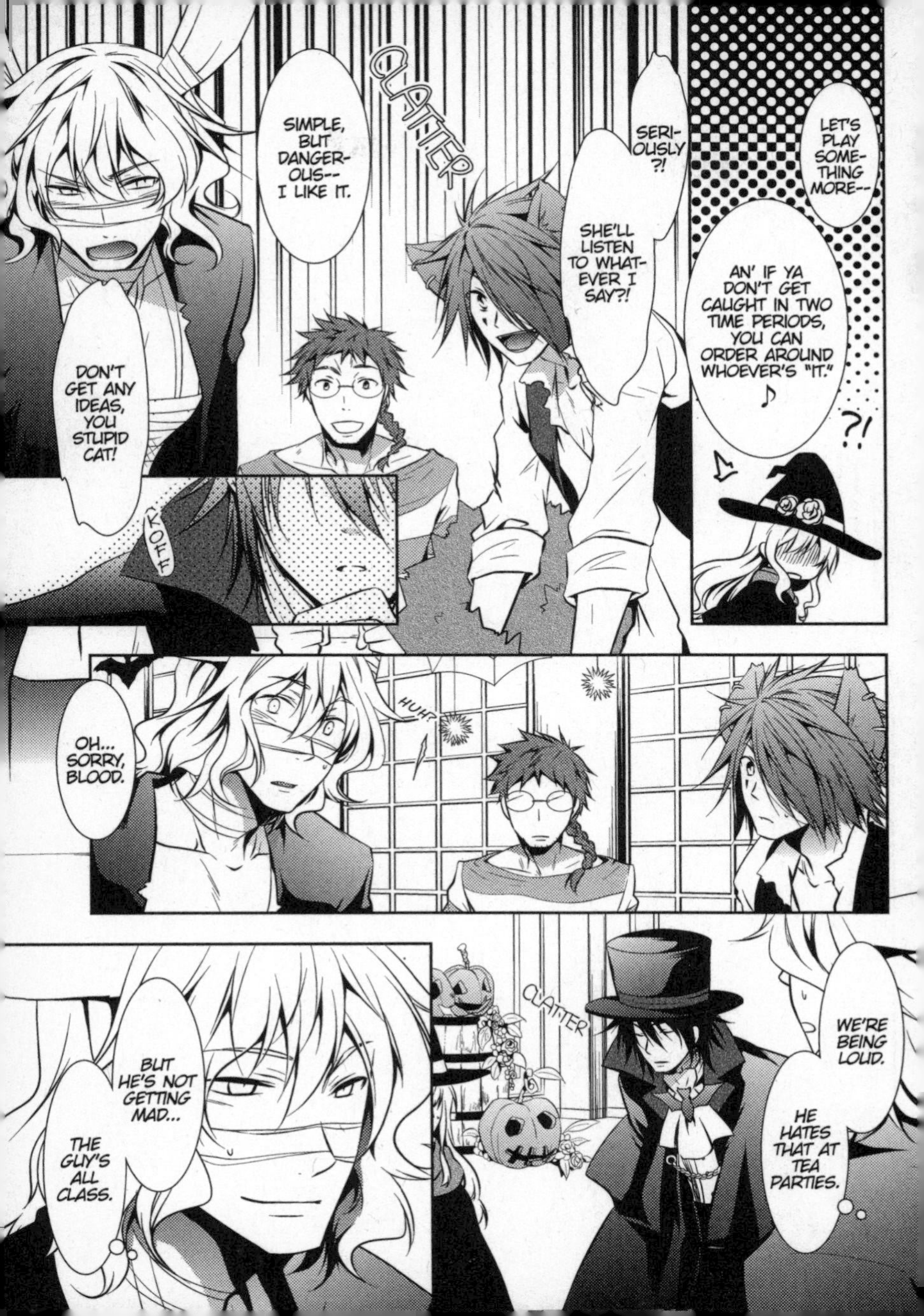
LET'S PLAY SOMETHING MORE--
AN' IF YA DON'T GET CAUGHT IN TWO TIME PERIODS, YOU CAN ORDER AROUND WHOEVER'S "IT." ♪
?!
SERIOUSLY ?!
SHE'LL LISTEN TO WHATEVER I SAY?!
CLATTER
SIMPLE, BUT DANGEROUS-- I LIKE IT.
DON'T GET ANY IDEAS, YOU STUPID CAT!
KOFF
HUH?
OH... SORRY, BLOOD.
WE'RE BEING LOUD.
HE HATES THAT AT TEA PARTIES.
CLATTER
BUT HE'S NOT GETTING MAD...
THE GUY'S ALL CLASS.

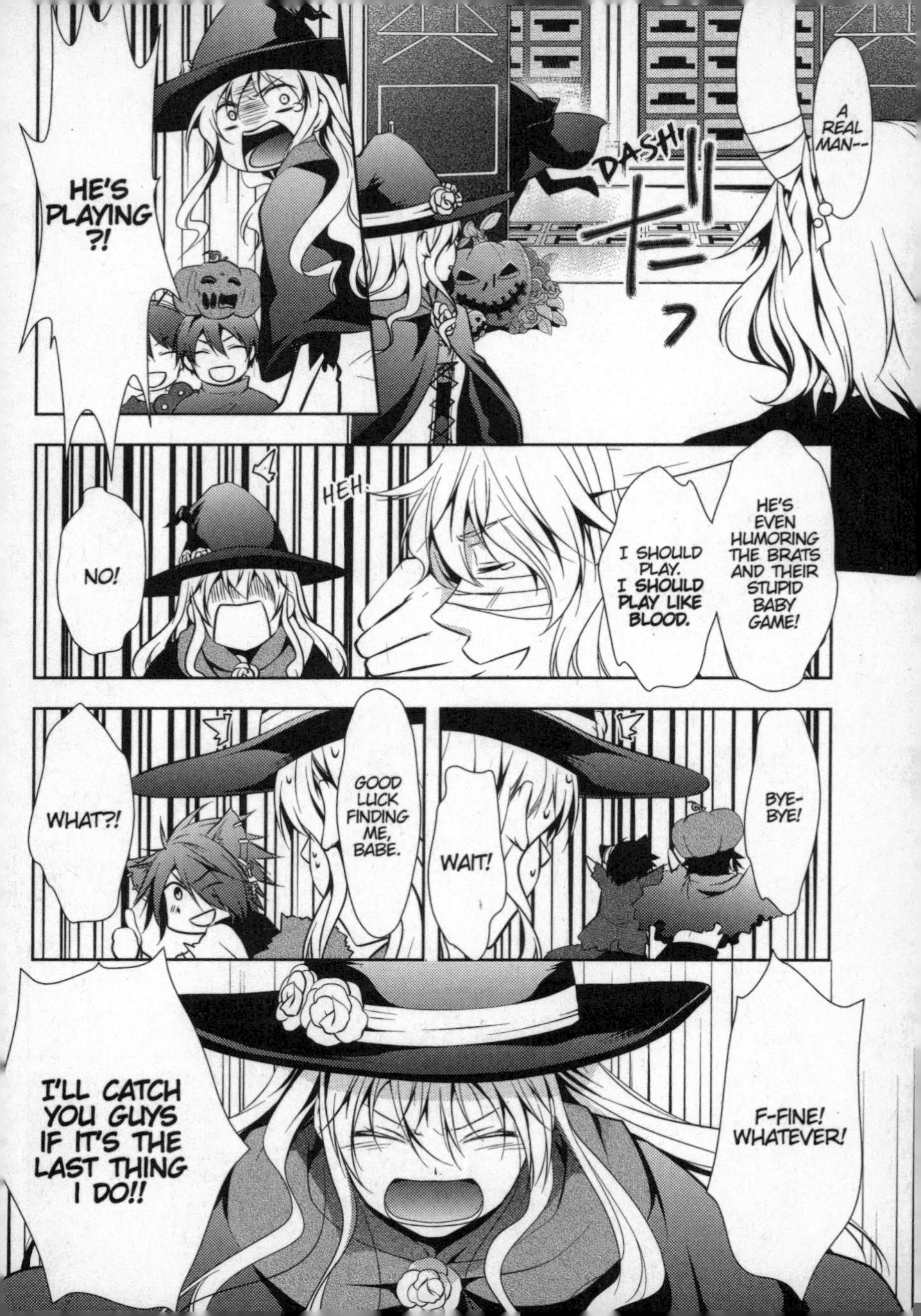
A REAL MAN--
DASH!
HE'S PLAYING ?!
HE'S EVEN HUMORING THE BRATS AND THEIR STUPID BABY GAME!
I SHOULD PLAY. I SHOULD PLAY LIKE BLOOD.
HEH.
NO!
BYE-BYE!
WAIT!
GOOD LUCK FINDING ME, BABE.
WHAT?!
F-FINE! WHATEVER!
I'LL CATCH YOU GUYS IF IT'S THE LAST THING I DO!!

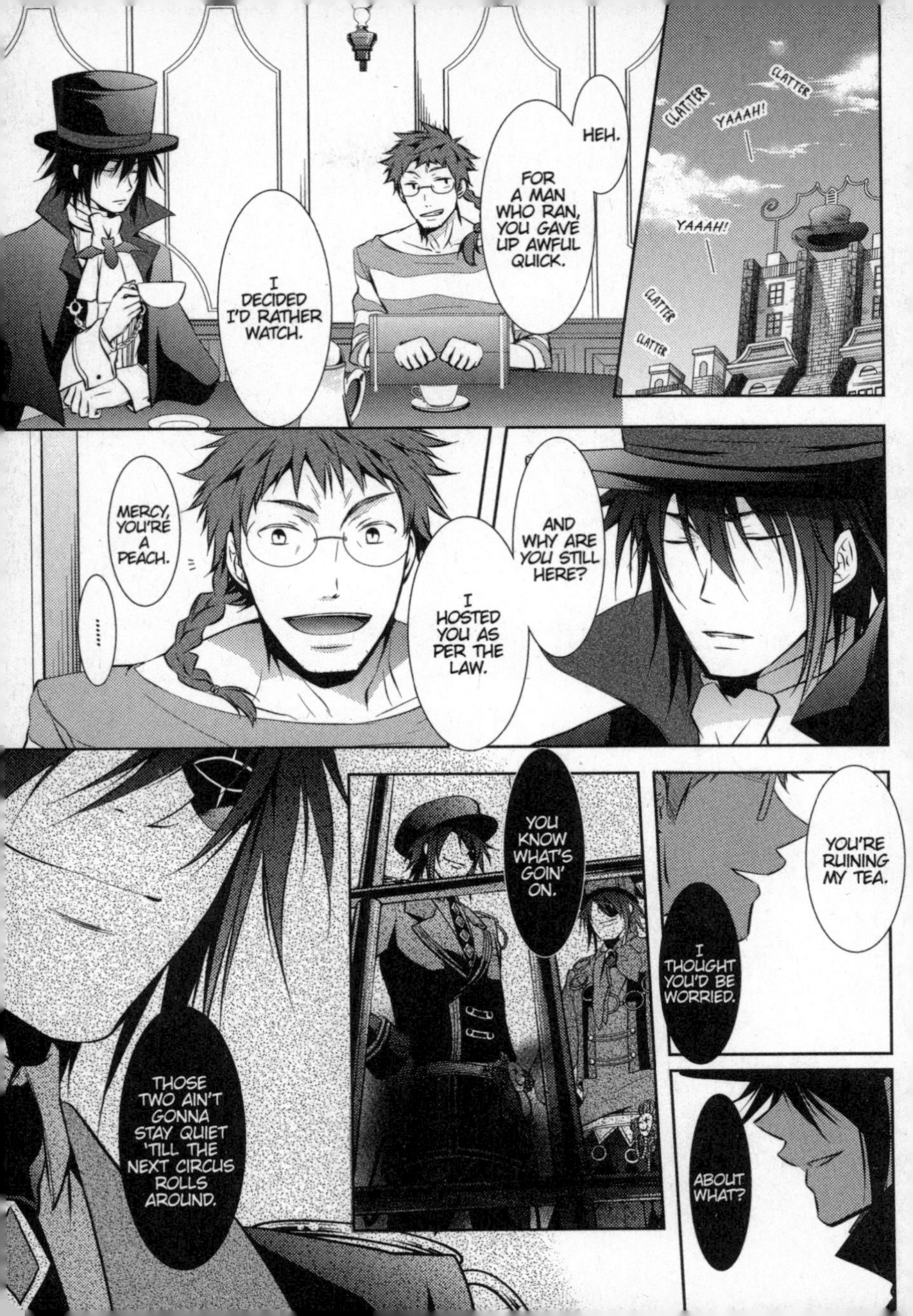
CLATTER
CLATTER
YAAAH!
YAAAH!
CLATTER
CLATTER
HEH.
FOR A MAN WHO RAN, YOU GAVE UP AWFUL QUICK.
I DECIDED I'D RATHER WATCH.
AND WHY ARE YOU STILL HERE?
I HOSTED YOU AS PER THE LAW.
MERCY, YOU'RE A PEACH.
......
YOU'RE RUINING MY TEA.
I THOUGHT YOU'D BE WORRIED.
ABOUT WHAT?
YOU KNOW WHAT'S GOIN' ON.
THOSE TWO AIN'T GONNA STAY QUIET 'TILL THE NEXT CIRCUS ROLLS AROUND.

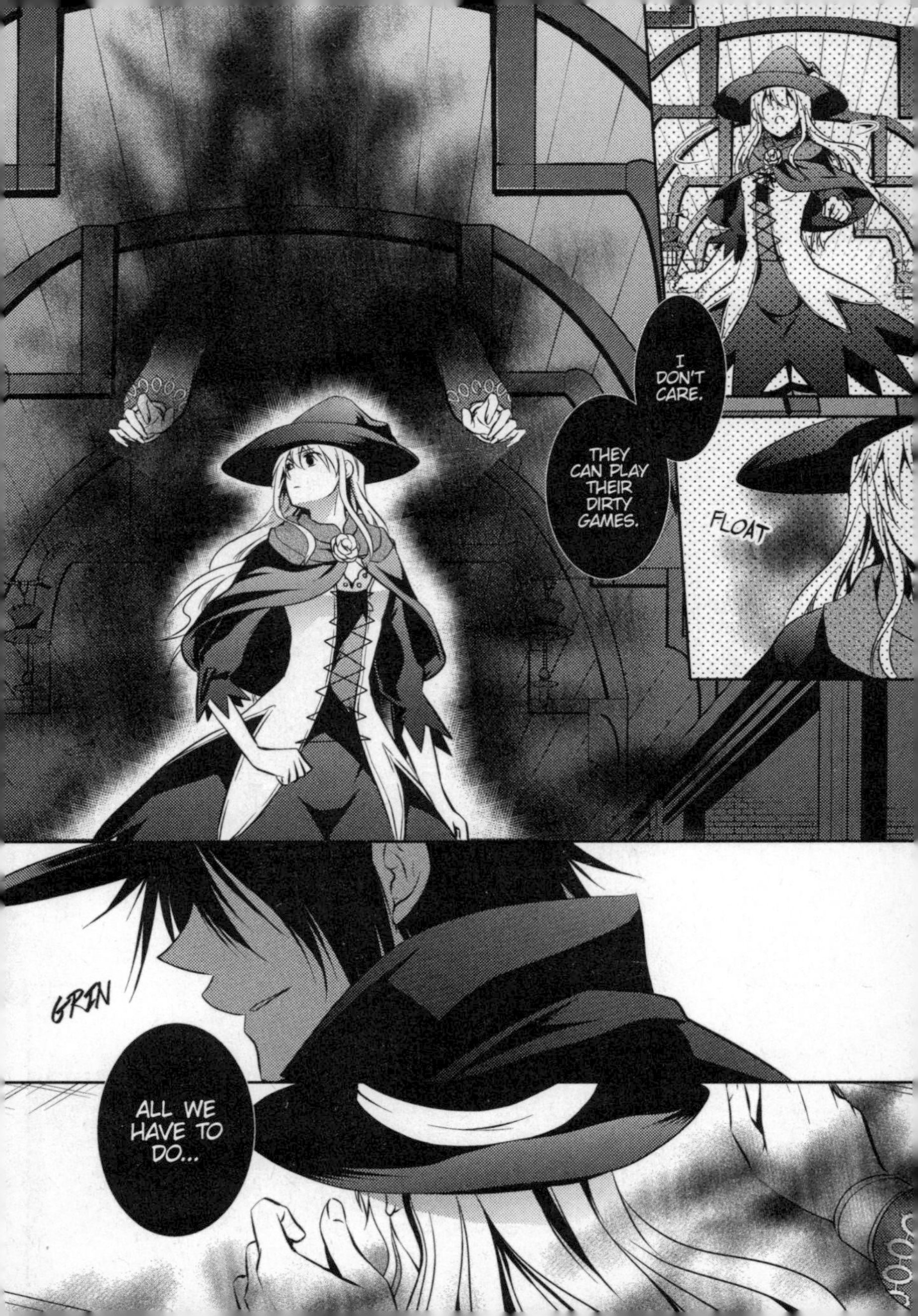
I DON'T CARE.
THEY CAN PLAY THEIR DIRTY GAMES.
FLOAT
GRIN
ALL WE HAVE TO DO...

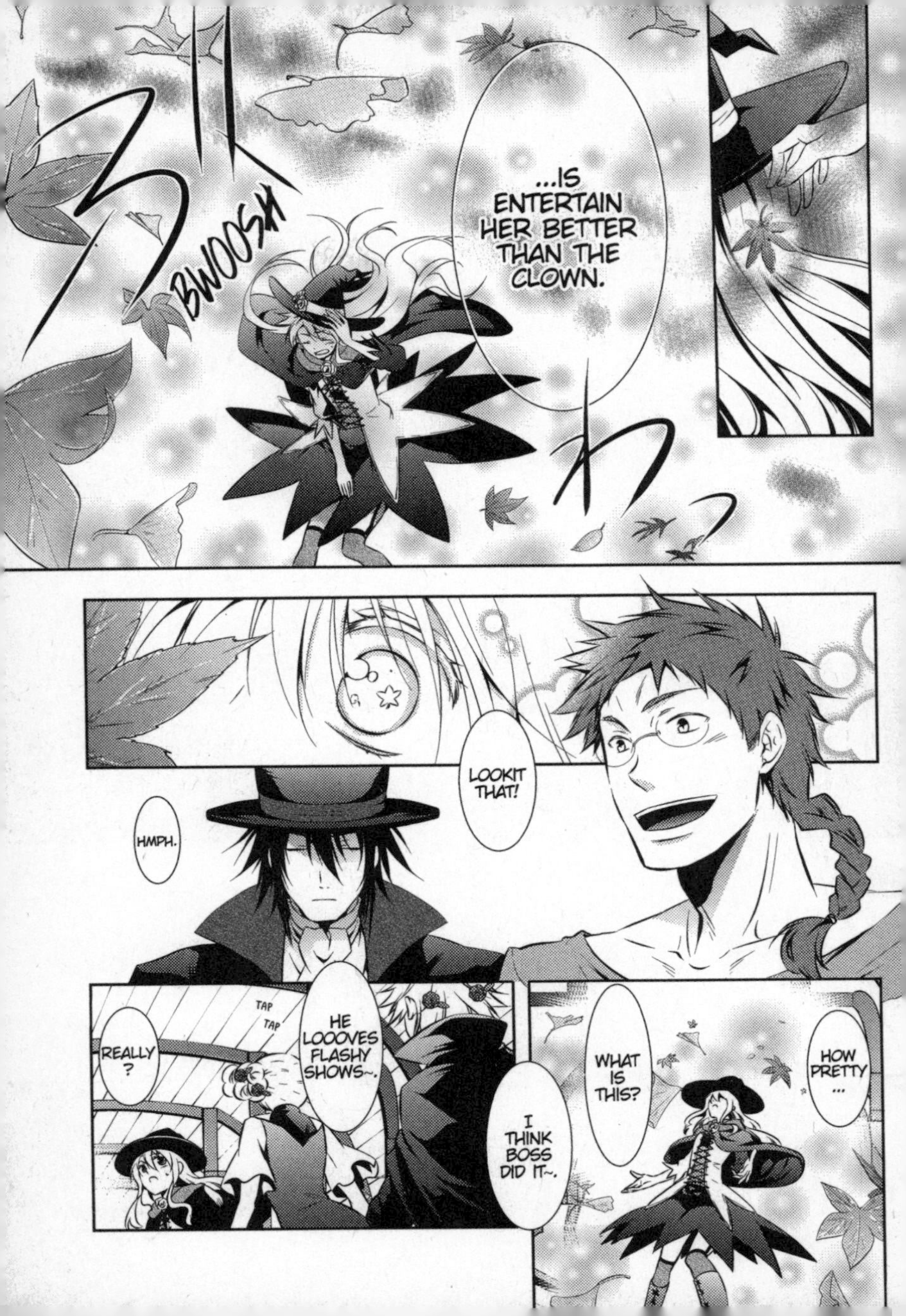
...IS ENTERTAIN HER BETTER THAN THE CLOWN.
BWOOSH
LOOKIT THAT!
HMPH.
HOW PRETTY...
WHAT IS THIS?
I THINK BOSS DID IT~.
HE LOOOVES FLASHY SHOWS~.
TAP TAP
REALLY?

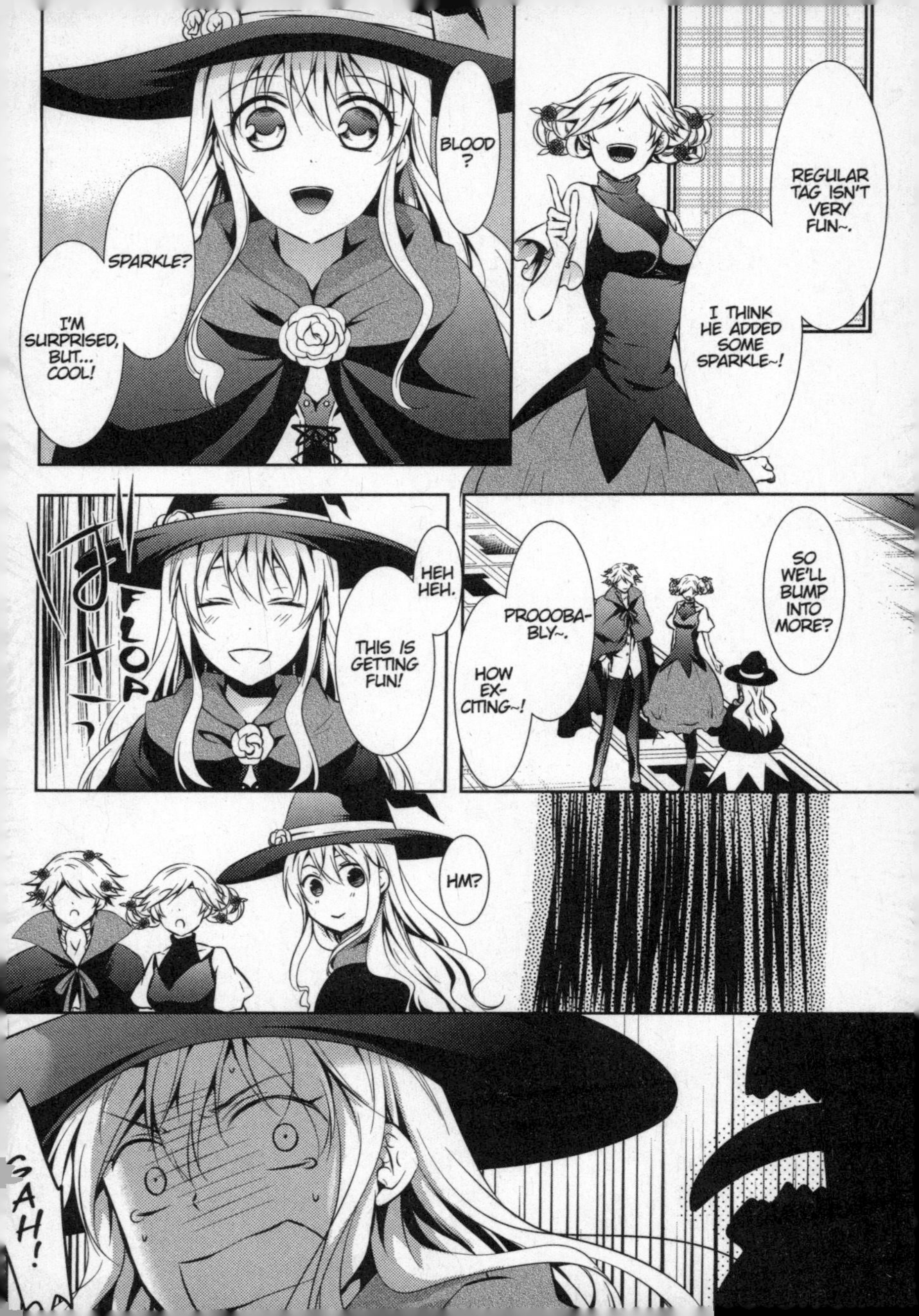
REGULAR TAG ISN'T VERY FUN~.
I THINK HE ADDED SOME SPARKLE~!
BLOOD?
SPARKLE?
I'M SURPRISED, BUT... COOL!
SO WE'LL BUMP INTO MORE?
PROOOBA-BLY~.
HOW EX-CITING~!
HEH HEH.
THIS IS GETTING FUN!
FLOP
HM?
GAH!

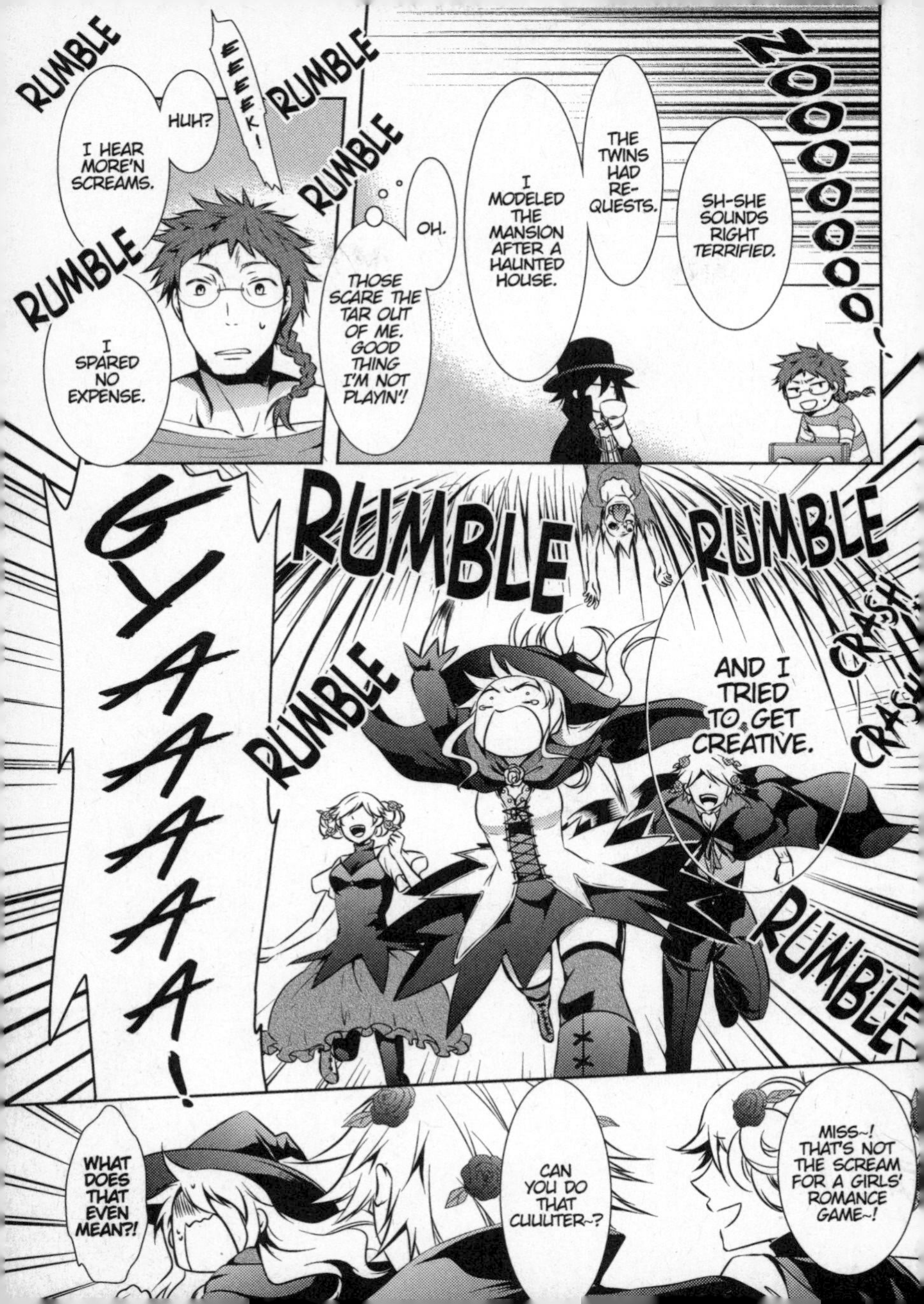
NOOOOOOO!
SH-SHE SOUNDS RIGHT TERRIFIED.
THE TWINS HAD RE-QUESTS.
I MODELED THE MANSION AFTER A HAUNTED HOUSE.
OH.
THOSE SCARE THE TAR OUT OF ME. GOOD THING I'M NOT PLAYIN'!
EEEEEK!
RUMBLE
RUMBLE
RUMBLE
RUMBLE
RUMBLE
HUH?
I HEAR MORE'N SCREAMS.
I SPARED NO EXPENSE.
RUMBLE
RUMBLE
CRASH
CRASH
AND I TRIED TO GET CREATIVE.
RUMBLE
RUMBLE
RUMBLE
GYAAAAAA!
MISS~! THAT'S NOT THE SCREAM FOR A GIRLS' ROMANCE GAME~!
CAN YOU DO THAT CUUUTER~?
WHAT DOES THAT EVEN MEAN?!

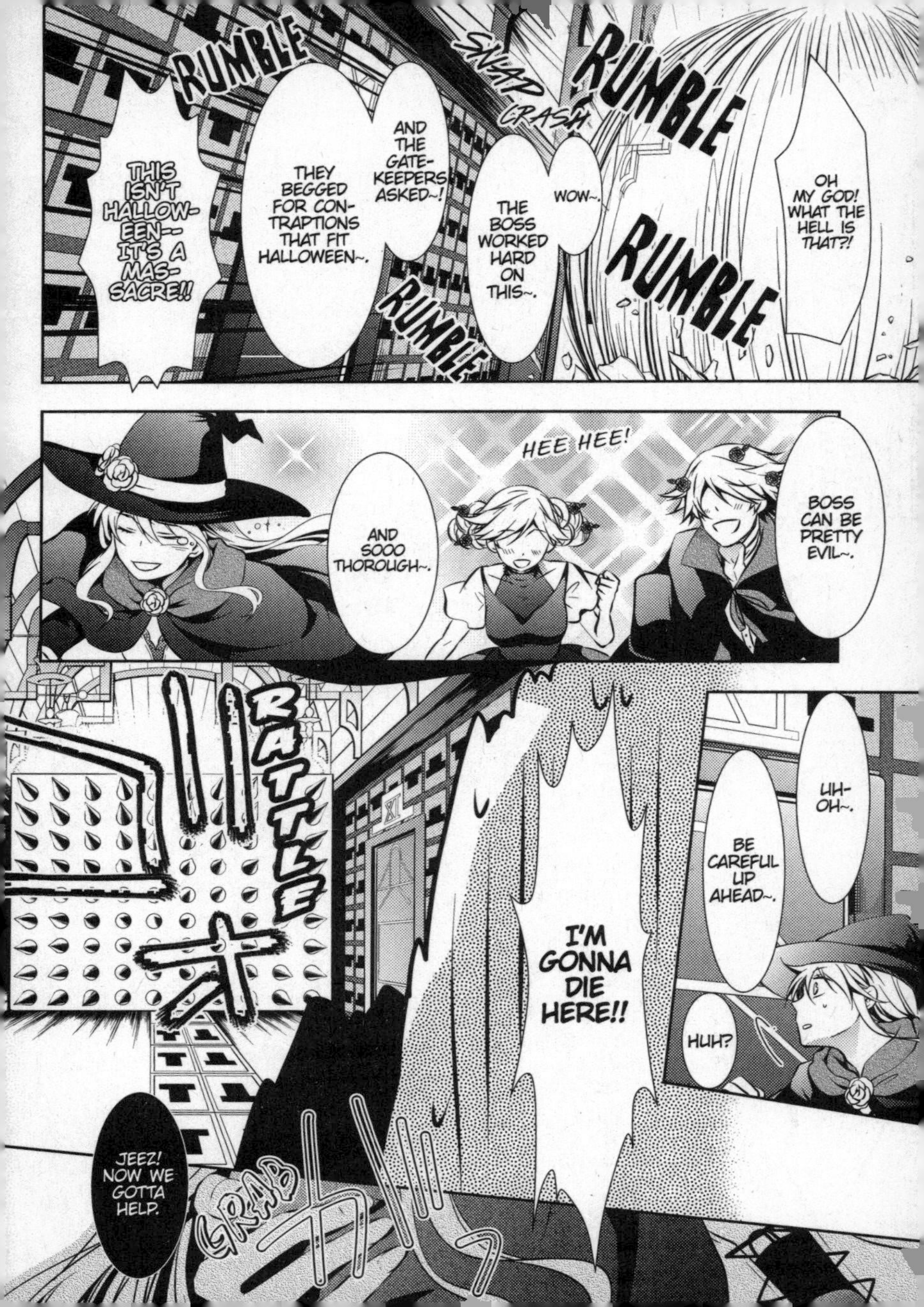
RUMBLE
RUMBLE
OH MY GOD! WHAT THE HELL IS THAT?!
WOW~.
SNAP
CRASH
THE BOSS WORKED HARD ON THIS~.
AND THE GATEKEEPERS ASKED~!
THEY BEGGED FOR CONTRAPTIONS THAT FIT HALLOWEEN~.
RUMBLE
RUMBLE
THIS ISN'T HALLOWEEN-- IT'S A MASSACRE!!
BOSS CAN BE PRETTY EVIL~.
HEE HEE!
AND SOOO THOROUGH~.
UH-OH~.
BE CAREFUL UP AHEAD~.
HUH?
I'M GONNA DIE HERE!!
RATTLE
GRAB
JEEZ! NOW WE GOTTA HELP.

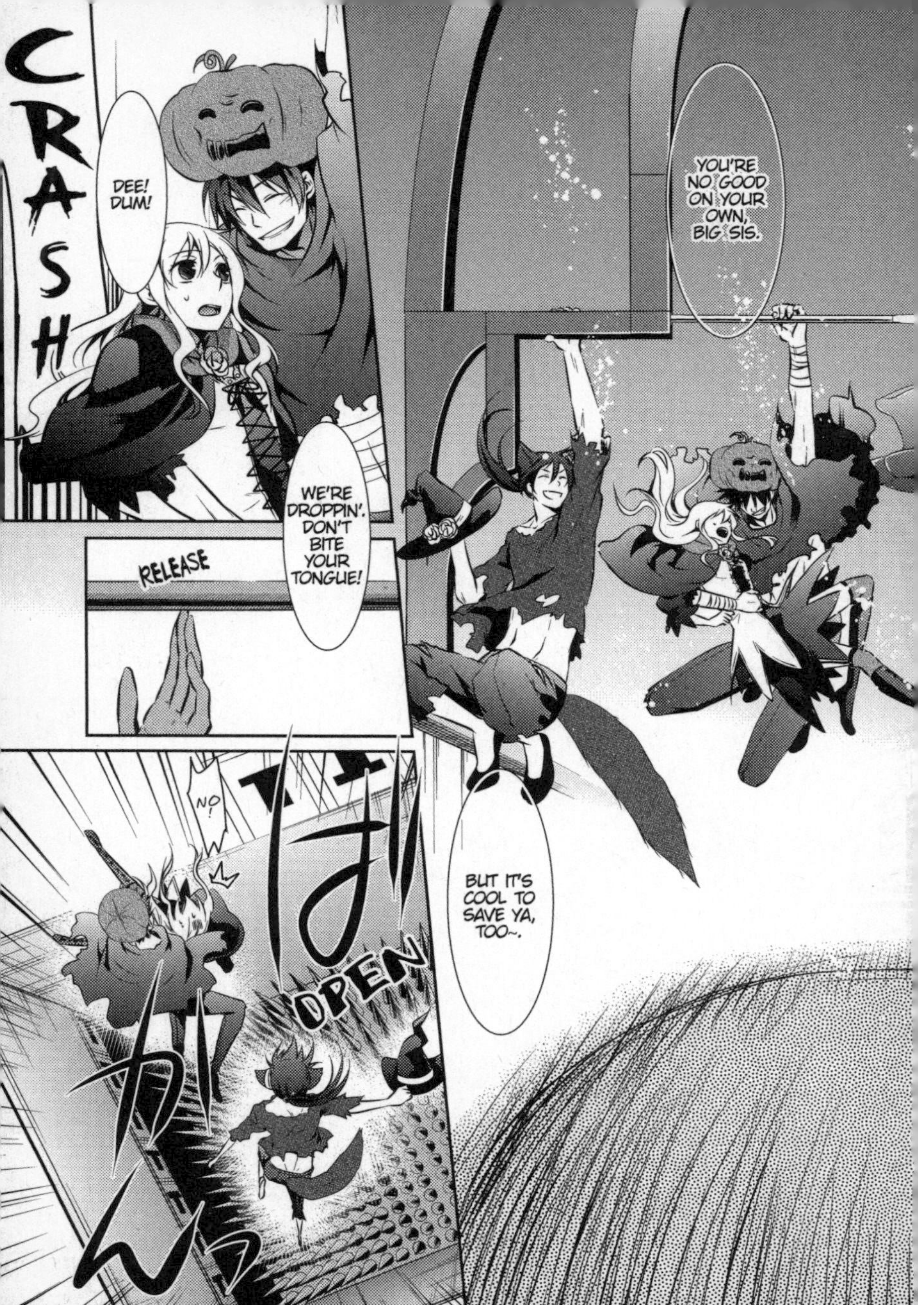
YOU'RE NO GOOD ON YOUR OWN, BIG SIS.
WE'RE DROPPIN'. DON'T BITE YOUR TONGUE!
BUT IT'S COOL TO SAVE YA, TOO~.
CRASH
DEE! DUM!
RELEASE
NO!
OPEN

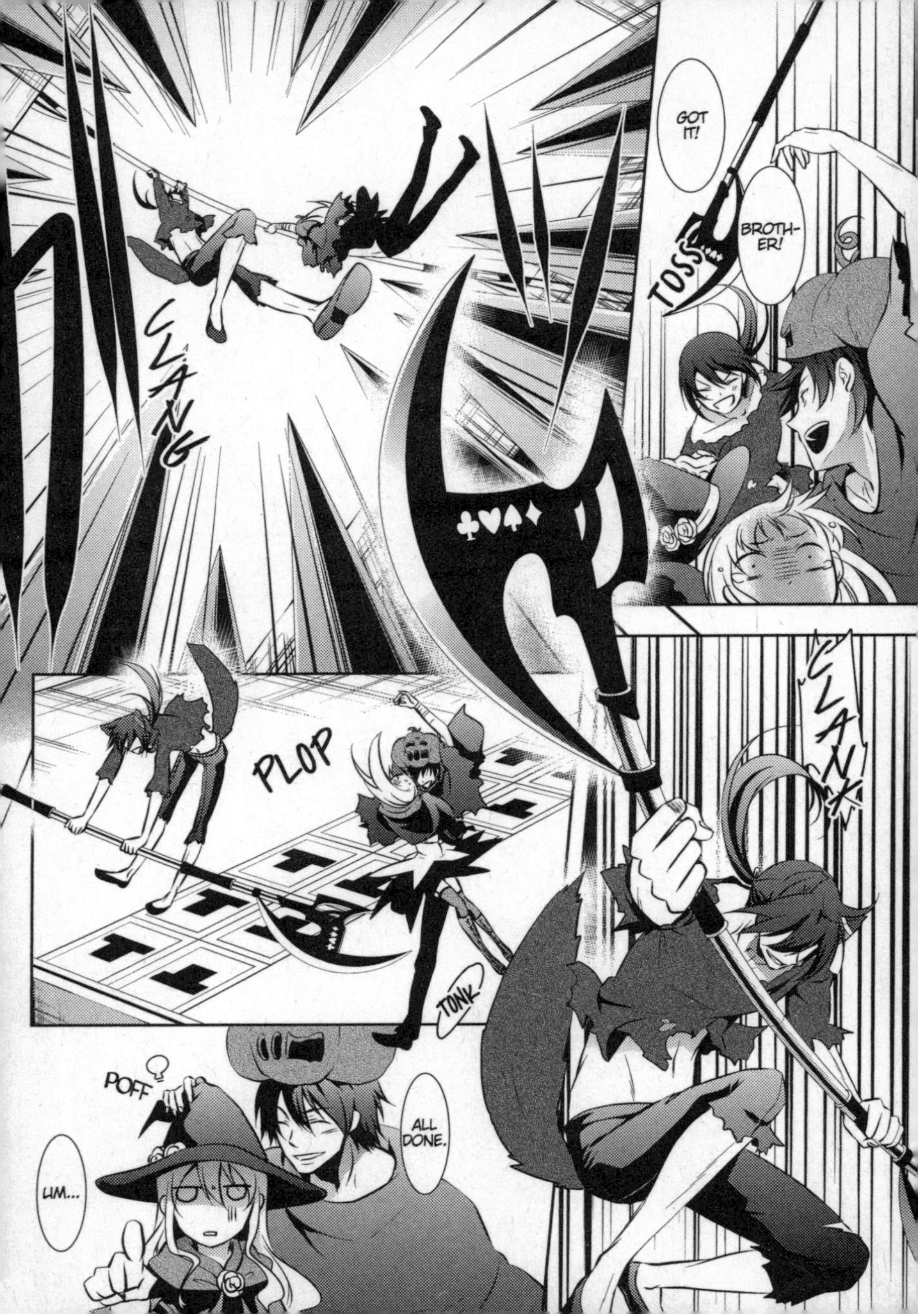
GOT IT!
BROTH-
ER!
TOSS
CLANG
CLANK
PLOP
TONK
ALL DONE.
POFF
UM...

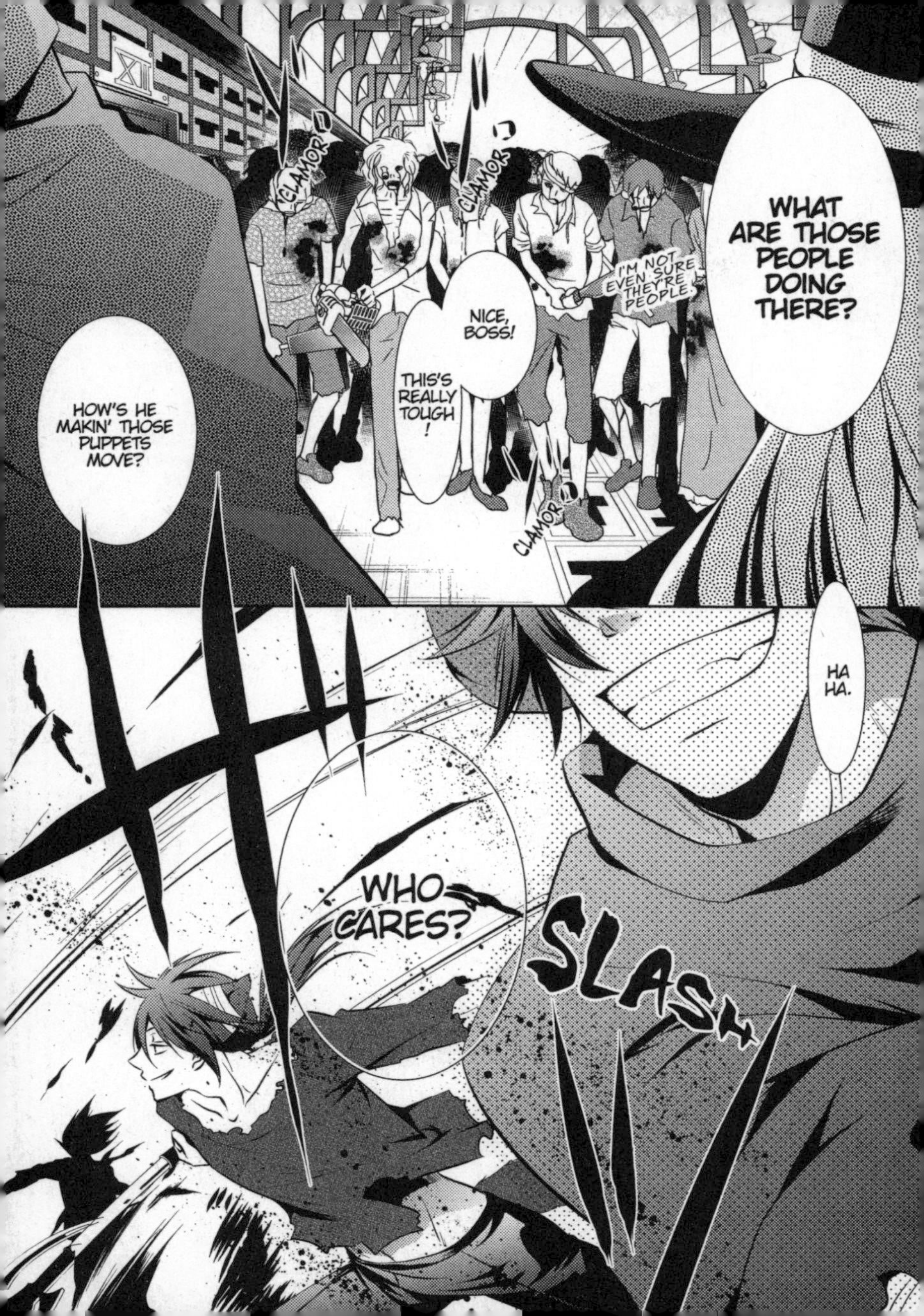
WHAT ARE THOSE PEOPLE DOING THERE?
CLAMOR
I'M NOT EVEN SURE THEY'RE PEOPLE.
NICE, BOSS!
THIS'S REALLY TOUGH!
CLAMOR
CLAMOR
HOW'S HE MAKIN' THOSE PUPPETS MOVE?
HA HA.
WHO CARES?
SLASH

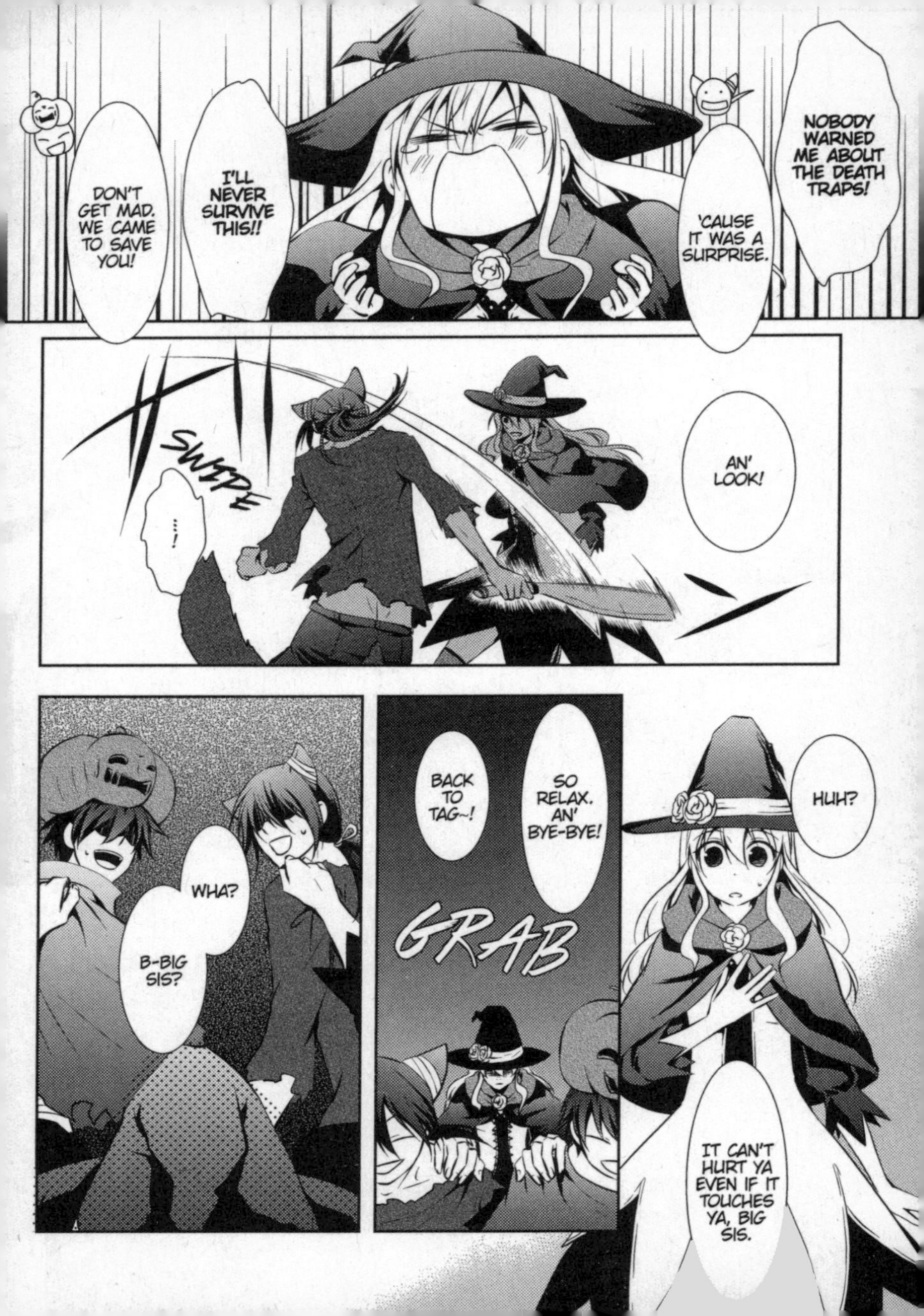
NOBODY WARNED ME ABOUT THE DEATH TRAPS!
'CAUSE IT WAS A SURPRISE.
I'LL NEVER SURVIVE THIS!!
DON'T GET MAD. WE CAME TO SAVE YOU!
AN' LOOK!
SWIPE
...!
HUH?
IT CAN'T HURT YA EVEN IF IT TOUCHES YA, BIG SIS.
SO RELAX. AN' BYE-BYE!
BACK TO TAG~!
GRAB
WHA?
B-BIG SIS?

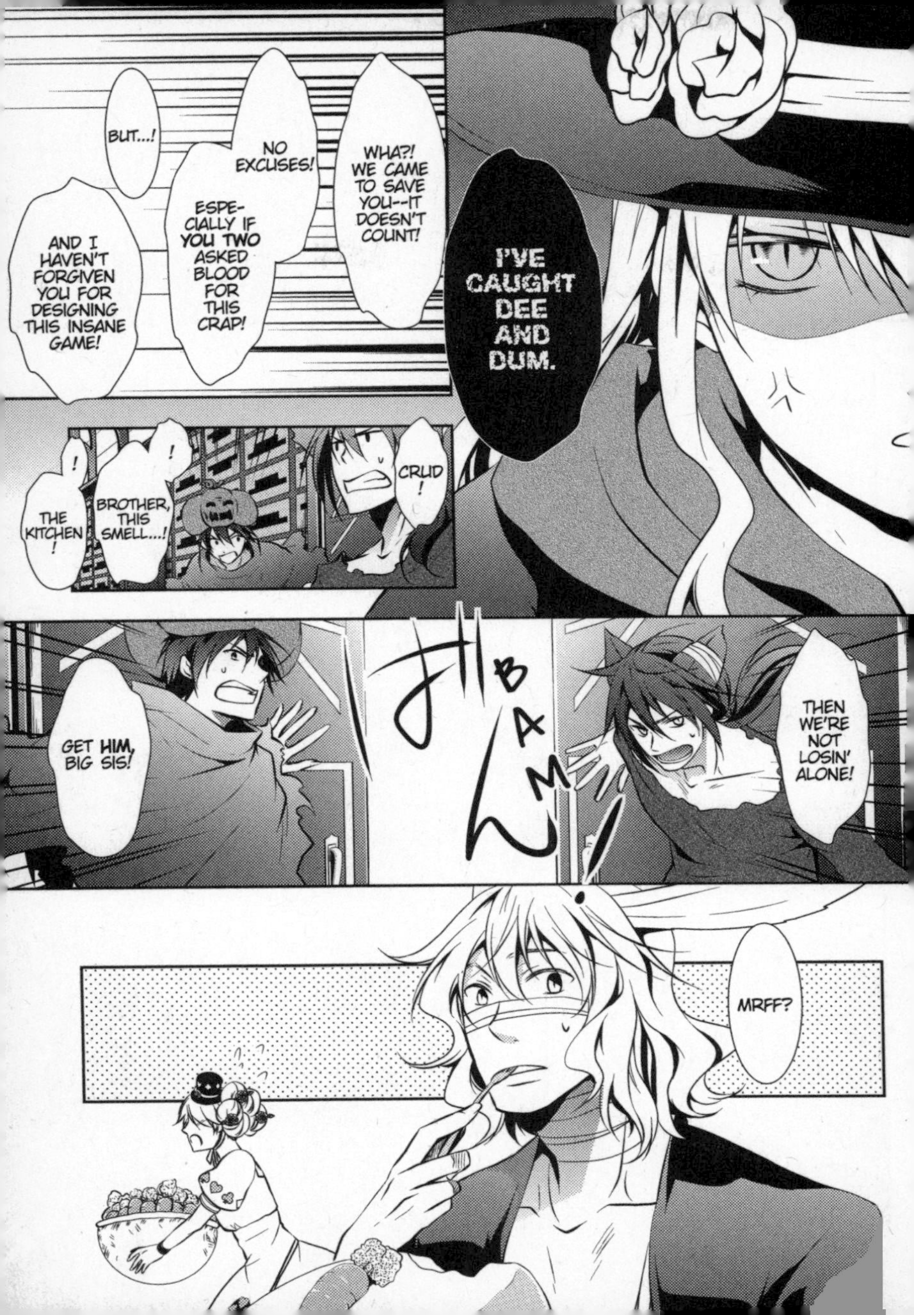
I'VE CAUGHT DEE AND DUM.
WHA?! WE CAME TO SAVE YOU--IT DOESN'T COUNT!
NO EXCUSES!
ESPE-CIALLY IF YOU TWO ASKED BLOOD FOR THIS CRAP!
BUT...!
AND I HAVEN'T FORGIVEN YOU FOR DESIGNING THIS INSANE GAME!
CRUD!
!
BROTHER, THIS SMELL...!
!
THE KITCHEN!
THEN WE'RE NOT LOSIN' ALONE!
BAM
GET HIM, BIG SIS!
MRFF?

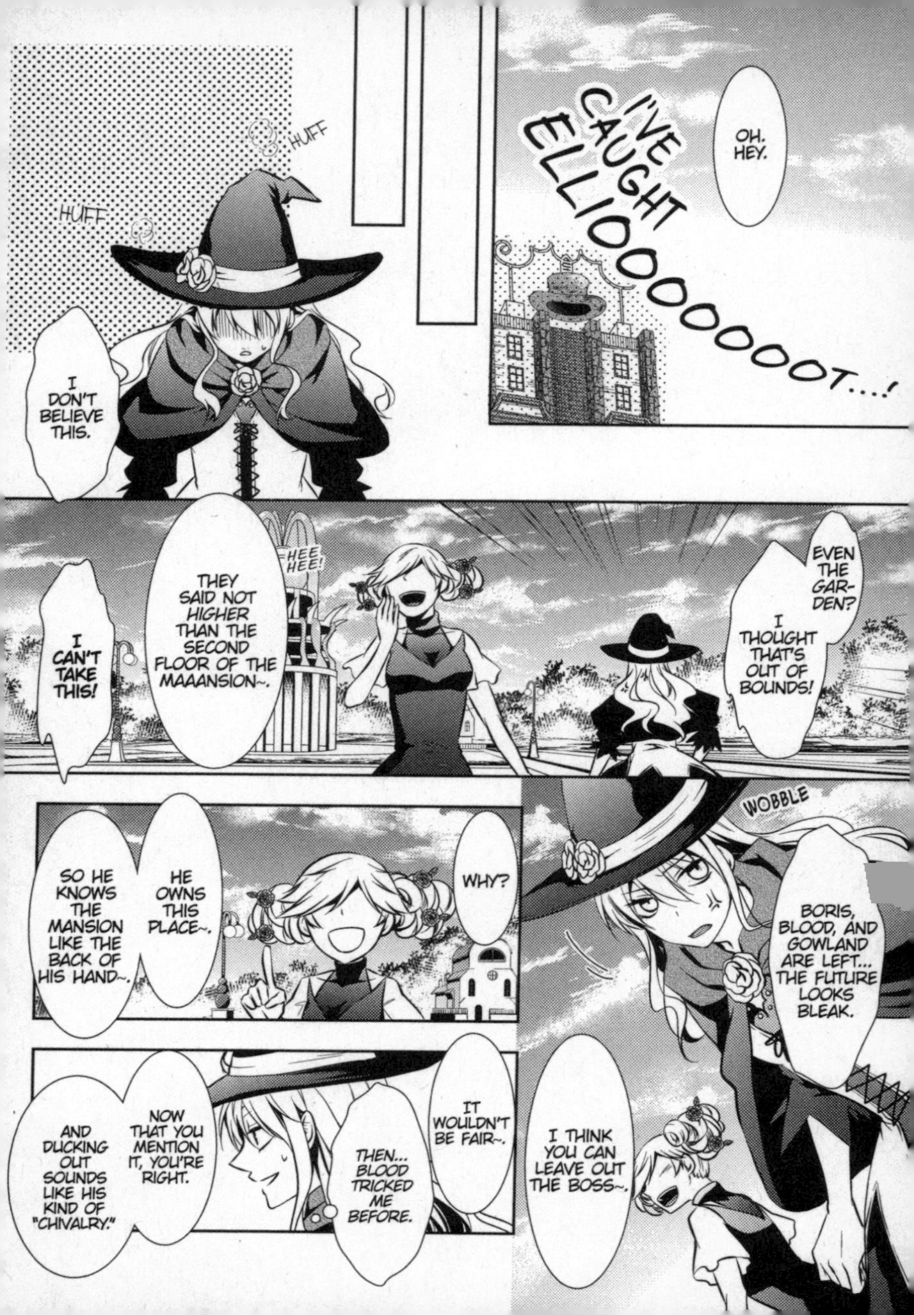
OH. HEY.
I'VE CAUGHT ELLIOOOOOOOOOT...!
HUFF
HUFF
I DON'T BELIEVE THIS.
EVEN THE GARDEN? I THOUGHT THAT'S OUT OF BOUNDS!
HEE HEE!
THEY SAID NOT HIGHER THAN THE SECOND FLOOR OF THE MAAANSION~.
I CAN'T TAKE THIS!
WOBBLE
BORIS, BLOOD, AND GOWLAND ARE LEFT... THE FUTURE LOOKS BLEAK.
I THINK YOU CAN LEAVE OUT THE BOSS~.
WHY?
HE OWNS THIS PLACE~.
SO HE KNOWS THE MANSION LIKE THE BACK OF HIS HAND~.
IT WOULDN'T BE FAIR~.
THEN... BLOOD TRICKED ME BEFORE.
NOW THAT YOU MENTION IT, YOU'RE RIGHT.
AND DUCKING OUT SOUNDS LIKE HIS KIND OF "CHIVALRY."

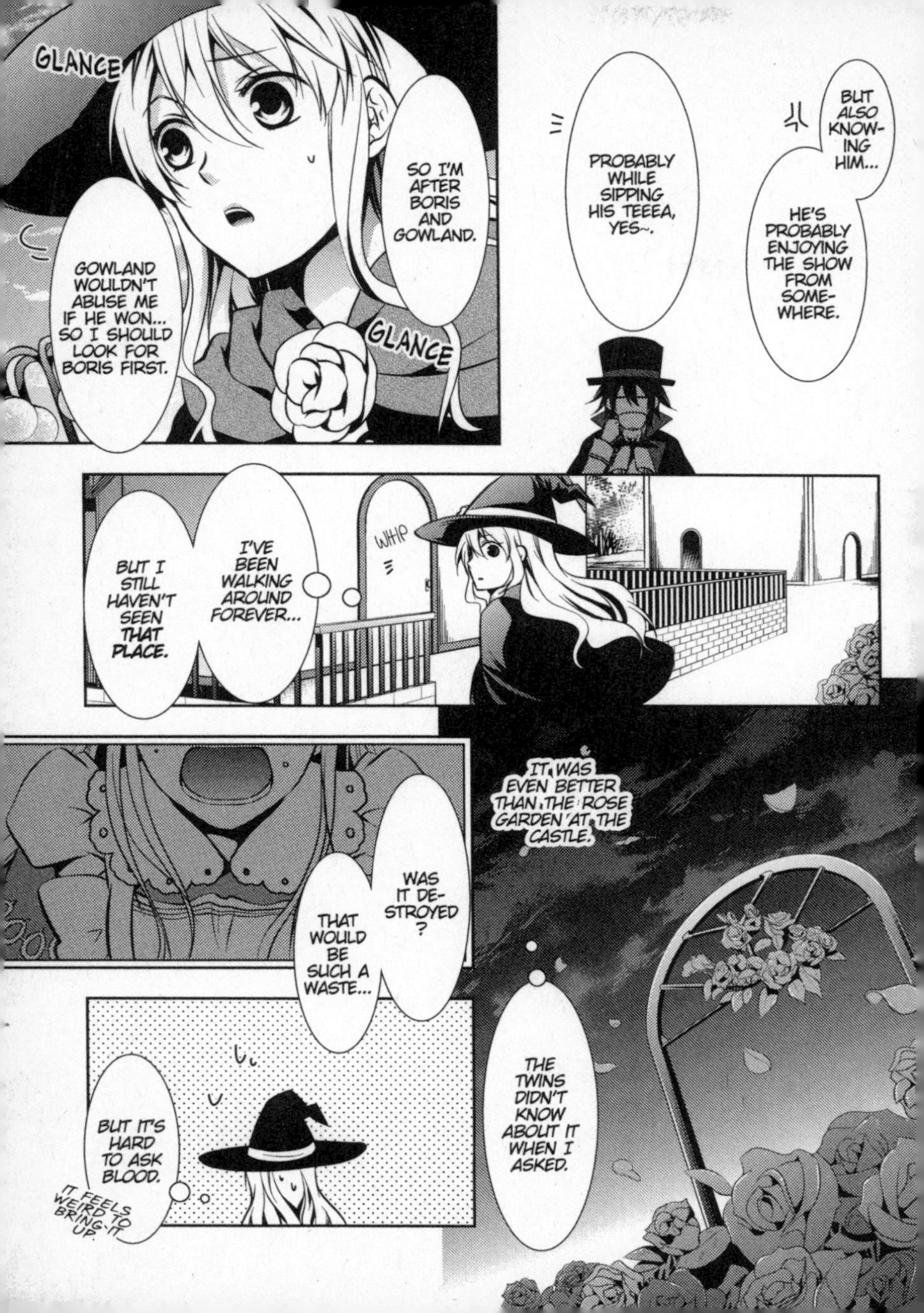
BUT ALSO KNOWING HIM...
HE'S PROBABLY ENJOYING THE SHOW FROM SOMEWHERE.
PROBABLY WHILE SIPPING HIS TEEEA, YES~.
GLANCE
SO I'M AFTER BORIS AND GOWLAND.
GLANCE
GOWLAND WOULDN'T ABUSE ME IF HE WON... SO I SHOULD LOOK FOR BORIS FIRST.
WHIP
I'VE BEEN WALKING AROUND FOREVER...
BUT I STILL HAVEN'T SEEN THAT PLACE.
IT WAS EVEN BETTER THAN THE ROSE GARDEN AT THE CASTLE.
THE TWINS DIDN'T KNOW ABOUT IT WHEN I ASKED.
WAS IT DESTROYED?
THAT WOULD BE SUCH A WASTE...
BUT IT'S HARD TO ASK BLOOD.
IT FEELS WEIRD TO BRING IT UP.

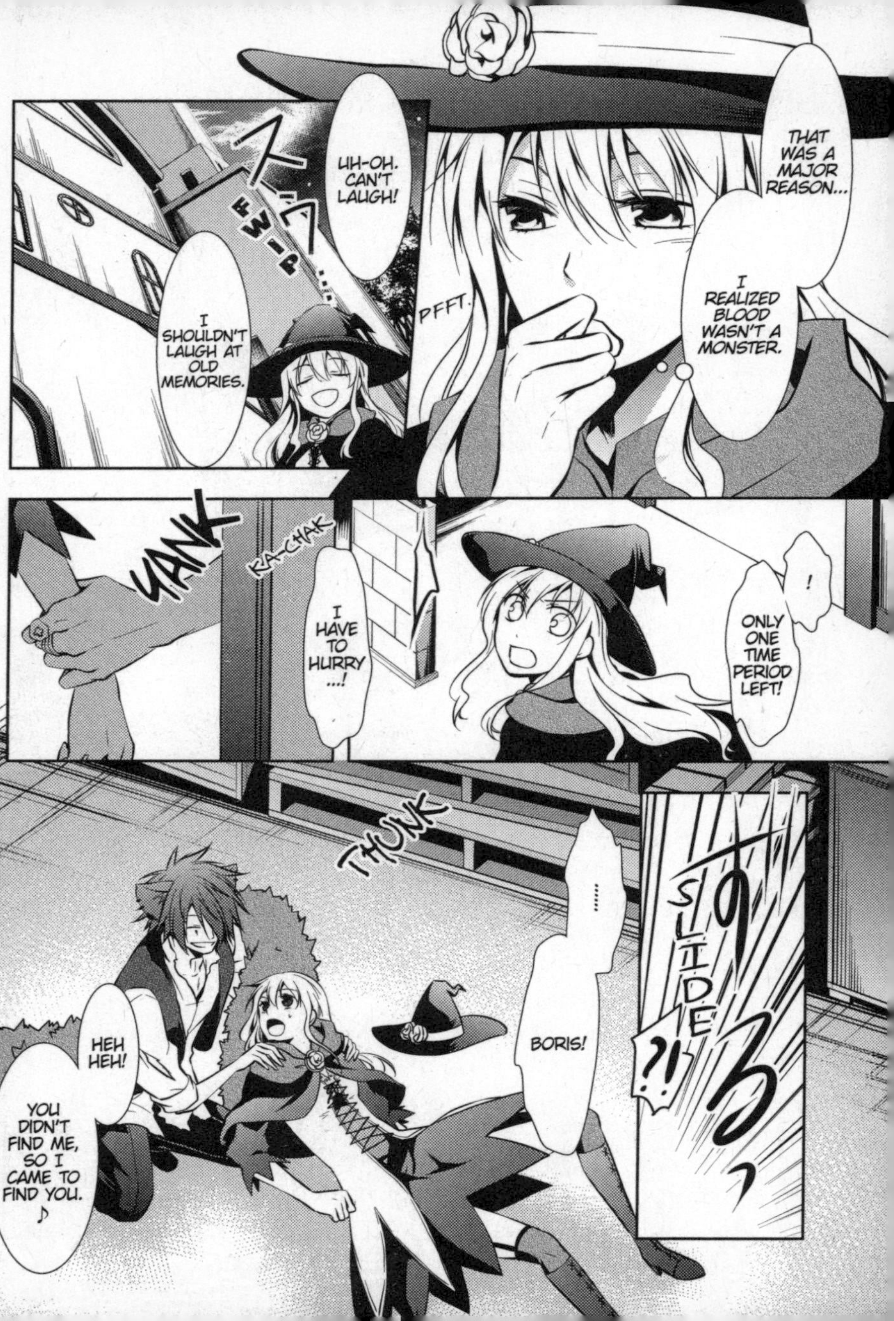
THAT WAS A MAJOR REASON...
I REALIZED BLOOD WASN'T A MONSTER.
PFFT.
UH-OH. CAN'T LAUGH!
FWIP...
I SHOULDN'T LAUGH AT OLD MEMORIES.
!
ONLY ONE TIME PERIOD LEFT!
I HAVE TO HURRY...!
KA-CHAK
YANK
SLIDE
?!
......
BORIS!
THUNK
HEH HEH!
YOU DIDN'T FIND ME, SO I CAME TO FIND YOU. ♪

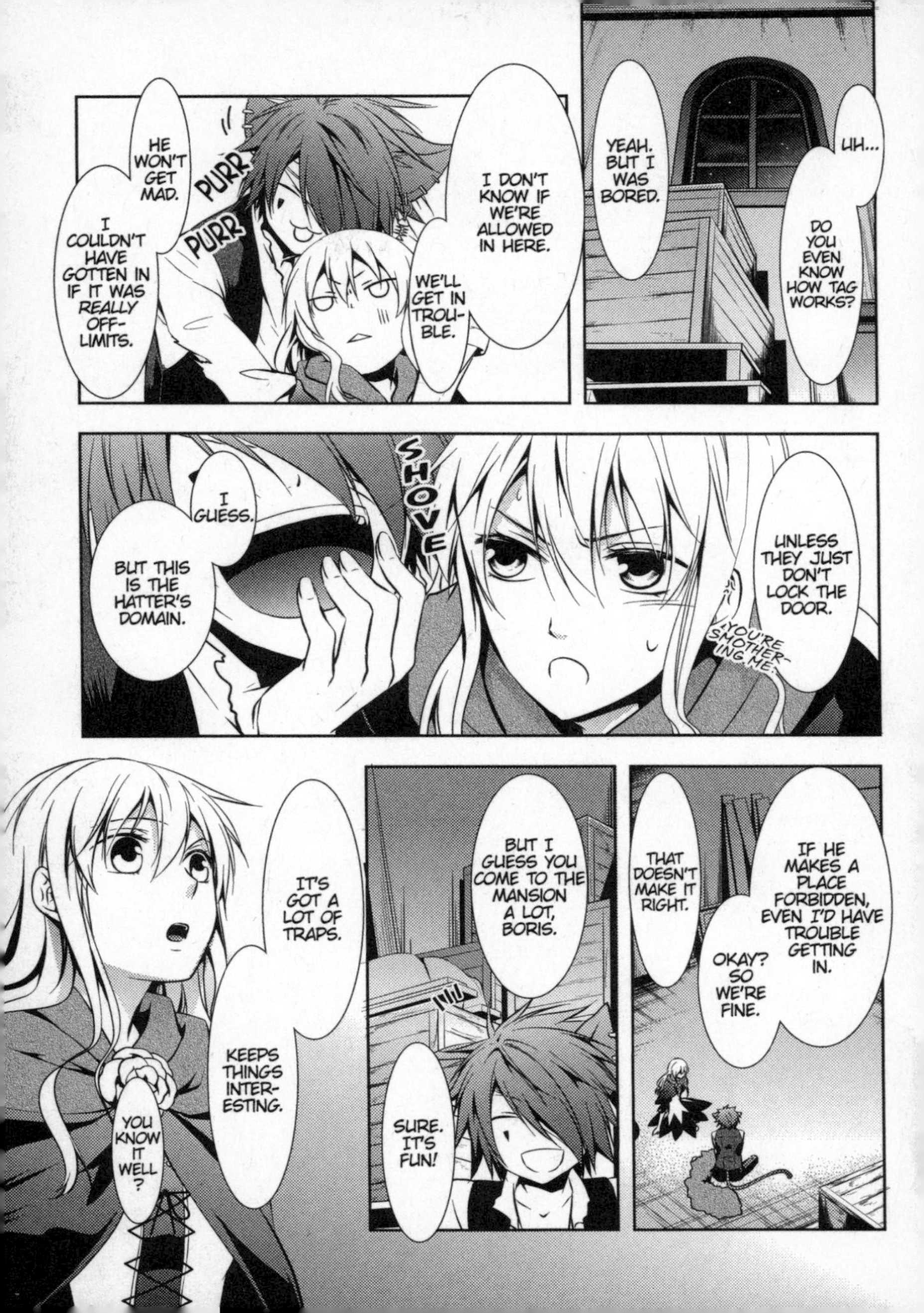
UH...
DO YOU EVEN KNOW HOW TAG WORKS?
YEAH. BUT I WAS BORED.
I DON'T KNOW IF WE'RE ALLOWED IN HERE.
WE'LL GET IN TROUBLE.
PURR
PURR
HE WON'T GET MAD.
I COULDN'T HAVE GOTTEN IN IF IT WAS *REALLY* OFF-LIMITS.
UNLESS THEY JUST DON'T LOCK THE DOOR.
YOU'RE SMOTHERING ME.
SHOVE
I GUESS.
BUT THIS IS THE HATTER'S DOMAIN.
IF HE MAKES A PLACE FORBIDDEN, EVEN *I'D* HAVE TROUBLE GETTING IN.
OKAY? SO WE'RE FINE.
THAT DOESN'T MAKE IT RIGHT.
BUT I GUESS YOU COME TO THE MANSION A LOT, BORIS.
NU
SURE. IT'S FUN!
IT'S GOT A LOT OF TRAPS.
KEEPS THINGS INTERESTING.
YOU KNOW IT WELL?

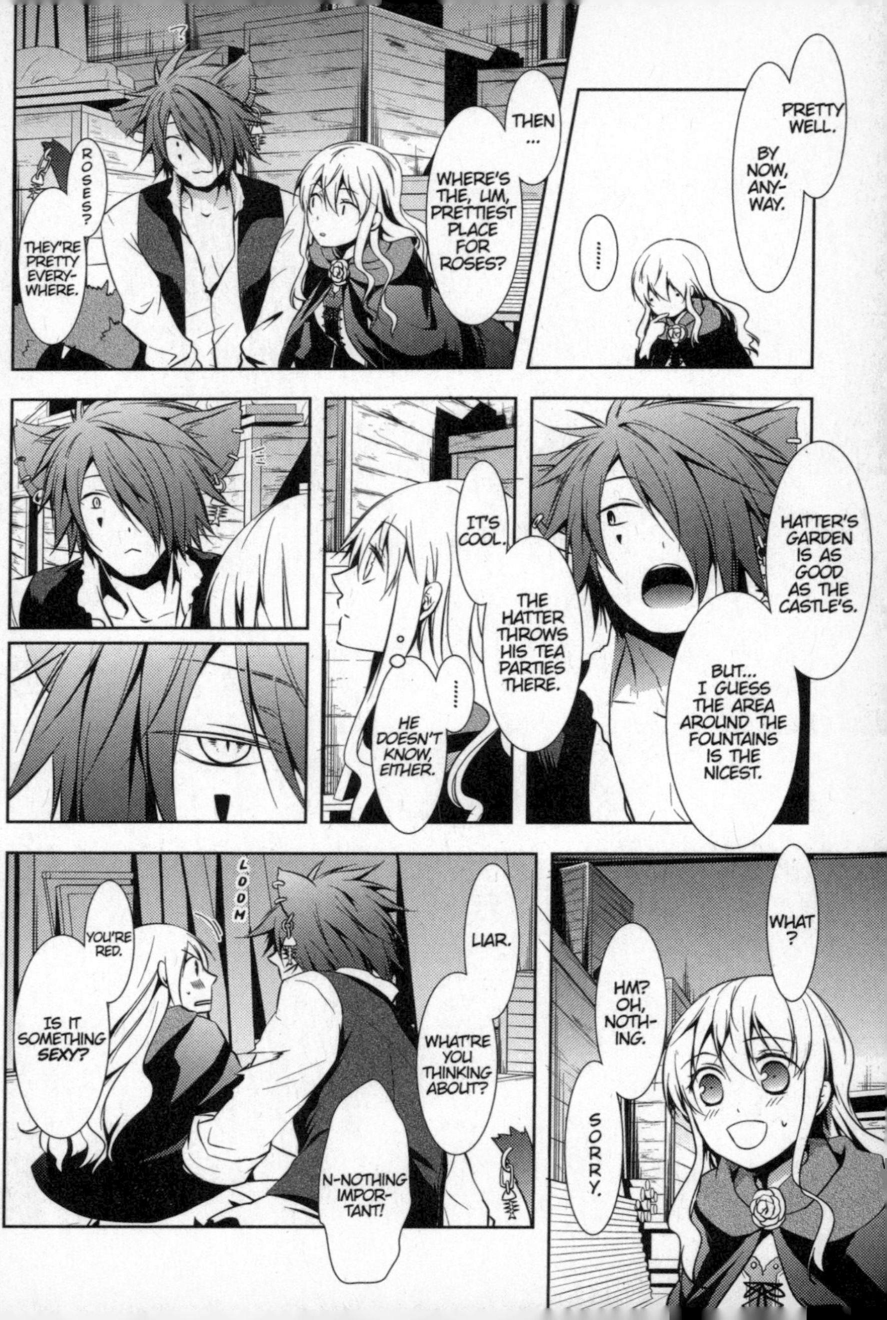
PRETTY WELL.
BY NOW, ANYWAY.
......
THEN ...
WHERE'S THE, UM, PRETTIEST PLACE FOR ROSES?
?
ROSES?
THEY'RE PRETTY EVERYWHERE.
HATTER'S GARDEN IS AS GOOD AS THE CASTLE'S.
BUT... I GUESS THE AREA AROUND THE FOUNTAINS IS THE NICEST.
IT'S COOL.
THE HATTER THROWS HIS TEA PARTIES THERE.
......
HE DOESN'T KNOW, EITHER.
WHAT?
HM? OH, NOTHING.
SORRY.
LIAR.
WHAT'RE YOU THINKING ABOUT?
N-NOTHING IMPORTANT!
LOOM
YOU'RE RED.
IS IT SOMETHING SEXY?

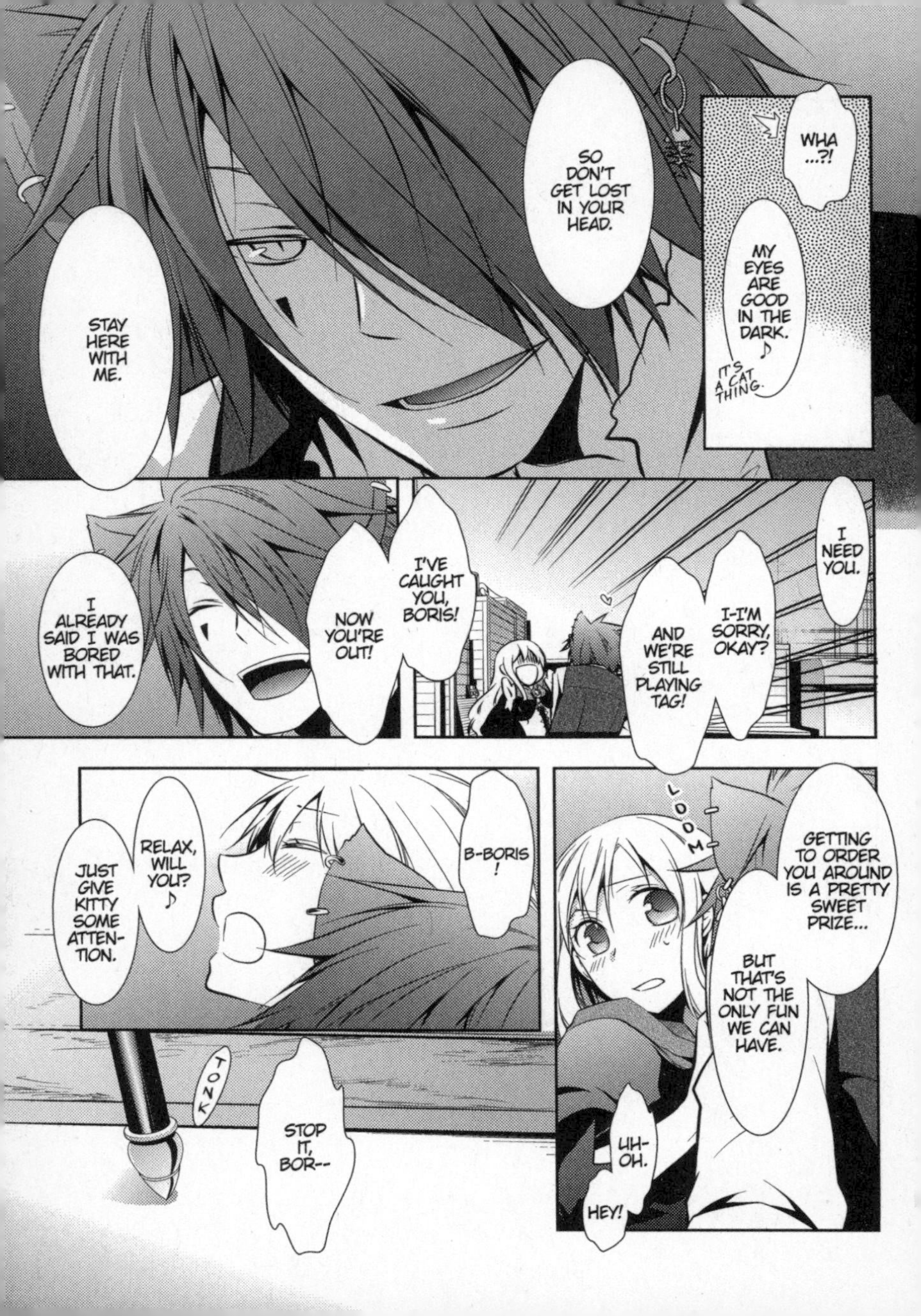
WHA ...?!
MY EYES ARE GOOD IN THE DARK. ♪
IT'S A CAT THING.
SO DON'T GET LOST IN YOUR HEAD.
STAY HERE WITH ME.
I NEED YOU.
I-I'M SORRY, OKAY?
AND WE'RE STILL PLAYING TAG!
I'VE CAUGHT YOU, BORIS!
NOW YOU'RE OUT!
I ALREADY SAID I WAS BORED WITH THAT.
LOOM
GETTING TO ORDER YOU AROUND IS A PRETTY SWEET PRIZE...
BUT THAT'S NOT THE ONLY FUN WE CAN HAVE.
UH-OH.
HEY!
B-BORIS!
RELAX, WILL YOU? ♪
JUST GIVE KITTY SOME ATTENTION.
TONK
STOP IT, BOR--

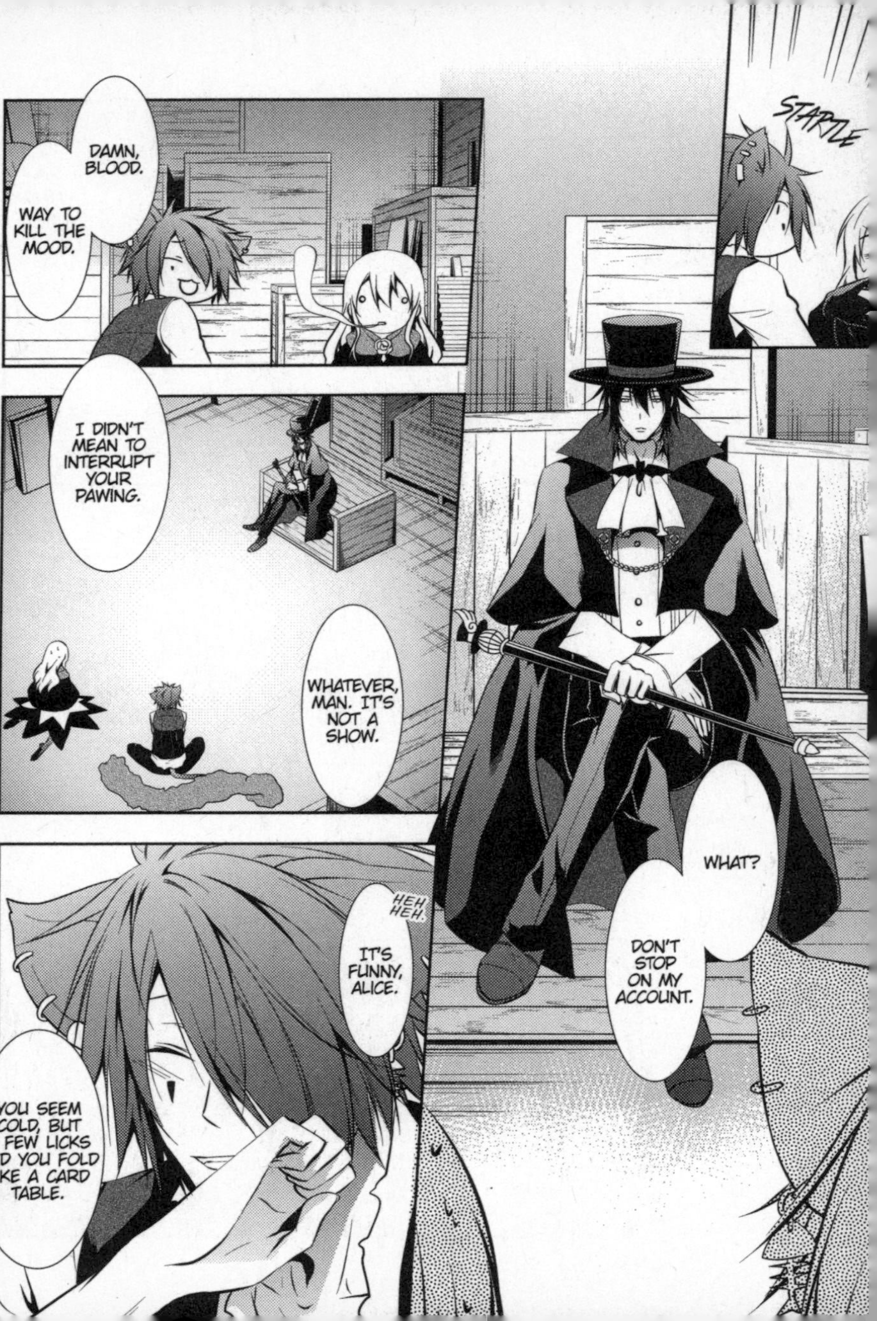
STARTLE
WHAT?
DON'T STOP ON MY ACCOUNT.
DAMN, BLOOD.
WAY TO KILL THE MOOD.
I DIDN'T MEAN TO INTERRUPT YOUR PAWING.
WHATEVER, MAN. IT'S NOT A SHOW.
HEH HEH.
IT'S FUNNY, ALICE.
YOU SEEM COLD, BUT A FEW LICKS AND YOU FOLD LIKE A CARD TABLE.

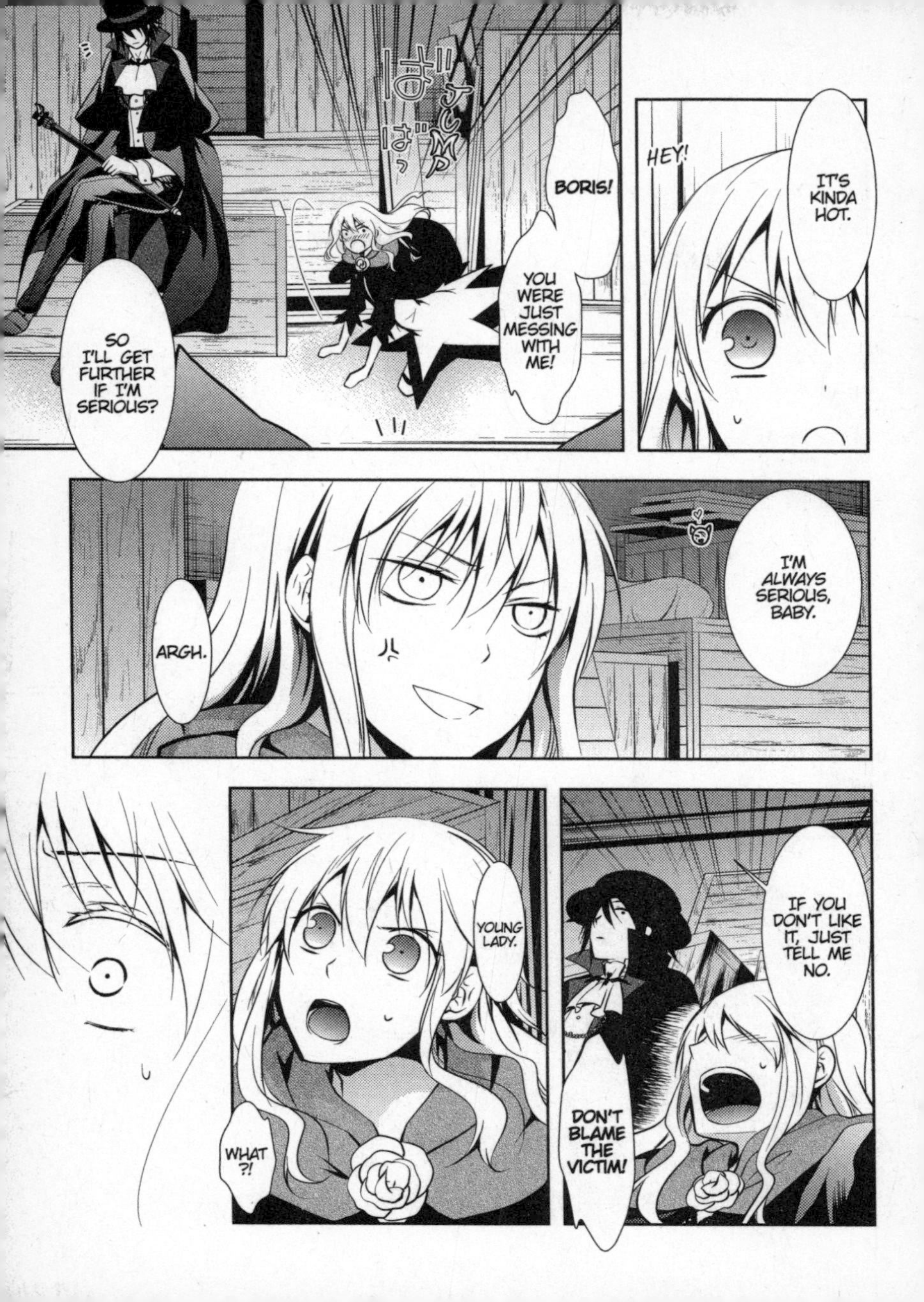
IT'S KINDA HOT.
HEY!
JUMP
BORIS!
YOU WERE JUST MESSING WITH ME!
SO I'LL GET FURTHER IF I'M SERIOUS?
I'M ALWAYS SERIOUS, BABY.
ARGH.
IF YOU DON'T LIKE IT, JUST TELL ME NO.
DON'T BLAME THE VICTIM!
YOUNG LADY.
WHAT ?!

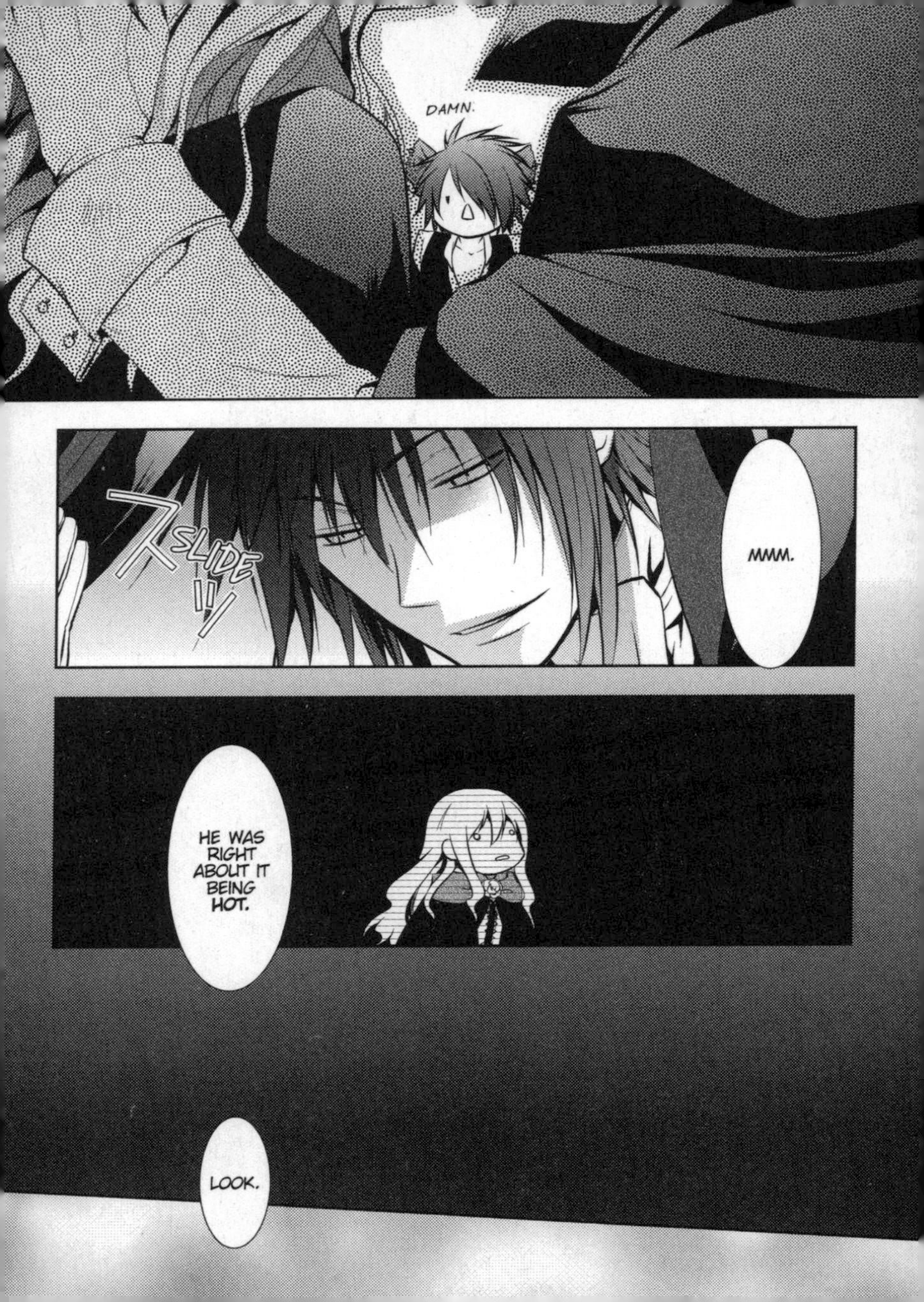
DAMN.
MMM.
SLIDE
HE WAS RIGHT ABOUT IT BEING HOT.
LOOK.

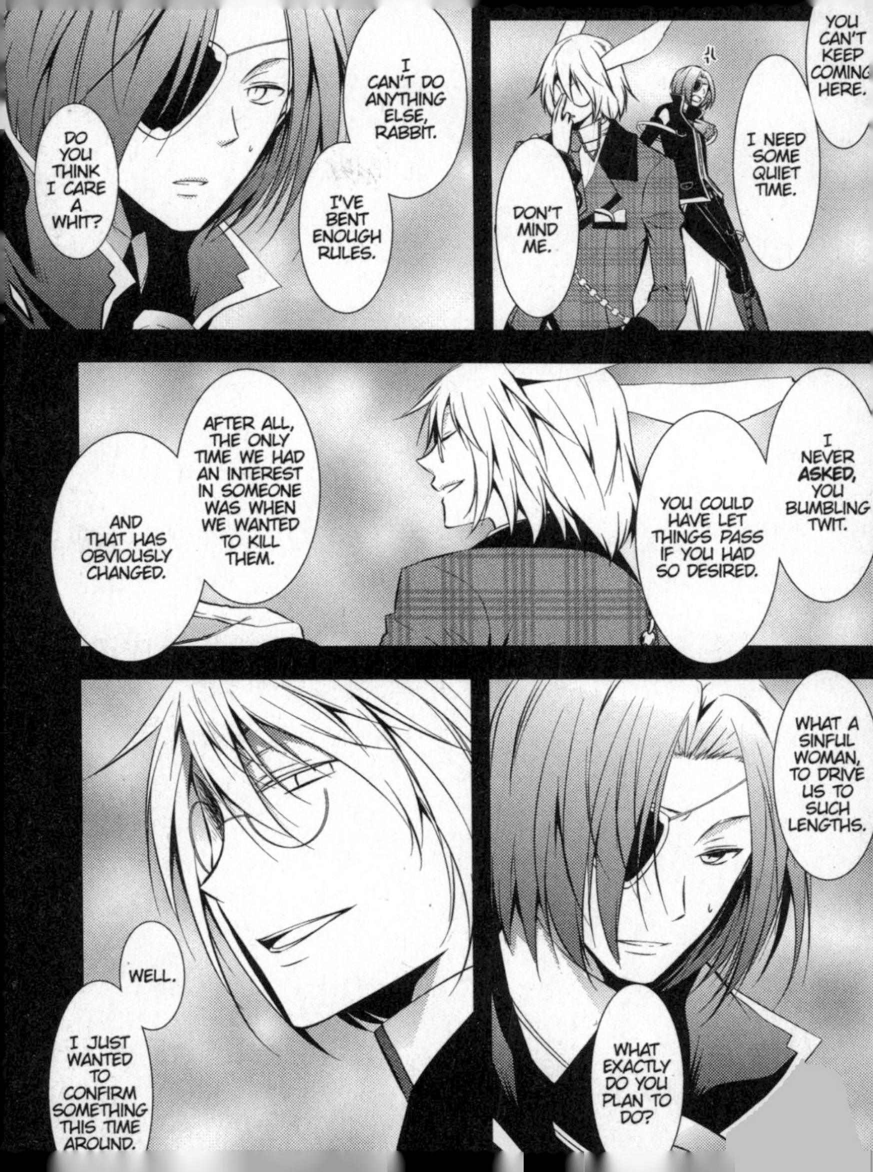
YOU CAN'T KEEP COMING HERE.
I NEED SOME QUIET TIME.
DON'T MIND ME.
I CAN'T DO ANYTHING ELSE, RABBIT.
I'VE BENT ENOUGH RULES.
DO YOU THINK I CARE A WHIT?
I NEVER **ASKED**, YOU BUMBLING TWIT.
YOU COULD HAVE LET THINGS PASS IF YOU HAD SO DESIRED.
AFTER ALL, THE ONLY TIME WE HAD AN INTEREST IN SOMEONE WAS WHEN WE WANTED TO KILL THEM.
AND THAT HAS OBVIOUSLY CHANGED.
WHAT A SINFUL WOMAN, TO DRIVE US TO SUCH LENGTHS.
WHAT EXACTLY DO YOU PLAN TO DO?
WELL.
I JUST WANTED TO CONFIRM SOMETHING THIS TIME AROUND.

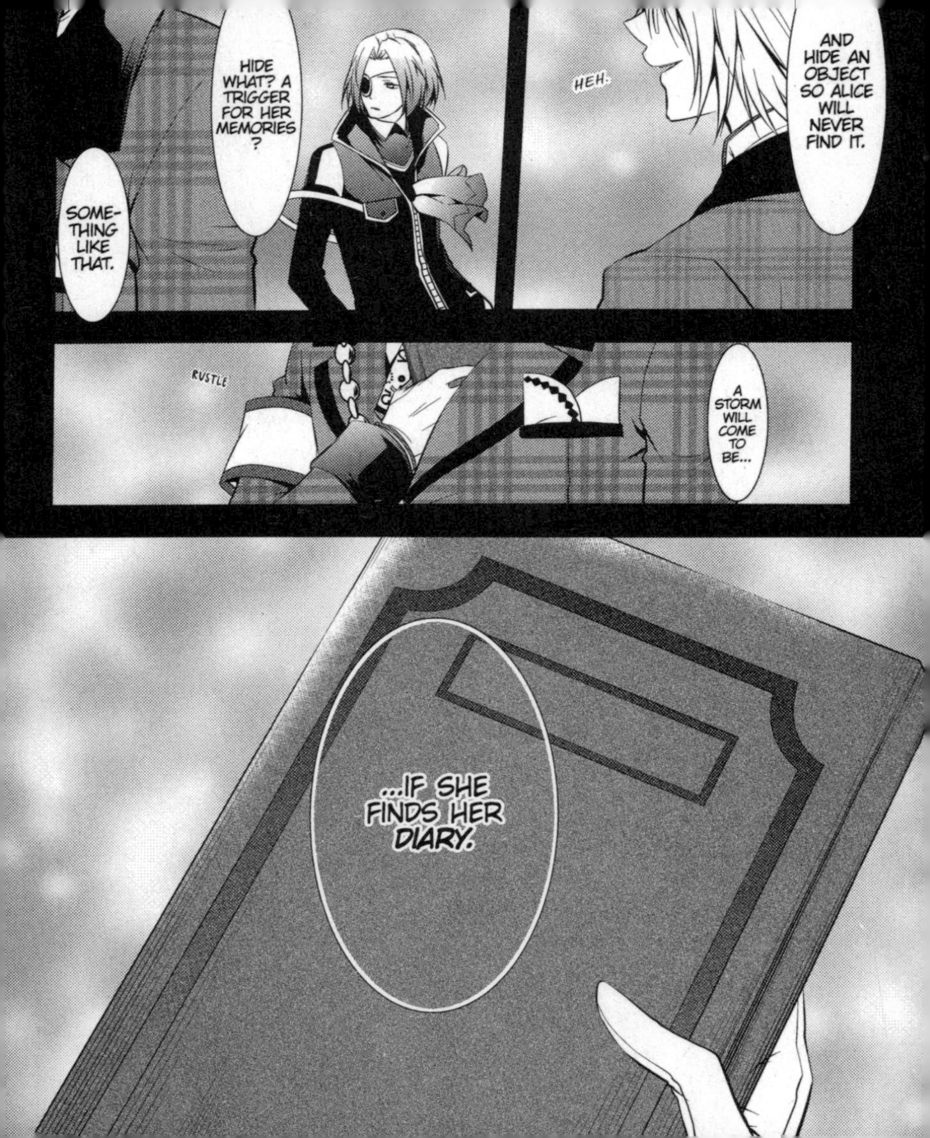
AND HIDE AN OBJECT SO ALICE WILL NEVER FIND IT.
HEH.
HIDE WHAT? A TRIGGER FOR HER MEMORIES?
SOMETHING LIKE THAT.
A STORM WILL COME TO BE...
RUSTLE
...IF SHE FINDS HER DIARY.

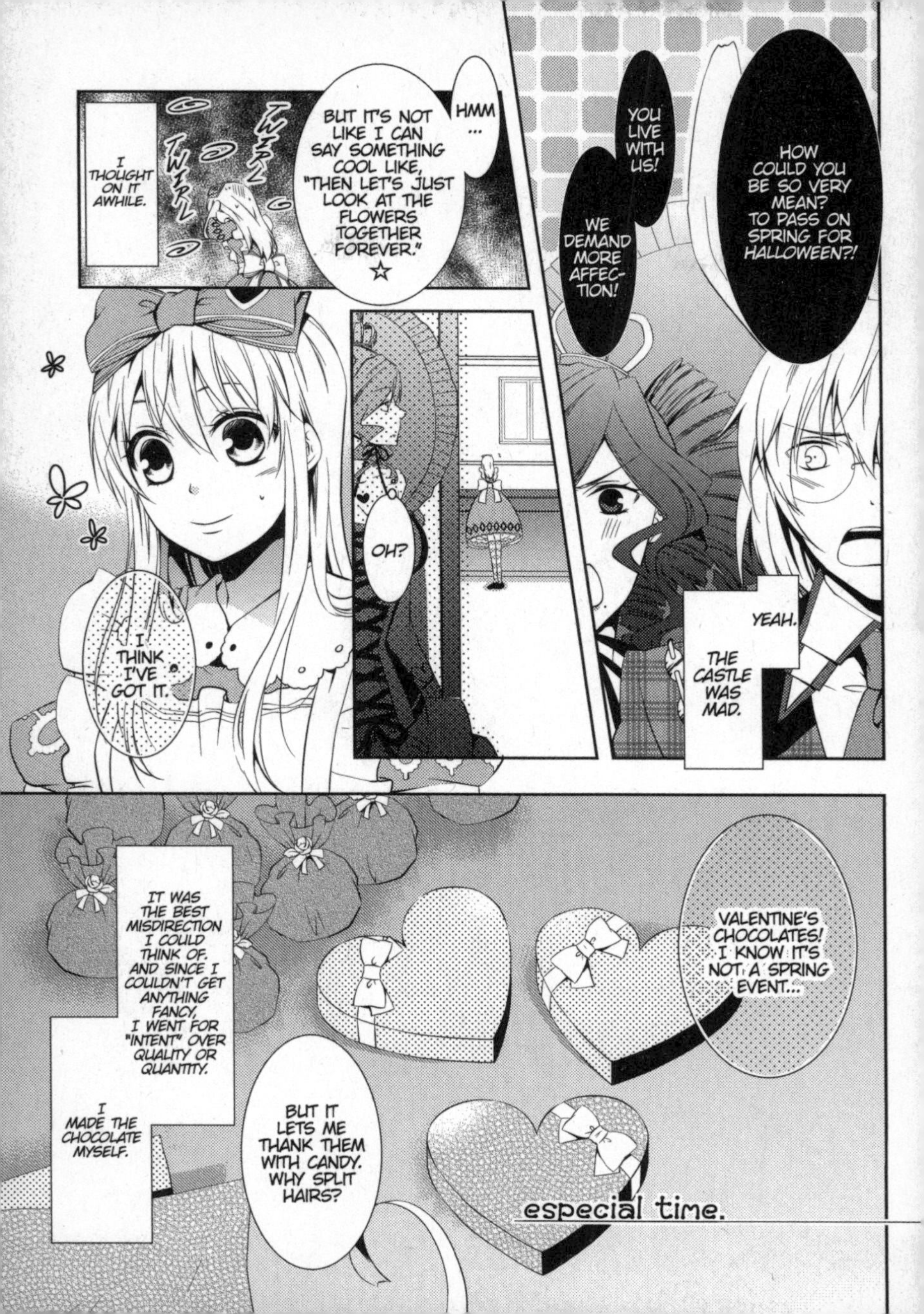
HOW COULD YOU BE SO VERY MEAN? TO PASS ON SPRING FOR HALLOWEEN?!
YOU LIVE WITH US!
WE DEMAND MORE AFFECTION!
YEAH.
THE CASTLE WAS MAD.
HMM ...
BUT IT'S NOT LIKE I CAN SAY SOMETHING COOL LIKE, "THEN LET'S JUST LOOK AT THE FLOWERS TOGETHER FOREVER." ☆
TWIRL TWIRL
I THOUGHT ON IT AWHILE.
OH?
I THINK I'VE GOT IT.
VALENTINE'S CHOCOLATES! I KNOW IT'S NOT A SPRING EVENT...
IT WAS THE BEST MISDIRECTION I COULD THINK OF. AND SINCE I COULDN'T GET ANYTHING FANCY, I WENT FOR "INTENT" OVER QUALITY OR QUANTITY.
BUT IT LETS ME THANK THEM WITH CANDY. WHY SPLIT HAIRS?
I MADE THE CHOCOLATE MYSELF.
especial time.

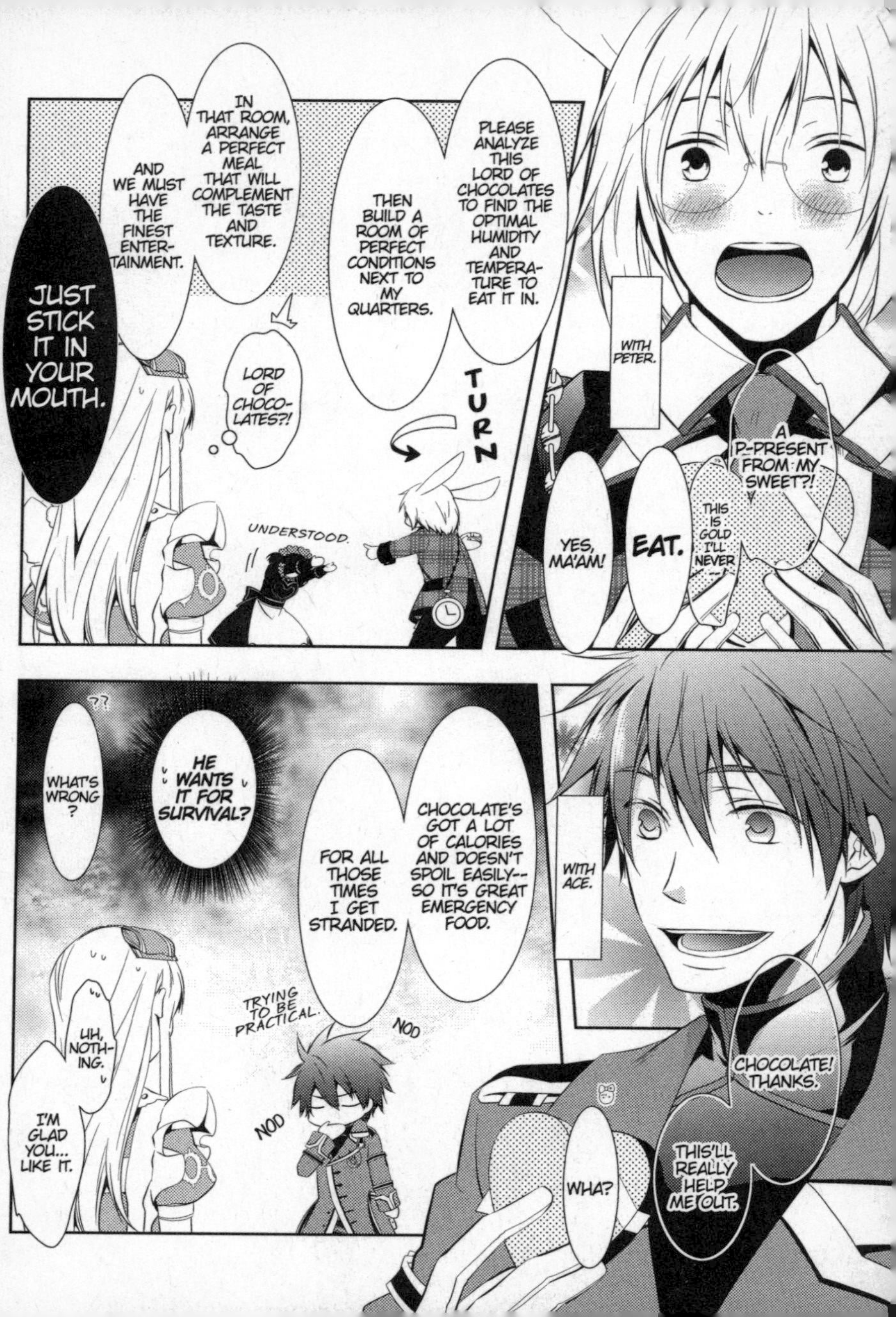
WITH PETER.
A P-PRESENT FROM MY SWEET?!
THIS IS GOLD I'LL NEVER --
EAT.
YES, MA'AM!
PLEASE ANALYZE THIS LORD OF CHOCOLATES TO FIND THE OPTIMAL HUMIDITY AND TEMPERA-TURE TO EAT IT IN.
THEN BUILD A ROOM OF PERFECT CONDITIONS NEXT TO MY QUARTERS.
IN THAT ROOM, ARRANGE A PERFECT MEAL THAT WILL COMPLEMENT THE TASTE AND TEXTURE.
AND WE MUST HAVE THE FINEST ENTER-TAINMENT.
LORD OF CHOCO-LATES?!
TURN
UNDERSTOOD.
JUST STICK IT IN YOUR MOUTH.
WITH ACE.
CHOCOLATE! THANKS.
THIS'LL REALLY HELP ME OUT.
WHA?
CHOCOLATE'S GOT A LOT OF CALORIES AND DOESN'T SPOIL EASILY-- SO IT'S GREAT EMERGENCY FOOD.
FOR ALL THOSE TIMES I GET STRANDED.
NOD
TRYING TO BE PRACTICAL.
NOD
HE WANTS IT FOR SURVIVAL?
WHAT'S WRONG?
UH, NOTHING.
I'M GLAD YOU... LIKE IT.

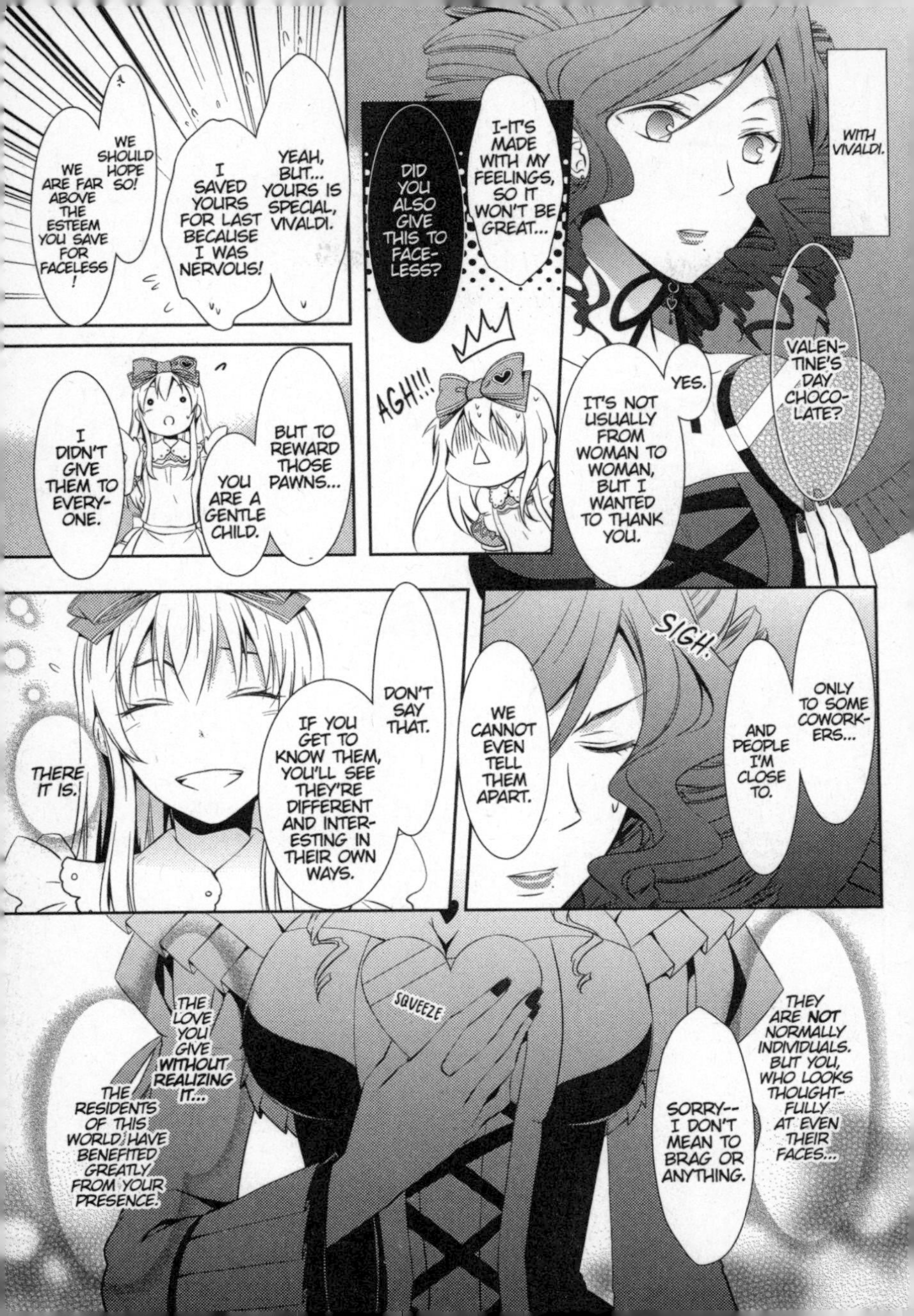
WITH VIVALDI.
VALENTINE'S DAY CHOCOLATE?
YES.
IT'S NOT USUALLY FROM WOMAN TO WOMAN, BUT I WANTED TO THANK YOU.
I-IT'S MADE WITH MY FEELINGS, SO IT WON'T BE GREAT...
DID YOU ALSO GIVE THIS TO FACELESS?
AGH!!!
YEAH, BUT... YOURS IS SPECIAL, VIVALDI.
I SAVED YOURS FOR LAST BECAUSE I WAS NERVOUS!
WE SHOULD HOPE SO!
WE ARE FAR ABOVE THE ESTEEM YOU SAVE FOR FACELESS!
BUT TO REWARD THOSE PAWNS...
YOU ARE A GENTLE CHILD.
I DIDN'T GIVE THEM TO EVERYONE.
SIGH.
ONLY TO SOME COWORKERS...
AND PEOPLE I'M CLOSE TO.
WE CANNOT EVEN TELL THEM APART.
DON'T SAY THAT.
IF YOU GET TO KNOW THEM, YOU'LL SEE THEY'RE DIFFERENT AND INTERESTING IN THEIR OWN WAYS.
THERE IT IS.
THEY ARE NOT NORMALLY INDIVIDUALS. BUT YOU, WHO LOOKS THOUGHTFULLY AT EVEN THEIR FACES...
SORRY-- I DON'T MEAN TO BRAG OR ANYTHING.
SQUEEZE
THE LOVE YOU GIVE WITHOUT REALIZING IT...
THE RESIDENTS OF THIS WORLD HAVE BENEFITED GREATLY FROM YOUR PRESENCE.

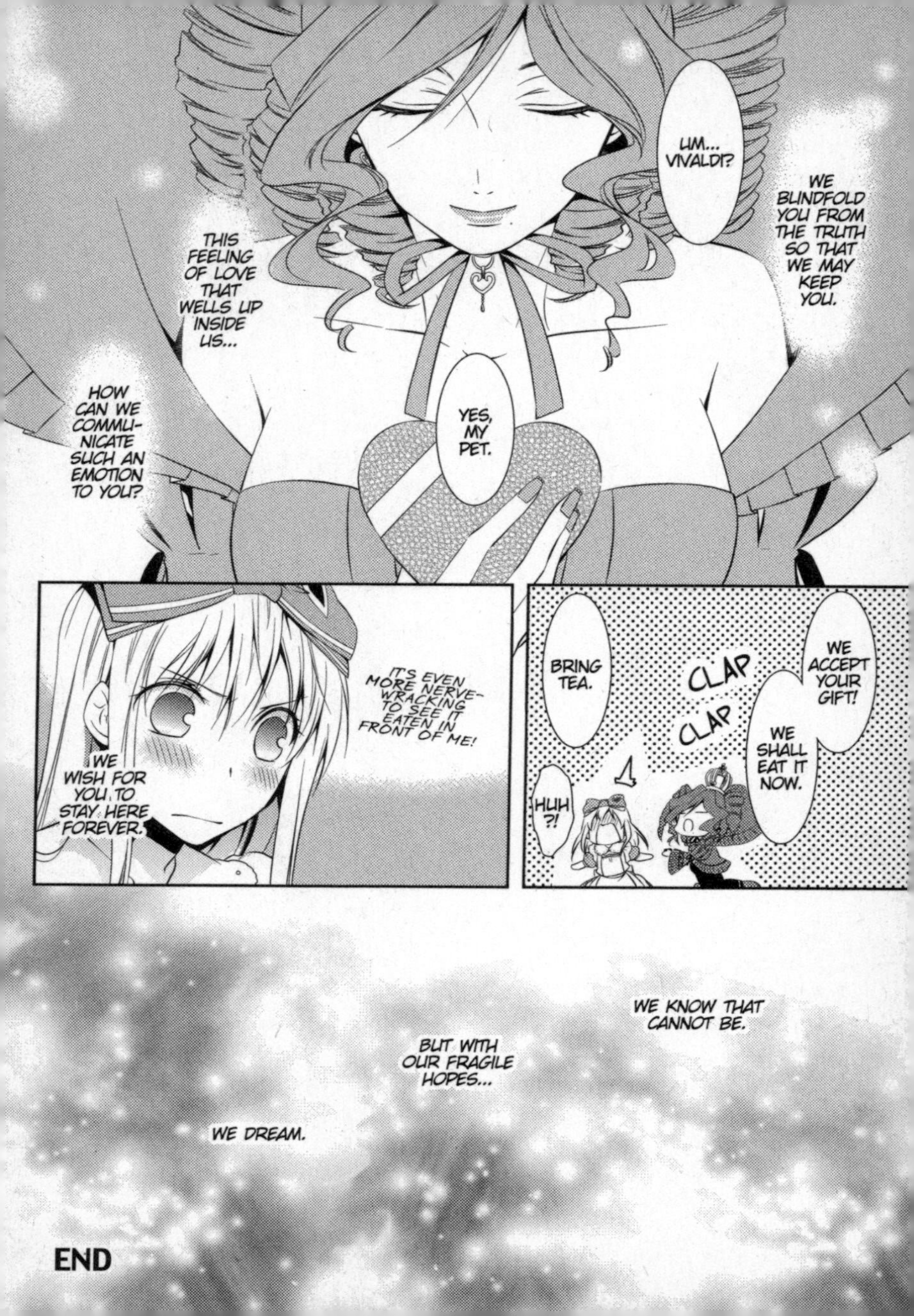
UM... VIVALDI?
WE BLINDFOLD YOU FROM THE TRUTH SO THAT WE MAY KEEP YOU.
THIS FEELING OF LOVE THAT WELLS UP INSIDE US...
YES, MY PET.
HOW CAN WE COMMUNICATE SUCH AN EMOTION TO YOU?
WE ACCEPT YOUR GIFT!
CLAP
CLAP
BRING TEA.
WE SHALL EAT IT NOW.
HUH ?!
IT'S EVEN MORE NERVE-WRACKING TO SEE IT EATEN IN FRONT OF ME!
WE WISH FOR YOU TO STAY HERE FOREVER.
WE KNOW THAT CANNOT BE.
BUT WITH OUR FRAGILE HOPES...
WE DREAM.
END

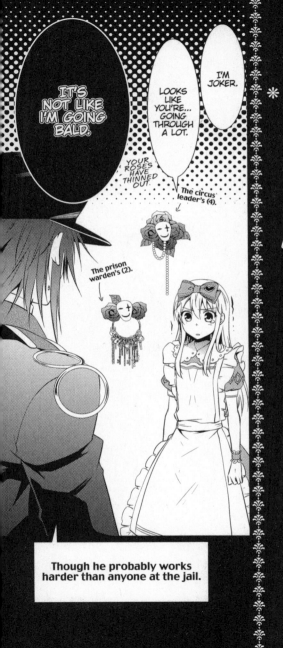

* THANK YOU VERY MUCH *

Everyone who helped me with the script

My friends & family

QuinRose-sama

My publisher

And most of all, the readers.

Mamenosuke Fujimaru

I'M JOKER.
LOOKS LIKE YOU'RE... GOING THROUGH A LOT.
YOUR ROSES HAVE THINNED OUT.
IT'S NOT LIKE I'M GOING BALD.
The circus leader's (4).
The prison warden's (2).
Though he probably works harder than anyone at the jail.

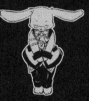

EVENT 1

IF ALICE WAS SMALL.

~Overflow of Volume 1 Edition~

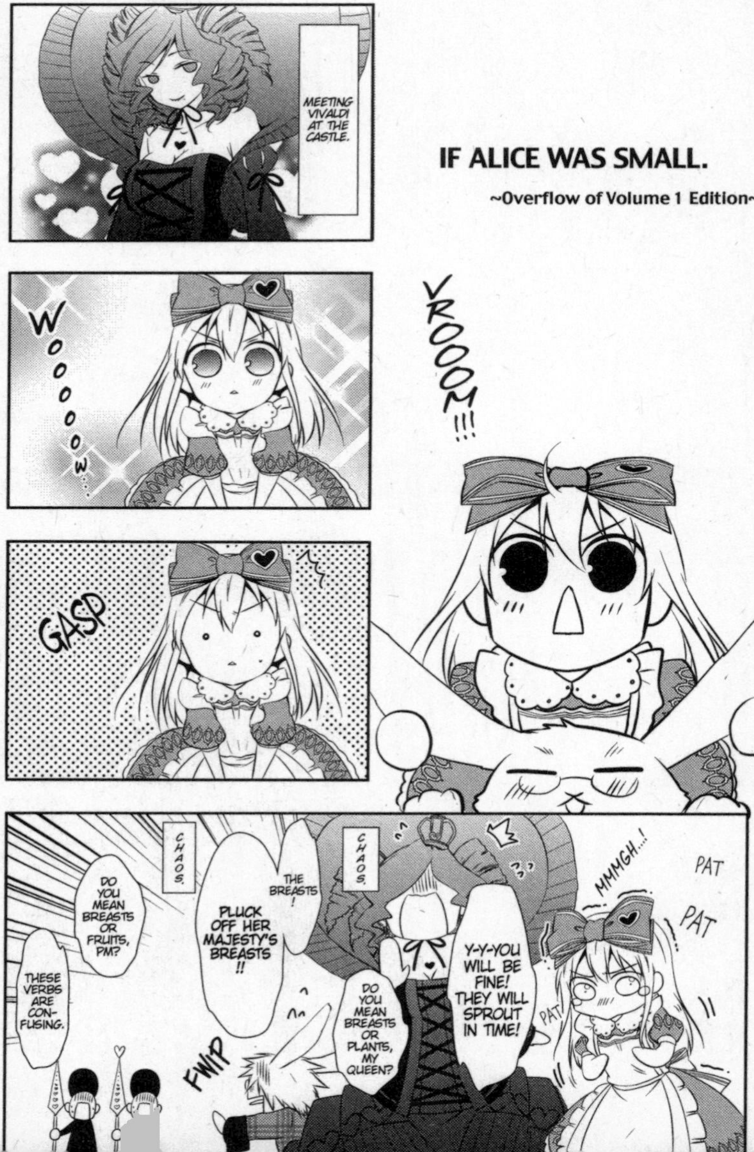
VROOOOM!!!
MEETING VIVALDI AT THE CASTLE.
WOOOOOOW...
GASP
MMMGH...!
PAT
PAT
Y-Y-YOU WILL BE FINE! THEY WILL SPROUT IN TIME!
CHAOS.
THE BREASTS!
PLUCK OFF HER MAJESTY'S BREASTS!!
DO YOU MEAN BREASTS OR PLANTS, MY QUEEN?
CHAOS.
DO YOU MEAN BREASTS OR FRUITS, PM?
THESE VERBS ARE CON-FUSING.
FWIP
PAT

EVENT 2

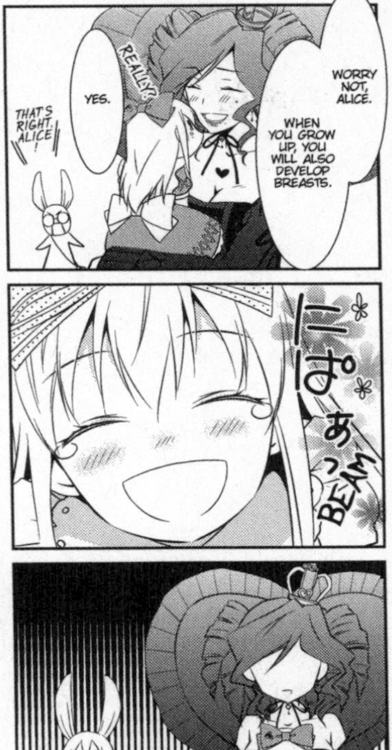
WORRY NOT, ALICE.
WHEN YOU GROW UP, YOU WILL ALSO DEVELOP BREASTS.
REALLY?
YES.
THAT'S RIGHT, ALICE!
にぱぁ
BEAM
?!
PULL
PULL
PULL
PULL

EVENT 3

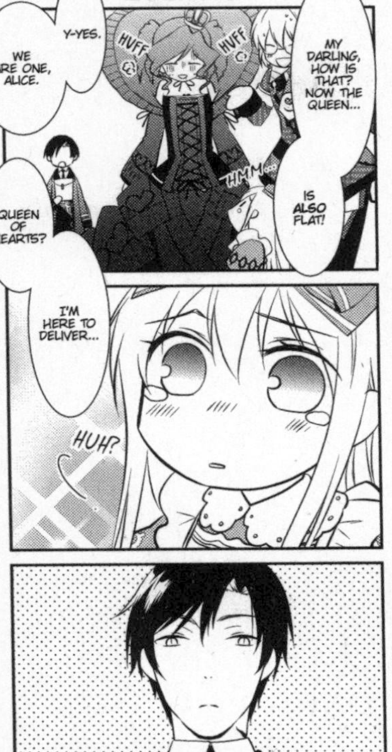
MY DARLING, HOW IS THAT? NOW THE QUEEN...
HUFF
HUFF
Y-YES.
WE ARE ONE, ALICE.
HMM...
IS ALSO FLAT!
QUEEN OF HEARTS?
I'M HERE TO DELIVER...
HUH?
SORRY FOR THE TROUBLE.
AND THANK YOU FOR FINDING MY LOVE CHILD.
GLANCE
GLANCE
OFF WITH HIS HEAD!
IF SHE WERE YOUR DAUGHTER, SHE WOULDN'T BE AN OUTSIDER, RINGMARC.
WHY IS HE HERE?!

A SUCKER FOR CUTE THINGS.

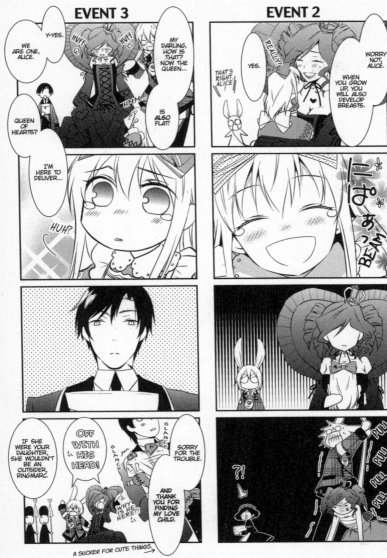

COMING SOON

JUNE 2013
Alice in the Country of Clover:
Ace of Hearts

JULY 2013
Alice in the Country of Clover:
Cheshire Cat Waltz Vol. 5

AUGUST 2013
Alice in the Country of Hearts:
The Clockmaker's Story

Crimson Empire Vol. 2

The Sacred Blacksmith

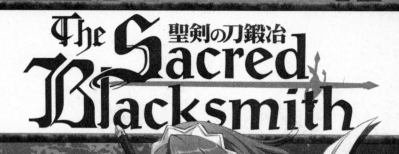

聖剣の刀鍛冶

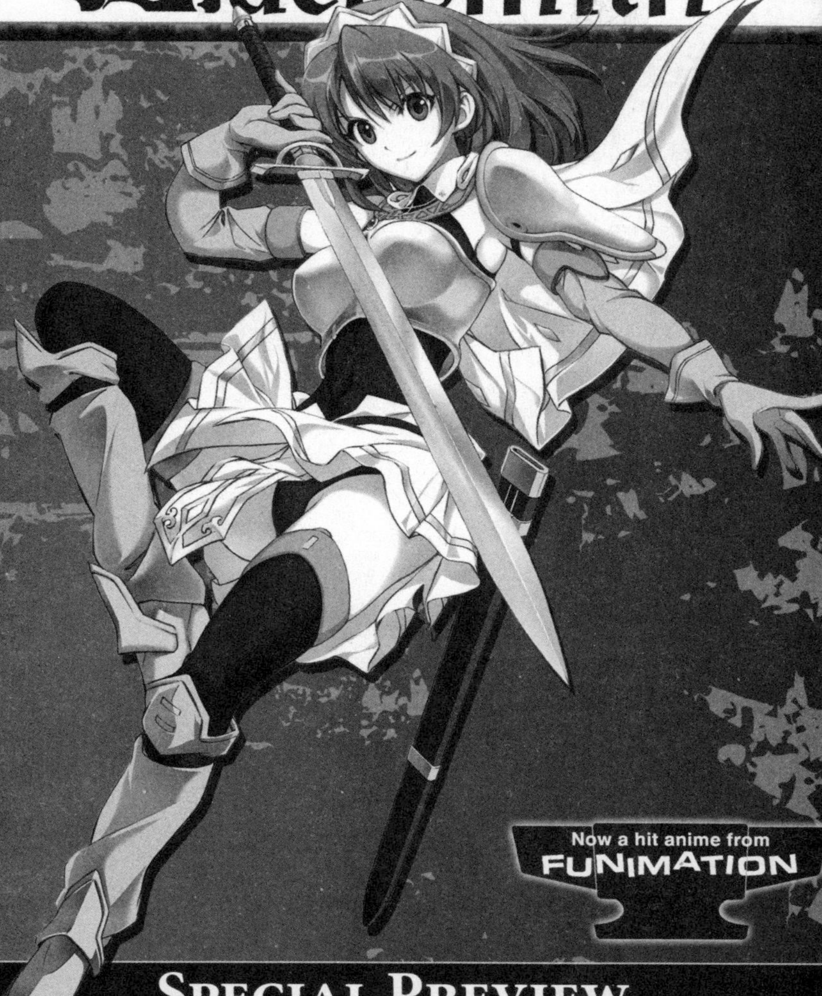
Now a hit anime from
FUNIMATION

SPECIAL PREVIEW

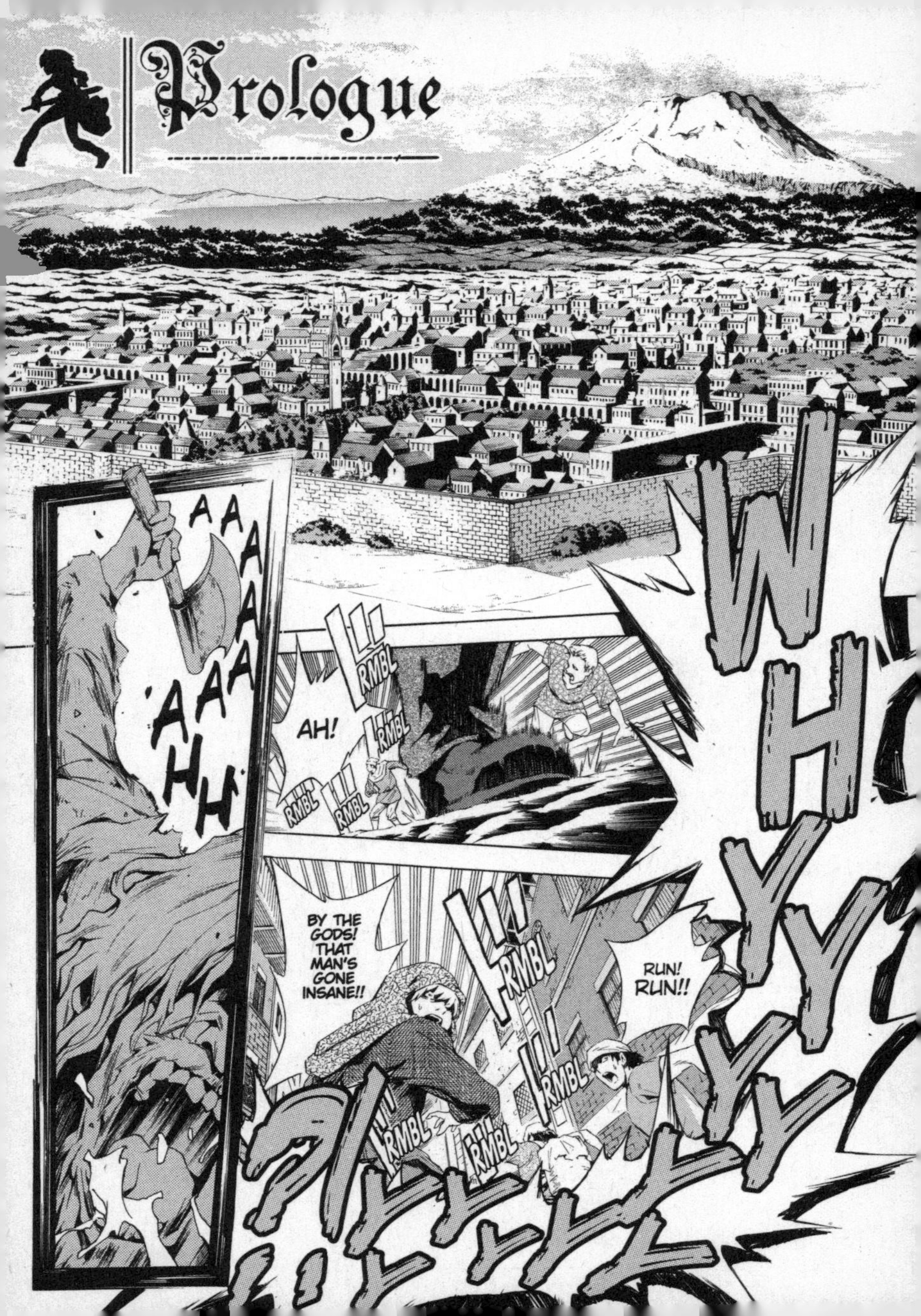
Prologue
RMBL
AH!
RMBL
RMBL
RMBL
RUN! RUN!!
BY THE GODS! THAT MAN'S GONE INSANE!!
RMBL
RMBL
RMBL
RMBL
AAAAAAAAAHH

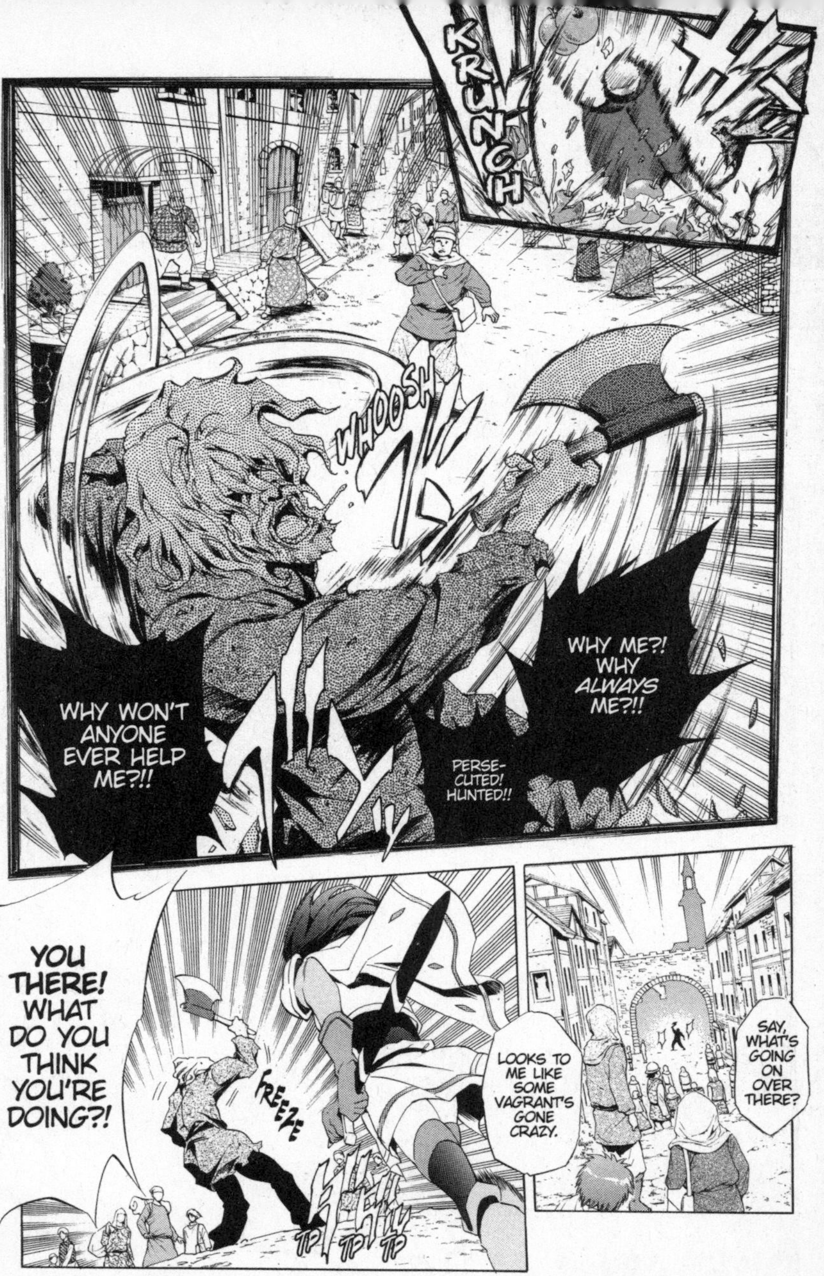
KRUNCH
WHOOSH
WHY ME?! WHY ALWAYS ME?!!
PERSE-CUTED! HUNTED!!
WHY WON'T ANYONE EVER HELP ME?!!
SAY, WHAT'S GOING ON OVER THERE?
LOOKS TO ME LIKE SOME VAGRANT'S GONE CRAZY.
YOU THERE! WHAT DO YOU THINK YOU'RE DOING?!
FREEZE
TP TP TP

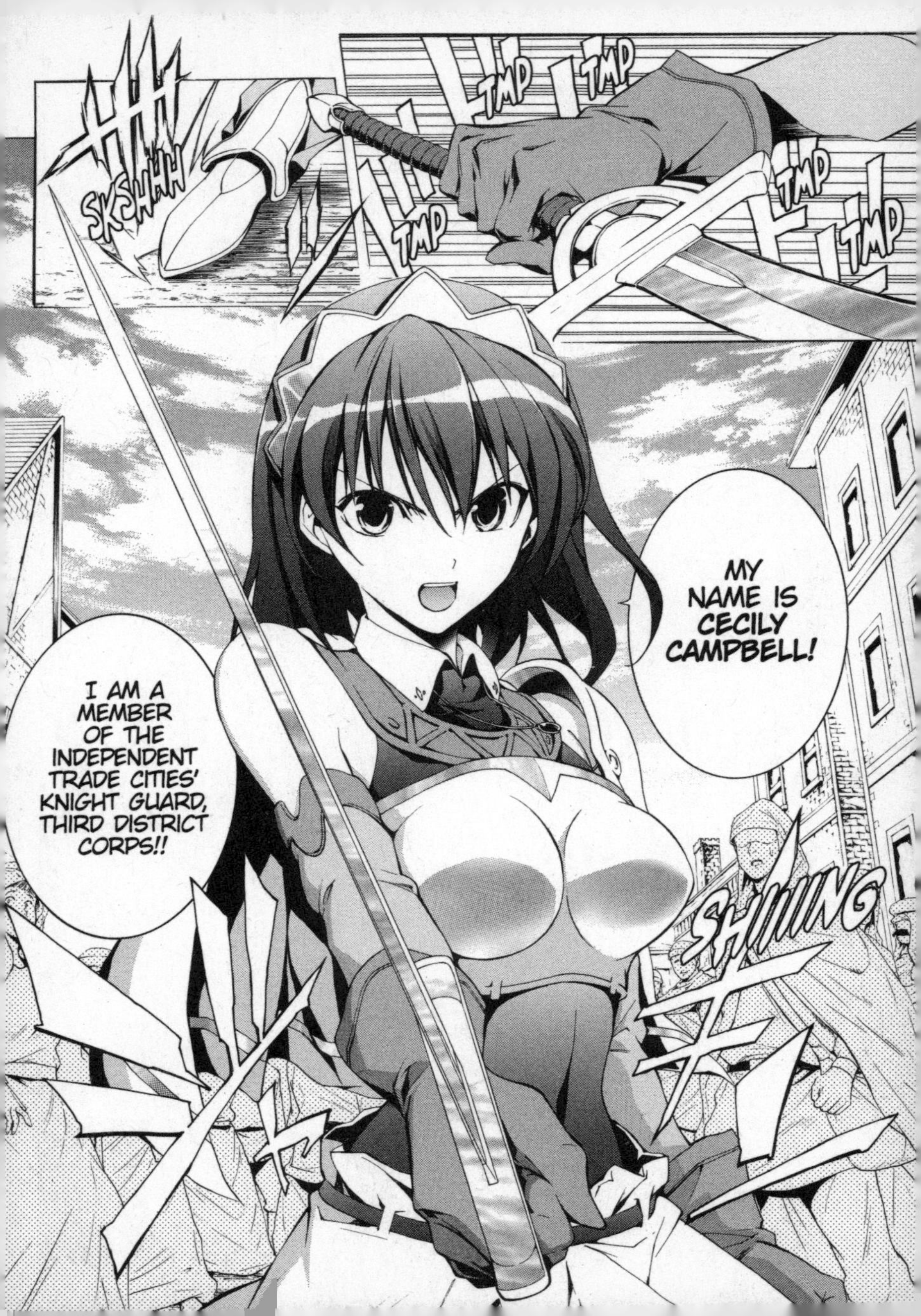

TMP
TMP
TMP
TMP
TMP
TMP
SKSHHH
MY NAME IS CECILY CAMPBELL!
I AM A MEMBER OF THE INDEPENDENT TRADE CITIES' KNIGHT GUARD, THIRD DISTRICT CORPS!!
SHIIING

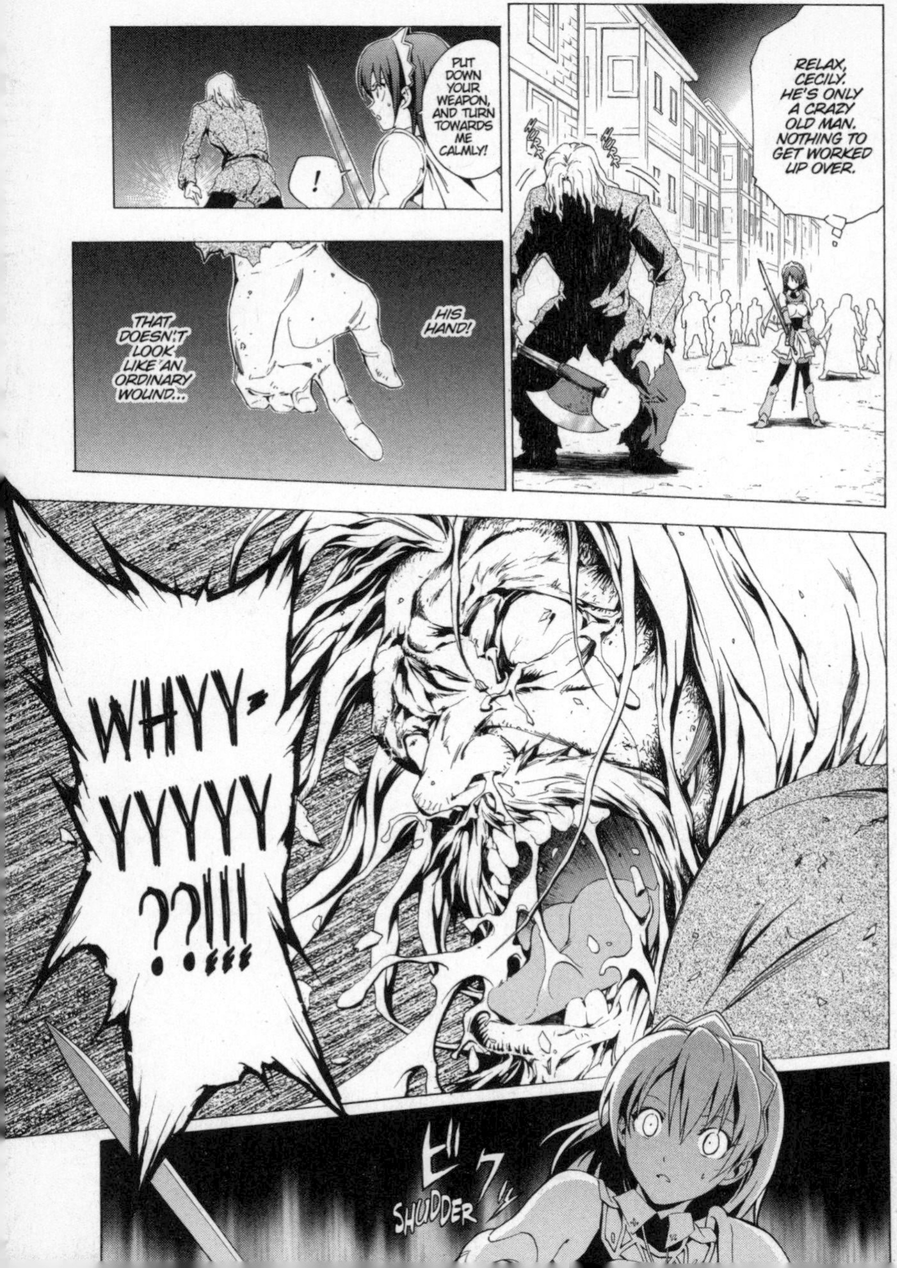
RELAX, CECILY. HE'S ONLY A CRAZY OLD MAN. NOTHING TO GET WORKED UP OVER.
HURR
HURR
PUT DOWN YOUR WEAPON, AND TURN TOWARDS ME CALMLY!
!
HIS HAND!
THAT DOESN'T LOOK LIKE AN ORDINARY WOUND...
WHYY-YYYYY??!!!!
ビクッ
SHUDDER

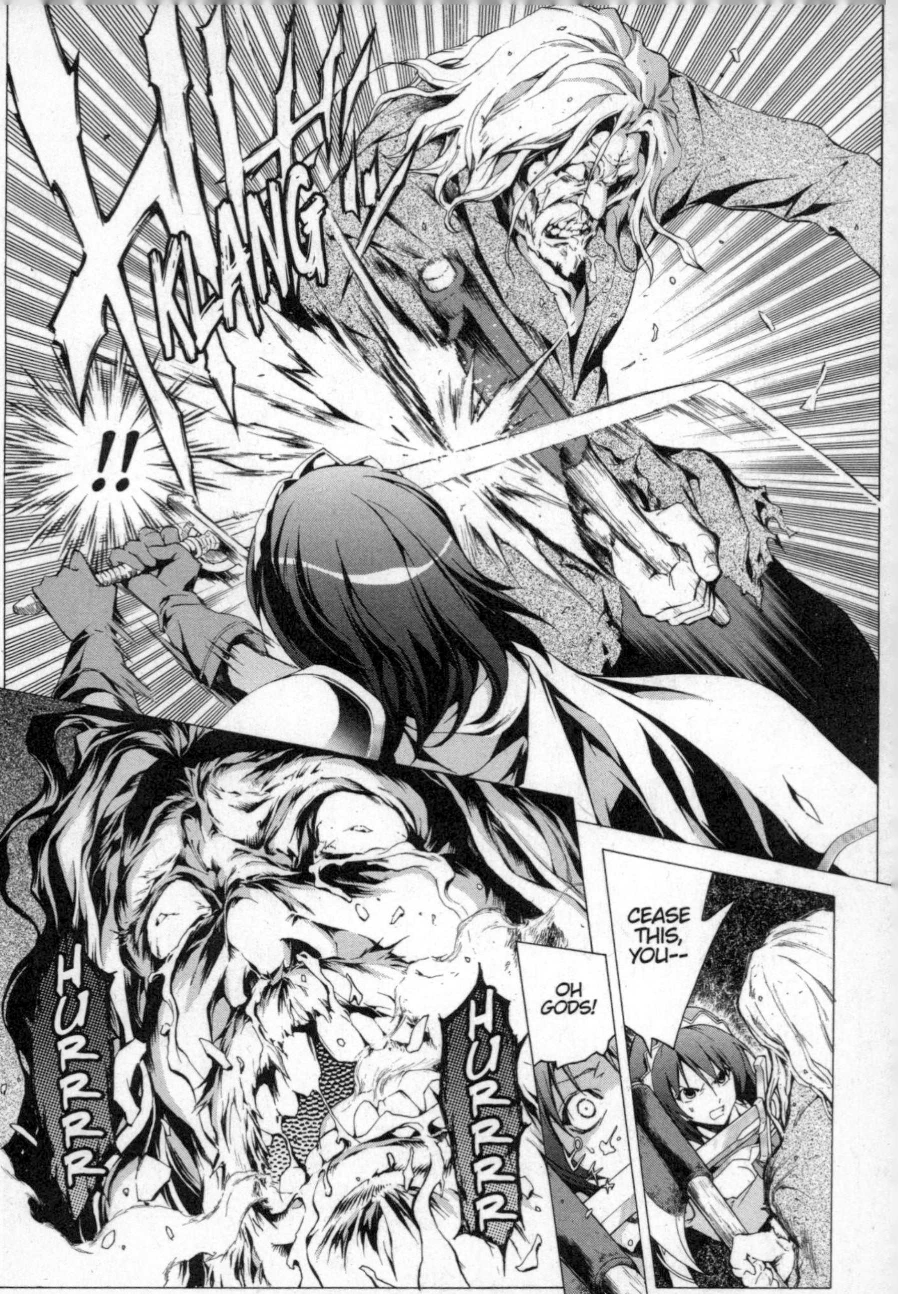
KLANG
!!
CEASE THIS, YOU--
OH GODS!
HURRRR
HURRRR

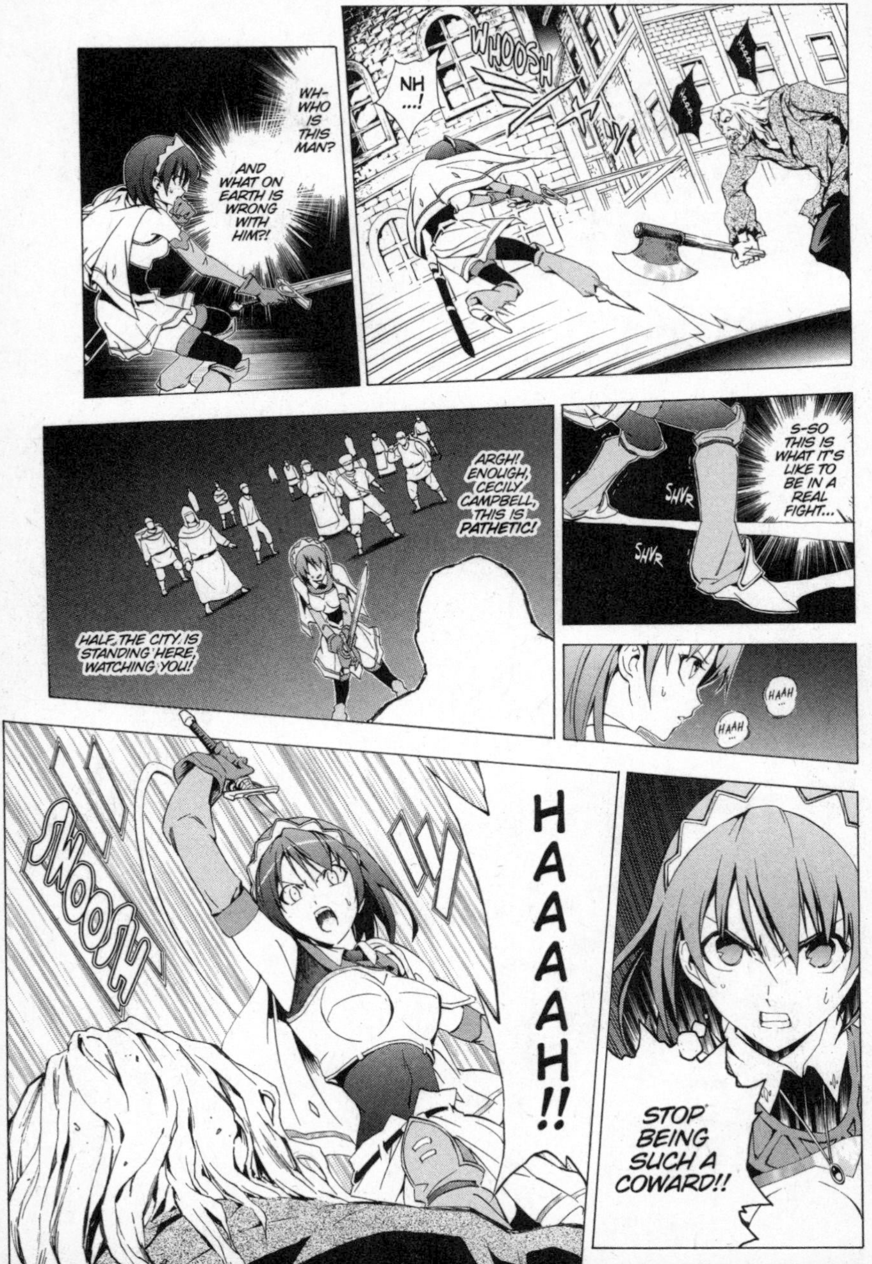
WHOOSH
NH ...!
WH-WHO IS THIS MAN?
AND WHAT ON EARTH IS WRONG WITH HIM?!
S-SO THIS IS WHAT IT'S LIKE TO BE IN A REAL FIGHT...
SHVR
SHVR
HAAH ...
HAAH ...
ARGH! ENOUGH, CECILY CAMPBELL, THIS IS PATHETIC!
HALF THE CITY IS STANDING HERE, WATCHING YOU!
STOP BEING SUCH A COWARD!!
HAAAAAH!!
SWOOSH

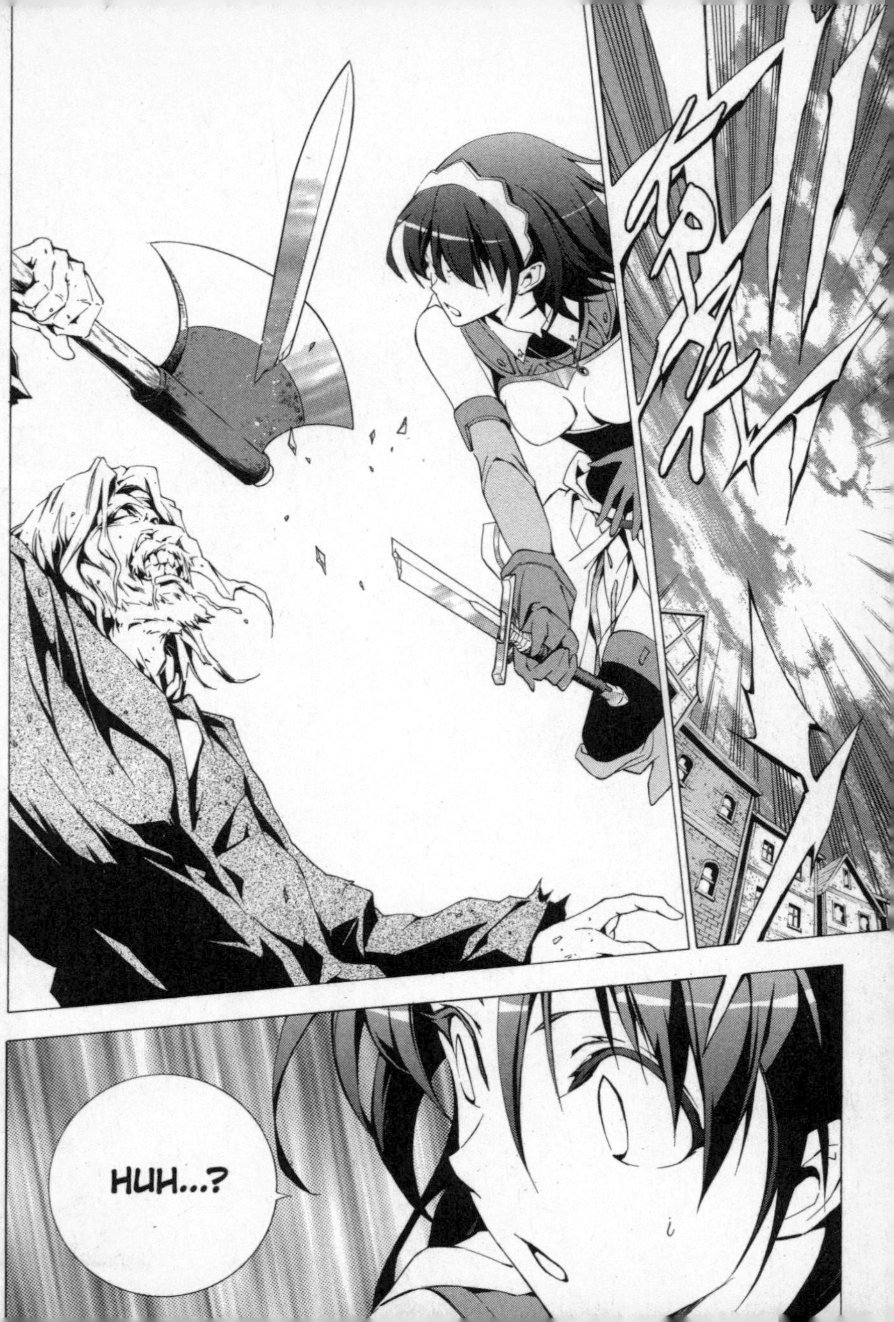
HUH...?

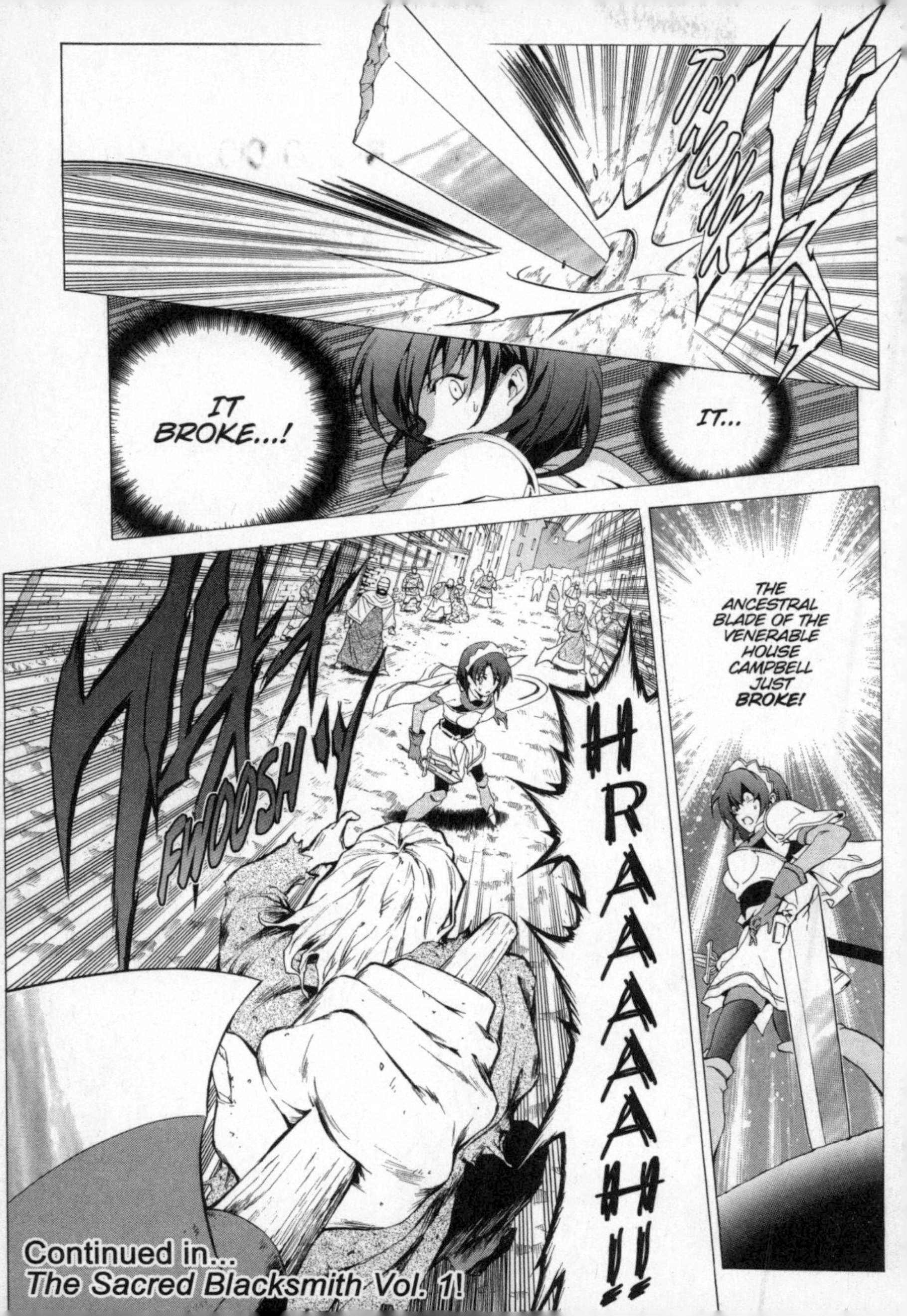
THUNK
IT...
IT BROKE...!
THE ANCESTRAL BLADE OF THE VENERABLE HOUSE CAMPBELL JUST BROKE!
HRAAAAAAH!!
FWOOSH

Continued in...
The Sacred Blacksmith Vol. 1!